Foundations of Modern Networking

SDN, NFV, QoE, IoT, and Cloud

William Stallings

With contributions by:
Florence Agboma
British Sky Broadcasting

Sofiene Jelassi
Assistant Professor
University of Monastir, Tunisia

800 East 96th Street, Indianapolis, Indiana 46240 USA

Foundations of Modern Networking: SDN, NFV, QoE, IoT, and Cloud

ISBN-13: 978-0-13-417539-3
ISBN-10: 0-13-417539-5

Library of Congress Control Number: 2015950673

Text printed in the United States on recycled paper at RR Donnelley, Crawfordsville, IN
First printing: November 2015

Trademarks

Many of the designations used by manufacturers and sellers to distinguish their products are claimed as trademarks. Where those designations appear in this book, and the publisher was aware of a trademark claim, the designations have been printed with initial capital letters or in all capitals.

Warning and Disclaimer

The author and publisher have taken care in the preparation of this book, but make no expressed or implied warranty of any kind and assume no responsibility for errors or omissions. No liability is assumed for incidental or consequential damages in connection with or arising out of the use of the information or programs contained herein.

Special Sales

For information about buying this title in bulk quantities, or for special sales opportunities (which may include electronic versions; custom cover designs; and content particular to your business, training goals, marketing focus, or branding interests), please contact our corporate sales department at corpsales@pearsoned.com or (800) 382-3419.

For government sales inquiries, please contact governmentsales@pearsoned.com.

For questions about sales outside the U.S., please contact international@pearsoned.com.

Visit us on the Web: informit.com/aw

Associate Publisher
Dave Dusthimer

Executive Editor
Brett Bartow

Senior Development Editor
Christopher Cleveland

Managing Editor
Sandra Schroeder

Project Editor
Mandie Frank

Copy Editor
Keith Cline

Indexer
Publishing Works

Proofreader
Katie Matejka

Technical Reviewers
Wendell Odom
Tim Szigeti

Editorial Assistant
Vanessa Evans

Designer
Alan Clements

Compositor
Mary Sudul

Contents at a Glance

Table of Contents

About the Author

Dr. William Stallings has made a unique contribution to understanding the broad sweep of technical developments in computer security, computer networking, and computer architecture. He has authored 18 textbooks, and, counting revised editions, a total of 70 books on various aspects of these subjects. His writings have appeared in numerous ACM and IEEE publications, including the *Proceedings of the IEEE* and *ACM Computing Reviews*. He has 13 times received the award for the best computer science textbook of the year from the Text and Academic Authors Association.

In over 30 years in the field, he has been a technical contributor, technical manager, and an executive with several high-technology firms. He has designed and implemented both TCP/IP-based and OSI-based protocol suites on a variety of computers and operating systems, ranging from microcomputers to mainframes. Currently, he is an independent consultant whose clients have included computer and networking manufacturers and customers, software development firms, and leading-edge government research institutions.

He created and maintains the Computer Science Student Resource Site at ComputerScienceStudent. com/. This site provides documents and links on a variety of subjects of general interest to computer science students (and professionals). He is a member of the editorial board of *Cryptologia*, a scholarly journal devoted to all aspects of cryptology.

Dr. Stallings holds a Ph.D. from M.I.T. in Computer Science and a B.S. from Notre Dame in electrical engineering.

About the Contributing Authors

Florence Agboma currently works as a Technology Analyst at British Sky Broadcasting (BSkyB), London. Her work includes streaming video quality improvements for different video platforms such as linear OTT, VoD, and broadcast. She is a member of the Video Quality Experts Group (VQEG). Dr. Agboma holds a Ph.D. from the University of Essex, United Kingdom, and her research focused on quality of experience for mobile content delivery systems.

Dr. Agboma has published a number of peer-reviewed articles in journal papers, book chapters, and international conference proceedings. Her interests include video quality assessments, psychophysical methods, pay TV analytics, quality of experience management, and emerging broadcast TV technologies such as high dynamic range and ultra HD.

Sofiene Jelassi received a Bachelor of Science and a Master of Science from the University of Monastir, Tunisia, in June 2003 and December 2005, respectively. He obtained a Ph.D. in Computer Science from the University of Pierre and Marie Curie, Paris, France, in February 2010. His doctoral thesis was titled *Adaptive Quality Control of Packetized Voice Conversations over Mobile Ad-Hoc Networks*. From June 2010 to December 2013, he worked as an R&D engineer at Inria within DIONYSOS research group. From January to December 2014, he worked as a post-doctoral fellow at GTA/ UFRJ in Rio de Janeiro, Brazil. Since January 2015, he has been working as Assistant Professor at University of Monastir, Tunisia. His research includes wired and wireless software-defined networks  (SDNs), server and network virtualization, network monitoring, content-oriented management of mobile networks and services, mobile virtual network operators (MVNO), customized voice and video systems, quality of user experience (QoE) measurement and modeling, in-lab and in-field usability testing, crowdsourcing, user profiling, context sensing, service gamification, and social-driven emergency services. Dr. Jelassi has more than 20 papers published in international journals and conferences.

Dedication

To Tricia, my loving wife, the kindest and gentlest person.

Acknowledgments

This book has benefited from review by a number of people who gave generously of their time and expertise. I especially thank Wendell Odom (Certskills, LLC) and Tim Szigeti (Cisco Systems), who each devoted an enormous amount of time to a detailed review of the entire manuscript.

Thanks also to the many people who provided detailed technical reviews of one or more chapters: Christian Adell (Corporació Catalana de Mitjans Audiovisuals), Eduard Dulharu (AT&T Germany), Cemal Duman (Ericsson), David L. Foote (NFV Forum (ATIS)), Harold Fritts, Scott Hogg (Global Technology Resources), Justin Kang (Accenture), Sergey Katsev (Fortinet), Raymond Kelly (Telecoms Now Ltd), Faisal Khan (Mobily Saudi Arabia), Epameinondas Kontothanasis (Unifys), Sashi Kumar (Intel), Hongwei Li (Hewlett-Packard), Cynthia Lopes (Maya Technologies), Simone Mangiante (EMC), Roberto Fuentes Martinez (Tecnocom), Mali Naghavi (Ericsson), Fatih Eyup Nar (Ericsson USA), Jimmy Ng (Huawei Technologies), Mark Noble (Salix Technology Services), Luke Reid (Sytel Reply UK), David Schuckman (State Farm Insurance), Vivek Srivastava (Zscaler), Istvan Teglas (Cisco Systems), and Paul Zanna (Northbound Networks).

Finally, I want to thank the many people at Pearson responsible for the publication of the book. This includes the staff at Pearson, particularly Senior Development Editor Chris Cleveland; Executive Editor Brett Bartow, and his assistant Vanessa Evans; and Project Editor Mandie Frank. Thanks also to the marketing and sales staffs at Pearson, without whose efforts this book would not be in front of you.

With all this assistance, little remains for which I can take full credit. However, I am proud to say that, with no help whatsoever, I selected all the quotations.

Preface

There is the book, Inspector. I leave it with you, and you cannot doubt that it contains a full explanation.

—*The Adventure of the Lion's Mane*, Sir Arthur Conan Doyle

Background

A host of factors have converged to produce the latest revolution in computer and communications networking:

- **Demand:** Enterprises are faced with a surge of demands that focus their attention on the need to design, evaluate, manage, and maintain sophisticated network infrastructures. These trends include the following:

  - **Big data:** Enterprises large and small increasingly rely on processing and analyzing massive amounts of data. To process large quantities of data within tolerable time periods, big data may need distributed file systems, distributed databases, cloud computing platforms, Internet storage, and other scalable storage technologies.

  - **Cloud computing:** There is an increasingly prominent trend in many organizations to move a substantial portion or even all information technology (IT) operations to an Internet-connected infrastructure known as enterprise cloud computing. This drastic shift in IT data processing is accompanied by an equally drastic shift in networking requirements.

  - **Internet of Things (IoT):** The IoT involves large numbers of objects that use standard communications architectures to provide services to end users. Billions of such devices will be interconnected in industrial, business, and government networks, providing new interactions between the physical world and computing, digital content, analysis, applications, and services. IoT provides unprecedented opportunities for users, manufacturers, and service providers in a wide variety of sectors. Areas that will benefit from IoT data collection, analysis, and automation capabilities include health and fitness, healthcare, home monitoring and automation, energy savings and smart grid, farming, transportation, environmental monitoring, inventory and product management, security, surveillance, education, and many others.

  - **Mobile devices:** Mobile devices are now an indispensable part of every enterprise IT infrastructure, including employer supplied and bring your own device (BYOD). The large population of mobile devices generates unique new demands on network planning and management.

- **Capacity:** Two interlocking trends have generated new and urgent requirements for intelligent and efficient network design and management:

- **Gigabit data rate networks:** Ethernet offerings have reached 100 Gbps with further increases in the works. Wi-Fi products at almost 7 Gbps are available. And 4G and 5G networks bring gigabit speeds to cellular networks.

- **High-speed, high-capacity servers:** Massive blade servers and other high-performance servers have evolved to meet the increasing multimedia and data processing requirements of enterprises, calling for a need for efficiently designed and managed networks.

- **Complexity:** Network designers and managers operate in a complex, dynamic environment, in which a range of requirements, most especially quality of service (QoS) and quality of experience (QoE) require flexible, manageable networking hardware and services.

- **Security:** With increasing reliance on networked resources, an increasing need emerges for networks that provide a range of security services.

With the development of new network technologies in response to these factors, it is imperative for system engineers, system analysts, IT managers, network designers, and product marketing specialists to have a firm grasp on modern networking. These professionals need to understand the implications of the factors listed above and how network designers have responded. Dominating this landscape are (1) two complementary technologies that are rapidly being developed and deployed (software-defined networking [SDN] and network functions virtualization [NFV]) and (2) the need to satisfy QoS and QoE requirements.

This book provides the reader with a thorough understanding of SDN and NFV and their practical deployment and use in today's enterprises. In addition, the book provides clear explanations of QoS/QoE and the whole range of related issues, such as cloud networking and IoT. This is a technical book, intended for readers with some technical background, but is sufficiently self-contained to be a valuable resource for IT managers and product marketing personnel, in addition to system engineers, network maintenance personnel, and network and protocol designers.

Organization of the Book

The book consists of six parts:

- **Modern Networking:** Provides an overview of modern networking and a context for the remainder of the book. Chapter 1 is a survey of the elements that make up the networking ecosystem, including network technologies, network architecture, services, and applications. Chapter 2 examines the requirements that have evolved for the current networking environment and provides a preview of key technologies for modern networking.

- **Software-Defined Networks:** Devoted to a broad and thorough presentation of SDN concepts, technology, and applications. Chapter 3 begins the discussion by laying out what the SDN approach is and why it is needed, and provides an overview of the SDN architecture. This chapter also looks at the organizations that are issuing specifications and standards for SDN. Chapter 4 is a detailed look at the SDN data plane, including the key components, how they interact, and how they are managed. Much of the chapter is devoted to OpenFlow, a vital data plane technology and an interface to the control plane. The chapter explains why OpenFlow is needed and then proceeds to provide a detailed technical explanation. Chapter 5 is devoted to the SDN control plane. It includes a discussion of OpenDaylight, an important open source implementation of the control plane. Chapter 6 covers the SDN application plane. In addition to examining the general SDN application plane architecture, the chapter discusses six major application areas that can be supported by SDN and provides a number of examples of SDN applications.

- **Virtualization:** Devoted to a broad and thorough presentation of network functions virtualization (NFV) concepts, technology, and applications, as well as a discussion of network virtualization. Chapter 7 introduces the concept of virtual machine, and then looks at the use of virtual machine technology to develop NFV-based networking environments. Chapter 8 provides a detailed discussion of NFV functionality. Chapter 9 looks at traditional concepts of virtual networks, then at the more modern approach to network virtualization, and finally introduces the concept of software defined infrastructure.

- **Defining and Supporting User Needs:** Equally as significant as the emergence of the SDN and NFV is the evolution of quality of service (QoS) and quality of experience (QoE) to determine customer needs and network design responses to those needs. Chapter 10 provides an overview of QoS concepts and standards. Recently QoS has been augmented with the concept of QoE, which is particularly relevant to interactive video and multimedia network traffic. Chapter 11 provides an overview of QoE and discusses a number of practical aspects of implementing QoE mechanisms. Chapter 12 looks further into the network design implications of the combined use of QoS and QoE.

- **Modern Network Architecture: Clouds and Fog:** The two dominant modern network architectures are cloud computing and the Internet of things (IoT), sometimes referred to as fog computing. The technologies and applications discussed in the preceding parts all provide a foundation for cloud computing and IoT. Chapter 13 is a survey of cloud computing. The chapter begins with a definition of basic concepts, and then covers cloud services, deployment models, and architecture. The chapter then discusses the relationship between cloud computing and SDN and NFV. Chapter 14 introduces IoT and provides a detailed look at the key components of IoT-enabled devices. Chapter 15 looks at several model IoT architectures and then describes three example IoT implementations.

- **Related Topics:** Discusses two additional topics that, although important, do not conveniently fit into the other Parts. Chapter 16 provides an analysis of security issues that have emerged with the evolution of modern networking. Separate sections deal with SDN, NFV, cloud, and IoT security, respectively. Chapter 17 discusses career-related issues, including the changing role of various network-related jobs, new skill requirements, and how the reader can continue his or her education to prepare for a career in modern networking.

Supporting Websites

I maintain a companion website at WilliamStallings.com/Network that includes a list of relevant links organized by chapter and an errata sheet for the book.

Companion website

I also maintain the Computer Science Student Resource Site, at ComputerScienceStudent.com. The purpose of this site is to provide documents, information, and links for computer science students and professionals. Links and documents are organized into seven categories:

Computer Science Student Resource Site

- **Math:** Includes a basic math refresher, a queuing analysis primer, a number system primer, and links to numerous math sites.

- **How-to:** Advice and guidance for solving homework problems, writing technical reports, and preparing technical presentations.

- **Research resources:** Links to important collections of papers, technical reports, and bibliographies.

- **Other useful:** A variety of other useful documents and links.

- **Computer science careers:** Useful links and documents for those considering a career in computer science.

- **Writing help:** Help in becoming a clearer, more effective writer.

- **Miscellaneous topics and humor:** You have to take your mind off your work once in a while.

PART I

Modern Networking

The whole of this operation is described in minute detail in the official British Naval History, and should be studied with its excellent charts by those who are interested in its technical aspect. So complicated is the full story that the lay reader cannot see the wood for the trees. I have endeavored to render intelligible the broad effects.

—*The World Crisis*, Winston Churchill

Part I provides an overview of modern networking and a context for the remainder of the book. Chapter 1 is a survey of the elements that make up the networking ecosystem, including network technologies, network architecture, services, and applications. In Chapter 2, we examine the requirements that have evolved for the current networking environment and provide a preview of key technologies for modern networking.

Chapter 1

Elements of Modern Networking

There is some evidence that computer networks will have a large impact on society. Likely areas are the economy, resources, small computers, human-to-human interaction, and computer research.

—*What Can Be Automated?*
The Computer Science and Engineering Research Study, National Science Foundation, 1980

Chapter Objectives

After studying this chapter, you should be able to

- Explain the key elements and their relationships of a modern networking ecosystem, including end users, network providers, application providers and application service providers.
- Discuss the motivation for the typical network hierarchy of access networks, distribution networks, and core networks.
- Present an overview of Ethernet, including a discussion of its application areas and common data rates.
- Present an overview of Wi-Fi, including a discussion of its application areas and common data rates.
- Understand the differences between the five generations of cellular networks.
- Present an overview of cloud computing concepts.
- Describe the Internet of Things.
- Explain the concepts of network convergence and unified communications.

Long gone are the days when a single vendor, such as IBM, could provide an enterprise with all the products and services required by their information technology (IT) department, including computer hardware, system software, applications software, and communications and networking equipment and services. Today, users and enterprises face complex, heterogeneous and diverse environments that require sophisticated and advanced solutions.

The focus of this book is twofold:

- The networking technologies that enable the design, development, deployment, and operation of complex modern networks, including and especially software-defined networks (SDN), network functions virtualization (NFV), quality of service (QoS), and quality of experience (QoE).

- The network architectures that have come to dominate modern networking, which are cloud networking and the Internet of Things (IoT), also known as fog networking.

But before diving into the details of these technologies, we need an overview of the current networking environment and the challenges it brings.

This chapter provides a brief survey of the key elements of modern networking. We begin with a top-level description of what might be considered the typical networking ecosystem. Then, Section 1.2 looks in more detail at the way in which the network elements are organized. Next, Sections 1.3 through 1.5 examine the key high-speed network technologies that support the modern networking ecosystem. The remainder of this chapter introduces important architectures and applications that are part of this ecosystem.

1.1   The Networking Ecosystem

Figure 1.1 depicts the modern networking ecosystem in very general terms. The entire ecosystem exists to provide services to end users. The term **end user**, or simply *user*, is used here as a very general term, to encompass users working within an enterprise or in a public setting or at home. The user platform can be fixed (for example, PC or workstation), portable (for example, laptop), or mobile (for example, tablet or smartphone).

end user

The ultimate consumer of applications, data and services on a computing platform.

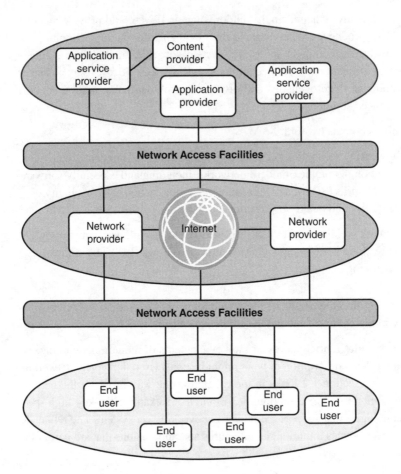

FIGURE 1.1   **The Modern Networking Ecosystem**

network provider

An organization that delivers communications services over a typically large geographic area. It provides, maintains, and manages network equipment and networks, either public or private.

application provider

An entity generating/selling user applications to be executed on the user's platform.

Users connect to network-based services and content through a wide variety of network access facilities. These include digital subscriber line (DSL) and cable modems, Wi-Fi and Worldwide Interoperability for Microwave Access (WiMAX) wireless modems, and cellular modems. Such network access facilities enable the use to connect directly to the Internet or to a variety of network providers, including Wi-Fi networks, cellular networks, and both private and shared network facilities, such as a premises enterprise network.

Ultimately, of course, users want to use network facilities to access applications and content. Figure 1.1 indicates three broad categories of interest to users. **Application providers** provide applications, or apps, that run on the user's platform, which is typically a mobile platform. More recently, the concept of an app store has become available for fixed and portable platforms as well.

A distinct category of provider is the **application service provider**. Whereas the application provider downloads software to the user's platform, the application service provider acts as a server or host of application software that is executed on the provider's platforms. Traditional examples of such software include web servers, e-mail servers, and database servers. The most prominent example now is the cloud computing provider. We discuss this latter category subsequently in this chapter and in Chapter 13, "Cloud Computing."

The final element shown in Figure 1.1 is the **content provider**. A content provider serves the data to be consumed on the user device (for example, e-mail, music, video). This data may be commercially provided intellectual property. In some instances, an enterprise may be an application or content provider. Examples of content providers are music record labels and movie studios.

Figure 1.1 is intended to provide a very general depiction of the networking ecosystem. It is worth pointing out here two major elements of modern networking not explicitly depicted in this figure:

- **Data center networking:** Both large enterprise data centers and cloud provider data centers consist of very large numbers of interconnected servers. Typically, as much as 80 percent of the data traffic is within the data center network, and only 20 percent relies on external networks to reach users.

- **IoT or fog networking:** An Internet of Things deployed by an enterprise may consist of hundreds, thousands, even millions of devices. The vast bulk of the data traffic to and from these devices is machine to machine, rather than user to machine.

Each of these networking environments creates its own particular requirements, which are discussed as the book progresses.

1.2 Example Network Architectures

This section introduces two example network architectures, and with them some of the networking terminology in common use. These examples give some idea of the range of network architectures covered in this book.

A Global Network Architecture

We begin with an architecture that could represent an enterprise network of national or global extent, or a portion of the Internet with some of its associated networks. Figure 1.2 illustrates some of the typical communications and network elements in use in such a context.

---

application service provider

An organization that hosts software applications within its own facilities. It provides network-accessible applications such as e-mail, web hosting, banking, and cloud-based services.

content provider

An organization or individual that creates information, including educational or entertainment content, distributed via the Internet or enterprise networks. A content provider may or may not provide the software used to access the material.

router

A network device that forwards data packets from one network to another. The forwarding decision is based on network layer information and routing tables, often constructed by outing protocols. Routers require packets formatted in a routable protocol, the global standard being the Internet Protocol (IP).

At the center of the figure is an IP backbone, or core, network, which could represent a portion of the Internet or an enterprise IP network. Typically, the backbone consists of high-performance routers, called **core routers**, interconnected with high-volume optical links. The optical links often make use of what is known as wavelength-division multiplexing (WDM), such that each link has multiple logical channels occupying different portions of the optical bandwidth.

At the periphery of an IP backbone are routers that provide connectivity to external networks and users. These routers are sometimes referred to as **edge routers** or **aggregation routers**. Aggregation routers are also used within an enterprise network to connect a number of routers and switches, to external resources, such as an IP backbone or a high-speed WAN. As an indication of the capacity requirements for core and aggregation routers, the IEEE Ethernet Bandwidth Assessments Group [XI11] reports on an analysis that projects these requirements for Internet backbone providers and large enterprise networks in China. The analysis concludes that aggregation router requirements will be in the range of 200 Gbps to 400 Gbps per optical link by 2020, and 400 Gbps to 1 Tbps per optical link for core routers by 2020.

The upper part of Figure 1.2 depicts a portion of what might be a large enterprise network. The figure shows two sections of the network connected via a private high-speed WAN, with switches interconnected with optical links. MPLS using IP is a common switching protocol used for such WANs; wide-area Ethernet is another option. Enterprise assets are connected to, and protected from, an IP backbone or the Internet via routers with firewall capability, a not uncommon arrangement for implementing the firewall.

core router

A router that resides within the middle of the network rather than at its periphery. The routers that make up the backbone of the Internet are core routers.

The lower left of the figure depicts what might be a layout for a small- or medium-size business, which relies on an Ethernet LAN. Connection to the Internet through a router could be through a cable or DSL connection or a dedicated high-speed link.

The lower portion of Figure 1.2 also shows an individual residential user connected to an Internet service provider (ISP) through some sort of subscriber connection. Common examples of such a connection are a DSL, which provides a high-speed link over telephone lines and requires a special DSL modem, and a cable TV facility, which requires a cable modem, or some type of wireless connection. In each case, there are separate issues concerning signal encoding, error control, and the internal structure of the subscriber network.

edge router

A router that sits at the periphery of a network. Also called an access router or aggregation router.

Finally, mobile devices, such as smartphones and tablets, can connect to the Internet through the public cellular network, which has a high-speed connection, typically optical, to the Internet.

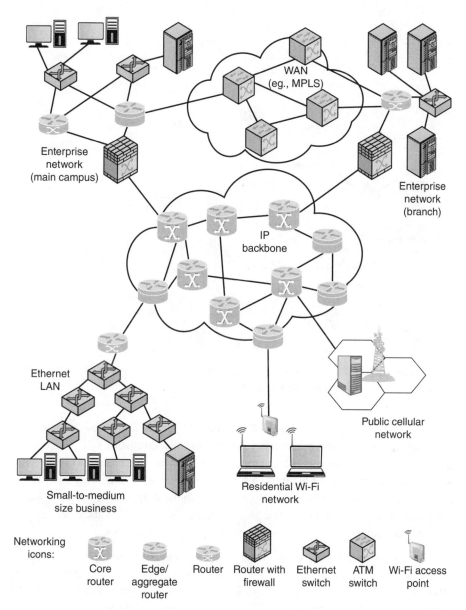

Enterprise
network
(main campus)

WAN
(eg., MPLS)

Enterprise
network
(branch)

IP
backbone

Ethernet
LAN

Public cellular
network

Residential Wi-Fi
network

Small-to-medium
size business

Networking
icons:

| Core router | Edge/ aggregate router | Router | Router with firewall | Ethernet switch | ATM switch | Wi-Fi access point |

FIGURE 1.2   A Global Networking Architecture

Multiprotocol Label Switching (MPLS)

A protocol developed by IETF for directing packets in a wide-area IP network, or other WAN. MPLS adds a 32-bit label to each packet to improve network efficiency and to enable routers to direct packets along predefined routes in accordance with the required quality of service.

A Typical Network Hierarchy

This section focuses in on a network architecture that, with some variation, is common in many enterprises. As Figure 1.3 illustrates, enterprises often design their network facilities in a three-tier hierarchy: access, distribution, and core.

Layer 3 (L3) switch

A high-performance device for network routing. Layer 3 switches are very similar to routers. The key difference between L3 switches and routers is that a L3 switch replaces some of a router's software logic with hardware to offer better performance. L3 switches often cost less than traditional routers. Designed for use within LANs, a L3 switch will typically not possess the WAN ports and WAN features a traditional router has.

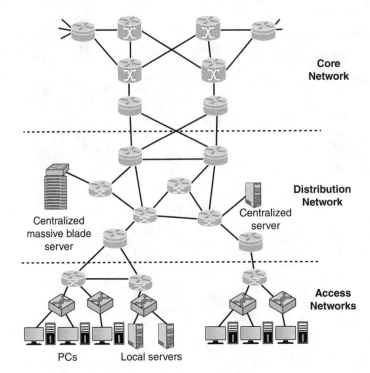

FIGURE 1.3   A Typical Network Hierarchy

Closest to the end user is the **access network**. Typically, an access network is a local-area network (LAN) or campus-wide network that consisting of LAN switches (typically Ethernet switches) and, in larger LANs, IP routers that provide connectivity among the switches. **Layer 3 switches** (not shown) are also commonly used within an LAN. The access network supports end user equipment, such as desktop and laptop computers and mobile devices. The access network also supports local servers that primarily or exclusively serve the users on the local access network.

access network

A network that connects directly to the end user or customer.

One or more access routers connect the local assets to the next higher level of the hierarchy, the distribution network. This connection may be via the Internet or some other public or private communications facility. Thus, as described in the preceding subsection, these access routers function as edge routers that forward traffic into and out of the access network. For a large local facility, there might be additional access routers that provide internal routing but do not function as edge routers (not shown in Figure 1.2).

distribution network

Connects access networks to a core network.

The **distribution network** connects access networks with each other and with the core network. An edge router in the distribution network connects to an edge router in an access network to provide connectivity. The two routers are configured to recognize each other and will generally exchange routing and connectivity information and, typically, some traffic-related information. This cooperation between routers is referred to as **peering**. The distribution network also serves to aggregate traffic destined for the core router, which protects the core from high-density peering. That is, the use of a distribution network limits the number of routers that establish peer relationships with edge routers in the core, saving memory, processing, and transmission capacity. A distribution network may also directly connect servers that are of use to multiple access networks, such as database servers and network management servers.

Again, as with access networks, some of the distribution routers may be purely internal and do not provide an edge router function.

The **core network**, also referred to as a **backbone network**, connects geographically dispersed distribution networks as well as providing access to other networks that are not part of the enterprise network. Typically, the core network will use very high performance routers, high-capacity transmission lines, and multiple interconnected routers for increased redundancy and capacity. The core network may also connect to high-performance, high-capacity servers, such as large database servers and private cloud facilities. Some of the core routers may be purely internal, providing redundancy and additional capacity without serving as edge routers.

A hierarchical network architecture is an example of a good modular design. With this design, the capacity, features, and functionality of network equipment (routers, switches, network management servers) can be optimized for their position in the hierarchy and the requirements at a given hierarchical level.

1.3 Ethernet

Continuing the top-down approach of the preceding two sections, the next three sections focus on key network transmission technologies of **Ethernet**, Wi-Fi, and 4G/5G cellular networks. Each of these technologies has evolved to support very high data rates. These data rates support the many multimedia applications required by enterprises and consumers and, at the same time, place great demands on network switching equipment and network management facilities. A full discussion of these network technologies is beyond the scope of this book. Here, we provide a brief survey.

This section begins with discussion of Ethernet applications, and then looks at standards and performance.

Applications of Ethernet

Ethernet is the predominant wired networking technology, used in homes, offices, data centers, enterprises, and WANs. As Ethernet has evolved to support data rates up to 100 Gbps and distances from a few meters to tens of kilometers, it has become essential for supporting personal computers, workstations, servers, and massive data storage devices in organizations large and small.

peering

An agreement between two routers to accept each other's data packets and forward them. A peer relationship generally involves the exchange of routing information.

core/ backbone network

A central network that provides networking services to attached distribution and access networks. Also referred to as a backbone network.

Ethernet

The commercial name for a wired local-area network technology. It involves the use of a shared physical medium, a medium access control protocol, and transmission of data in packets. Standards for Ethernet products are defined by the IEEE 802.3 committee.

Ethernet in the Home

Ethernet has long been used in the home to create a local network of computers with access to the Internet via a broadband modem/router. With the increasing availability of high-speed, low-cost Wi-Fi on computers, tablets, smartphones, modem/routers, and other devices, home reliance on Ethernet has declined. Nevertheless almost all home networking setups include some use of Ethernet.

Two recent extensions of Ethernet technology have enhanced and broadened the use of Ethernet in the home: powerline carrier (PLC) and Power over Ethernet (PoE). Powerline modems take advantage of existing power lines and use the power wire as a communication channel to transmit Ethernet packets on top of the power signal. This makes it easy to include Ethernet-capable devices throughout the home into the Ethernet network. PoE acts in a complementary fashion, distributing power over the Ethernet data cable. PoE uses the existing Ethernet cables to distribute power to devices on the network, thus simplifying the wiring for devices such as computers and televisions.

With all of these Ethernet options, Ethernet will retain a strong presence in home networking, complementing the advantages of Wi-Fi.

Ethernet in the Office

Ethernet has also long been the dominant network technology for wired local-area networks (LANs) in the office environment. Early on there were some competitors, such as IBM's Token Ring LAN and the Fiber Distributed Data Interface (FDDI), but the simplicity, performance, and wide availability of Ethernet hardware eventually made Ethernet the winner. Today, as with home networks, the wired Ethernet technology exists side by side with the wireless Wi-Fi technology. Much of the traffic in a typical office environment now travels on Wi-Fi, particularly to support mobile devices. Ethernet retains its popularity because it can support many devices at high speeds, is not subject to interference, and provides a security advantage because it is resistant to eavesdropping. Therefore, a combination of Ethernet and Wi-Fi is the most common architecture.

Figure 1.4 provides a simplified example of an enterprise LAN architecture. The LAN connects to the Internet/WANs via a firewall. A hierarchical arrangement of routers and switches provides the interconnection of servers, fixed user devices, and wireless devices. Typically, wireless devices are only attached at the edge or bottom of the hierarchical architecture; the rest of the campus infrastructure is all Ethernet. There may also be an IP telephony server that provides call control functions (voice switching) for the telephony operations in an enterprise network, with connectivity to the public switched telephone network (PTSN).

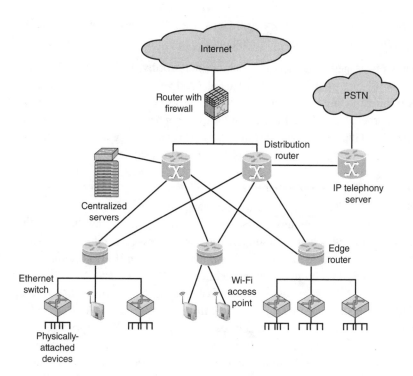

FIGURE 1.4 **A Basic Enterprise LAN Architecture**

Ethernet in the Enterprise

A tremendous advantage of Ethernet is that it is possible to scale the network, both in terms of distance and data rate, with the same Ethernet protocol and associated quality of service (QoS) and security standards. An enterprise can easily extend an Ethernet network among a number of buildings on the same campus or even some distance apart, with links ranging from 10 Mbps to 100 Gbps, using a mixture of cable types and Ethernet hardware. Because all the hardware and communications software conform to the same standard, it is easy to mix different speeds and different vendor equipment. The same protocol is used for intensive high-speed interconnections of data servers in a single room, workstations and servers distributed throughout the building, and links to Ethernet networks in other buildings up to 100 km away.

Ethernet in the Data Center

As in other areas, Ethernet has come to dominate in the data center, where very high data rates are needed to handle massive volumes of data among networked servers and storage units. Historically, data centers have employed various technologies to support high-volume, short-distance needs, including InfiniBand and Fiber Channel.

blade server

A server architecture that houses multiple server modules (blades) in a single chassis. It is widely used in data centers to save space and improve system management. Either self-standing or rack mounted, the chassis provides the power supply, and each blade has its own CPU, memory, and hard disk.

But now that Ethernet can scale up to 100 Gbps, with 400 Gbps on the horizon, the case for a unified protocol approach throughout the enterprise is compelling.

Two features of the new Ethernet approach are noteworthy. For co-located servers and storage units, high-speed Ethernet fiber links and switches provided the needed networking infrastructure. Another important version of Ethernet is known as backplane Ethernet. Backplane Ethernet runs over copper jumper cables that can provide up to 100 Gbps over very short distances. This technology is ideal for **blade servers**, in which multiple server modules are housed in a single chassis.

Ethernet for Wide-Area Networking

Until fairly recently, Ethernet was not a significant factor in wide-area networking. But gradually, more telecommunications and network providers have switched to Ethernet from alternative schemes to support wide-area access (also referred to as first mile or last mile). Ethernet is supplanting a variety of other wide-area options, such as dedicated T1 lines, synchronous digital hierarchy (SDH) lines, and Asynchronous Transfer Mode (ATM). When used in this fashion, the term *carrier Ethernet* is applied. The term *metro Ethernet*, or *metropolitan-area network (MAN) Ethernet*, is also used. Ethernet has the advantage that it seamlessly fits into the enterprise network for which it provides wide-area access. But a more important advantage is that carrier Ethernet provides much more flexibility in terms of the data rate capacity that is used, compared to traditional wide-area alternatives.

Carrier Ethernet is one of the fastest-growing Ethernet technologies, destined to become the dominant means by which enterprises access wide-area networking and Internet facilities.

IEEE 802

A committee of the Institute of Electrical and Electronics Engineers (IEEE) responsible for developing standards for wireless LANs.

IEEE 802.3
Committee

Standards

Within the **IEEE 802** LAN standards committee, the 802.3 group is responsible for issuing standards for LANs that are referred to commercially as Ethernet. Complementary to the efforts of the 802.3 committee, the industry consortium known as The Ethernet Alliance supports and originates activities that span from incubation of new Ethernet technologies to interoperability testing to demonstrations to education.

Ethernet Data Rates

Currently, Ethernet systems are available at speeds up to 100 Gbps. Here's a brief chronology.

- **1983:** 10 Mbps (megabit per second, million bits per second)
- **1995:** 100 Mbps
- **1998:** 1 Gbps (gigabits per second, billion bits per second)

- **2003:** 10 Gbps

- **2010:** 40 Gbps and 100 Gbps

Coming soon (as of this writing) are standards at 2.5, 5, 25, 50, and 400 Gbps (see Figure 1.5).

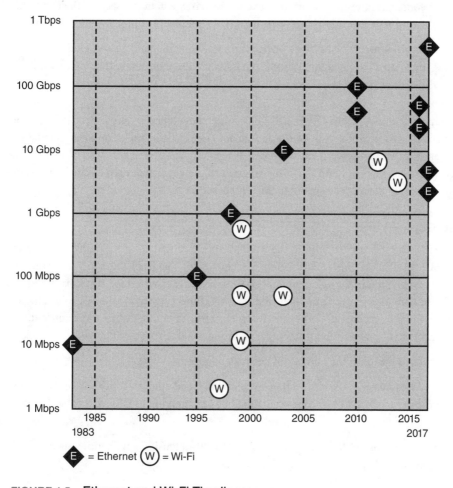

FIGURE 1.5 **Ethernet and Wi-Fi Timelines**

1-Gbps Ethernet

For a number of years, the initial standard of Ethernet, at 10 Mbps, was adequate for most office environments. By the early 1990s, it was clear that higher data rates were needed to support the growing traffic load on the typical LAN. Key drivers included the following:

- **Centralized server farms:** In many multimedia applications, there is a need for client system to be able to draw huge amounts of data from multiple, centralized servers, called server farms. As the performance of the servers has increased, the network becomes the bottleneck.

- **Power workgroups:** These groups typically consist of a small number of cooperating users who need to exchange massive data files across the network. Example applications are software development and computer-aided design.

- **High-speed local backbone:** As processing demand grows, enterprises develop an architecture of multiple LANs interconnected with a high-speed backbone network.

To meet such needs, the IEEE 802.3 committee developed a set of specifications for Ethernet at 100 Mbps, followed a few years later by a 1-Gbps family of standards. In each case, the new specifications defined transmission media and transmission encoding schemes built on the basic Ethernet framework, making the transition easier than if a completely new specification were issued.

10-Gbps Ethernet

Even as the ink was drying on the 1-Gbps specification, the continuing increase in local traffic made this specification inadequate for needs in the short-term future. Accordingly, the IEEE 802.3 committee soon issued a standard for 10-Gbps Ethernet. The principle driving requirement for 10-Gbps Ethernet was the increase in intranet (local interconnected networks) and Internet traffic. A number of factors contribute to the explosive growth in both Internet and intranet traffic:

- An increase in the number of network connections

- An increase in the connection speed of each end-station (for example, 10-Mbps users moving to 100 Mbps, analog 56k users moving to DSL and cable modems)

- An increase in the deployment of bandwidth-intensive applications such as high-quality video

- An increase in web hosting and application hosting traffic

Initially, network managers used 10-Gbps Ethernet to provide high-speed, local backbone interconnection between large-capacity switches. As the demand for bandwidth increased, 10-Gbps Ethernet began to be deployed throughout the entire network, to include server farm, backbone, and campus-wide connectivity. This technology enables ISPs and network service providers (NSPs) to create very high-speed links at a very low cost between co-located carrier-class switches and routers.

The technology also allows the construction of MANs and WANs that connect geographically dispersed LANs between campuses or points of presence (PoPs).

100-Gbps Ethernet

The IEEE 802.3 committee soon realized the need for a greater data rate capacity than 10-Gbps Ethernet offers, to support Internet exchanges, high-performance computing, and video-on-demand delivery. The authorization request justified the need for two different data rates in the new standard (40 Gbps and 100 Gbps) by recognizing that aggregate network requirements and end-station requirements are increasing at different rates.

The following are market drivers for 100-Gbps Ethernet:

- **Data center/Internet media providers:** To support the growth of Internet multimedia content and web applications, content providers have been expanding data centers, pushing 10-Gbps Ethernet to its limits. Likely to be high-volume early adopters of 100-Gbps Ethernet.

- **Metro video/service providers:** Video on demand has been driving a new generation of 10-Gbps Ethernet metropolitan/core network buildouts. Likely to be high-volume adopters in the medium term.

- **Enterprise LANs:** Continuing growth in convergence of voice/video/data and in unified communications is driving up network switch demands. However, most enterprises still rely on 1-Gbps or a mix of 1-Gbps and 10-Gbps Ethernet, and adoption of 100-Gbps Ethernet is likely to be slow.

- **Internet exchanges/ISP core routing:** With the massive amount of traffic flowing through these nodes, these installations are likely to be early adopters of 100-Gbps Ethernet.

Figure 1.6 shows an example of the application of 100-Gbps Ethernet. The trend at large data centers, with substantial banks of blade servers, is the deployment of 10-Gbps ports on individual servers to handle the massive multimedia traffic provided by these servers. Typically, a single blade server rack will contain multiple servers and one or two 10-Gbps Ethernet switches to interconnect all the servers and provide connectivity to the rest of the facility. The switches are often mounted in the rack and referred to as top-of-rack (ToR) switches. The term *ToR* has become synonymous with server access switch, even if it is not located "top of rack." For very large data centers, such as cloud providers, the interconnection of multiple blade server racks with additional 10-Gbps switches is increasingly inadequate. To handle the increased traffic load, switches operating at greater than 10 Gbps are needed to support the interconnection of server racks and to provide adequate capacity for connecting offsite through network interface controllers (NICs).

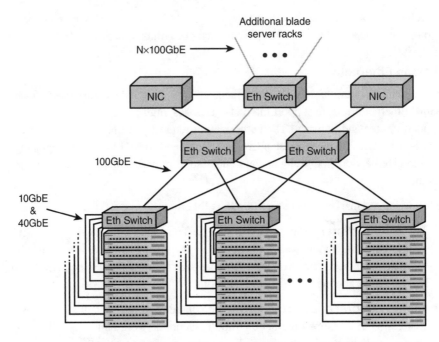

FIGURE 1.6   **Configuration for Massive Blade Server Cloud Site**

25/50-Gbps Ethernet

One of the options for implementing 100-Gbps is as four 25-Gbps physical lanes. Therefore, it would be relatively easy to develop standards for 25-Gbps and 50-Gbps Ethernet, using one or two lanes, respectively. Having these two lower-speed alternatives, based on the 100-Gbps technology, would give users more flexibility in meeting existing and near-term demands with a solution that would scale easily to higher data rates.

Such considerations have led to the form of the 25 Gigabit Ethernet Consortium by a number of leading cloud networking providers, including Google and Microsoft. The objective of the Consortium is to support an industry-standard, interoperable Ethernet specification that boosts the performance and slashes the interconnect cost per Gbps between the NIC and ToR switch. The specification adopted by the Consortium prescribes a single-lane 25-Gbps Ethernet and dual-lane 50-Gbps Ethernet link protocol, enabling up to 2.5 times higher performance per physical lane on twinax copper wire between the rack endpoint and switch compared to 10-Gbps and 40-Gbps Ethernet links. The IEEE 802.3 committee is at work developing the needed standards for 25 Gbps and may include 50 Gbps.

It is too early to say how these various options (25, 40, 50, 100 Gbps) will play out in the marketplace. In the intermediate term, the 100-Gbps switch is likely to predominate at large sites, but the availability of these slower and cheaper alternatives gives enterprises a number of paths for scaling up to meet increasing demand.

400-Gbps Ethernet

The growth in demand never lets up. IEEE 802.3 is currently exploring technology options for producing a 400-Gbps Ethernet standard, although no timetable is yet in place. Looking beyond that milestone, there is widespread acknowledgment that a 1-Tbps (terabits per second, trillion bits per second) standard will eventually be produced.

2.5/5-Gbps Ethernet

As a testament to the versatility and ubiquity of Ethernet, and at the same time that ever higher data rates are being standardized, consensus is developing to standardize two lower rates: 2.5 Gbps and 5 Gbps. These relatively low speeds are also known as Multirate Gigabit BASE-T (MGBASE-T). Currently, the MGBASE-T Alliance is overseeing the development of these standards outside of IEEE. It is likely that the IEEE 802.3 committee will ultimately issue standards based on these industry efforts.

These new data rates are mainly intended to support IEEE 802.11ac wireless traffic into a wired network. IEEE 802.11ac is a 3.2-Gbps Wi-Fi standard that is gaining acceptance where more than 1 Gbps of throughput is needed, such as to support mobile users in the office environment. This new wireless standard overruns 1-Gbps Ethernet link support but may not require the next step up, which is 10 Gbps. Assuming that 2.5 and 5 Gbps can be made to work over the same cable that supports 1 Gbps, this would provide a much needed uplink speed improvement for access points supporting 802.11ac radios with their high bandwidth capabilities.

1.4 Wi-Fi

Just as Ethernet has become the dominant technology for wired LANs, so **Wi-Fi**, standardized by the IEEE 802.11 committee, has become the dominant technology for wireless LANs. This overview section discusses applications of Wi-Fi and then looks at standards and performance.

Applications of Wi-Fi

Wi-Fi is the predominant wireless Internet access technology, used in homes, offices, and public spaces. Wi-Fi in the home now connects computers, tablets, smartphones, and a host of electronic devices, such as video cameras, TVs, and thermostats. Wi-Fi

Wi-Fi

Refers to the wireless LAN technology standardized by the IEEE 802.11 committee. The term *Wi-Fi* designates products that have been certified by the Wi-Fi Alliance to conform to the 802.11 standards and have passed interoperability tests.

in the enterprise has become an essential means of enhancing worker productivity and network effectiveness. And public Wi-Fi hotspots have expanded dramatically to provide free Internet access in must public places.

Wi-Fi in the Home

The first important use of Wi-Fi in the home was to replace Ethernet cabling for connecting desktop and laptop computers with each other and with the Internet. A typical layout is a desktop computer with an attached router/modem that provides an interface to the Internet. Other desktop and laptop computers connect either via Ethernet or Wi-Fi to the central router, so that all the home computers can communicate with each other and with the Internet. Wi-Fi greatly simplified the hookup. Not only is there no need for a physical cable hookup, but the laptops can be moved easily from room to room or even outside the house.

Today, the importance of Wi-Fi in the home has expanded tremendously. Wi-Fi remains the default scheme for interconnecting a home computer network. Because both Wi-Fi and cellular capability are now standard on both smartphones and tablets, the home Wi-Fi provides a cost-effective way to the Internet. The smartphone or tablet will automatically use a Wi-Fi connection to the Internet if available, and only switch to the more expensive cellular connection if the Wi-Fi connection is not available. And Wi-Fi is essential to implementing the latest evolution of the Internet: the Internet of Things.

Public Wi-Fi

Access to the Internet via Wi-Fi has expanded dramatically in recent years, as more and more facilities provide a Wi-Fi hotspot, which enables any Wi-Fi device to attach. Wi-Fi hotspots are provided in coffee shops, restaurants, train stations, airports, libraries, hotels, hospitals, department stores, RV parks, and many other places. So many hotspots are available that it is rare to be too far from one. There are now numerous tablet and smartphone apps that increase their convenience.

Even very remote places will be able to support hotspots with the development of the satellite Wi-Fi hotspot. The first company to develop such a product is the satellite communications company Iridium. The satellite modem will initially provide a relatively low-speed connection, but the data rates will inevitably increase.

Enterprise Wi-Fi

The economic benefit of Wi-Fi is most clearly seen in the enterprise. Wi-Fi connections to the enterprise network have been offered by many organizations of all sizes, including public and private sector. But in recent years, the use of Wi-Fi has expanded dramatically, to the point that now approximately half of all enterprise network traffic is via Wi-Fi rather then the traditional Ethernet. Two trends have driven the transition to a Wi-Fi-centered enterprise. First, the demand has increased, with more and more employees preferring to use laptops, tablets, and smartphones to connect to the enterprise network, rather than a desktop computer. Second, the arrival of Gigabit Ethernet, especially the IEEE 802.ac standard, allows the enterprise network to support high-speed connections to many mobile devices simultaneously.

Whereas Wi-Fi once merely provided an accessory network designed to cover meetings and public areas, enterprise Wi-Fi deployment now generally provides ubiquitous coverage, to include main offices and remote facilities, and both indoor locations and outdoor spaces surrounding them. Enterprises accepted the need for, and then began to encourage, the practice known as bring your own device (BYOD). The almost universal availability of Wi-Fi capability on laptops, tablets, and smartphones, in addition to the wide availability of home and public Wi-Fi networks, has greatly benefited the organization. Employees can use the same devices and the same applications to continue their work or check their e-mail from wherever they are— home, at their local coffee shop, or while traveling. From the enterprise perspective, this means higher productivity and efficiency and lower costs.

Standards

Essential to the success of Wi-Fi is interoperability. Wi-Fi-enabled devices must be able to communicate with Wi-Fi access points, such as the home router, the enterprise access point, and public hotspots, regardless of the manufacturer of the device or access point. Such interoperability is guaranteed by two organizations. First, the IEEE 802.11 wireless LAN committee develops the protocol and signaling standards for Wi-Fi. Then, the Wi-Fi Alliance creates test suites to certify interoperability for commercial products that conform to various IEEE 802.11 standards. The term *Wi-Fi* (wireless fidelity) is used for products certified by the Alliance.

IEEE 802.11
Wireless LAN
Working Group

Wi-Fi Alliance

Wi-Fi Data Rates

Just as businesses and home users have generated a need to extend the Ethernet standard to speeds in the gigabits per second (Gbps) range, the same requirement exists for Wi-Fi. As the technology of antennas, wireless transmission techniques, and wireless protocol design has evolved, the IEEE 802.11 committee has been able to introduce standards for new versions of Wi-Fi at ever-higher speeds. Once the standard is issued, industry quickly develops the products. Here's a brief chronology, starting with the original standard, which was simply called IEEE 802.11, and showing the maximum data rate for each version (Figure 1.5):

- **802.11 (1997):** 2 Mbps (megabits per second, million bits per second)
- **802.11a (1999):** 54 Mbps

- **802.11b (1999):** 11 Mbps

- **802.11n (1999):** 600 Mbps

- **802.11g (2003):** 54 Mbps

- **802.11ad (2012):** 6.76 Gbps (billion bits per second)

- **802.11ac (2014):** 3.2 Gbps

IEEE 802.11ac operates in the 5-GHz band, as does the older and slower standards 802.11a and 802.11n. It is designed to provide a smooth evolution from 802.11n. This new standard makes use of advanced technologies in antenna design and signal processing to achieve much greater data rates, at lower battery consumption, all within the same frequency band as the older versions of Wi-Fi.

IEEE 802.11ad is a version of 802.11 operating in the 60-GHz frequency band. This band offers the potential for much wider channel bandwidth than the 5-GHz band, enabling high data rates with relatively simple signal encoding and antenna characteristics. Few devices operate in the 60-GHz band, which means communication experiences less interference than in the other bands used for Wi-Fi.

Because of the inherent transmission limitations of the 60-GHz band, 802.11ad is likely to be useful only within a single room. Because it can support high data rates and, for example, could easily transmit uncompressed high-definition video, it is suitable for applications such as replacing wires in a home entertainment system, or streaming high-definition movies from your cell phone to your television.

Gigabit Wi-Fi holds attractions for both office and residential environments and commercial products are beginning to roll out. In the office environment, the demand for ever greater data rates has led to Ethernet offerings at 10 Gbps, 40 Gbps, and most recently 100 Gbps. These stupendous capacities are needed to support blade servers, heavy reliance on video and multimedia, and multiple broadband connections offsite. At the same time, the use of wireless LANs has grown dramatically in the office setting to meet needs for mobility and flexibility. With the gigabit-range data rates available on the fixed portion of the office LAN, gigabit Wi-Fi is needed to enable mobile users to effectively use the office resources. IEEE 802.11ac is likely to be the preferred gigabit Wi-Fi option for this environment.

In the consumer and residential market, IEEE 802.11ad is likely to be popular as a low-power, short-distance wireless LAN capability with little likelihood of interfering with other devices. IEEE 802.11ad is also an attractive option in professional media production environments in which massive amounts of data need to be moved short distances.

1.5 4G/5G Cellular

Cellular technology is the foundation of mobile wireless communications and supports users in locations that are not easily served by wired networks. Cellular technology is the underlying technology for mobile telephones, personal communications systems, wireless Internet and wireless web applications, and much more. This section looks at how cellular technology has evolved through four generations and is poised for a fifth generation.

First Generation

The original cellular networks, now dubbed 1G, provided analog traffic channels and were designed to be an extension of the public switched telephone networks. Users with brick-sized cell phones placed and received calls in the same fashion as landline subscribers. The most widely deployed 1G system was the Advanced Mobile Phone Service (AMPS), developed by AT&T. Voice transmission was purely analog and control signals were sent over a 10-kbps analog channel.

Second Generation

First-generation cellular networks quickly became highly popular, threatening to swamp available capacity. Second-generation (2G) systems were developed to provide higher-quality signals, higher data rates for support of digital services, and greater capacity. Key differences between 1G and 2G networks include the following:

- **Digital traffic channels:** The most notable difference between the two generations is that 1G systems are almost purely analog, whereas 2G systems are digital. In particular, 1G systems are designed to support voice channels; digital traffic is supported only by the use of a modem that converts the digital data into analog form. 2G systems provide digital traffic channels. These systems readily support digital data; voice traffic is first encoded in digital form before transmitting.

- **Encryption:** Because all the user traffic, and the control traffic, is digitized in 2G systems, it is a relatively simple matter to encrypt all the traffic to prevent eavesdropping. All 2G systems provide this capability, whereas 1G systems send user traffic in the clear, providing no security.

- **Error detection and correction:** The digital traffic stream of 2G systems also lends itself to the use of error detection and correction techniques. The result can be very clear voice reception.

- **Channel access:** In 1G systems, each cell supports a number of channels. At any given time a channel is allocated to only one user. 2G systems also provide multiple channels per cell, but each channel is dynamically shared by a number of users.

Third Generation

The objective of the third generation (3G) of wireless communication is to provide fairly high-speed wireless communications to support multimedia, data, and video in addition to voice. 3G systems share the following design features:

- **Bandwidth:** An important design goal for all 3G systems is to limit channel usage to 5 MHz. There are several reasons for this goal. On the one hand, a bandwidth of 5 MHz or more improves the receiver's ability to resolve multipath when compared to narrower bandwidths. On the other hand, the available spectrum is limited by competing needs, and 5 MHz is a reasonable upper limit on what can be allocated for 3G. Finally, 5 MHz is adequate for supporting data rates of 144 and 384 kbps, the main targets for 3G services.

- **Data rate:** Target data rates are 144 and 384 kbps. Some 3G systems also provide support up to 2 Mbps for office use.

- **Multirate:** The term *multirate* refers to the provision of multiple fixed-data-rate logical channels to a given user, in which different data rates are provided on different logical channels. Further, the traffic on each logical channel can be switched independently through the wireless and fixed networks to different destinations. The advantage of multirate is that the system can flexibly support multiple simultaneous applications from a given user and can efficiently use available capacity by only providing the capacity required for each service.

Fourth Generation

The evolution of smartphones and cellular networks has ushered in a new generation of capabilities and standards, which is collectively called 4G. 4G systems provide ultra-broadband Internet access for a variety of mobile devices including laptops, smartphones, and tablets. 4G networks support Mobile web access and high-bandwidth applications such as high-definition mobile TV, mobile video conferencing, and gaming services.

These requirements have led to the development of a fourth generation (4G) of mobile wireless technology that is designed to maximize bandwidth and throughput while also maximizing spectral efficiency. 4G systems have the following characteristics:

- Based on an all-IP packet switched network

- Support peak data rates of up to approximately 100 Mbps for high-mobility mobile access and up to approximately 1 Gbps for low-mobility access such as local wireless access

- Dynamically share and use the network resources to support more simultaneous users per cell

- Support smooth handovers across heterogeneous networks

- Support high QoS for next-generation multimedia applications

In contrast to earlier generations, 4G systems do not support traditional circuit-switched telephony service, providing only IP telephony services.

Fifth Generation

5G systems are still some years away (perhaps 2020), but 5G technologies are likely an area of active research. By 2020, the huge amounts of data traffic generated by tablets and smartphones will be augmented by an equally huge, and perhaps much larger, amount of traffic from the *Internet of Things*, which includes shoes, watches, appliances, cars, thermostats, door locks, and much more.

With 4G, we may have reached a point of diminishing returns on network efficiency. There will be incremental improvements in the future, but significant increases in transmission efficiency seem unlikely. Instead, the focus for 5G will be on building more intelligence into the network, to meet service quality demands by dynamic use of priorities, adaptive network reconfiguration, and other network management techniques.

1.6 Cloud Computing

This section provides a brief overview of cloud computing, which is dealt with in greater detail later in the book.

Although the general concepts for cloud computing go back to the 1950s, cloud computing services first became available in the early 2000s, particularly targeted at large enterprises. Since then, cloud computing has spread to small- and medium-size businesses, and most recently to consumers. Apple's iCloud was launched in 2012 and had 20 million users within a week of launch. Evernote, the cloud-based note-taking and archiving service, launched in 2008, approached 100 million users in less than six years. In late 2014, Google announced that Google Drive had almost a quarter of a billion active users. Here, we look at the key elements of clouds, including cloud computing, cloud networking, and cloud storage.

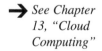

See Chapter 13, "Cloud Computing"

Cloud Computing Concepts

There is an increasingly prominent trend in many organizations to move a substantial portion or even all IT operations to an Internet-connected infrastructure known as enterprise **cloud computing**. At the same time, individual users of PCs and mobile devices are relying more and more on cloud computing services to back up data, sync devices, and share, using personal cloud computing.

The National Institute of Standards and Technology (NIST) defines the essential characteristics of cloud computing as follows:

Cloud computing

A loosely defined term for any system providing access via the Internet to processing power, storage, software, or other computing services, often via a web browser. Often, these services are rented from an external company that hosts and manages them.

- **Broad network access:** Capabilities are available over the network and accessed through standard mechanisms that promote use by heterogeneous thin or thick client platforms (for example, mobile phones, laptops, and personal digital assistants [PDAs]) and other traditional or cloud-based software services.

- **Rapid elasticity:** Cloud computing enables you to expand and reduce resources according to your specific service requirement. For example, you may need a large number of server resources for the duration of a specific task. You can then release these resources upon completion of the task.

- **Measured service:** Cloud systems automatically control and optimize resource use by leveraging a metering capability at some level of abstraction appropriate to the type of service (for example, storage, processing, bandwidth, and active user accounts). Resource usage can be monitored, controlled, and reported, providing transparency for both the provider and consumer of the utilized service.

- **On-demand self-service:** A consumer can unilaterally provision computing capabilities, such as server time and network storage, as needed automatically without requiring human interaction with each service provider. Because the service is on demand, the resources are not permanent parts of your IT infrastructure.

- **Resource pooling:** The provider's computing resources are pooled to serve multiple consumers using a multitenant model, with different physical and virtual resources dynamically assigned and reassigned according to consumer demand. There is a degree of location independence in that the customer generally has no control or knowledge over the exact location of the provided resources, but may be able to specify location at a higher level of abstraction (for example, country, state, or data center). Examples of resources include storage, processing, memory, network bandwidth, and virtual machines. Even private clouds tend to pool resources between different parts of the same organization.

Figure 1.7 illustrates the typical cloud service context. An enterprise maintains workstations within an enterprise LAN or set of LANs, which are connected by a router through a network or the Internet to the cloud service provider. The cloud service provider maintains a massive collection of servers, which it manages with a variety of network management, redundancy, and security tools. In the figure, the cloud infrastructure is shown as a collection of blade servers, which is a common architecture.

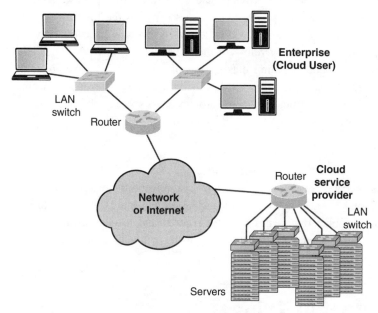

FIGURE 1.7   Cloud Computing Context

The Benefits of Cloud Computing

Cloud computing provides economies of scale, professional network management, and professional security management. These features can be attractive to companies large and small, government agencies, and individual PC and mobile users. The individual or company needs to pay only for the storage capacity and services they need. The user, be it company or individual, does not have the hassle of setting up a database system, acquiring the hardware they need, doing maintenance, and backup up the data; all this is part of the cloud service.

In theory, another big advantage of using cloud computing to store your data and share it with others is that the cloud provider takes care of security. Alas, the customer is not always protected. There have been a number of security failures among cloud providers. Evernote made headlines in early 2013 when it told all of its users to reset their passwords after an intrusion was discovered. Cloud security is addressed in Chapter 16, "Security."

Cloud Networking

Cloud networking refers to the networks and network management functionality that must be in place to enable cloud computing. Many cloud computing solutions rely on the Internet, but that is only a piece of the networking infrastructure.

One example of cloud networking is the provisioning high-performance/high-reliability networking between the provider and subscriber. In this case, some or all of the traffic between an enterprise and the cloud bypasses the Internet and uses dedicated private network facilities owned or leased by the cloud service provider. More generally, cloud networking refers to the collection of network capabilities required to access a cloud, including making use of specialized services over the Internet, linking enterprise data centers to a cloud, and using firewalls and other network security devices at critical points to enforce access security policies.

Cloud Storage

We can think of cloud storage as a subset of cloud computing. In essence, cloud storage consists of database storage and database applications hosted remotely on cloud servers. Cloud storage enables small businesses and individual users to take advantage of data storage that scales with their needs and to take advantage of a variety of database applications without having to buy, maintain, and manage the storage assets.

Internet of Things (IoT)
The expanding connectivity, particularly via the Internet of a wide range of sensors, actuators, and other embedded systems. In almost all cases, there is no human user, with interaction fully automated.

1.7   Internet of Things

The **Internet of Things (IoT)** is the latest development in the long and continuing revolution of computing and communications. Its size, ubiquity, and influence on everyday lives, business, and government dwarf any technical advance that has gone before. This section provides a brief overview of the IoT, which is dealt with in greater detail later in the book.

→ *See Chapter 14, "The Internet of Things"*

Things on the Internet of Things

The *Internet of Things (IoT)* is a term that refers to the expanding interconnection of smart devices, ranging from appliances to tiny sensors. A dominant theme is the embedding of short-range mobile transceivers into a wide array of gadgets and everyday items, enabling new forms of communication between people and things, and between things themselves. The Internet now supports the interconnection of billions of industrial and personal objects, usually through cloud systems. The objects deliver sensor information, act on their environment, and in some cases modify themselves, to create overall management of a larger system, like a factory or city.

The IoT is primarily driven by deeply embedded devices. These devices are low-bandwidth, low-repetition data-capture and low-bandwidth data-usage appliances that communicate with each other and provide data via user interfaces. Embedded appliances, such as high-resolution video security cameras, Video over IP (VoIP) phones, and a handful of others, require high-bandwidth streaming capabilities. Yet countless products simply require packets of data to be intermittently delivered.

Evolution

With reference to the end systems supported, the Internet has gone through roughly four generations of deployment culminating in the IoT:

1. **Information technology (IT):** PCs, servers, routers, firewalls, and so on, bought as IT devices by enterprise IT people, primarily using wired connectivity.

2. **Operational technology (OT):** Machines/appliances with embedded IT built by non-IT companies, such as medical machinery, SCADA (supervisory control and data acquisition), process control, and kiosks, bought as appliances by enterprise OT people and primarily using wired connectivity.

3. **Personal technology:** Smartphones, tablets, and ebook readers bought as IT devices by consumers (employees) exclusively using wireless connectivity and often multiple forms of wireless connectivity.

4. **Sensor/actuator technology:** Single-purpose devices bought by consumers, IT, and OT people exclusively using wireless connectivity, generally of a single form, as part of larger systems.

It is the fourth generation that is usually thought of as the IoT, and which is marked by the use of billions of embedded devices.

Layers of the Internet of Things

Both the business and technical literature often focus on two elements of the Internet of Things—the "things" that are connected, and the Internet that interconnects them. It is better to view the IoT as a massive system, which consists of five layers:

- **Sensors and actuators:** These are the things. Sensors observe their environment and report back quantitative measurements of such variables as temperature, humidity, presence or absence of some observable, and so on.

Actuators operate on their environment, such as changing a thermostat setting or operating a valve.

- **Connectivity:** A device may connect via either a wireless or wired link into a network to send collected data to the appropriate data center (sensor) or receive operational commands from a controller site (actuator).

- **Capacity:** The network supporting the devices must be able to handle a potentially huge flow of data.

- **Storage:** There needs to be a large storage facility to store and maintain backups of all the collected data. This is typically a cloud capability.

- **Data analytics**. For large collections of devices, "big data" is generated, requiring a data analytics capability to process the data flow.

All of these layers are essential to an effective use of the IoT concept.

1.8 Network Convergence

network convergence

The provision of telephone, video, and data communication services within a single network.

Network convergence refers to the merger of previously distinct telephony and information technologies and markets. You can think of this convergence in terms of a three-layer model of enterprise communications:

- **Application convergence:** These are seen by the end users of a business. Convergence integrates communications applications, such as voice calling (telephone), voice mail, e-mail, and instant messaging, with business applications, such as workgroup collaboration, customer relationship management, and back-office functions. With convergence, applications provide rich features that incorporate voice, data, and video in a seamless, organized, and value-added manner. One example is multimedia messaging, which enables a user to use a single interface to access messages from a variety of sources (for example, office voice mail, e-mail, SMS text messages, and mobile voice mail).

- **Enterprise services:** At this level, the manager deals with the information network in terms of the services that must be available to ensure that users can take full advantage of the applications that they use. For example, network managers need to make sure that appropriate privacy mechanisms and authentication services are in place to support convergence-based applications. They may also be able to track user locations to support remote print services and network storage facilities for mobile workers. Enterprise network management services may also include setting up collaborative environments for various users, groups, and applications and QoS provision.

- **Infrastructure:** The network and communications infrastructure consists of the communication links, LANs, WANs, and Internet connections available to the enterprise. Increasingly, enterprise network infrastructure also includes private/public cloud connections to data centers that host high-volume data storage and web services. A key aspect of convergence at this level is the ability to carry voice, image, and video over networks that were originally designed to carry data traffic. Infrastructure convergence has also occurred for networks that were designed for voice traffic. For example, video, image, text, and data are routinely delivered to smartphone users over cell phone networks.

Figure 1.8 illustrates the major attributes of the three-layer model of enterprise communications. In simple terms, convergence involves moving an organization's voice, video, and image traffic to a single network infrastructure. This often involves integrating distinct voice and data networks into a single network infrastructure and extending the infrastructure to support mobile users. The foundation of this convergence is packet-based transmission using the Internet Protocol (IP). Using IP packets to deliver all varieties of communications traffic, sometimes referred to as everything over IP, enables the underlying infrastructure to deliver a wide range of useful applications to business users.

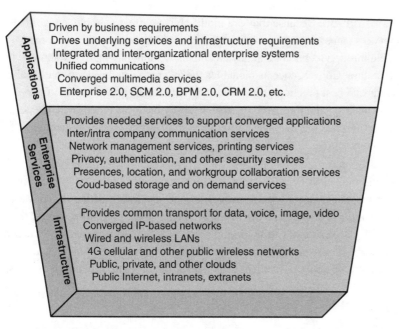

Applications
Driven by business requirements
Drives underlying services and infrastructure requirements
Integrated and inter-organizational enterprise systems
Unified communications
Converged multimedia services
Enterprise 2.0, SCM 2.0, BPM 2.0, CRM 2.0, etc.

Enterprise Services
Provides needed services to support converged applications
Inter/intra company communication services
Network management services, printing services
Privacy, authentication, and other security services
Presences, location, and workgroup collaboration services
Coud-based storage and on demand services

Infrastructure
Provides common transport for data, voice, image, video
Converged IP-based networks
Wired and wireless LANs
4G cellular and other public wireless networks
Public, private, and other clouds
Public Internet, intranets, extranets

FIGURE 1.8   **Business-Driven Convergence**

Convergence brings many benefits, including simplified network management, increased efficiency, and greater flexibility at the application level. For example, a converged network infrastructure provides a predictable platform on which to build new add applications that combine video, data, and voice. This makes it easier for developers to create innovative mash-ups and other value-added business applications and services. The following list summarizes three key benefits of IP network convergence:

- **Cost savings:** A converged network can provide significant double-digit percent reductions in network administration, maintenance, and operating costs; converging legacy networks onto a single IP network enables better use of existing resources, and implementation of centralized capacity planning, asset management, and policy management.

- **Effectiveness:** The converged environment has the potential to provide users with great flexibility, irrespective of where they are. IP convergence allows companies to create a more mobile workforce. Mobile workers can use a virtual private network (VPN) to remotely access business applications and communication services on the corporate network. A VPN helps maintain enterprise network security by separating business traffic from other Internet traffic.

- **Transformation:** Because they are modifiable and interoperable, converged IP networks can easily adapt to new functions and features as they become available through technological advancements without having to install new infrastructure. Convergence also enables the enterprise-wide adoption of global standards and best practices, thus providing better data, enhanced real-time decision making, and improved execution of key business processes and operations. The end result is enhanced agility and innovation, the key ingredients of business innovation.

These compelling business benefits are motivating companies to invest in converged network infrastructures. Businesses, however, are keenly aware of the downside of convergence: having a single network means a single point of failure. Given their reliance on ICT (information and communications technology), today's converged enterprise network infrastructures typically include redundant components and back up systems to increase network resiliency and lessen the severity of network outages.

1.9 Unified Communications

A concept related to network convergence is **unified communications** (UC). Whereas enterprise network convergence focuses on the consolidation of traditionally distinct voice, video, and data communications networks into a common infrastructure, UC focuses on the integration of real-time communication services to optimize business processes. As with converged enterprise networks, IP is the cornerstone on which UC systems are built. Key elements of UC include the following:

1. UC systems typically provide a unified user interface and consistent user experience across multiple devices and media.

2. UC merges real-time communications services with non-real-time services and business process applications.

Figure 1.9 shows the typical components of a UC architecture and how they relate to one another.

unified communications

The integration of real-time enterprise communication services such as instant messaging, presence information, voice (including IP telephony), web and video conferencing, and speech recognition with non-real-time communication services such as unified messaging (integrated voice mail, e-mail, SMS, and fax).

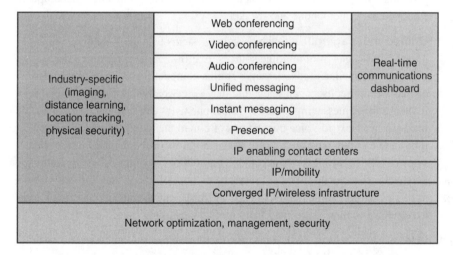

FIGURE 1.9 Elements of a Unified Communications Architecture

The key elements of this architecture are as follows:

- **Real-time communications (RTC) dashboard:** An RTC dashboard is a key component of UC architecture. This is the element that provides UC users with a unified user interface across communication devices. Ideally, the user has a consistent interface no matter what communication device the user is currently using, whether it is a cell phone, wireless tablet computer, desktop system, or office telephone attached to the corporate private branch exchange (PBX). As you can see in Figure 1.9, RTC dashboards provide access to real-time communication services such as instant messaging, audio and video conferencing, and interactive whiteboards; RTC dashboards also provide access to non-real-time services such as unified messaging (e-mail, voice mail, fax, and SMS) in unified view. An RTC dashboard includes presence information about co-workers and partners so that users can know on the fly which colleagues are available to communicate or join a collaborative communication session. RTC dashboards have become necessities in organizations that require high levels of communication and collaboration to support business processes.

- **Web conferencing:** Refers to live meetings or presentations in which participants access the meeting or presentation via a mobile device or the web, either over the Internet, or corporate intranet. Web conferences often include data sharing through web-connected interactive white boards (IWBs).

- **Audio conferencing:** Also called conference calling, refers to a live meeting in which participants are linked together for audio transmission and reception. A participant may be on a landline, mobile phone, or at a "softphone"—a computer equipped with microphone and speaker.

- **Unified messaging:** Unified messaging systems provide a common repository for messages from multiple sources. It allows users to retrieve saved e-mail, voice mail, and fax messages from a computer, telephone, or mobile device. Computer users can select and play voice-mail recordings that appear in their unified messaging inboxes. Telephone users can both retrieve voice mail and hear text-to-voice translations of e-mail messages. Messages of any type can be saved, answered, filed, sorted, and forwarded. Unified messaging systems relieve business users from having to monitor multiple voice mailboxes by enabling voicemail messages received by both office phones and cell phones to be saved to the same mailbox. With UC, users can use any device at any time to retrieve e-mail or voice-mail from unified messaging mailboxes.

- **Instant messaging (IM):** Real-time text-based messaging between two or more participants. IM is similar to online chat because it is text-based and exchanged bidirectionally in real time. IM is distinct from chat in that IM clients use contact (or buddy) lists to facilitate connections between known users, whereas online chat can include text-based exchanges between anonymous users.

- **Video teleconferencing (VTC):** Videoconferencing allows users in two or more locations to interact simultaneously via two-way video and audio transmission. UC systems enable users to participate in video conferences via desktop computers, smartphones, and mobile devices.

- **Presence:** The capability to determine, in real time, where someone is, how that person prefers to be reached, and even what the person is currently doing. Presence information shows the individual's availability state before co-workers attempt to contact them person. It was once considered simply an underlying technology to instant messaging (for example, "available to chat" or "busy") but has been broadened to include whether co-workers are currently on office or mobile phones, logged in to a computer, involved in a video call or in a meeting, or out of the office for lunch or vacation. A co-worker's geographic location is becoming more common as an element in presence information for a number of business reasons, including the capability to quickly respond to customer emergencies. Business has embraced presence information because it facilitates more efficient and effective communication. It helps eliminate inefficiencies associated with "phone tag" or composing and sending e-mails to someone who could more quickly answer a question over the phone or with a quick meeting.

- **IP enabling contact centers:** Refers to the use of IP-based unified communications to enhance customer contact center functionality and performance. The unified communications infrastructure makes use of presence technology to enable customers and internal enterprise employees to be quickly connected to the required expert or support person. In addition, this technology supports mobility, so that call center personnel need not be located at a particular office or remain in a particular place. Finally, the UC infrastructure enables the call center employee to quickly access other employees and information assets, including data, video, image, and audio.

- **IP/mobility:** Refers to the delivery of information to and collection of information from enterprise personnel who are usually mobile, using an IP network infrastructure. In a typical enterprise, upward of 30 percent of employees use some form of weekly remote access technology in the performance of their jobs.

- **Converged IP/wireless infrastructure:** A unified networking and communications-based IP packet transfer to support voice, data, and video transmission and can be extended to include local- and wide-area wireless communications. UC-enabled mobile devices are able to switch between Wi-Fi and cellular systems in the middle of a communication session. For example, a UC user could receive a co-worker's call via a smartphone connected to Wi-Fi network at home, continue the conversation while driving to work over a cellular network connection, and could end the call at the office while connected to the business's Wi-Fi network. Both handoffs (home Wi-Fi to cellular and cellular to office Wi-Fi) would take place seamlessly and transparently without dropping the call.

The importance of UC is not only that it integrates communication channels but also that it offers a way to integrate communication functions and business applications. Three major categories of benefits are typically realized by organizations that use UC:

- **Personal productivity gains:** Presence information helps employees find each other and choose the most effective way to communicate in real time. Less time is wasted calling multiple numbers to locate co-workers or checking multiple worked-related voice mailboxes. Calls from VIP contacts can be routed simultaneously to all of a UC user's phone devices (office phone, softphone, smartphone, home phone) to ensure faster responsiveness to customers, partners, and co-workers. With mobile presence information capabilities, employees who are geographically closest can be dispatched to address a problem.

- **Workgroup performance gains:** UC systems support real-time collaboration among team members, which facilitates workgroup performance improvements. Examples include the use of presence information to speed identification of an available individual with the right skills a work team needs to address a problem. Enhanced conferencing capabilities with desktop VTC and interactive white boards and automated business rules to route or escalate communications also help to increase workgroup performance.

- **Enterprise-level process improvements:** IP convergence enables UC to be integrated with enterprise-wide and departmental-level applications, business processes, and workflows. UC-enabled enhanced communications with customers, suppliers, and business partners are redefining best practices for customer relationship management (CRM), supply chain management (SCM), and other enterprise-wide applications and are transforming relationships among members of business networks. Communication-enabled business processes (CEBP) are fueling competition in several industries, including financial services, healthcare, and retail.

1.10   Key Terms

After completing this chapter, you should be able to define the following terms.

3G	cloud storage	network convergence
4G	content provider	network provider
5G	core network	peering
access network	core router	Power over Ethernet (PoE)
aggregation router	distribution network	powerline carrier (PLC)
application provider	edge router	top-of-rack (ToR) switch
application service provider	end users	unified communications
backbone network	IEEE 802.3	Wi-Fi
blade server	IEEE 802.11	
cloud computing	Internet of Things (IoT)	
cloud networking	Ethernet	

1.11   References

XI11: Xi, H. "Bandwidth Needs in Core and Aggregation Nodes in the Optical Transport Network." IEEE 802.3 Industry Connections Ethernet Bandwidth Assessment Meeting, November 8, 2011. http://www.ieee802.org/3/ad_hoc/bwa/public/nov11/index_1108.html

Chapter 2

Requirements and Technology

Networks will make possible many straightforward and significant economies. There will be problems such as loss of control, a potential lack of responsiveness to changing needs, and priority conflicts; but many of these problems have already been solved to a considerable degree.

—*What Can Be Automated?*
The Computer Science and Engineering Research Study, National Science Foundation, 1980

Chapter Objectives

After studying this chapter, you should be able to

- Present an overview of the major categories of packet traffic on the Internet and internets, including elastic, inelastic, and real-time traffic.
- Discuss the traffic demands placed on contemporary networks by big data, cloud computing, and mobile traffic.
- Explain the concept of quality of service.
- Explain the concept of quality of experience.
- Understand the essential elements of routing.
- Understand the effects of congestion and the types of techniques used for congestion control.
- Compare and contrast software-defined networking and network functions virtualization.

Chapter 1, "Elements of Modern Networking," provided a survey of the elements that make up the networking ecosystem, including network technologies, network architecture, services, and applications. In a concise fashion, this chapter provides motivation, technical background, and an overview of the key topics covered in this book.

2.1 Types of Network and Internet Traffic

Traffic on the Internet and enterprise networks can be divided into two broad categories: elastic and inelastic. A consideration of their differing requirements clarifies the need for an enhanced networking architecture.

Elastic Traffic

Elastic traffic is that which can adjust, over wide ranges, to changes in delay and throughput across an **internet** and still meet the needs of its applications. This is the traditional type of traffic supported on TCP/IP-based internets and is the type of traffic for which internets were designed. Applications that generate such traffic typically use Transmission Control Protocol (TCP) or User Datagram Protocol (UDP) as a transport protocol. In the case of UDP, the application will use as much capacity as is available up to the rate that the application generates data. In the case of TCP, the application will use as much capacity as is available up to the maximum rate that the end-to-end receiver can accept data. Also with TCP, traffic on individual connections adjusts to congestion by reducing the rate at which data are presented to the network.

Internet

A worldwide internetwork based on TCP/IP that interconnects thousands of public and private networks and millions of users.

internet (with lower case *i*)

A large network made up of a number of smaller networks. Also referred to as an internetwork.

Applications that can be classified as elastic include the common applications that operate over TCP or UDP, including file transfer (File Transfer Protocol / Secure FTP [FTP/SFTP]), electronic mail (Simple Mail Transport Protocol [SMTP]), remote login (Telnet, Secure Shell [SSH]), network management (Simple Network Management Protocol [SNMP]), and web access (Hypertext Transfer Protocol / HTTP Secure [HTTP/HTTPS]). However, there are differences among the requirements of these applications, including the following:

- E-mail is generally insensitive to changes in delay.

- When file transfer is done via user command rather than as an automated background task, the user expects the delay to be proportional to the file size and so is sensitive to changes in throughput.

- With network management, delay is generally not a serious concern. However, if failures in an internet are the cause of congestion, then the need for SNMP messages to get through with minimum delay increases with increased congestion.

- Interactive applications, such as remote logon and web access, are sensitive to delay.

It is important to realize that it is not per-packet delay that is the quantity of interest. Observation of real delays across the Internet suggest that wide variations in delay do not occur. Because of the congestion control mechanisms in TCP, when congestion develops, delays only increase modestly before the arrival rate from the various TCP connections slow down. Instead, the quality of service (QoS) perceived by the user relates to the total elapsed time to transfer an element of the current application. For an interactive Telnet-based application, the element may be a single keystroke or single line. For web access, the element is a web page, which could be as little as a few kilobytes or could be substantially larger for an image-rich page. For a scientific application, the element could be many megabytes of data.

For very small elements, the total elapsed time is dominated by the delay time across the Internet. However, for larger elements, the total elapsed time is dictated by the sliding-window performance of TCP and is therefore dominated by the throughput achieved over the TCP connection. Thus, for large transfers, the transfer time is proportional to the size of the file and the degree to which the source slows because of congestion.

It should be clear that even if you confine your attention to elastic traffic, some service prioritizing and controlling traffic could be of benefit. Without such a service, routers are dealing evenhandedly with arriving IP packets, with no concern for the type of application and whether a particular packet is part of a large transfer element or a small one. Under such circumstances, and if congestion develops, it is unlikely that resources will be allocated in such a way as to meet the needs of all applications fairly. When inelastic traffic is added to the mix, the results are even more unsatisfactory.

Inelastic Traffic

Inelastic traffic does not easily adapt, if at all, to changes in delay and throughput across an internet. Examples of inelastic traffic include multimedia transmission, such as voice and video, and high-volume interactive traffic, such as an interactive simulation application (for example, airline pilot simulation). The requirements for inelastic traffic may include the following:

- **Throughput:** A minimum throughput value may be required. Unlike most elastic traffic, which can continue to deliver data with perhaps degraded service, many inelastic applications absolutely require a given minimum throughput.

- **Delay**: Also called latency. An example of a delay-sensitive application is stock trading; someone who consistently receives later service will consistently act later, and with greater disadvantage.

delay jitter
The variation in delay associated with the transfer of packets between two points. Typically measured as the maximum variation in delay experienced by packets in a single session.

- **Delay jitter:** The magnitude of delay variation, called **delay jitter**, or simply jitter, is a critical factor in real-time applications. Because of the variable delay imposed by an internet, the interarrival times between packets are not maintained at a fixed interval at the destination. To compensate for this, the incoming packets are buffered, delayed sufficiently to compensate for the jitter, and then released at a constant rate to the software that is expecting a steady real-time stream. The larger the allowable delay variation, the longer the real delay in delivering the data and the greater the size of the delay buffer required at receivers. Real-time interactive applications, such as teleconferencing, may require a reasonable upper bound on jitter.

- **Packet loss**: Real-time applications vary in the amount of packet loss, if any, that they can sustain.

Table 2.1 shows the loss, delay, and jitter characteristics of various classes of traffic, as specified in RFC 4594 (*Configuration Guidelines for DiffServ Service Classes*, August 2006). Table 2.2 gives examples of QoS requirements for various media-oriented applications [SZIG14].

Table 2.1 Service Class Characteristics

Application Category	Service Class	Traffic Characteristics	Tolerance to Loss	Tolerance to Delay	Tolerance to Jitter
Control	Network control	Variable-size packets, mostly inelastic short messages, but traffic can also burst (BGP)	Low	Low	Yes
	OA&M	Variable-size packets, elastic and inelastic flows	Low	Medium	Yes
Media-Oriented	Telephony	Fixed-size small packets, constant emission rate, inelastic and low-rate flows	Very low	Very low	Very low
	Real-time interactive	RTP/UDP streams, inelastic, mostly variable rate	Low	Very low	Low
	Multimedia conferencing	Variable-size packets, constant transmit interval, rate adaptive, reacts to loss	Low-medium	Very low	Low
	Broadcast video	Constant and variable rate, inelastic, nonbursty flows	Very low	Medium	Low
	Multimedia Streaming	Variable-size packets, elastic with variable rate	Low-medium	Medium	Yes

Application Category	Service Class	Traffic Characteristics	Tolerance to Loss	Tolerance to Delay	Tolerance to Jitter
Data	Low-latency data	Variable rate, bursty short-lived elastic flows	Low	Low-medium	Yes
	High-throughput data	Variable rate, bursty long-lived elastic flows	Low	Medium-high	Yes
	Low-priority data	Non-real-time and elastic	High	High	Yes
Best effort	Standard	A bit of everything	Not specified		

BGP = Border Gateway Protocol

OA&M = Operations, administration, and management

RTP = Real-time Transport Protocol

UDP = User Datagram Protocol

Table 2.2   QoS Requirements by Application Class

Voice	One-way latency ≤ 150 ms
	One-way peak-to-peak jitter ≤ 30 ms
	Per-hop peak-to-peak jitter ≤ 10 ms
	Packet loss ≤ 1 percent
Broadcast video	Packet loss ≤ 0.1 percent
Real-time interactive video	One-way latency ≤ 200 ms
	One-way peak-to-peak jitter ≤ 50 ms
	Per-hop peak-to-peak jitter ≤ 10 ms
	Packet loss ≤ 0.1 percent
Multimedia conferencing	One-way latency ≤ 200 ms
	Packet loss ≤ 1 percent
Multimedia streaming	One-way latency ≤ 400 ms
	Packet loss ≤ 1 percent

These requirements are difficult to meet in an environment with variable queuing delays and congestion losses. Accordingly, inelastic traffic introduces two new requirements into the internet architecture. First, some means is needed to give preferential treatment to applications with more demanding requirements. Applications need to be able to state their requirements, either ahead of time in some sort of service request function, or on the fly, by means of fields in the IP packet header. The former approach provides more flexibility in stating requirements, and it enables the network to anticipate demands and deny new requests if the required resources are unavailable. This approach implies the use of some sort of resource reservation protocol.

An additional requirement in supporting inelastic traffic in an internet architecture is that elastic traffic must still be supported. Inelastic applications typically do not back off and reduce demand in the face of congestion, in contrast to TCP-based applications. Therefore, in times of congestion, inelastic traffic will continue to supply a high load, and elastic traffic will be crowded off the internet. A reservation protocol can help control this situation by denying service requests that would leave too few resources available to handle current elastic traffic.

Real-Time Traffic Characteristics

As mentioned, a common example of inelastic traffic is **real-time traffic**. With traditional elastic applications, such as file transfer, electronic mail, and client/server applications including the web, the performance metrics of interest are generally throughput and delay. There is also a concern with reliability, and mechanisms are used to make sure that no data are lost, corrupted, or misordered during transit. By contrast, **real-time** applications are concerned with timing issues as well as packet loss. In most cases, there is a requirement that data be delivered at a constant rate equal to the sending rate. In other cases, a deadline is associated with each block of data, such that the data are not usable after the deadline has expired.

real time

As fast as required. A real-time system must respond to a signal, event or request fast enough to satisfy some requirement.

real-time traffic

A data flow that must meet real-time requirements, such as low jitter and low delay.

Figure 2.1 illustrates a typical real-time environment. Here, a server is generating audio to be transmitted at 64 kbps. The digitized audio is transmitted in packets containing 160 octets of data, so that one packet is issued every 20 ms. These packets are passed through an internet and delivered to a multimedia PC, which plays the audio in real time as it arrives. However, because of the variable delay imposed by the internet, the interarrival times between packets are not maintained at a fixed 20 ms at the destination. To compensate for this, the incoming packets are buffered, delayed slightly, and then released at a constant rate to the software that generates the audio. The buffer may be internal to the destination machine or in an external network device.

The compensation provided by the delay buffer is limited. For example, if the minimum end-to-end delay seen by any packet is 1 ms and the maximum is 6 ms, the delay jitter is 5 ms. As long as the time delay buffer delays incoming packets by at least 5 ms, the output of the buffer will include all incoming packets. However, if the buffer delayed packets by only 4 ms, any incoming packets that had experienced a relative delay of more than 4 ms (an absolute delay of more than 5 ms) would have to be discarded so as not to be played back out of order.

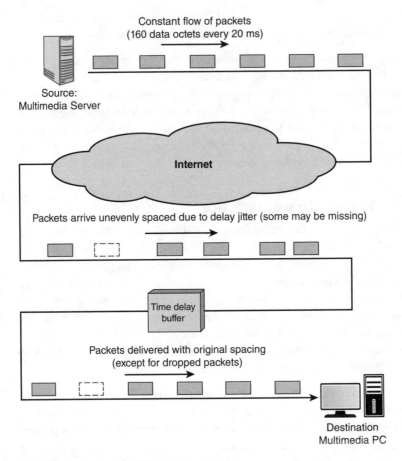

FIGURE 2.1   Real-Time Traffic

The description of real-time traffic so far implies a series of equal-size packets generated at a constant rate. This is not always the profile of the traffic. Figure 2.2 illustrates some of the common possibilities, as described in the list that follows.

- **Continuous data source:** Fixed-size packets are generated at fixed intervals. This characterizes applications that are constantly generating data, have few redundancies, and that are too important to compress in a lossy way. Examples are air traffic control radar and real-time simulations.

- **On/off source:** The source alternates between periods when fixed-size packets are generated at fixed intervals and periods of inactivity. A voice source, such as in telephony or audio conferencing, fits this profile.

- **Variable packet size**: The source generates variable-length packets at uniform intervals. An example is digitized video in which different frames may experience different compression ratios for the same output quality level.

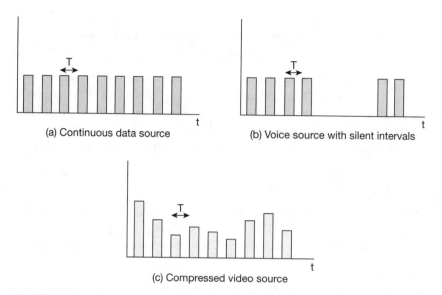

FIGURE 2.2   Real-Time Packet Transmission

2.2   Demand: Big Data, Cloud Computing, and Mobile Traffic

Having looked at the types of traffic presented to the Internet and other IP-based networks, consider the application areas that are generating the greatest stress on network resources and management. Three areas stand out: big data, cloud computing, and mobility. All of these areas suggest the need for using powerful tools such as software-defined networking (SDN) and network functions virtualization (NFV) for network operation and management, and for using comprehensive QoS and quality of experience (QoE) systems for effective delivery of services over IP-based networks.

Big Data

In simple terms, **big data** refers to everything that enables an organization to create, manipulate, and manage very large data sets (measured in terabytes, petabytes, exabytes, and so on) and the facilities in which these are stored. Distributed data centers, data warehouses, and cloud-based storage are common aspects of today's enterprise networks. Many factors have contributed to the merging of "big data" and business networks, including continuing declines in storage costs, the maturation of data mining and business intelligence (BI) tools, and government regulations and court cases that have caused organizations to stockpile large masses of structured and unstructured data, including documents, e-mail messages, voice-mail messages, text messages, and social media data. Other data sources being captured, transmitted,

big data

A collection of data on such a large scale that standard data analysis and management tools are not adequate. More broadly, big data refers to the volume, variety, and velocity of structured and unstructured data pouring through networks into processors and storage devices, along with the conversion of such data into business advice for enterprises.

and stored include web logs, Internet documents, Internet search indexing, call detail records, scientific research data and results, military surveillance, medical records, video archives, and e-commerce transactions.

Data sets continue to grow with more and more being gathered by remote sensors, mobile devices, cameras, microphones, radio frequency identification (RFID) readers, and similar technologies. One study from a few years ago estimated that 2.5 exabytes (2.5×10^{18} bytes) of data are created each day, and 90 percent of the data in the world was created in the past two years [IBM11]. Those numbers are likely higher today.

Big Data Infrastructure Considerations

Traditional business data storage and management technologies include relational database management systems (RDBMS), network-attached storage (NAS), storage-area networks (SANs), data warehouses (DWs), and business intelligence (BI) analytics.

analytics

Analysis of massive amounts of data, particularly with a focus on decision making.

Traditional data warehouse and BI analytics systems tend to be highly centralized within an enterprise infrastructure. These often include a central data repository with a RDBMS, high-performance storage, and **analytics** software, such as online analytical processing (OLAP) tools for mining and visualizing data.

Increasingly, big data applications are becoming a source of competitive value for businesses, especially those that aspire to build data products and services to profit from the huge volumes of data that they capture and store. There is every indication that the exploitation of data will become increasingly important to enterprises in the years ahead as more and more businesses reap the benefits of big data applications.

Big Data Networking Example

To get some feel for the networking requirements for a typical big data system, consider the example ecosystem of Figure 2.3 (compared to Figure 1.1 from Chapter 1).

Key elements within the enterprise include the following:

- **Data warehouse:** The DW holds integrated data from multiple data sources, used for reporting and data analysis.

- **Data management servers:** Large banks of servers serve multiple functions with respect to big data. The servers run data analysis applications, such as data integration tools and analytics tools. Other applications integrate and structure data from enterprise activity, such as financial data, point-of-sale data, and e-commerce activity.

- **Workstations / data processing systems:** Other systems involved in the use of big data applications and in the generation of input to big data warehouses.

■ **Network management server:** One or more servers responsible for network management, control, and monitoring.

Not shown in Figure 2.3 are other important network devices, including firewalls,
intrusion detection/prevention systems (IDS/IPS), LAN switches, and routers.

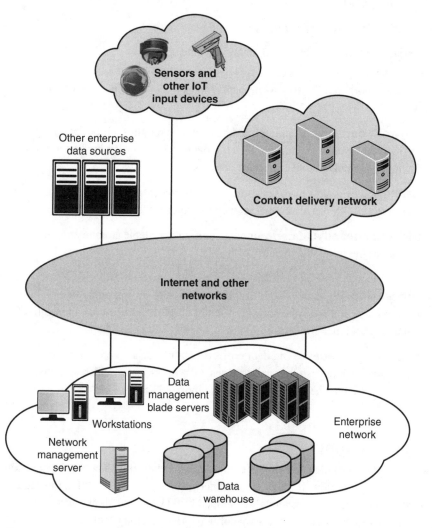

FIGURE 2.3   Big Data Networking Ecosystem

The enterprise network can involve multiple sites distributed regionally, nationally, or
globally. In addition, depending on the nature of the big data system, an enterprise can
receive data from other enterprise servers, from dispersed sensors and other devices

in an Internet of Things, in addition to multimedia content from content delivery networks.

The networking environment for big data is complex. The impact of big data on an enterprise's networking infrastructure is driven by the so-called three *V*'s:

- Volume (growing amounts of data)

- Velocity (increasing speed in storing and reading data)

- Variability (growing number of data types and sources)

Based on a Network World 2014 white paper, areas of concern include the following [NETW14]:

- **Network capacity:** Running big data analytics requires a lot of capacity on its own; the issue is magnified when big data and day-to-day application traffic are combined over an enterprise network.

- **Latency:** The real or near-real-time nature of big data demands a network architecture with consistent low latency to achieve optimal performance.

- **Storage capacity:** Massive amounts of highly scalable storage are required to address the insatiable appetite of big data, yet these resources must be flexible enough to handle many different data formats and traffic loads.

- **Processing:** Big data can add significant pressure on computational, memory, and storage systems, which, if not properly addressed, can negatively impact operational efficiency.

- **Secure data access:** Big data projects combine sensitive information from many sources like customer transactions, GPS coordinates, video streams, and so on, which must be protected from unauthorized access.

Cloud Computing

As with big data installations, cloud computing presents imposing challenges for effective and efficient flow of traffic through networks. It will be helpful in this regard to consider the cloud network model developed by ITU-T, and shown in Figure 2.4 [ITUT12]. This figure indicates the scope of network concerns for cloud network and service providers and for cloud service users.

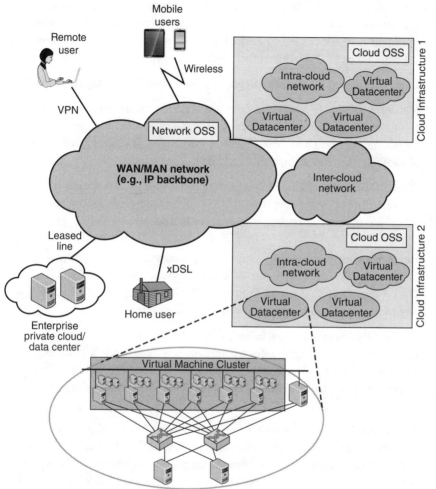

FIGURE 2.4   Cloud Network Model

A cloud service provider maintains one or more local or regional cloud infrastructures. An intracloud network connects the elements of the infrastructure, including database servers, storage arrays, and other servers (for example, firewalls, load balancers, application acceleration devices, and IDS/IPS). The intracloud network will likely include a number of LANs interconnected with IP routers. Within the infrastructure, database servers are organized as a cluster of **virtual machines**, providing virtualized, isolated computing environments for different users.

virtual machine

One instance of an operating system along with one or more applications running in an isolated partition within the computer. It enables different operating systems to run in the same computer at the same time and prevents applications from interfering with each other.

➔ *See Chapter 7, "Network Functions Virtualization: Concepts and Architecture"*

Intercloud networks interconnect cloud infrastructures together. These cloud infrastructures may be owned by the same cloud provider or by different ones. Finally, a core transport network is used by customers to access and consume cloud services deployed within the cloud provider's data center.

Also depicted in Figure 2.4 are two categories of operations support system (OSS):

- **Network OSS:** The traditional OSS is a system dedicated to providers of telecommunication services. The processes supported by a network OSS include service management and maintenance of the network inventory, configuration of particular network components, and fault management.

- **Cloud OSS:** OSS of cloud infrastructure is the system dedicated to providers of cloud computing services. Cloud OSS supports processes for the maintenance, monitoring, and configuration of cloud resources.

These three network components (intracloud, intercloud, core), together with the OSS components, are the foundation of cloud services composition and delivery. The ITU-T Focus Group on Cloud Computing Technical Report [ITUT12] lists the following functional requirements for this network capability:

- **Scalability:** Networks must be able to scale easily to meet the demands of moving from current cloud infrastructures of hundreds or a few thousand servers to networks of tens or even hundreds of thousands of servers. This scaling presents challenges in areas such as addressing, routing, and congestion control.

- **Performance:** Traffic in both big data installations and cloud provider networks is unpredictable and quite variable [KAND12]. There are sustained spikes between nearby servers within the same rack and intermittent heavy traffic with a single source server and multiple destination servers. Intracloud networks need to provide reliable high-speed direct (logical point-to-point) communications between servers with congestion-free links, and uniform capacity between any two arbitrary servers within the data center. The ITU-T report concludes that the current three-tier topology (access, aggregation, and core) used in data centers is not well adapted to provide these requirements. A more flexible and dynamic control of data flows, in addition to virtualization of network devices, provides a better foundation for providing the desired quality of service.

- **Agility and flexibility**: The cloud-based data center needs to be able to respond and manage the highly dynamic nature of cloud resource utilization. This includes the ability to adapt to virtual machine mobility and to provide fine-grained control of flows routing through the data center.

➜ *See Chapter 13, "Cloud Computing"*

We return to this discussion in Chapter 13, "Cloud Computing." For now, it suffices to point out that as the book unfolds, it should be clear that the combination of SDN and NFV are well suited to meeting the requirements in the preceding list.

Mobile Traffic

Technical innovations have contributed to the success of what were originally just mobile phones. The prevalence of the latest devices, with multimegabit Internet access, mobile apps, high megapixel digital cameras, access to multiple types of wireless networks (for example, Wi-Fi, Bluetooth, 3G, 4G), and several onboard sensors, all add to this momentous achievement. Devices have become increasingly powerful while staying easy to carry. Battery life has increased (even though device energy usage has also expanded), and digital technology has improved reception and allowed better use of a finite spectrum. As with many types of digital equipment, the costs associated with mobile devices have been decreasing.

The first rush to wireless was for voice. Now, the attention is on data; some wireless devices are only rarely used for voice. Figure 2.5 shows the dramatic trend in world total mobile traffic in 2G, 3G, and 4G networks (not including DVB-H, Wi-Fi, and Mobile WiMAX) estimated by Ericsson [AKAM15]. Ericsson's presence in more than 180 countries and its customer base representing more than 1000 networks enable it to measure mobile voice and data volumes. The result is a representative base for calculating world total mobile traffic.

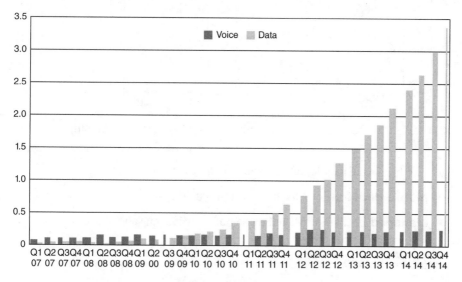

FIGURE 2.5　World Total Monthly Mobile Voice and Data Traffic (exabytes/month) [AKAM15]

A big part of the mobile market is the wireless Internet. Wireless users use the Internet differently than fixed users, but in many ways no less effectively. Wireless smartphones have limited displays and input capabilities compared with larger devices such as laptops or PCs, but mobile apps give quick access to intended information without using websites. Because wireless devices are location aware, information can be tailored to the geographic location of the user. Information finds users, instead of users searching for information. Tablet devices provide a happy medium between the larger screens and better input capabilities of PCs and the portability of smartphones.

Figure 2.6 shows a projection for mobile enterprise IP traffic [CISC14], where the term *enterprise* refers to businesses and governments. Cisco's methodology rests on a combination of analyst projections, in-house estimates and forecasts, and direct data collection. As with mobile data traffic over cellular networks, mobile enterprise IP traffic is on a strong growth curve.

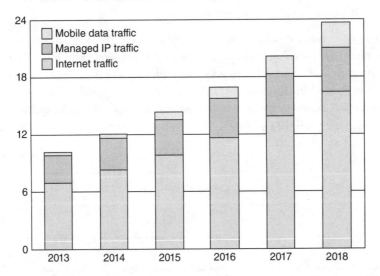

FIGURE 2.6   Forecast Monthly Enterprise IP Traffic (Exabytes/Month) [CISC14]

Figure 2.6 breaks the mobile traffic down into three categories:

- **Mobile data traffic:** All enterprise traffic that crosses a mobile access point

- **Managed IP traffic:** All enterprise traffic that is transported over IP but remains within the corporate WAN

- **Internet traffic:** All enterprise traffic that crosses the public Internet

Although mobile traffic is the smallest of the three categories of enterprise traffic, it is growing much more rapidly than the other two categories. Based on Cisco's projections, the compound annual growth rate over the period 2013 to 2018 for enterprise traffic is as follows:

Mobile Data Traffic	Managed IP Traffic	Internet Traffic	Total Traffic
55 percent	10 percent	18 percent	18 percent

Enterprise networks need to be flexible enough to handle the rapidly growing mobile data load. Such a load is characterized by dynamically changing physical access points into the network and a wide variety of elastic and inelastic traffic types. As you will learn, SDN and NFV are well suited to coping with this highly dynamic load.

2.3 Requirements: QoS and QoE

So far, this chapter has focused on the types of traffic the enterprise networks and the Internet carry and looked at three areas of demand that create significant challenges for providing effective and efficient network service to users. This section briefly introduces two concepts that provide a way of quantifying the network performance that the enterprise desires to achieve: quality of service (QoS) and quality of experience (QoE). QoS and QoE enable the network manager to determine whether the network is meeting user needs and to diagnose problem areas that require adjustment to network management and network traffic control. QoS and QoE are treated in detail in Part IV of the book.

→ *See Part IV, "Defining and Supporting User Needs"*

Quality of Service

You can define QoS as the measurable end-to-end performance properties of a network service, which can be guaranteed in advance by a service level agreement (SLA) between a user and a service provider, so as to satisfy specific customer application requirements. Commonly specified properties include the following:

- **Throughput**: A minimum or average throughput, in bytes per second or bits per second, for a given logical connection or traffic flow.
- **Delay:** The average or maximum delay. Also called latency.
- **Packet jitter:** Typically, the maximum allowable jitter.
- **Error rate:** Typically maximum error rate, in terms of fraction of bits delivered in error.
- **Packet loss:** Fraction of packets lost.

- **Priority:** A network may offer a given number of levels of priority. The assigned level for various traffic flows influences the way in which the different flows are handled by the network.

- **Availability:** Expressed as a percentage of time available.

- **Security:** Different levels or types of security may be defined.

QoS mechanisms ensure that business applications continue to receive the necessary performance guarantee even though they no longer run on dedicated hardware, such as when applications are transferred to a cloud. The QoS provided by an infrastructure is partially determined by its overall performance and efficiency. However, QoS is also the ability to prioritize specific workloads and allocate the needed resources to meet required service levels. It can offer a powerful way to allocate processor, memory, I/O, and network traffic resources among applications and virtual guests.

Quality of Experience

QoE is a subjective measure of performance as reported by the user. Unlike QoS, which can be precisely measured, QoE relies on human opinion. QoE is important particularly when we deal with multimedia applications and multimedia content delivery. QoS provides measurable, quantitative targets that guide the design and operation of a network and enable customer and provider to agree on what quantitative performance the network will deliver for give applications and traffic flows.

However, QoS processes by themselves are not sufficient in that they do not take into account the user's perception of network performance and service quality. Although the maximum capacity may be fixed at a certain value by a media transmission system, this does not necessarily fix the quality of the multimedia content at, say, "high." This is because there are numerous ways the multimedia content could have been encoded, giving rise to differing perceived qualities. The ultimate measure of a network and the services it offers is how subscribers perceive the performance. QoE augments the traditional QoS by providing information regarding the delivered services from an end user point of view.

There is a wide range of factors and features that can be included in a requirement for QoE, which can, roughly, be classified into the following categories:

- **Perceptual:** This category encompasses the quality of the sensory aspects of the user experience. For video, examples include sharpness, brightness, contrast, flicker, and distortion. Audio examples include clarity and timbre.

- **Psychological:** This category deals with the user's feeling about the experience. Examples include ease of use, joy of use, usefulness, perceived quality, satisfaction, annoyance, and boredom.

- **Interactive:** This category deals with aspects of an experience related to the interaction between the user and the application or device, such as responsiveness, naturalness of interaction, communication efficiency, and accessibility.

For practical application, these features need to be converted to quantitative measures.

The management of QoE has become a crucial concept in the deployment of future successful applications, services, and products. The greatest challenges in providing QoE are developing effective methods for converting QoE features to quantitative measures and translating QoE measures to QoS measures. Whereas QoS can now easily be measured, monitored, and controlled at both the networking and application layers, and at both the end system and network sides, QoE is something that is still quite intricate to manage.

2.4 Routing

This section and the next briefly introduce two mechanisms that are fundamental to the operation of a network and its capability to transmit and deliver packet traffic: routing and congestion control. A detailed look is beyond the scope of the book. The purpose here is to indicate the basic concepts of routing and congestion control, because these are the basic tools needed to support network traffic and to provide QoS and QoE.

Characteristics

The primary function of an internet is to accept packets from a source station and deliver them to a destination station. To accomplish this, a path or route through the network must be determined; generally, more than one route is possible. Therefore, a routing function must be performed.

The selection of a route is generally based on some performance criterion. The simplest criterion is to choose the minimum-hop route (one that passes through the least number of nodes) through the network. This is an easily measured criterion and should minimize the consumption of network resources. A generalization of the minimum-hop criterion is least-cost routing. In this case, a cost is associated with each link, and, for any pair of attached stations, the route through the network that accumulates the least cost is sought.

Figure 2.7 illustrates a network in which the two arrowed lines between a pair of nodes represent a link between these nodes, and the corresponding numbers represent the current link cost in each direction. Our concern, of course, is with an internet, in which each node is a router and the links between adjacent routers are networks or direct communications links. The shortest path (fewest hops) from node 1 to node 6 is 1-3-6 (Cost = 5 + 5 = 10), but the least-cost path is 1-4-5-6 (Cost = 1 + 1 + 2 = 4).

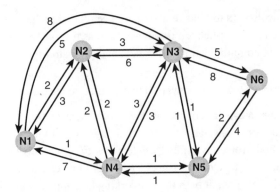

FIGURE 2.7   Network Architecture Example

Costs are assigned to links to support one or more design objectives. For example, the cost could be inversely related to the data rate (that is, the higher the data rate on a link, the lower the assigned cost of the link) or the current link delay. In the first case, the least-cost route should provide the highest throughput. In the second case, the least-cost route should minimize delay. Routing decisions can be based on other criteria as well. For example, a routing policy may dictate that certain types of traffic be restricted to certain routes for security concerns.

Packet Forwarding

The key function of any router is to accept incoming packets and forward them. For this purpose, a router maintains forwarding tables. Figure 2.8 shows a simplified example of how this might be implemented for the network, with its associated link costs, of Figure 2.7. A router's forwarding table shows, for each destination, the identity of the next node on the router. Each router may be responsible for discovering the appropriate routes. Alternatively, a network control center may be responsible for designing routes for all routers and maintaining a central forwarding table, providing each router with individual forwarding tables relevant only to that router.

Note that it is not necessary to store the complete route for each possible pair of nodes. Rather, it is sufficient to know, for each pair of nodes, the identity of the first node on the route.

In the simple example of Figure 2.8, forwarding decisions are based solely on the identity of the destination system. Additional information is often used to determine the forwarding decision, such as the source address, packet flow identifier, or security level of the packet:

- **Failure:** When a node or link fails, it can no longer be used as part of a route.

- **Congestion:** When a particular portion of the network is heavily congested, it is desirable to route packets around rather than through the area of congestion.

- **Topology change**: The insertion of new links or nodes affects routing.

CENTRAL FORWARDING TABLE

From Node

	1	2	3	4	5	6
1	–	1	5	2	4	5
2	2	–	5	2	4	5
3	4	3	–	5	3	5
4	4	4	5	–	4	5
5	4	4	5	5	–	5
6	4	4	5	5	6	–

To Node (rows 1–6)

Node 1 Table

Destination	Next Node
2	2
3	4
4	4
5	4
6	4

Node 2 Table

Destination	Next Node
1	1
3	3
4	4
5	4
6	4

Node 3 Table

Destination	Next Node
1	5
2	5
4	5
5	5
6	5

Node 4 Table

Destination	Next Node
1	2
2	2
3	5
5	5
6	5

Node 5 Table

Destination	Next Node
1	4
2	4
3	3
4	4
6	6

Node 6 Table

Destination	Next Node
\\\\	5
2	5
3	5
4	5
5	5

FIGURE 2.8   Packet Forwarding Tables (using Figure 2.7)

For adaptive routing to be possible, information about the state of the network must be exchanged among the nodes or between the nodes and a central controller.

Routing Protocols

The routers in an internet are responsible for receiving and forwarding packets through the interconnected set of networks. Each router makes routing decisions based on knowledge of the topology and traffic/delay conditions of the internet. Accordingly, a degree of dynamic cooperation is needed among the routers. In particular, the router must avoid portions of the network that have failed and should avoid portions

autonomous system (AS)

A network that is administered by a single set of management rules that are controlled by one person, group, or organization. Autonomous systems often use only one routing protocol, although multiple protocols can be used. The core of the Internet is made up of many autonomous systems.

interior router protocol (IRP)

A protocol that distributes routing information to collaborating routers within an AS. Routing Information Protocol (RIP) and Open Shortest Path First (OSPF) Protocol are examples of IRPs. Historically, an IRP was referred to as an interior gateway protocol.

of the network that are congested. To make such dynamic routing decisions, routers exchange routing information using a routing protocol. Information is needed about the status of the internet, in terms of which networks can be reached by which routes, and the delay characteristics of various routes.

There are essentially two categories of routing protocols, which are based on the concept of an **autonomous system (AS)**. We first define AS and then look at the two categories. An AS exhibits the following characteristics:

1. An AS is a set of routers and networks managed by a single organization.

2. An AS consists of a group of routers exchanging information via a common routing protocol.

3. Except in times of failure, an AS is connected (in a graph-theoretic sense); that is, there is a path between any pair of nodes.

A shared routing protocol, called here an **interior router protocol (IRP)**, passes routing information between routers within an AS. The protocol used within the AS does not need to be implemented outside of the system. This flexibility allows IRPs to be custom tailored to specific applications and requirements.

It may happen, however, that an internet will be constructed of more than one AS. For example, all the LANs at a site, such as an office complex or campus, could be linked by routers to form an AS. This system might be linked through a wide-area network to other autonomous systems. Figure 2.9 illustrates this situation.

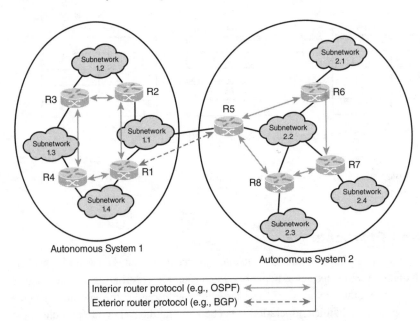

FIGURE 2.9   Use of Exterior and Interior Routing Protocols

In this case, the routing algorithms and information in routing tables used by routers in different autonomous systems may differ. Nevertheless, the routers in one AS need at least a minimal level of information concerning networks outside the system that can be reached. We refer to the protocol used to pass routing information between routers in different autonomous systems as an **exterior router protocol (ERP)**.

> **Note**
>
> In the literature, the terms *interior gateway protocol (IGP)* and *exterior gateway protocol (EGP)* are often used for what are referred to here as IRP and ERP. However, because the terms *IGP* and *EGP* also refer to specific protocols, we avoid their use when referring to the general concepts.

exterior router protocol (ERP)

A protocol that distributes routing information to collaborating routers that connect autonomous systems. BGP is an example of an ERP. Historically, an ERP was referred to as an exterior gateway protocol.

You can expect that an ERP will need to pass less information than an IRP for the following reason. If a packet is to be transferred from a host in one AS to a host in another AS, a router in the first system need only determine the target AS and devise a route to get into that target system. Once the packet enters the target AS, the routers within that system can cooperate to deliver the packet; the ERP is not concerned with, and does not know about, the details of the route followed within the target AS.

Elements of a Router

Figure 2.10 depicts the principal elements of a router, from the point of view of its routing function.

Any given router has a number of I/O ports attached to it: one or more to other routers, and zero or more to end systems. On each port, packets arrive and depart. You can consider that there are two buffers, or queues, at each port: one to accept arriving packets, and one to hold packets that are waiting to depart. In practice, there might be two fixed-size buffers associated with each port, or there might be a pool of memory available for all buffering activities. In the latter case, you can think of each port having two variable-size buffers associated with it, subject to the constraint that the sum of all buffer sizes is a constant.

In any case, as packets arrive, they are stored in the input buffer of the corresponding port. The router examines each incoming packet, makes a routing decision based on the forwarding tables, and then moves the packet to the appropriate output buffer. Packets queued for output are transmitted as rapidly as possible. Each output queue can be operated as a simple first-in, first-out (FIFO) queue. More commonly, a more complex queuing discipline is used, to take into account the relative priority of the queued packets. A set of routing policies may also influence the construction of the forwarding tables and how various packets are to be treated. Policies may determine routing not just on the destination address but other factors, such as source address, packet size, and protocol of the payload.

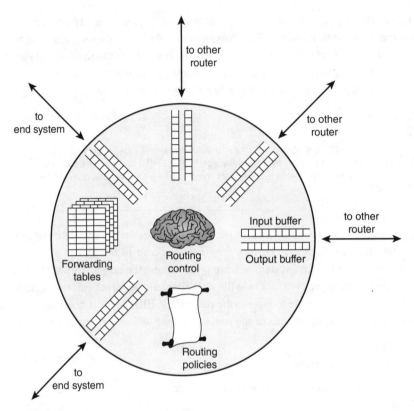

FIGURE 2.10   Elements of a Router

The final element shown in Figure 2.10 is a routing control function. This function includes execution of routing protocols, adaptive maintenance of the routing tables, and supervising congestion control policies.

2.5   Congestion Control

If the traffic demand on an internet exceeds capacity, or if the internet does not manage the traffic efficiently, congestion will occur. This section provides a brief overview of the effects of congestion and a general introduction to approaches to congestion control.

Effects of Congestion

If packets arrive too fast for a router to process them (that is, make routing decisions) or faster than packets can be cleared from the outgoing buffers, eventually packets will arrive for which no memory is available. When such a saturation point is reached, one of two general strategies can be adopted. The first such strategy is to discard any incoming packet for which there is no available buffer space. The alternative is for the node that is experiencing these problems to exercise some sort of flow control over its neighbors so that the traffic flow remains manageable. But, as Figure 2.11 illustrates, each of a node's neighbors is also managing a number of queues. If node 6 restrains the flow of packets from node 5, this causes the output buffer in node 5 for the port to node 6 to fill up. Thus, congestion at one point in the network can quickly propagate throughout a region or the entire network. Although flow control is indeed a powerful tool, you need to use it in such a way as to manage the traffic on the entire network.

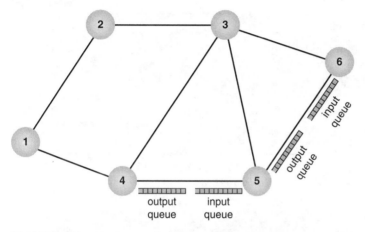

FIGURE 2.11   Interaction of Queues in a Data Network

Ideal Performance

Figure 2.12 suggests the ideal goal for network utilization.

The top graph plots the steady-state total throughput (number of packets delivered to destination end systems) through the network as a function of the offered load (number of packets transmitted by source end systems), both normalized to the maximum theoretical throughput of the network. In the ideal case, the throughput of the network increases to accommodate load up to an offered load equal to the full capacity of the network; then normalized throughput remains at 1.0 at higher input loads. Note, however, what happens to the end-to-end delay experienced by the average packet even with this assumption of ideal performance. At negligible load, there is some small constant amount of delay that consists of the propagation delay through the network from source to destination plus processing delay at each node. As the load on the network increases, queuing delays at each node are added to this fixed amount of delay. The reason for the increase in delay even when the total network capacity is not exceeded has to do with the variability in load at each node. With multiple sources supplying data to the network, even if each source produced packets at fixed intervals, there will be fluctuation in the input rate at each individual network node. When a burst of packets arrives at a node, it will take some time to clear the backlog. As it is clearing the backlog, it is sending out a sustained burst of packets, thus imposing packet bursts on downstream node. And once a queue builds up at a node, even if packets only arrive at a rate the node can handle during a given time period, those packets have to wait their turn in the queue, and thus experience additional delay. This is a standard result of queuing theory: delays will grow with increasing load if the arrival rate is not constant.

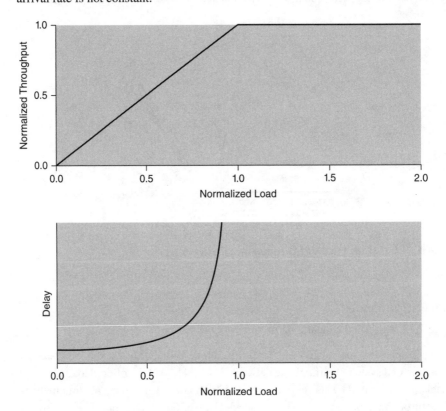

FIGURE 2.12 Ideal Network Utilization

When the load exceeds the network capacity, delays increase without bound. Here is a simple intuitive explanation of why delay must go to infinity. Suppose that each node in the network is equipped with buffers of infinite size and suppose that the input load exceeds network capacity. Under ideal conditions, the network will continue to sustain a normalized throughput of 1.0. Therefore, the rate of packets leaving the network is 1.0. Because the rate of packets entering the network is greater than 1.0, internal queue sizes grow. In the steady state, with input greater than output, these queue sizes grow without bound and therefore queuing delays grow without bound.

It is important to grasp the meaning of Figure 2.12 before looking at real-world conditions. This figure represents the ideal, but unattainable, goal of all traffic and congestion control schemes. No scheme can exceed the performance depicted in Figure 2.12.

Practical Performance

The ideal case reflected in Figure 2.12 assumes infinite buffers and no overhead related to congestion control. In practice, buffers are finite, leading to buffer overflow, and attempts to control congestion consume network capacity in the exchange of control signals.

Consider what happens in a network with finite buffers if no attempt is made to control congestion or to restrain input from end systems. The details, of course, differ depending on network architecture and on the statistics of the presented traffic; however, the graphs in Figure 2.13 depict the devastating outcome in general terms.

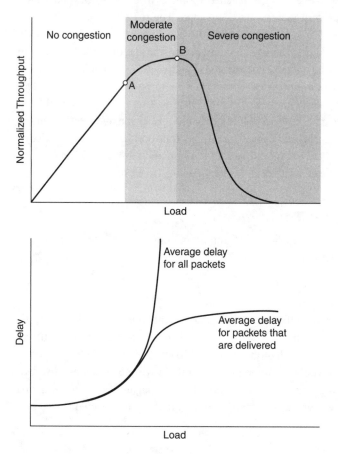

FIGURE 2.13   The Effects of Congestion

At light loads, throughput and hence network utilization increases as the offered load increases. As the load continues to increase, a point is reached (point A in the plot) beyond which the throughput of the network increases at a rate slower than the rate at which offered load is increased. This is because of network entry into a moderate congestion state. In this region, the network continues to cope with the load, although with increased delays. The departure of throughput from the ideal is accounted for by a number of factors. For one thing, the load is unlikely to be spread uniformly throughout the network. Therefore, while some nodes may experience moderate congestion, others may be experiencing severe congestion and may need to discard traffic. In addition, as the load increases, the network attempts to balance the load by routing packets through areas of lower congestion. For the routing function to work, an increased number of routing messages must be exchanged between nodes to alert each other to areas of congestion; this overhead reduces the capacity available for data packets.

As the load on the network continues to increase, the queue lengths of the various nodes continue to grow. Eventually, a point is reached (point B in the plot) beyond which throughput actually drops with increased offered load. The reason for this is that the buffers at each node are of finite size. When the buffers at a node become full, the node must discard packets. Therefore, the sources must retransmit the discarded packets in addition to new packets. This only exacerbates the situation: As more and more packets are retransmitted, the load on the system grows, and more buffers become saturated. While the system is trying desperately to clear the backlog, users are pumping old and new packets into the system. Even successfully delivered packets may be retransmitted because it takes too long, at a higher layer (for example, transport layer), to acknowledge them: The sender assumes the packet did not get through and retransmits. Under these circumstances, the effective capacity of the system declines to zero.

Congestion Control Techniques

Figure 2.14 provides a general depiction of important congestion control techniques. This section examines each of these.

Backpressure

Backpressure can be exerted on the basis of links or logical connections (for example, virtual circuits). Referring again to Figure 2.11, if node 6 becomes congested (buffers fill up), node 6 can slow down or halt the flow of all packets from node 5 (or node 3, or both nodes 5 and 3). If this restriction persists, node 5 will need to slow down or halt traffic on its incoming links. This flow restriction propagates backward (against the flow of data traffic) to sources, which are restricted in the flow of new packets into the network.

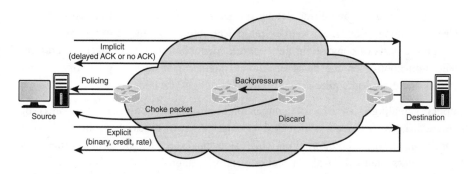

FIGURE 2.14   Mechanisms for Congestion Control

Backpressure for all traffic on a particular link is automatically invoked by the flow control mechanisms of data link layer protocols. Backpressure can also be selectively applied to logical connections, so that the flow from one node to the next is only restricted or halted on some connections, generally the ones with the most traffic. In this case, the restriction propagates back along the connection to the source. Such a mechanism is used in Frame Relay and Asynchronous Transfer Mode (ATM) networks. However, the use of these networks has declined considerably in favor of Ethernet carrier networks and IP-based Multiprotocol Label Switching (MPLS) networks.

Choke Packet

A choke packet is a control packet generated at a congested node and transmitted back to a source node to restrict traffic flow. Either a router or a destination end system may send this message to a source end system, requesting that it reduce the rate at which it is sending traffic to the internet destination. On receipt of a choke packet, the source host should cut back the rate at which it is sending traffic to the specified destination until it no longer receives choke packets. The choke packet can be used by a router or host that must discard IP datagrams because of a full buffer. In that case, the router or host will issue a choke packet for every packet that it discards. In addition, a system may anticipate congestion and issue choke packets when its buffers approach capacity. In that case, the packet referred to in the choke packet may well be delivered. Therefore, receipt of a choke packet does not imply delivery or nondelivery of the corresponding packet.

Implicit Congestion Signaling

When network congestion occurs, two things may happen:

1. The transmission delay for an individual packet from source to destination increases, so that it is noticeably longer than the fixed propagation delay, and

2. Packets are discarded.

If a source can detect increased delays and packet discards, it has implicit evidence of network congestion. If all sources can detect congestion and, in response, reduce flow on the basis of congestion, the network congestion will be relieved. Therefore, congestion control on the basis of implicit signaling is the responsibility of end systems and does not require action on the part of network nodes.

Implicit signaling is an effective congestion control technique in connectionless, or datagram, networks, such as IP-based internets. In such cases, there are no logical connections through the internet on which flow can be regulated. However, between the two end systems, logical connections can be established at the TCP level. TCP includes mechanisms for acknowledging receipt of TCP segments and for regulating the flow of data between source and destination on a TCP connection.

Explicit Congestion Signaling

It is desirable to use as much of the available capacity in a network as possible but still react to congestion in a controlled and fair manner. This is the purpose of explicit congestion avoidance techniques. In general terms, for explicit congestion avoidance, the network alerts end systems to growing congestion within the network and the end systems take steps to reduce the offered load to the network.

Explicit congestion signaling approaches can work in one of two directions:

- **Backward:** Notifies the source that congestion avoidance procedures should be initiated where applicable for traffic in the opposite direction of the received notification. It indicates that the packets that the user transmits on this logical connection may encounter congested resources. Backward information is transmitted either by altering bits in a header of a data packet headed for the source to be controlled or by transmitting separate control packets to the source.

- **Forward**: Notifies the user that congestion avoidance procedures should be initiated where applicable for traffic in the same direction as the received notification. It indicates that this packet, on this logical connection, has encountered congested resources. Again, this information may be transmitted either as altered bits in data packets or in separate control packets. In some schemes, when a forward signal is received by an end system, it echoes the signal back along the logical connection to the source. In other schemes, the end system is expected to exercise flow control upon the source end system at a higher layer (for example, TCP).

You can divide explicit congestion signaling approaches into three general categories:

- **Binary:** A bit is set in a data packet as it is forwarded by the congested node. When a source receives a binary indication of congestion on a logical connection, it may reduce its traffic flow.

- **Credit based:** These schemes are based on providing an explicit credit to a source over a logical connection. The credit indicates how many octets or how many packets the source may transmit. When the credit is exhausted, the source must await additional credit before sending additional data. Credit-based schemes are common for end-to-end flow control, in which a destination system uses credit to prevent the source from overflowing the destination buffers, but credit-based schemes have also been considered for congestion control. Credit-based schemes are defined in Frame Relay and ATM networks.

- **Rate based**: These schemes are based on providing an explicit data rate limit to the source over a logical connection. The source may transmit data at a rate up to the set limit. To control congestion, any node along the path of the connection can reduce the data rate limit in a control message to the source.

2.6 SDN and NFV

With the ever-increasing volume and variety of network traffic, generated by such high-demand sources as big data, cloud computing, and mobile traffic, it becomes increasingly difficult to meet stringent QoS and QoE requirements. Networks need to be more adaptable and scalable. To provide adaptability and scalability, two key technologies that are rapidly being deployed by a variety of network service and application providers are software-defined networking (SDN) and network functions virtualization (NFV). Because these two topics occupy a large portion of this book, only a brief introduction is appropriate here.

Software-Defined Networking

SDN has reached a tipping point at which it is replacing the traditional networking model. Software-defined networks provide an enhanced level of flexibility and customizability to meet the needs of newer networking and IT trends such as cloud, mobility, social networking, and video.

SDN Functionality

The two elements involved in forwarding packets through routers are a control function, which decides the route the traffic takes and the relative priority of traffic, and a data function, which forwards data based on control-function policy. Prior to SDN, these functions were performed in an integrated fashion at each network device (router, bridge, packet switch, and so on). Control in such a traditional network is

---

software-defined networking (SDN)

An approach to designing, building and operating large-scale networks based on programming the forwarding decisions in routers and switches via software from a central server. SDN differs from traditional networking, which requires configuring each device separately and which relies on protocols that cannot be altered.

See Part II, "Software-Defined Networks"

exercised by means of a routing and control network protocol that is implemented in each network node. This approach is relatively inflexible and requires all the network nodes to implement the same protocols. With SDN, a central controller performs all complex functionality, including routing, naming, policy declaration, and security checks (see Figure 2.15).

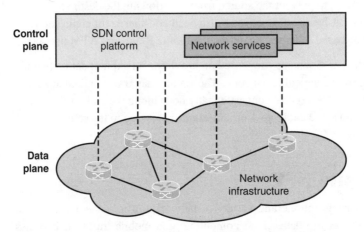

FIGURE 2.15   Software-Defined Networking

This constitutes the SDN **control plane**, and consists of one or more SDN controllers. The SDN controller defines the data flows that occur in the SDN data plane. Each flow through the network is configured by the controller, which verifies that the communication is permissible by the network policy. If the controller allows a flow requested by an end system, it computes a route for the flow to take, and adds an entry for that flow in each of the switches along the path. With all complex function subsumed by the controller, switches simply manage flow tables whose entries can only be populated by the controller. The switches constitute the **data plane**. Communication between the controller and the switches uses a standardized protocol.

Key Drivers

One driving factor for SDN is the increasingly widespread use of server virtualization. In essence, server virtualization masks server resources, including the number and identity of individual physical servers, processors, and operating systems, from server users. This makes it possible to partition a single machine into multiple, independent servers, conserving hardware resources. It also makes it possible to quickly migrate a server from one machine to another for load balancing or for dynamic switchover in the case of machine failure. Server virtualization has become a central element in dealing with big data applications and in implementing cloud computing infrastructures. But it creates problems with traditional network architectures. One problem is configuring virtual LANs. Network managers need to make sure the VLAN used by the virtual machine (VM) is assigned to the same switch port as the physical server running the VM. But with the VM being movable, it is necessary to reconfigure the VLAN every time that a virtual server is moved. In general terms, to match the flexibility of server virtualization, the network manager needs to be able to dynamically add, drop, and change network resources and profiles. This is difficult to do with conventional network switches, in which the control logic for each switch is collocated with the switching logic.

Another effect of server virtualization is that traffic flows differ substantially from the traditional client/server model. Typically, there is a considerable amount of traffic among virtual servers, for such purposes as maintaining consistent images of database and invoking security functions such as access control. These server-to-server flows change in location and intensity over time, demanding a flexible approach to managing network resources.

Another factor leading to the need for rapid response in allocating network resources is the increasing use by employees of mobile devices, such as smartphones, tablets, and notebooks to access enterprise resources. These devices can add fast-changing and unpredictable large loads on the network, and can rapidly change their network attachment point. Network managers must be able to respond to rapidly changing resource, QoS, and security requirements for mobile devices.

Existing network infrastructures can respond to changing requirements for the management of traffic flows, providing differentiated QoS levels and security levels for individual flows, but the process can be very time-consuming if the enterprise network is large or involves network devices from multiple vendors. The network manager must configure each vendor's equipment separately, and adjust performance and security parameters on a per-session, per-application basis. In a large enterprise, every time a new VM is brought up, it can take hours or even days for network managers to do the necessary reconfiguration.

Network Functions Virtualization

The discussion of SDN mentioned that a key driving factor in the deployment of SDN is the need to provide flexible network response to the widespread use of virtualized servers. VM technology over the Internet or an enterprise network has, until recently, been used for application-level server functions such as database servers, cloud servers, web servers, e-mail servers, and so on. This same technology, however, can equally be applied to network devices, such as routers, LAN switches, firewalls, and IDS/IPS servers (see Figure 2.16).

➔ *See Part III, "Virtualization"*

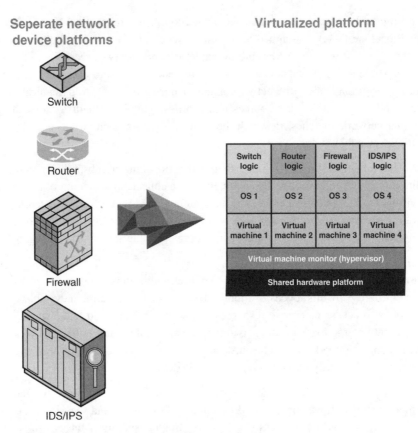

FIGURE 2.16 Network Functions Virtualization

network functions virtualization (NFV)

The virtualization of network functions by implementing these functions in software and running them on virtual machines.

Network functions virtualization (NFV) decouples network functions, such as routing, firewalling, intrusion detection, and Network Address Translation from proprietary hardware platforms and implements these functions in software. It utilizes standard virtualization technologies that run on high-performance hardware to virtualize network functions. It is applicable to any data plane processing or control plane function in both wired and wireless network infrastructures.

NFV has a number of features in common with SDN. They share the following objectives:

- Move functionality to software

- Use commodity hardware platforms instead of proprietary platforms

- Use standardized or open application program interfaces (APIs)

- Support more efficient evolution, deployment, and repositioning of network functions

NFV and SDN are independent but complementary schemes. SDN decouples the data and control planes of network traffic control, making the control and routing of network traffic more flexible and efficient. NFV decouples network functions from specific hardware platforms via virtualization to make the provision of these functions more efficient and flexible. Virtualization can be applied to the data plane functions of the routers and other network functions, including SDN controller functions. So, either can be used alone, but the two can be combined to reap greater benefits.

2.7 Modern Networking Elements

This chapter ends with a rough depiction of how the major elements of modern networking treated in this book fit together (see Figure 2.17). The discussion that follows works through this figure from the bottom up.

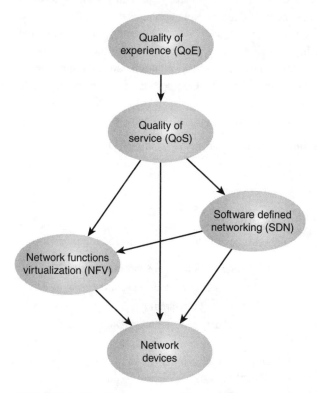

FIGURE 2.17   Modern Networking Schema

Ultimately, the concern of a network service provider is about the set of network devices (such as routers) and the control and management of the functions they perform (such as packet forwarding). If NFV is used, these network functions are implemented in software and executed on VMs. If instead the network functions are implemented on dedicated machines and SDN is used, the control functions are implemented on central SDN controllers, which interact with the network devices.

However, SDN and NFV are not mutually exclusive. If both SDN and NFV are implemented for a network, the following relationships hold:

- Network data plane functionality is implemented on VMs.

- The control plane functionality may be implemented on a dedicated SDN platform or on an SDN VM.

In either case, the SDN controller interacts with the data plane functions running on VMs.

QoS measures are commonly used to specify the service required by various network customers or users and to dictate the traffic management policies used on the network. The common case, until recently, is that QoS was implemented on network that used neither NFV nor SDN. In this case, routing and traffic control policies must be configured directly on network devices using a variety of automated and manual techniques. If NFV but not SDN is implemented, the QoS settings are communicated to the VMs. With SDN, regardless of whether NFV is used, it is the SDN controller that is responsible for enforcing QoS parameters for the various network users.

If QoE considerations come into play, these are used to adjust QoS parameters to satisfy the users' QoE requirements.

2.8 Key Terms

After completing this chapter, you should be able to define the following terms.

analytics	network functions virtualization (NFV)
autonomous system	operations support system (OSS)
big data	packet forwarding
cloud computing	quality of experience (QoE)
congestion	quality of service (QoS)
delay jitter	real-time traffic
elastic traffic	router
exterior router protocol (ERP)	routing
inelastic traffic	routing protocol
interior router protocol (IRP)	software-defined networking (SDN)
internet	virtual machine (VM)
Internet	

2.9 References

AKAM15: Akamai Technologies. *Akamai's State of the Internet*. Akamai Report, Q4|2014. 2015.

CISC14: Cisco Systems. *Cisco Visual Networking Index: Forecast and Methodology*, 2013–2018. White Paper, 2014.

IBM11: IBM Study, "Every Day We Create 2.5 Quintillion Bytes of Data." Storage Newsletter, October 21, 2011. http://www.storagenewsletter.com/rubriques/market-reportsresearch/ibm-cmo-study/

ITUT12: ITU-T. Focus Group on Cloud Computing Technical Report Part 3: Requirements and Framework Architecture of Cloud Infrastructure. FG Cloud TR, February 2012.

KAND12: Kandula, A., Sengupta, S., and Patel, P. "The Nature of Data Center Traffic: Measurements and Analysis." ACM SIGCOMM Internet Measurement Conference, November 2009.

NETW14: Network World. *Survival Tips for Big Data's Impact on Network Performance*. White paper. April 2014.

SZIG14: Szigeti, T., Hattingh, C., Barton, R., and Briley, K. *End-to-End QoS Network Design: Quality of Service for Rich-Media & Cloud Networks*. Englewood Cliffs, NJ: Pearson. 2014.

PART II

Software-Defined Networks

One man had a vision of railways that would link all the mainline railroad termini. His name was Charles Pearson and, though born the son of an upholsterer, he became Solicitor to the city of London. There had previously been a plan for gaslit subway streets through which horse-drawn traffic could pass. This was rejected on the grounds that such sinister tunnels would become lurking places for thieves. Twenty years before his system was built, Pearson envisaged a line running through "a spacious archway," well-lit and well-ventilated.

His was a scheme for trains in a drain.

—*King Solomon's Carpet*, Barbara Vine (Ruth Rendell)

The heart of modern networking is software-defined networking (SDN). Part II is devoted to a broad and thorough presentation of SDN concepts, technology, and applications. Chapter 3 begins the discussion by laying out what the SDN approach is and why it is needed, and provides an overview of the SDN architecture. This chapter also looks at the organizations that are issuing specifications and standards for SDN. Chapter 4 is a detailed look at the SDN data plane, including the key components, how they interact, and how they are managed. Much of the chapter is devoted to OpenFlow, a vital data plane technology as well as an interface to the control plane. The chapter explains why Open-Flow is needed and then proceeds to provide a detailed technical explanation. Chapter 5 is devoted to the SDN control plane. It includes a discussion of OpenDaylight, an important open source implementation of the control plane. Chapter 6 covers the SDN application plane. In addition to examining the general SDN application plane architecture, the chapter discusses six major application areas that can be supported by SDN and provides a number of examples of SDN applications.

Chapter | **3**

SDN: Background and Motivation

The requirements for a future all-digital-data distributed network which provides common user service for a wide range of users having different requirements is considered. The use of a standard format message block permits building relatively simple switching mechanisms using an adaptive store-and-forward routing policy to handle all forms of digital data including "real-time" voice. This network rapidly responds to changes in network status.

—On Distributed Communications: Introduction to Distributed Communications Networks, Rand Report RM-3420-PR, Paul Baran, August 1964

Chapter Objectives

After studying this chapter, you should be able to

- Make a presentation justifying the position that traditional network architectures are inadequate for modern networking needs.
- List and explain the key requirements for an SDN architecture.
- Present an overview of an SDN architecture, to include explaining the significance of northbound and southbound APIs.
- Summarize the work being done on SDN and NFV standardization by various organizations.

This chapter begins the discussion of software-defined networks (SDNs) by providing some background and motivation for the SDN approach.

3.1   Evolving Network Requirements

A number of trends are driving network providers and users to reevaluate traditional approaches to network architecture. These trends can be grouped under the categories of demand, supply, and traffic patterns.

Demand Is Increasing

As was described in Chapter 2, "Requirements and Technology," a number of trends are increasing the load on enterprise networks, the Internet, and other internets. Of particular note are the following:

- **Cloud computing:** There has been a dramatic shift by enterprises to both public and private cloud services.

- **Big data:** The processing of huge data sets requires massive parallel processing on thousands of servers, all of which require a degree of inter-connection to each other. Therefore, there is a large and constantly growing demand for network capacity within the data canter.

- **Mobile traffic:** Employees are increasingly accessing enterprise network resources via mobile personal devices, such as smartphones, tablets, and notebooks. These devices support sophisticated apps that can consume and generate image and video traffic, placing new burdens on the enterprise network.

- **The Internet of Things (IoT):** Most "things" in the IoT generate modest traffic, although there are exceptions, such as surveillance video cameras. But the sheer number of such devices for some enterprises results in a significant load on the enterprise network.

Supply Is Increasing

As the demand on networks is rising, so is the capacity of network technologies to absorb rising loads. In terms of transmission technology, Chapter 1, "Elements of Modern Networking," established that the key enterprise wired and wireless network technologies, Ethernet and Wi-Fi respectively, are well into the gigabits per second (Gbps) range. Similarly, 4G and 5G cellular networks provide greater capacity for mobile devices from remote employees who access the enterprise network via cellular networks rather than Wi-Fi.

The increase in the capacity of the network transmission technologies has been matched by an increase in the performance of network devices, such as LAN switches, routers, firewalls, intrusion detection system/intrusion prevention systems (IDS/IPS), and network monitoring and management systems. Year by year, these devices have larger, faster memories, enabling greater buffer capacity and faster buffer access, as well as faster processor speeds.

Traffic Patterns Are More Complex

If it were simply a matter of supply and demand, it would appear that today's networks should be able to cope with today's data traffic. But as traffic patterns have changed and become more complex, traditional enterprise network architectures are increasingly ill suited to the demand.

Until recently, and still common today, the typical enterprise network architecture consisted of a local or campus-wide tree structure of Ethernet switches with routers connecting large Ethernet LANs and connecting to the Internet and WAN facilities. This architecture is well suited to the client/server computing model that was at one time dominant in the enterprise environment. With this model, interaction, and therefore traffic, was mostly between one client and one server. In such an environment, networks could be laid out and configured with relatively static client and server locations and relatively predictable traffic volumes between clients and servers.

A number of developments have resulted in far more dynamic and complex traffic patterns within the enterprise data center, local and regional enterprise networks, and carrier networks. These include the following:

- Client/server applications typically access multiple databases and servers that must communicate with each other, generating "horizontal" traffic between servers as well as "vertical" traffic between servers and clients.

- Network convergence of voice, data, and video traffic creates unpredictable traffic patterns, often of large multimedia data transfers.

- Unified communications (UC) strategies involve heavy use of applications that trigger access to multiple servers.

- The heavy use of mobile devices, including personal bring your own device (BYOD) policies, results in user access to corporate content and applications from any device anywhere any time. As illustrated previously in Figure 2.6 in Chapter 2, this mobile traffic is becoming an increasingly significant fraction of enterprise network traffic.

- The widespread use of public clouds has shifted a significant amount of what previously had been local traffic onto WANs for many enterprises, resulting in increased and often very unpredictable loads on enterprise routers.

- The now-common practice of application and database server virtualization has significantly increased the number of hosts requiring high-volume network access and results in every-changing physical location of server resources.

Traditional Network Architectures are Inadequate

Even with the greater capacity of transmission schemes and the greater performance of network devices, traditional network architectures are increasingly inadequate in the face of the growing complexity, variability, and high volume of the imposed load. In addition, as quality of service (QoS) and quality of experience (QoE) requirements imposed on the network are expanded as a result of the variety of applications, the traffic load must be handled in an increasingly sophisticated and agile fashion.

The traditional internetworking approach is based on the **TCP/IP protocol architecture**. Three noteworthy characteristics of this approach are as follows:

- Two-level end system addressing

- Routing based on destination

- Distributed, autonomous control

Let's look at each of these characteristics in turn.

The traditional architecture relies heavily on the network interface identity. At the physical layer of the TCP/IP model, devices attached to networks are identified by hardware-based identifiers, such as Ethernet MAC addresses. At the internetworking level, including both the Internet and private internets, the architecture is a network of networks. Each attached device has a physical layer identifier recognized within its immediate network and a logical network identifier, its IP address, which provides global visibility.

The design of TCP/IP uses this addressing scheme to support the networking of autonomous networks, with distributed control. This architecture provides a high level of resilience and scales well in terms of adding new networks. Using IP and distributed routing protocols, routes can be discovered and used throughout an internet. Using transport-level protocols such as TCP, distributed and decentralized algorithms can be implemented to respond to congestion.

Traditionally, routing was based on each packet's destination address. In this **datagram** approach, successive packets between a source and destination may follow different routes through the internet, as routers constantly seek to find the minimum-delay path for each individual **packet**. More recently, to satisfy QoS requirements, packets are often treated in terms of **flows** of packets. Packets associated with a given flow have defined QoS characteristics, which affect the routing for the entire flow.

However, this distributed, autonomous approach developed when networks were predominantly static and end systems predominantly of fixed location. Based on these characteristics, the Open Networking Foundation (ONF) cites four general limitations of traditional network architectures [ONF12]:

TCP/IP protocol architecture

The protocol architecture built around the TCP and IP protocols, consisting of five layers: physical, data link, network/Internet (usually IP), transport (usually TCP or UDP), and application.

packet

A unit of data sent across a network. A packet is a group of bits that includes data plus protocol control information. The term generally applies to protocol data units at the network layer.

packet switching

A method of transmitting messages through a communications network, in which long messages are subdivided into short packets. Each packet is passed from source to destination through intermediate nodes. At each node, the entire message is received, stored briefly, and then forwarded to the next node.

Datagram

A packet that is treated independently of other packets for packet switching. A datagram carries information sufficient for routing from the source to the destination without the necessity of establishing a logical connection between the endpoints.

flow

A sequence of packets between a source and destination that are recognized by the network as related and are treated in a uniform fashion.

- **Static, complex architecture:** To respond for demands such as differing levels of QoS, high and fluctuating traffic volumes, and security requirements, networking technology has grown more complex and difficult to manage. This has resulted in a number of independently defined protocols each of which addresses a portion of networking requirements. An example of the difficulty this presents is when devices are added or moved. The network management staff must use device-level management tools to make changes to configuration parameters in multiple switches, routers, firewalls, web authentication portals, and so on. The updates include changes to access control lists (ACLs), virtual LAN settings, QoS settings in numerous devices, and other protocol-related adjustments. Another example is the adjustment of QoS parameters to meet changing user requirements and traffic patterns. Manual procedures must be used to configure each vendor's equipment on a per-application and even per-session basis.

- **Inconsistent policies:** To implement a network-wide security policy, staff may have to make configuration changes to thousands of devices and mechanisms. In a large network, when a new virtual machine is activated, it can take hours or even days to reconfigure ACLs across the entire network.

- **Inability to scale:** Demands on networks are growing rapidly, both in volume and variety. Adding more switches and transmission capacity, involving multiple vendor equipment, is difficult because of the complex, static nature of the network. One strategy enterprises have used is to oversubscribe network links based on predicted traffic patterns. But with the increased use of virtualization and the increasing variety of multimedia applications, traffic patterns are unpredictable.

- **Vendor dependence:** Given the nature of today's traffic demands on networks, enterprises and carriers need to deploy new capabilities and services rapidly in response to changing business needs and user demands. A lack of open interfaces for network functions leaves the enterprises limited by the relatively slow product cycles of vendor equipment.

3.2 The SDN Approach

This section provides an overview of SDN and shows how it is designed to meet evolving network requirements.

Requirements

Based on the narrative of Section 3.1, we are now in a position to detail the principal requirements for a modern networking approach. The Open Data Center Alliance (ODCA) provides a useful, concise list of requirements, which include the following [ODCA14]:

- **Adaptability:** Networks must adjust and respond dynamically, based on application needs, business policy, and network conditions.

- **Automation:** Policy changes must be automatically propagated so that manual work and errors can be reduced.

- **Maintainability**. Introduction of new features and capabilities (software upgrades, patches) must be seamless with minimal disruption of operations.

- **Model management:** Network management software must allow management of the network at a model level, rather than implementing conceptual changes by reconfiguring individual network elements.

- **Mobility:** Control functionality must accommodate mobility, including mobile user devices and virtual servers.

- **Integrated security:** Network applications must integrate seamless security as a core service instead of as an add-on solution.

- **On-demand scaling:** Implementations must have the ability to scale up or scale down the network and its services to support on-demand requests.

SDN Architecture

An analogy can be drawn between the way in which computing evolved from closed, vertically integrated, proprietary systems into an open approach to computing and the evolution coming with SDN (see Figure 3.1). In the early decades of computing, vendors such as IBM and DEC provided a fully integrated product, with a proprietary processor hardware, unique assembly language, unique operating system (OS), and the bulk if not all of the application software. In this environment, customers, especially large customers, tended to be locked in to one vendor, dependent primarily on the applications offered by that vendor. Migration to another vendor's hardware platform resulted in major upheaval at the application level.

Today, the computing environment is characterized by extreme openness and great customer flexibility. The bulk of computing hardware consists of x86 and x86-compatible processors for standalone systems and ARM processors for embedded systems. This makes it easy to port operating systems implemented in C, C++, Java, and the like. Even proprietary hardware architectures, such as IBM's zEnterprise line, provide standardized compilers and programming environments and so can easily run open sources operating systems such as Linux. Therefore, applications written for Linux or other open operating systems can easily be moved from one vendor platform to another. Even proprietary systems such as Windows and Mac OS provide programming environments to make porting of applications an easy matter. It also enables the development of virtual machines that can be moved from one server to another across hardware platforms and operating systems.

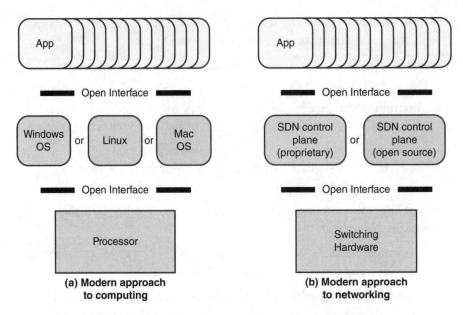

FIGURE 3.1   The Modern Approach to Computing and Networking

The networking environment today faces some of the same limitations faced in the pre-open era of computing. Here the issue is not developing applications that can run on multiple platforms. Rather, the difficulty is the lack of integration between applications and network infrastructure. As demonstrated in the preceding section, traditional network architectures are inadequate to meet the demands of the growing volume and variety of traffic.

The central concept behind SDN is to enable developers and network managers to have the same type of control over network equipment that they have had over x86 servers. As discussed in Section 2.6 in Chapter 2, the SDN approach splits the switching function between a data plane and a control plane that are on separate devices (see Figure 3.2). The data plane is simply responsible for forwarding packets, whereas the control plane provides the "intelligence" in designing routes, setting priority and routing policy parameters to meet QoS and QoE requirements and to cope with the shifting traffic patterns. Open interfaces are defined so that the switching hardware presents a uniform interface regardless of the details of internal implementation. Similarly, open interfaces are defined to enable networking applications to communicate with the SDN controllers.

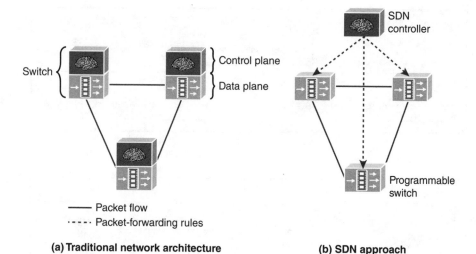

(a) Traditional network architecture

(b) SDN approach

FIGURE 3.2 Control and Data Planes

← *See Figure 2.15, Software Defined Networking*

Figure 3.3 elaborates on the structure shown in Figure 2.15, showing more detail of the SDN approach. The data plane consists of physical switches and virtual switches. In both cases, the switches are responsible for forwarding packets. The internal implementation of buffers, priority parameters, and other data structures related to forwarding can be vendor dependent. However, each switch must implement a model, or abstraction, of packet forwarding that is uniform and open to the SDN controllers. This model is defined in terms of an open **application programming interface (API)** between the control plane and the data plane (southbound API). The most prominent example of such an open API is OpenFlow, discussed in Chapter 4, "SDN Data Plane and OpenFlow." As Chapter 4 explains, the OpenFlow specification defines both a protocol between the control and data planes and an API by which the control plane can invoke the OpenFlow protocol.

application programming interface (API)

A language and message format used by an application program to communicate with the operating system or some other control program such as a database management system (DBMS) or communications protocol. APIs are implemented by writing function calls in the program, which provide the linkage to the required subroutine for execution. An open or standardized API can ensure the portability of the application code and the vendor independence of the called service.

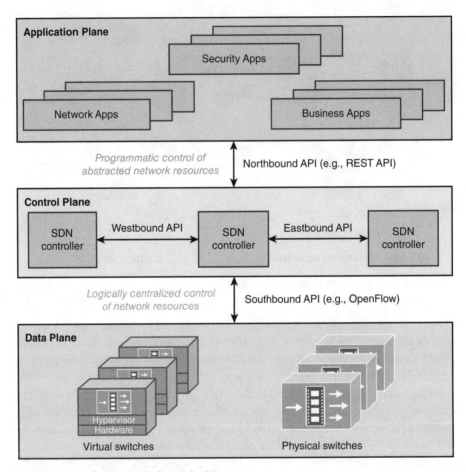

FIGURE 3.3   Software-Defined Architecture

→ *See Chapter 5, "SDN Control Plane"*

SDN controllers can be implemented directly on a server or on a virtual server. OpenFlow or some other open API is used to control the switches in the data plane. In addition, controllers use information about capacity and demand obtained from the networking equipment through which the traffic flows. SDN controllers also expose northbound APIs, which allow developers and network managers to deploy a wide range of off-the-shelf and custom-built network applications, many of which were not feasible before the advent of SDN. As yet there is no standardized northbound API nor a consensus on an open northbound API. A number of vendors offer a REpresentational State Transfer (REST)-based API to provide a programmable interface to their SDN controller.

Also envisioned but not yet defined are horizontal APIs (east/westbound), which would enable communication and cooperation among groups or federations of controllers to synchronize state for high availability.

At the application plane are a variety of applications that interact with SDN controllers. SDN applications are programs that may use an abstract view of the network for their decision-making goals. These applications convey their network requirements and desired network behavior to the SDN controller via a northbound API. Examples of applications are energy-efficient networking, security monitoring, access control, and network management.

Characteristics of Software-Defined Networking

Putting it all together, the key characteristics of SDN are as follows:

- The control plane is separated from the data plane. Data plane devices become simple packet-forwarding devices (refer back to Figure 3.2).

- The control plane is implemented in a centralized controller or set of coordinated centralized controllers. The SDN controller has a centralized view of the network or networks under its control. The controller is portable software that can run on commodity servers and is capable of programming the forwarding devices based on a centralized view of the network.

- Open interfaces are defined between the devices in the control plane (controllers) and those in the data plane.

- The network is programmable by applications running on top of the SDN controllers. The SDN controllers present an abstract view of network resources to the applications.

3.3   SDN- and NFV-Related Standards

Unlike some technology areas, such as Wi-Fi, there is no single standards body responsible for developing open **standards** for SDN and NFV. Rather, there is a large and evolving collection of standards-developing organizations (SDOs), industrial consortia, and open development initiatives involved in creating standards and guidelines for SDN and NFV. Table 3.1 lists the main SDOs and other organizations involved in the effort and the main outcomes so far produced. This section covers some of the most prominent efforts.

standards

Documents that provide requirements, specifications, guidelines, or characteristics that can be used consistently to ensure that materials, products, processes, and services are fit for their purpose. Standards are established by consensus among those participating in a standards-making organization and are approved by a generally recognized body.

open standard

A standard that is: developed on the basis of an open decision-making procedure available to all interested parties, is available for implementation to all on a royalty-free basis, and is intended to promote interoperability among products from multiple vendors.

TABLE 3.1   SDN and NFV Open Standards Activities

Organization	Mission	SDN- and NFV-Related Effort
Open Networking Foundation (ONF)	An industry consortium dedicated to the promotion and adoption of SDN through open standard development.	OpenFlow
Internet Engineering Task Force (IETF)	The Internet's technical standards body. Produces RFCs and Internet standards.	Interface to routing systems (I2RS) Service function chaining
European Telecommunications Standards Institute (ETSI)	An EU-sponsored standards organization that produces globally applicable standards for information and communications technologies.	NFV architecture
OpenDaylight	A collaborative project under the auspices of the Linux Foundation.	OpenDaylight
International Telecommunication Union— Telecommunication Standardization Sector (ITU-T)	United Nations agency that produces Recommendations with a view to standardizing telecommunications on a worldwide basis.	SDN functional requirements and architecture
Internet Research Task Force (IRTF) Software Defined Networking Research Group (SDNRG)	Research group within IRTF. Produces SDN-related RFCs.	SDN architecture
Broadband Forum (BBF)	Industry consortium developing broadband packet networking specifications.	Requirements and framework for SDN in telecommunications broadband networks
Metro Ethernet Forum (MEF)	Industry consortium that promotes the use of Ethernet for metropolitan and wide-area applications.	Defining APIs for service orchestration over SDN and NFV
IEEE 802	An IEEE committee responsible for developing standards for LANs.	Standardize SDN capabilities on access networks.
Optical Internetworking Forum (OIF)	Industry consortium promoting development and deployment of interoperable networking solutions and services for optical networking products.	Requirements on transport networks in SDN architectures

Organization	Mission	SDN- and NFV-Related Effort
Open Data Center Alliance (ODCA)	Consortium of leading IT organizations developing interoperable solutions and services for cloud computing.	SDN usage model
Alliance for Telecommunications Industry Solutions (ATIS)	A standards organization that develops standards for the unified communications (UC) industry.	Operational opportunities and challenges of SDN/NFV programmable infrastructure
Open Platform for NFV (OPNFV)	An open source project focused on accelerating the evolution of NFV.	NFV infrastructure

Standards-Developing Organizations

The Internet Society, ITU-T, and ETSI are all making key contributions to the standardization of SDN and NFV.

Internet Society

A number of **standards-developing organizations (SDOs)** are looking at various aspects of SDN. Perhaps the most active are two groups within the Internet Society (ISOC): IETF and IRTF. ISOC is the coordinating committee for Internet design, engineering, and management. Areas covered include the operation of the Internet itself and the standardization of protocols used by end systems on the Internet for interoperability. Various organizations under the ISOC are responsible for the actual work of standards development and publication.

The Internet Engineering Task Force (IETF) has working groups developing SDN-related specifications in the following areas:

- **Interface to routing systems (I2RS):** Develop capabilities to interact with routers and routing protocols to apply routing policies.

- **Service function chaining:** Develop an architecture and capabilities for controllers to direct subsets of traffic across the network in such a way that each virtual service platform sees only the traffic it must work with.

The Internet Research Task Force (IRTF) has published *Software-Defined Networking (SDN): Layers and Architecture Terminology* (RFC 7426, January 2015). The document provides a concise reference that reflects current approaches regarding the SDN layer architecture. The **Request For Comments (RFC)** also provides a useful discussion of the southbound API (Figure 3.3) and describes some specific APIs, such as for I2RS.

standards-developing organization (SDO)

An official national, regional, or international standards body that develops standards and coordinates the standard activities of a specific country, region or the world. Some SDOs facilitate the development of standards through support of technical committee activities, and some may be directly involved in standards development.

Request For Comments (RFC)

A document in the archival series that is the official channel for publications of the Internet Society, including IETF and IRTF publications. An RFC may be informational, best practice, draft standard, or an official Internet standard.

IRTF also sponsors the Software Defined Networking Research Group (SDNRG). This group investigates SDN from various perspectives with the goal of identifying the approaches that can be defined, deployed, and used in the near term and identifying future research challenges.

ITU-T

The International Telecommunication Union—Telecommunication Standardization Sector (ITU-T) is a UN agency that issues standards, called recommendations, in the telecommunications area. So far, their only published contribution to SDN is Recommendation Y.3300 (*Framework of Software-Defined Networking*, June 2014). The document addresses definitions, objectives, high-level capabilities, requirements, and high-level architecture of SDN. It provides a valuable framework for standards development.

ITU-T has established a Joint Coordination Activity on Software-Defined Networking (JCA-SDN) and begun work on developing SDN-related standards.

Four ITU-T study groups (SGs) are involved in SDN-related activities:

- **SG 13 (Future networks, including cloud computing, mobile, and next-generation networks):** This is the lead study group of SDN in ITU-T and developed Y.3300. This group is studying SDN and virtualization aspects for next-generation networks (NGNs).

- **SG 11 (Signaling requirements, protocols, and test specifications):** This group is studying the framework for SDN signaling and how to apply SDN technologies for IPv6.

- **SG 15 (Transport, access, and home):** This group looks at optical transport networks, access networks, and home networks. The group is investigating transport aspects of SDN, aligned with the Open Network Foundation's SDN architecture.

- **SG 16 (Multimedia):** This group is evaluating OpenFlow as a protocol to control multimedia packet flows, and is studying virtual content delivery networks.

European Telecommunications Standards Institute

ETSI is recognized by the European Union as a European Standards Organization. However, this not-for-profit SDO has member organizations worldwide and its standards have international impact.

ETSI has taken the lead role in defining standards for NFV. ETSI's Network Functions Virtualisation (NFV) Industry Specification Group (ISG) began work in January 2013 and produced a first set of specifications in January 2015. The 11 specifications

include an NFV's architecture, infrastructure, service quality metrics, management
and orchestration, resiliency requirements, and security guidance.

Industry Consortia

Consortia for open standards began to appear in the late 1980s. There was a growing
feeling within private-sector multinational companies that the SDOs acted too slowly
to provide useful standards in the fast-paced world of technology. Recently, a number
of consortia have become involved in the development of SDN and NFV standards.
We mention here three of the most significant efforts.

➔ *See Chapter
4, "SDN
Data
Plane and
OpenFlow"*

By far the most important **consortium** involved in SDN standardization is the
Open Networking Foundation (ONF). ONF is an industry consortium dedicated to
the promotion and adoption of SDN through open standards development. Its most
important contribution to date is the OpenFlow protocol and API. The OpenFlow
protocol is the first standard interface specifically designed for SDN and is already
being deployed in a variety of networks and networking products, both hardware
based and software based. The standard enables networks to evolve by giving logically centralized control software the power to modify the behavior of network
devices through a well-defined "forwarding instruction set." Chapter 4 is devoted to
this protocol.

consortium

A group of inde-
pendent organiza-
tions joined by
common interests.
In the area of stan-
dards development,
a consortium typi-
cally consists of
individual corpora-
tions and trade
groups concerned
with a specific area
of technology.

The Open Data Center Alliance (ODCA) is a consortium of leading global IT
organizations dedicated to accelerating adoption of interoperable solutions and
services for cloud computing. Through the development of usage models for SDN and
NFV, ODCA is defining requirements for SDN and NFV cloud deployment.

The Alliance for Telecommunications Industry Solutions (ATIS) is a membership
organization that provides the tools necessary for the industry to identify standards,
guidelines, and operating procedures that make the interoperability of existing and
emerging telecommunications products and services possible. Although ATIS is
accredited by ANSI, it is best viewed as a consortium rather than an SDO. So far,
ATIS has issued a document that identifies operational issues and opportunities associated with increasing programmability of the infrastructure using SDN and NFV.

Open Development Initiatives

There are a number of other organizations that are not specifically created by industry
members and are not official bodies such as SDOs. Generally, these organizations are
user created and driven and have a particular focus, always with the goal of developing open standards or open source software. A number of such groups have become

active in SDN and NFV standardization. This section lists three of the most significant efforts.

OpenDaylight

➔ *See Section 5.3, "Open-Daylight"*

OpenDaylight is an open source software activity under the auspices of the Linux foundation. Its member companies provide resources to develop an SDN controller for a wide range of applications. Although the core membership consists of companies, individual developers and users can also participate, so OpenDaylight is more in the nature of an open development initiative than a consortium. ODL also supports network programmability via southbound protocols, a bunch of programmable network services, a collection of northbound APIs, and a set of applications.

OpenDaylight is composed of about 30 projects, and releases their outputs in simultaneous manner. After its first release, Hydrogen, in February 2014, it successfully delivered the second one, Helium, at the end of September 2014.

Open Platform for NFV

➔ *See Section 7.4, "NFV Benefits and Requirements"*

Open Platform for NFV is an open source project dedicated to acceleration the adoption of standardized NFV elements. OPNFV will establish a carrier-grade, integrated, open source reference platform that industry peers will build together to advance the evolution of NFV and to ensure consistency, performance, and interoperability among multiple open source components. Because multiple open source NFV building blocks already exist, OPNFV will work with upstream projects to coordinate continuous integration and testing while filling development gaps.

OpenStack

OpenStack is an open source software project that aims to produce an open source cloud operating system. It provides multitenant Infrastructure as a Service (IaaS), and aims to meets the needs of public and private clouds regardless of size, by being simple to implement and massively scalable. SDN technology is expected to contribute to its networking part, and to make the cloud operating system more efficient, flexible, and reliable.

OpenStack is composed of a number of projects. One of them, Neutron, is dedicated for networking. It provides Network as a Service (NaaS) to other OpenStack services. Almost all SDN controllers have provided plug-ins for Neutron, and through them services on OpenStack and other OpenStack services can build rich networking topologies and can configure advanced network policies in the cloud.

3.4   Key Terms

After completing this chapter, you should be able to define the following terms.

application programming interface (API)	REpresentational State Transfer (REST)
consortium	Request For Comments (RFC)
datagram	service function chaining
flow	southbound API
IEEE 802	standard
northbound API	standards-developing organization (SDO)
open standard	TCP/IP protocol architecture
packet switching	

3.5   References

ODCA14: Open Data Center Alliance. *Open Data Center Alliance Master Usage Model: Software-Defined Networking Rev. 2.0.* White Paper. 2014.

ONF12: Open Networking Foundation. *Software-Defined Networking: The New Norm for Networks.* ONF White Paper, April 13, 2012.

Chapter 4

SDN Data Plane and OpenFlow

"I tell you," went on Syme with passion, "that every time a train comes in I feel that it has broken past batteries of besiegers, and that man has won a battle against chaos. You say contemptuously that when one has left Sloane Square one must come to Victoria. I say that one might do a thousand things instead, and that whenever I really come there I have the sense of hairbreadth escape. And when I hear the guard shout out the word 'Victoria', it is not an unmeaning word. It is to me the cry of a herald announcing conquest. It is to me indeed 'Victoria'; it is the victory of Adam."

—*The Man Who Was Thursday*, G. K. Chesterton

Chapter Objectives

After studying this chapter, you should be able to

- Present an overview of the functions of the SDN data plane.
- Understand the concept of an OpenFlow logical network device.
- Describe and explain the OpenFlow flow table entry structure.
- Summarize the operation of the OpenFlow pipeline.
- Explain the operation of the group table.
- Understand the basic elements of the OpenFlow protocol.

Section 4.1 of this chapter begins the detailed study of software-defined networking (SDN) with a discussion of the data plane (Figure 4.1). The remainder of the chapter is devoted to OpenFlow, the most widely used implementation of the SDN data plane. OpenFlow is both a specification of the logical structure of data plane functionality and a protocol between SDN controllers and network devices. Sections 4.2 and 4.3, respectively, examine the OpenFlow logical network device and the OpenFlow protocol in more detail.

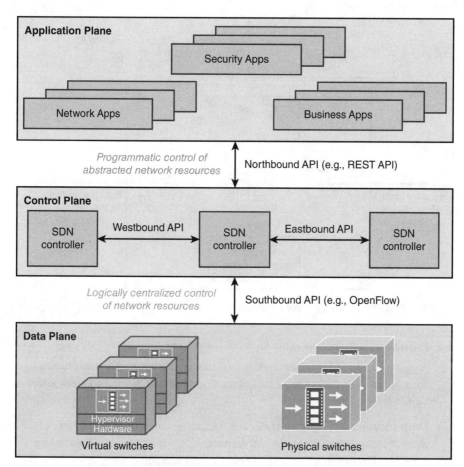

FIGURE 4.1 SDN Architecture

4.1 SDN Data Plane

The SDN data plane, referred to as the resource layer in ITU-T Y.3300 and also often referred to as the infrastructure layer, is where network forwarding devices perform the transport and processing of data according to decisions made by the SDN control plane. The important characteristic of the network devices in an SDN network is that these devices perform a simple forwarding function, without embedded software to make autonomous decisions.

Data Plane Functions

Figure 4.2 illustrates the functions performed by the data plane network devices (also called data plane network elements or switches). The principal functions of the network device are the following:

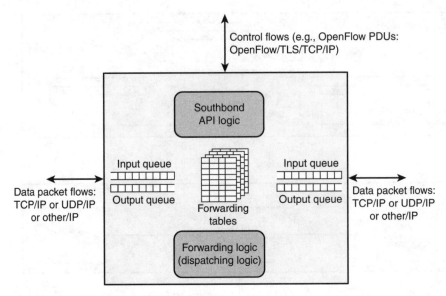

FIGURE 4.2   Data Plane Network Device

- **Control support function:** Interacts with the SDN control layer to support programmability via resource-control interfaces. The switch communicates with the controller and the controller manages the switch via the OpenFlow switch protocol.

- **Data forwarding function:** Accepts incoming data flows from other network devices and end systems and forwards them along the data forwarding paths that have been computed and established according to the rules defined by the SDN applications.

These forwarding rules used by the network device are embodied in forwarding tables that indicate for given categories of packets what the next hop in the route should be. In addition to simple forwarding of a packet, the network device can alter the packet header before forwarding, or discard the packet. As shown, arriving packets may be placed in an input queue, awaiting processing by the network device, and forwarded packets are generally placed in an output queue, awaiting transmission.

The network device in Figure 4.2 is shown with three I/O ports: one providing control communication with an SDN controller, and two for the input and output of data packets. This is a simple example. The network device may have multiple ports to communicate with multiple SDN controllers, and may have more than two I/O ports for packet flows into and out of the device.

Data Plane Protocols

Figure 4.2 suggests the protocols supported by the network device. Data packet flows consist of streams of IP packets. It may be necessary for the forwarding table to define entries based on fields in upper-level protocol headers, such as TCP, UDP, or some other transport or application protocol. The network device examines the IP header and possibly other headers in each packet and makes a forwarding decision.

The other important flow of traffic is via the southbound application programming interface (API), consisting of OpenFlow protocol data units (PDUs) or some similar southbound API protocol traffic.

4.2 OpenFlow Logical Network Device

To turn the concept of SDN into practical implementation, two requirements must be met:

- There must be a common logical architecture in all switches, routers, and other network devices to be managed by an SDN controller. This logical architecture may be implemented in different ways on different vendor equipment and in different types of network devices, as long as the SDN controller sees a uniform logical switch functionality.

- A standard, secure protocol is needed between the SDN controller and the network device.

These requirements are addressed by OpenFlow, which is both a protocol between SDN controllers and network devices and a specification of the logical structure of the network switch functionality. OpenFlow is defined in the *OpenFlow Switch Specification*, published by the Open Networking Foundation (ONF).

Open Network
Foundation
OpenFlow Definition

This section covers the logical switch architecture defined by OpenFlow. Our discussion is based on the OpenFlow specification current at the time of this writing: Version 1.5.1, March 26, 2015.

Figure 4.3 indicates the main elements of an OpenFlow environment, consisting of SDN controllers that include OpenFlow software, OpenFlow switches, and end systems.

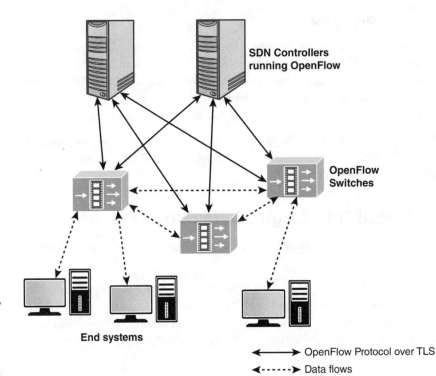

End systems

$\longleftrightarrow$ OpenFlow Protocol over TLS

$\blacktriangleleft\text{-----}\blacktriangleright$ Data flows

OpenFlow switch

A set of OpenFlow resources that can be managed as a single entity, includes a data path and a control channel. OpenFlow switches connect logically to each other via their OpenFlow ports.

OpenFlow port

Where packets enter and exit the OpenFlow pipeline. A packet can be forwarded from one OpenFlow switch to another OpenFlow switch only via an output OpenFlow port on the first switch and an ingress OpenFlow port on the second switch.

OpenFlow channel

Interface between an OpenFlow switch and an OpenFlow controller, used by the controller to manage the switch.

FIGURE 4.3   OpenFlow Switch Context

Figure 4.4 displays the main components of an OpenFlow switch. An SDN controller communicates with OpenFlow-compatible switches using the OpenFlow protocol running over Transport Layer Security (TLS). Each switch connects to other **OpenFlow switches** and, possibly, to end-user devices that are the sources and destinations of packet flows. On the switch side, the interface is known as an **OpenFlow channel**. These connections are via OpenFlow ports. An **OpenFlow port** also connects the switch to the SDN controller. OpenFlow defines three types of ports:

- **Physical port:** Corresponds to a hardware interface of the switch. For example, on an Ethernet switch, physical ports map one to one to the Ethernet interfaces.

- **Logical port:** Does not correspond directly to a hardware interface of the switch. Logical ports are higher-level abstractions that may be defined in the switch using non-OpenFlow methods (for example, link aggregation groups, tunnels, loopback interfaces). Logical ports may include packet encapsulation and may map to various physical ports. The processing done by the logical port is implementation dependent and must be transparent to OpenFlow processing, and those ports must interact with OpenFlow processing like OpenFlow physical ports.

- **Reserved port:** Defined by the OpenFlow specification. It specifies generic forwarding actions such as sending to and receiving from the controller, flooding, or forwarding using non-OpenFlow methods, such as "normal" switch processing.

Within each switch, a series of tables is used to manage the flows of packets through the switch.

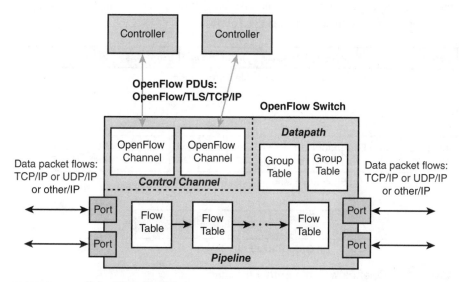

FIGURE 4.4   OpenFlow Switch

The OpenFlow specification defines three types of tables in the logical switch architecture. A **flow table** matches incoming packets to a particular flow and specifies what functions are to be performed on the packets. There may be multiple flow tables that operate in a pipeline fashion, as explained subsequently. A flow table may direct a flow to a **group table**, which may trigger a variety of actions that affect one or more flows. A **meter table** can trigger a variety of performance-related actions on a flow. Meter tables are discussed in Chapter 10. Using the OpenFlow switch protocol, the controller can add, update, and delete flow entries in tables, both reactively (in response to packets) and proactively.

→ *See Chapter 10, "Quality of Service"*

Before proceeding, it is helpful to define what is meant by the term *flow*. Curiously, this term is not defined in the OpenFlow specification, nor is there an attempt to define it in virtually all of the literature on OpenFlow. In general terms, a flow is a sequence of packets traversing a network that share a set of header field values. For example, a flow could consist of all packets with the same source and destination IP addresses or all packets with the same virtual LAN (VLAN) identifier. The sections that follow provide a more specific definition of this concept.

Flow Table Structure

The basic building block of the logical switch architecture is the **flow table**. Each packet that enters a switch passes through one of more flow tables. Each flow table consists of a number of rows, called **entries**, consisting of seven components (see part a of Figure 4.5), as defined in the list that follows.

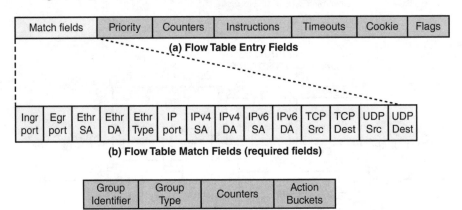

FIGURE 4.5   OpenFlow Table Entry Formats

- **Match fields:** Used to select packets that match the values in the fields.

- **Priority:** Relative priority of table entries. This is a 16-bit field with 0 corresponding to the lowest priority. In principle, there could be $2^{16} = 64k$ priority levels.

- **Counters:** Updated for matching packets. The OpenFlow specification defines a variety of counters. Table 4.1 lists the counters that must be supported by an OpenFlow switch.

- **Instructions:** Instructions to be performed if a match occurs.

- **Timeouts:** Maximum amount of idle time before a flow is expired by the switch. Each flow entry has an idle_timeout and a hard_timeout associated with it. A nonzero hard_timeout field causes the flow entry to be removed after the given number of seconds, regardless of how many packets it has matched.

A nonzero idle_timeout field causes the flow entry to be removed when it has matched no packets in the given number of seconds.

- **Cookie:** 64-bit opaque data value chosen by the controller. May be used by the controller to filter flow statistics, flow modification and flow deletion; not used when processing packets.

- **Flags**: Flags alter the way flow entries are managed; for example, the flag OFPFF_SEND_FLOW_REM triggers flow removed messages for that flow entry.

TABLE 4.1 Required OpenFlow Counters

Counter	Usage	Bit Length
Reference count (active entries)	Per flow table	32
Duration (seconds)	Per flow entry	32
Received packets	Per port	64
Transmitted packets	Per port	64
Duration (seconds)	Per port	32
Transmit packets	Per queue	64
Duration (seconds)	Per queue	32
Duration (seconds)	Per group	32
Duration (seconds)	Per meter	32

Match Fields Component

The match fields component of a table entry consists of the following required fields (see part b of Figure 4.5):

- **Ingress port:** The identifier of the port on this switch on which the packet arrived. This may be a physical port or a switch-defined virtual port. Required in ingress tables.

- **Egress port:** The identifier of the egress port from action set. Required in egress tables.

- **Ethernet source and destination addresses:** Each entry can be an exact address, a bitmasked value for which only some of the address bits are checked, or a wildcard value (match any value).

- **Ethernet type field:** Indicates type of the Ethernet packet payload.

- **IP:** Version 4 or 6.

- **IPv4 or IPv6 source address, and destination address:** Each entry can be an exact address, a bitmasked value, a subnet mask value, or a wildcard value.

- **TCP source and destination ports:** Exact match or wildcard value.

- **UDP source and destination ports:** Exact match or wildcard value.

The preceding match fields must be supported by any OpenFlow-compliant switch. The following fields may be optionally supported.

- **Physical port:** Used to designate underlying physical port when packet is received on a logical port.

- **Metadata:** Additional information that can be passed from one table to another during the processing of a packet. Its use is discussed subsequently.

- **VLAN ID and VLAN user priority:** Fields in the IEEE 802.1Q virtual LAN header. SDN support for VLANs is discussed in Chapter 8, " NFV Functionality."

- **IPv4 or IPv6 DS and ECN:** Differentiated Services and Explicit Congestion Notification fields.

- **SCTP source and destination ports:** Exact match or wildcard value for Stream Transmission Control Protocol.

- **ICMP type and code fields:** Exact match or wildcard value.

- **ARP opcode:** Exact match in Ethernet Type field.

- **Source and target IPv4 addresses in ARP payload:** Can be an exact address, a bitmasked value, a subnet mask value, or a wildcard value.

- **IPv6 flow label:** Exact match or wildcard.

- **ICMPv6 type and code fields:** Exact match or wildcard value.

- **IPv6 neighbor discovery target address:** In an IPv6 Neighbor Discovery message.

- **IPv6 neighbor discovery source and target addresses:** Link-layer address options in an IPv6 Neighbor Discovery message.

- **MPLS label value, traffic class, and BoS:** Fields in the top label of an MPLS label stack.

- **Provider bridge traffic ISID:** Service instance identifier.

- **Tunnel ID:** Metadata associated with a logical port.

- **TCP flags:** Flag bits in the TCP header. May be used to detect start and end of TCP connections.

- **IPv6 extension**: Extension header.

Thus, OpenFlow can be used with network traffic involving a variety of protocols and network services. Note that at the MAC/link layer, only Ethernet is supported. Therefore, OpenFlow as currently defined cannot control Layer 2 traffic over wireless networks.

Each of the fields in the match fields component either has a specific value or a wildcard value, which matches any value in the corresponding packet header field. A flow table may include a table-miss flow entry, which wildcards all match fields (every field is a match regardless of value) and has the lowest priority.

We can now offer a more precise definition of the term *flow*. From the point of view of an individual switch, a flow is a sequence of packets that matches a specific entry in a flow table. The definition is packet oriented, in the sense that it is a function of the values of header fields of the packets that constitute the flow, and not a function of the path they follow through the network. A combination of flow entries on multiple switches defines a flow that is bound to a specific path.

Instructions Component

The instructions component of a table entry consists of a set of instructions that are executed if the packet matches the entry. Before describing the types of instructions, we need to define the terms *action* and *action set*. Actions describe packet forwarding, packet modification, and group table processing operations. The OpenFlow specification includes the following actions:

- **Output:** Forward packet to specified port. The port could be an output port to another switch or the port to the controller. In the latter case, the packet is encapsulated in a message to the controller.

- **Set-Queue:** Sets the queue ID for a packet. When the packet is forwarded to a port using the output action, the queue ID determines which queue attached to this port is used for scheduling and forwarding the packet. Forwarding behavior is dictated by the configuration of the queue and is used to provide basic QoS support. SDN support for QoS is discussed in Chapter 10.

- **Group:** Process packet through specified group.

- **Push-Tag/Pop-Tag:** Push or pop a tag field for a VLAN or Multiprotocol Label Switching (MPLS) packet.

- **Set-Field:** The various Set-Field actions are identified by their field type and modify the values of respective header fields in the packet.

- **Change-TTL:** The various Change-TTL actions modify the values of the IPv4 TTL (time to live), IPv6 hop limit, or MPLS TTL in the packet.

- **Drop**: There is no explicit action to represent drops. Instead, packets whose action sets have no output action should be dropped.

An action set is a list of actions associated with a packet that are accumulated while the packet is processed by each table and that are executed when the packet exits the processing pipeline.

The types of instructions can be grouped into four categories:

- **Direct packet through pipeline:** The Goto-Table instruction directs the packet to a table farther along in the pipeline. The Meter instruction directs the packet to a specified meter.

- **Perform action on packet:** Actions may be performed on the packet when it is matched to a table entry. The Apply-Actions instruction applies the specified actions immediately, without any change to the action set associated with this packet. This instruction may be used to modify the packet between two tables in the pipeline.

- **Update action set:** The Write-Actions instruction merges specified actions into the current action set for this packet. The Clear-Actions instruction clears all the actions in the action set.

- **Update metadata**: A metadata value can be associated with a packet. It is used to carry information from one table to the next. The Write-Metadata instruction updates an existing metadata value or creates a new value.

Flow Table Pipeline

A switch includes one or more flow tables. If there is more than one flow table, they are organized as a pipeline, with the tables labeled with increasing numbers starting with zero. The use of multiple tables in a pipeline, rather than a single flow table, provides the SDN controller with considerable flexibility.

The OpenFlow specification defines two stages of processing:

- **Ingress processing:** Ingress processing always happens, beginning with Table 0, and uses the identity of the input port. Table 0 may be the only table, in which case the ingress processing is simplified to the processing performed on that single table, and there is no egress processing.

- **Egress processing:** Egress processing is the processing that happens after the determination of the output port. It happens in the context of the output port. This stage is optional. If it occurs, it may involve one or more tables. The separation of the two stages is indicated by the numerical identifier of the first egress table. All tables with a number lower than the first egress table must be used as ingress tables, and no table with a number higher than or equal to the first egress table can be used as an ingress table.

Pipeline processing always starts with ingress processing at the first flow table; the packet must be first matched against flow entries of flow Table 0. Other ingress flow tables may be used depending on the outcome of the match in the first table. If the outcome of ingress processing is to forward the packet to an output port, the OpenFlow switch may perform egress processing in the context of that output port.

When a packet is presented to a table for matching, the input consists of the packet, the identity of the ingress port, the associated metadata value, and the associated action set. For Table 0, the metadata value is blank and the action set is null. At each table, processing proceeds as follows (see Figure 4.6):

1. If there is a match on one or more entries, other than the table-miss entry, the match is defined to be with the highest-priority matching entry. As mentioned in the preceding discussion, the priority is a component of a table entry and is set via OpenFlow; the priority is determined by the user or application invoking OpenFlow. The following steps may then be performed:

   a. Update any counters associated with this entry.

   b. Execute any instructions associated with this entry. This may include updating the action set, updating the metadata value, and performing actions.

   c. The packet is then forwarded to a flow table further down the pipeline, to the group table, to the meter table, or directed to an output port.

2. If there is a match only on a table-miss entry, the table entry may contain instructions, as with any other entry. In practice, the table-miss entry specifies one of three actions:

   a. Send packet to controller. This will enable the controller to define a new flow for this and similar packets, or decide to drop the packet.

   b. Direct packet to another flow table farther down the pipeline.

   c. Drop the packet.

3. If there is no match on any entry and there is no table-miss entry, the packet is dropped.

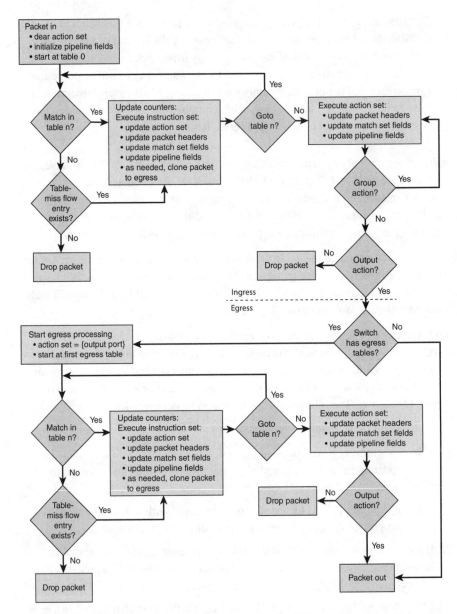

FIGURE 4.6   Simplified Flowchart Detailing Packet Flow Through an OpenFlow Switch

For the final table in the pipeline, forwarding to another flow table is not an option. If and when a packet is finally directed to an output port, the accumulated action set is executed and then the packet is queued for output. Figure 4.7 illustrates the overall ingress pipeline process.

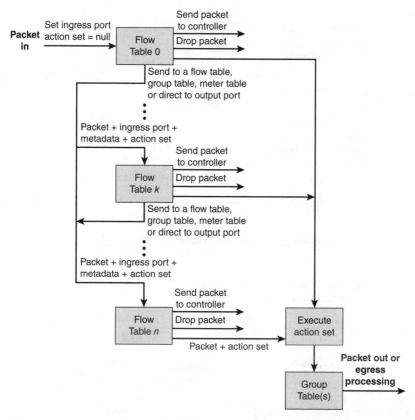

FIGURE 4.7   Packet Flow Through an OpenFlow Switch: Ingress Processing

If egress processing is associated with a particular output port, then after a packet is directed to an output port at the completion of the ingress processing, the packet is directed to the first flow table of the egress pipeline. Egress pipeline processing proceeds in the same fashion as for ingress processing, except that there is no group table processing at the end of the egress pipeline. Egress processing is shown in Figure 4.8.

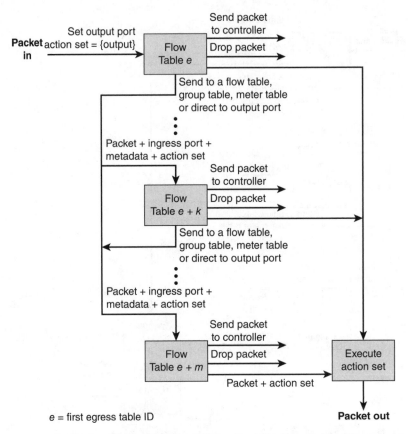

FIGURE 4.8   Packet Flow Through OpenFlow Switch: Egress Processing

The Use of Multiple Tables

The use of multiple tables enables the nesting of flows, or put another way, the breaking down of a single flow into a number of parallel subflows. Figure 4.9 illustrates this property. In this example, an entry in Table 0 defines a flow consisting of packets traversing the network from a specific source IP address to a specific destination IP address. Once a least-cost route between these two endpoints is established, it might make sense for all traffic between these two endpoints to follow that route, and the next hop on that route from this switch can be entered in Table 0. In Table 1, separate entries for this flow can be defined for different transport layer protocols, such as TCP and UDP. For these subflows, the same output port might be retained so that the subflows all follow the same route. However, TCP includes elaborate congestion control mechanisms not normally found with UDP, so it might be reasonable to handle the TCP and UDP subflows differently in terms of quality of service (QoS)-related parameters. Any of the Table 1 entries could immediately route its respective subflow to the output port, but some or all of the entries may invoke Table 2, further dividing each subflow. The figure shows that the TCP subflow could be divided on the basis of the protocol running on top of TCP, such as Simple Mail Transfer Protocol (SMTP) or File Transfer Protocol (FTP). Similarly, the UDP flow could be subdivided based on protocols running on UDP, such as Simple Network Management Protocol (SNMP). The figure also indicates other subflows at Table 1 and 2, which may be used for other purposes.

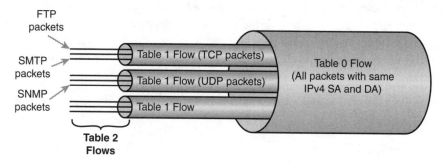

FIGURE 4.9 Example of Nested Flows

For this example, it would be possible to define each of these fine-grained subflows in Table 0. The use of multiple tables simplifies the processing in both the SDN controller and the OpenFlow switch. Actions such as next hop that apply to the aggregate flow can be defined once by the controller and examined and performed once by the switch. The addition of new subflows at any level involves less setup. Therefore, the use of pipelined, multiple tables increases the efficiency of network operations, provides granular control, and enables the network to respond to real-time changes at the application, user, and session levels.

Group Table

In the course of pipeline processing, a flow table may direct a flow of packets to the group table rather than another flow table. The group table and group actions enable OpenFlow to represent a set of ports as a single entity for forwarding packets. Different types of groups are provided to represent different forwarding abstractions, such as multicasting and broadcasting.

Each group table consists of a number of rows, called group entries, consisting of four components (refer back to part c of Figure 4.5):

- **Group identifier:** A 32-bit unsigned integer uniquely identifying the group. A **group** is defined as an entry in the group table.

- **Group type:** To determine group semantics, as explained subsequently.

- **Counters:** Updated when packets are processed by a group.

- **Action buckets:** An ordered list of action buckets, where each action bucket contains a set of actions to execute and associated parameters.

Each group includes a set of one or more action buckets. Each bucket contains a list of actions. Unlike the action set associated with a flow table entry, which is a list of actions that accumulate while the packet is processed by each flow table, the action list in a bucket is executed when a packet reaches a bucket. The action list is executed in sequence and generally ends with the Output action, which forwards the packet to a specified port. The action list may also end with the Group action, which sends the packet to another group. This enables the chaining of groups for more complex processing.

A group is designated as one of the types depicted in Figure 4.10: all, select, fast failover, and indirect.

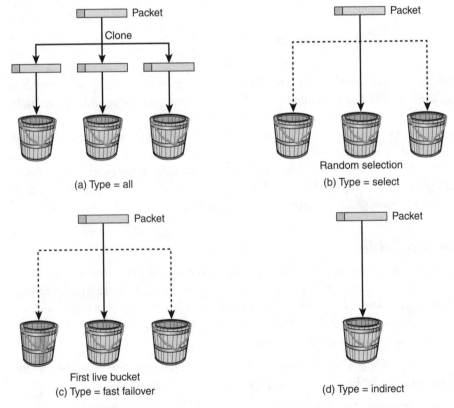

(a) Type = all

(b) Type = select

(c) Type = fast failover

(d) Type = indirect

FIGURE 4.10   Group Types

The **all type** executes all the buckets in the group. Thus, each arriving packet is effectively cloned. Typically, each bucket will designate a different output port, so that the incoming packet is then transmitted on multiple output ports. This group is used for multicast or broadcast forwarding.

The **select type** executes one bucket in the group, based on a switch-computed selection algorithm (for example, hash on some user-configured tuple or simple round-robin). The selection algorithm should implement equal load sharing or, optionally, load sharing based on bucket weights assigned by the SDN controller.

The **fast failover type** executes the first live bucket. Port liveness is managed by code outside of the scope of OpenFlow and may have to do with routing algorithms or congestion control mechanisms. The buckets are evaluated in order, and the first live bucket is selected. This group type enables the switch to change forwarding without requiring a round trip to the controller.

The three just-mentioned types all work with a single packet flow. The **indirect type** allows multiple packet flows (that is, multiple flow table entries) to point to a common group identifier. This type provides for more efficient management by the controller in certain situations. For example, suppose that there are 100 flow entries that have the same match value in the IPv4 destination address match field, but differ in some other match field, but all of them forward the packet to port X by including the action Output X on the action list. We can instead replace this action with the action Group GID, where GID is the ID of an indirect group entry that forwards the packet to port X. If the SDN controller needs to change from port X to port Y, it is not necessary to update all 100 flow table entries. All that is required is to update the group entry.

4.3 OpenFlow Protocol

The OpenFlow protocol describes message exchanges that take place between an OpenFlow controller and an OpenFlow switch. Typically, the protocol is implemented on top of TLS, providing a secure OpenFlow channel.

The OpenFlow protocol enables the controller to perform add, update, and delete actions to the flow entries in the flow tables. It supports three types of messages (see Table 4.2):

- **Controller to switch:** These messages are initiated by the controller and, in some cases, require a response from the switch. This class of messages enables the controller to manage the logical state of the switch, including its configuration and details of flow and group table entries. Also included in this class is the Packet-out message. This message is sent by the controller to a switch when that switch sends a packet to the controller and the controller decides not to drop the packet but to direct it to a switch output port.

- **Asynchronous:** These types of messages are sent without solicitation from the controller. This class includes various status messages to the controller.

Also included is the Packet-in message, which may be used by the switch to send a packet to the controller when there is no flow table match.

- **Symmetric**: These messages are sent without solicitation from either the controller or the switch. They are simple yet helpful. Hello messages are typically sent back and forth between the controller and switch when the connection is first established. Echo request and reply messages can be used by either the switch or controller to measure the latency or bandwidth of a controller-switch connection or just verify that the device is up and running. The Experimenter message is used to stage features to be built in to future versions of OpenFlow.

TABLE 4.2   OpenFlow Messages

Message	Description
Controller to Switch	
Features	Request the capabilities of a switch. Switch responds with a features reply that specifies its capabilities.
Configuration	Set and query configuration parameters. Switch responds with parameter settings.
Modify-State	Add, delete, and modify flow/group entries and set switch port properties.
Read-State	Collect information from switch, such as current configuration, statistics, and capabilities.
Packet-out	Direct packet to a specified port on the switch.
Barrier	Barrier request/reply messages are used by the controller to ensure message dependencies have been met or to receive notifications for completed operations.
Role-Request	Set or query role of the OpenFlow channel. Useful when switch connects to multiple controllers.
Asynchronous-Configuration	Set filter on asynchronous messages or query that filter. Useful when switch connects to multiple controllers.
Asynchronous	
Packet-in	Transfer packet to controller.
Flow-Removed	Inform the controller about the removal of a flow entry from a flow table.
Port-Status	Inform the controller of a change on a port.
Role-Status	Inform controller of a change of its role for this switch from master controller to slave controller.
Controller-Status	Inform the controller when the status of an OpenFlow channel changes. This can assist failover processing if controllers lose the ability to communicate among themselves.
Flow-monitor	Inform the controller of a change in a flow table. Allows a controller to monitor in real time the changes to any subsets of the flow table done by other controllers.

Message	Description
Symmetric	
Hello	Exchanged between the switch and controller upon connection startup.
Echo	Echo request/reply messages can be sent from either the switch or the controller, and must return an echo reply.
Error	Used by the switch or the controller to notify problems to the other side of the connection.
Experimenter	For additional functionality.

In general terms, the OpenFlow protocol provides the SDN controller with three types of information to be used in managing the network:

- **Event-based messages:** Sent by the switch to the controller when a link or port change occurs.

- **Flow statistics:** Generated by the switch based on traffic flow. This information enables the controller to monitor traffic, reconfigure the network as needed, and adjust flow parameters to meet QoS requirements.

- **Encapsulated packets:** Sent by the switch to the controller either because there is an explicit action to send this packet in a flow table entry or because the switch needs information for establishing a new flow.

The OpenFlow protocol enables the controller to manage the logical structure of a switch, without regard to the details of how the switch implements the OpenFlow logical architecture.

4.4 Key Terms

After completing this chapter, you should be able to define the following terms.

action bucket	flow table	OpenFlow instruction
action list	group table	OpenFlow message
action set	ingress table	OpenFlow port
egress table	match fields	OpenFlow switch
flow	OpenFlow action	SDN data plane

Chapter 5

SDN Control Plane

The organization for the control and guidance of the trade should therefore be of so complete a character that the trade may be either dispersed about the ocean or concentrated along particular routes; or in some places dispersed and in others concentrated; and that changes from one policy to the other can be made when necessary at any time.

—*The World Crisis*, Winston Churchill, 1923

Chapter Objectives

After studying this chapter, you should be able to

- List and explain the key functions of the SDN control plane.
- Discuss the routing function in the SDN controller.
- Understand the ITU-T Y.3300 layered SDN model.
- Present an overview of OpenDaylight.
- Present an overview of REST.
- Compare centralized and distributed SDN controller architectures.
- Explain the role of BGP in an SDN network.

This chapter continues our study of software-defined networking (SDN), focusing on the control plane (see Figure 5.1). Section 5.1 provides an overview of SDN control plane architecture, discussing the functions and interface capabilities of a typical SDN control plane implementation. Next, we summarize the ITU-T layered SDN model, which provides additional insight into the role of the control plane. This is followed by a description of one of the most significant open source SDN controller efforts, known as OpenDaylight. Then Section 5.4 describes the REST northbound interface, which has become common in SDN implementations. Finally, Section 5.5 discusses issues relating to cooperation and coordination among multiple SDN controllers.

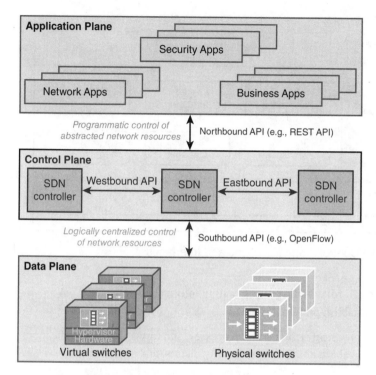

FIGURE 5.1   SDN Architecture

5.1   SDN Control Plane Architecture

The SDN control layer maps application layer service requests into specific commands and directives to data plane switches and supplies applications with information about data plane topology and activity. The control layer is implemented as a server or cooperating set of servers known as SDN controllers. This section provides an overview of control plane functionality. Later, we look at specific protocols and standards implemented within the control plane.

Control Plane Functions

Figure 5.2 illustrates the functions performed by SDN controllers. The figure illustrates the essential functions that any controller should provide, as suggested in a paper by Kreutz [KREU15], which include the following:

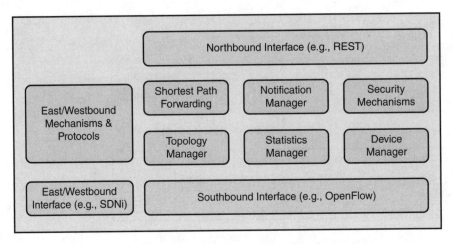

FIGURE 5.2   SDN Control Plane Functions and Interfaces

- **Shortest path forwarding:** Uses routing information collected from switches to establish preferred routes.

- **Notification manager:** Receives, processes, and forwards to an application events, such as alarm notifications, security alarms, and state changes.

- **Security mechanisms:** Provides isolation and security enforcement between applications and services.

- **Topology manager:** Builds and maintains switch interconnection topology information.

- **Statistics manager:** Collects data on traffic through the switches.

- **Device manager:** Configures switch parameters and attributes and manages flow tables.

network operating system (NOS)

A server-based operating system oriented to computer networking. It may include directory services, network management, network monitoring, network policies, user group management, network security and other network-related functions.

The functionality provided by the SDN controller can be viewed as a **network operating system (NOS)**. As with a conventional OS, an NOS provides essential services, common application programming interfaces (APIs), and an abstraction of lower-layer elements to developers. The functions of an SDN NOS, such as those in the preceding list, enable developers to define network policies and manage networks without concern for the details of the network device characteristics, which may be heterogeneous and dynamic. The northbound interface, discussed subsequently, provides a uniform means for application developers and network managers to access SDN service and perform network management tasks. Further, well-defined northbound interfaces enable developers to create software that is independent not only of data plane details but to a great extent usable with a variety of SDN controller servers.

A number of different initiatives, both commercial and open source, have resulted in SDN controller implementations. The following list describes a few prominent ones:

- **OpenDaylight:** An open source platform for network programmability to enable SDN, written in Java. OpenDaylight was founded by Cisco and IBM, and its membership is heavily weighted toward network vendors. OpenDaylight can be implemented as a single centralized controller, but enables controllers to be distributed where one or multiple instances may run on one or more clustered servers in the network.

- **Open Network Operating System (ONOS):** An open source SDN NOS, initially released in 2014. It is a nonprofit effort funded and developed by a number of carriers, such as AT&T and NTT, and other service providers. Significantly, ONOS is supported by the Open Networking Foundation, making it likely that ONOS will be a major factor in SDN deployment. ONOS is designed to be used as a distributed controller and provides abstractions for partitioning and distributing network state onto multiple distributed controllers.

- **POX:** An open source OpenFlow controller that has been implemented by a number of SDN developers and engineers. POX has a well written API and documentation. It also provides a web-based graphical user interface (GUI) and is written in Python, which typically shortens its experimental and developmental cycles compared to some other implementation languages, such as C++.

- **Beacon:** An open source package developed at Stanford. Written in Java and highly integrated into the Eclipse integrated development environment (IDE). Beacon was the first controller that made it possible for beginner programmers to work with and create a working SDN environment.

- **Floodlight:** An open source package developed by Big Switch Networks. Although its beginning was based on Beacon, it was built using Apache Ant, which is a very popular software build tool that makes the development of Floodlight easier and more flexible. Floodlight has an active community and has a large number of features that can be added to create a system that best meets the requirements of a specific organization. Both a web-based and Java-based GUI are available and most of its functionality is exposed through a REST API.

- **Ryu:** An open source component-based SDN framework developed by NTT Labs. It is open sourced and fully developed in python.

- **Onix:** Another distributed controller, jointly developed by VMWare, Google, and NTT. Onix is a commercially available SDN controller.

→ *See Section 5.3, "Open-Daylight"*

Perhaps the most significant controller on this list is OpenDaylight, described subsequently in Section 5.3.

Southbound Interface

The southbound interface provides the logical connection between the SDN controller and the data plane switches (see Figure 5.3). Some controller products and configurations support only a single southbound protocol. A more flexible approach is the use of a southbound abstraction layer that provides a common interface for the control plane functions while supporting multiple southbound APIs.

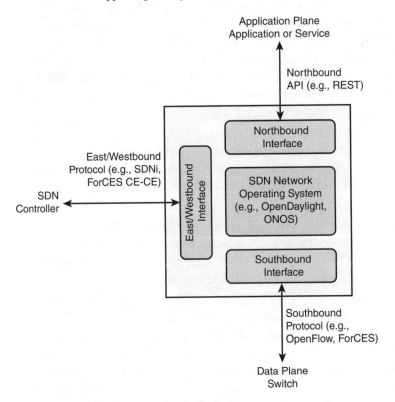

FIGURE 5.3   SDN Controller Interfaces

The most commonly implemented southbound API is OpenFlow, covered in some detail in Chapter 4, "SDN Data Plane and OpenFlow." Other southbound interfaces include the following:

- **Open vSwitch Database Management Protocol (OVSDB):** Open vSwitch (OVS) an open source software project which implements virtual switching that is interoperable with almost all popular hypervisors. OVS uses

OpenFlow for message forwarding in the control plane for both virtual and physical ports. OVSDB is the protocol used to manage and configure OVS instances.

- **Forwarding and Control Element Separation (ForCES):** An IETF effort that standardizes the interface between the control plane and the data plane for IP routers.

- **Protocol Oblivious Forwarding (POF):** This is advertised as an enhancement to OpenFlow that simplifies the logic in the data plane to a very generic forwarding element that need not understand the protocol data unit (PDU) format in terms of fields at various protocol levels. Rather, matching is done by means of (offset, length) blocks within a packet. Intelligence about packet format resides at the control plane level.

Northbound Interface

The northbound interface enables applications to access control plane functions and services without needing to know the details of the underlying network switches. The northbound interface is more typically viewed as a software API rather than a protocol.

Unlike the southbound and eastbound/westbound interfaces, where a number of heterogeneous interfaces have been defined, there is no widely accepted standard for the northbound interface. The result has been that a number of unique APIs have been developed for various controllers, complicating the effort to develop SDN applications. To address this issue the Open Networking Foundation formed the Northbound Interface Working Group (NBI-WG) in 2013, with the objective of defining and standardizing a number of broadly useful northbound APIs. As of this writing, the working group has not issued any standards.

A useful insight of the NBI-WG is that even in an individual SDN controller instance, APIs are needed at different "latitudes." That is, some APIs may be "further north" than others, and access to one, several, or all of these different APIs could be a requirement for a given application.

Figure 5.4, from the NBI-WG charter document (October 2013), illustrates the concept of multiple API latitudes. For example, an application may need one or more APIs that directly expose the functionality of the controller, to manage a network domain, and use APIs that invoke analytic or reporting services residing on the controller.

Figure 5.5 shows a simplified example of an architecture with multiple levels of northbound APIs, the levels of which are described in the list that follows.

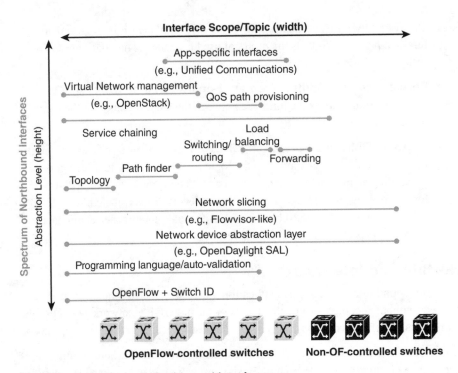

FIGURE 5.4   Latitude of Northbound Interfaces

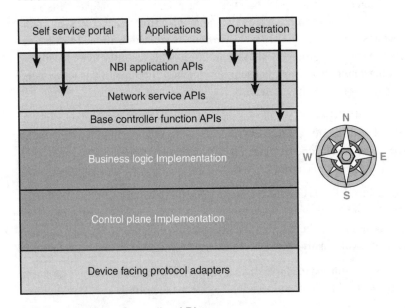

FIGURE 5.5   SDN Controller APIs

- **Base controller function APIs:** These APIs expose the basic functions of the controller and are used by developers to create network services.

- **Network service APIs:** These APIs expose network services to the north.

- **Northbound interface application APIs:** These APIs expose application-related services that are built on top of network services.

A common architectural style used for defining northbound APIs is REpresentational State Transfer (REST). Section 5.4 discusses REST.

→ *See Section 5.4, "REST"*

Routing

As with any network or internet, an SDN network requires a routing function. In general terms, the routing function comprises a protocol for collecting information about the topology and traffic conditions of the network, and an algorithm for designing routes through the network. Recall from Chapter 2, "Requirements and Technology," that there are two categories of routing protocols: interior router protocols (IRPs) that operate within an autonomous system (AS), and exterior router protocols (ERPs) that operate between autonomous systems.

← *See Section 2.4, "Routing"*

An IRP is concerned with discovering the topology of routers within an AS and then determining the best route to each destination based on different metrics. Two widely used IRPs are Open Shortest Path First (OSPF) Protocol and Enhanced Interior Gateway Routing Protocol (EIGRP). An ERP need not collect as much detailed traffic information. Rather, the primary concern with an ERP is to determine reachability of networks and end systems outside of the AS. Therefore, the ERP is typically executed only in edge nodes that connect one AS to another. Border Gateway Protocol (BGP) is commonly used for the ERP.

Traditionally, the routing function is distributed among the routers in a network. Each router is responsible for building up an image of the topology of the network. For interior routing, each router as well must collect information about connectivity and delays and then calculate the preferred route for each IP destination address. However, in an SDN-controlled network, it makes sense to centralize the routing function within the SDN controller. The controller can develop a consistent view of the network state for calculating shortest paths, and can implement application-aware routing policies. The data plane switches are relieved of the processing and storage burden associated with routing, leading to improved performance.

The centralized routing application performs two distinct functions: link discovery and topology manager.

For **link discovery**, the routing function needs to be aware of links between data plane switches. Note that in the case of an internetwork, the links between routers are networks, whereas for Layer 2 switches, such as Ethernet switches, the links are direct physical links. In addition, link discovery must be performed between a router and a host system and between a router in the domain of this controller and a router in a neighboring domain. Discovery is triggered by unknown traffic entering the controller's network domain either from an attached host or from a neighboring router.

The **topology manager** maintains the topology information for the network and calculates routes in the network. Route calculation involves determining the shortest path between two data plane nodes or between a data plane node and a host.

5.2   ITU-T Model

Before proceeding to a discussion of an SDN controller design, it will be useful to look at the SDN high-level architecture defined in ITU-T Y.3300 (see Figure 5.6). As was depicted in Figure 3.3, the Y.3300 model consists of three layers, or planes: application, control, and resource. As defined in Y.3300, the **application layer** is where SDN applications specify network services or business applications by defining a service-aware behavior of network resources. The applications interact with the SDN control layer via APIs that form an application-control interface. The applications make use of an abstracted view of the network resources provided by the SDN control layer by means of information and data models exposed via the APIs.

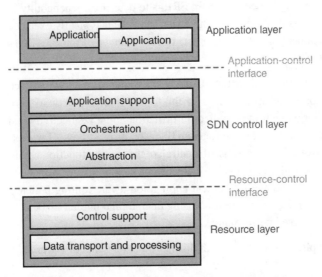

FIGURE 5.6   High-Level Architecture of SDN (ITU-T Y.3300)

The control layer provides a means to dynamically control the behavior of network resources, as instructed by the application layer. The control layer can be viewed as having the following sublayers:

- **Application support:** Provides an API for SDN applications to access network information and program application-specific network behavior.

- **Orchestration:** Provides the automated control and management of network resources and coordination of requests from the application layer for network resources. Orchestration encompasses physical and virtual network topologies, network elements, traffic control, and other network-related aspects.

- **Abstraction:** Interacts with network resources, and provides an abstraction of the network resources, including network capabilities and characteristics, to support management and orchestration of physical and virtual network resources. Such abstraction relies upon standard information and data models and is independent of the underlying transport infrastructure.

The **resource layer** consists of an interconnected set of data plane forwarding elements (switches). Collectively, these switches perform the transport and processing of data packets according to decisions made by the SDN control layer and forwarded to the resource layer via the resource-control interface. Most of this control is on behalf of applications. However, the SDN control layer, on its own behalf, may execute control of the resource layer for the sake of performance (for example, traffic engineering). The resource layer can be viewed as having the following sublayers:

- **Control support:** Supports programmability of resource-layer functions via the resource-control interface.

- **Data transport and processing:** Provides data forwarding and data routing functions.

The SDN design philosophy seeks to minimize the complexity and processing burden on the data switches. Accordingly, we can expect that many, if not most, of the commercial SDN switches will be equipped with a single southbound interface, such as OpenFlow, for simplicity of implementation and configuration. But different switches may support different southbound interfaces to the controller. Therefore, the SDN controller should support multiple protocols and interfaces to the data plane and be able to abstract all of these interfaces to a uniform network model to be used the application layer.

5.3 OpenDaylight

OpenDaylight

The OpenDaylight Project is an open source project hosted by the Linux Foundation and includes the involvement of virtually every major networking organization, including users of SDN technology and vendors of SDN products. Rather than hammer out new standards, the project aims to produce an extensible, open source, virtual networking platform atop such existing standards as OpenFlow. The approach of OpenDaylight is to enable industry participants to come together to develop core open source modules collaboratively, around which participants can add unique value. The goal is a common and open SDN platform for developers to utilize, contribute to, and build commercial products and technologies upon.

It is worthwhile to examine OpenDaylight in some detail, as it gives the reader a good idea of the scope of functionality of a typical SDN controller.

OpenDaylight Architecture

Figure 5.7 provides a top-level view of the OpenDaylight architecture. It consists of five logical layers, as further described in the list that follows.

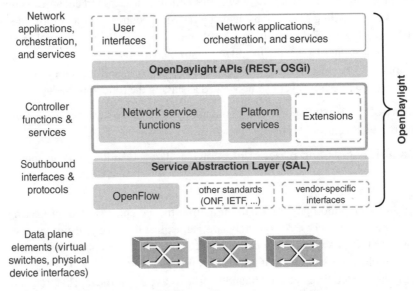

FIGURE 5.7   OpenDaylight Architecture

- **Network applications, orchestration, and services:** Consists of business and network logic applications that control and monitor network behavior. These applications use the controller to gather network intelligence, run algorithms to perform analytics, and then use the controller to orchestrate the new rules, if any, throughout the network.

- **APIs:** A set of common interfaces to OpenDaylight controller functions. OpenDaylight supports the **Open Service Gateway Initiative (OSGi)** framework and bidirectional REST for the northbound API. The OSGi framework is used for applications that will run in the same address space as the controller, while the REST (web-based) API is used for applications that do not run in the same address space (or even necessarily on the same machine) as the controller.

- **Controller functions and services:** SDN control plane functions and services.

- **Service abstraction layer (SAL):** Provides a uniform view of data plane resources, so that control plane functions can be implemented independent of the specific southbound interface and protocol.

- **Southbound interfaces and protocols:** Supports OpenFlow, other standard southbound protocols, and vendor-specific interfaces.

Open Service Gateway Initiative (OSGi)

A set of specifications that defines a dynamic component system for Java. These specifications reduce software complexity by providing a modular architecture for large-scale distributed systems as well as small, embedded applications.

There are several noteworthy aspects to the OpenDaylight architecture. First, OpenDaylight encompasses both control plane and application plane functionality. Thus, OpenDaylight is more than just an SDN controller implementation. This enables enterprise and telecommunications network managers to host open source software on their own servers to construct an SDN configuration. Vendors can use this software to create products with value-added additional application plane functions and services.

A second significant aspect of the OpenDaylight design is that it is not tied to OpenFlow or any other specific southbound interface. This provides greater flexibility in constructing SDN network configurations. The key element in this design is the SAL, which enables the controller to support multiple protocols on the southbound interface and provide consistent services for controller functions and for SDN applications. Figure 5.8 illustrates the operation of the SAL. The OSGi framework provides for dynamically linking plug-ins for the available southbound protocols. The capabilities of these protocols are abstracted to a collection of features that can be invoked by control plane services via a services manager in the SAL. The services manager maintains a registry that maps service requests to feature requests. Based on the service request, the SAL maps to the appropriate plug-in and thus uses the most appropriate southbound protocol to interact with a given network device.

The emphasis in the OpenDaylight project is that the software suite be modular, pluggable, and flexible. All of the code is implemented in Java and is contained within its own Java Virtual Machine (JVM). As such, it can be deployed on any hardware and operating system platform that supports Java.

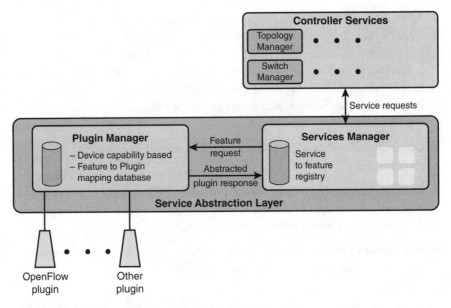

FIGURE 5.8   Service Abstraction Layer Model

OpenDaylight Helium

At the time of this writing, the most recent release of OpenDaylight is the Helium release, illustrated in Figure 5.9. The controller platform (exclusive of applications, which may also run on the controller) consists of a growing collection of dynamically pluggable modules, each of which performs one or more SDN-related functions and services. Five modules are considered base network service functions, likely to be included in any OpenDaylight implementation, as described in the list that follows.

- **Topology manager:** A service for learning the network layout by subscribing to events of node addition and removal and their interconnection. Applications requiring network view can use this service.

- **Statistics manager:** Collects switch-related statistics, including flow statistics, node connector, and queue occupancy.

- **Switch manager:** Holds the details of the data plane devices. As a switch is discovered, its attributes (for example, what switch/router it is, software version, capabilities) are stored in a database by the switch manager.

- **Forwarding rules manager:** Installs routes and tracks next-hop information. Works in conjunction with switch manager and topology manager to register and maintain network flow state. Applications using this need not have visibility of network device specifics.

- **Host tracker:** Tracks and maintains information about connected hosts.

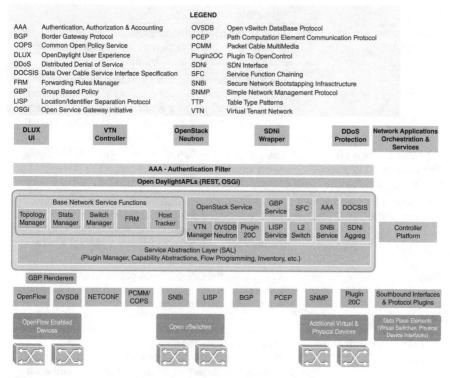

LEGEND

AAA	Authentication, Authorization & Accounting	OVSDB	Open vSwitch DataBase Protocol
BGP	Border Gateway Protocol	PCEP	Path Computation Element Communication Protocol
COPS	Common Open Policy Service	PCMM	Packet Cable MultiMedia
DLUX	OpenDaylight User Experience	Plugin2OC	Plugin To OpenControl
DDoS	Distributed Denial of Service	SDNi	SDN Interface
DOCSIS	Data Over Cable Service Interface Specification	SFC	Service Function Chaining
FRM	Forwarding Rules Manager	SNBi	Secure Network Bootstapping Infrasctructure
GBP	Group Based Policy	SNMP	Simple Network Management Protocol
LISP	Location/Identifier Separation Protocol	TTP	Table Type Patterns
OSGi	Open Service Gateway initiative	VTN	Virtual Tenant Network

FIGURE 5.9   OpenDaylight Structure (Helium)

To augment these base services, a number of other modules have been developed to enable implementation of more sophisticated and feature-rich controllers, as described in Table 5.1.

TABLE 5.1   OpenDaylight Modules

Feature	Description
Southbound Interfaces and Protocol Plug-Ins	
OpenFlow	The OpenFlow protocol.
Open vSwitch DataBase Protocol (OVSDB)	A network configuration protocol for virtual switching.
NETCONF	A network management protocol developed by IETF. NETCONF provides mechanisms to install, manipulate, and delete the configuration of network devices.
Packet Cable MultiMedia (PCMM)	PCMM provides an interface to control and manage service flow for cable modem network elements.
Secure Network Bootstrapping Infrastructure (SNBi)	Provides a secure channel that can be used by other applications to securely connect to various devices.

Feature	Description
Location/Identifier Separation Protocol (LISP)	An IETF proposed standard that separates the current IP address into two separate name spaces to show an IP location and identifier separately.
BGP	For routing service across multicarrier networks, the BGP-Link State (BGP-LS) protocol is run on the controller. BGP-LS learns the route information from adjacent autonomous systems and builds a consolidated and centralized routing database.
Path Computation Element Communication Protocol (PCEP)	Used to provision virtual private network (VPN) configuration information.
Simple Network Management Protocol (SNMP)	A collection of specifications for network management that include the protocol itself, the definition of a database, and associated concepts. SNMP enables a management station to monitor and control a network of devices.
Plugin2OC	A plug-in to the OpenContrail platform. OpenContrail is an open source project whose focus is as a network platform for cloud infrastructure.

Controller Modules

OpenStack service	OpenStack is an open source project to develop a massively scalable cloud operating system platform. SDN architectures that enable virtual networks are a good fit for OpenStack.
Group Based Policy (GBP) service	GBP is an application-centric policy model for OpenDaylight that separates information about application connectivity requirements from information about the underlying details of the network infrastructure.
Service function chaining (SFC)	An IETF proposed standard for combining service functions. In the SFC model, service functions, whether physical or virtualized, are not required to reside on the direct data path, and traffic is instead steered through required service functions, wherever they are deployed.
Authentication, authorization, and accounting (AAA)	Provides three basic security services: Authentication means to authenticate the identity of both human and machine users independent of choice of binding (direct or federated); authorization means to authorize human or machine user access to resources, including RPCs, notification subscriptions, and subsets of the data tree; accounting means to record and access the records of human or machine user access to resources, including RPCs, notifications, and subsets of the data tree.
Data Over Cable Service Interface Specification (DOCSIS)	A standard protocol stack for cable modem interface to digital networks.

Feature	Description
Virtual Tenant Network (VTN) Manager	VTN is an application that provides multitenant virtual networks on an SDN controller.
Open vSwitch DataBase (OVSDB) Protocol Neutron	Neutron interface to OVSDB.
Plugin2OC	Service interface to the Plugin2OC plug-in.
LISP service	Service interface to LISP plug-in.
L2Switch	This is an OSI Layer 2 switch routing functionality. The basic concept is to use controller intelligence to design routes through an Ethernet switched network that avoid the use of broadcast when the route to the destination is known.
SNBi service	Service interface to the SNBi plug-in.
SDN interface (SDNi) aggregator	The OpenDaylight- SDN Interface Application project aims at enabling inter-SDN controller communication by developing SDNi (Software-Defined Networking interface) as an application (ODL-SDNi App). This service acts as an aggregator for collecting network information such as topology, statistics, and host identity and location.
AAA authentication filter	Intercept requests or responses to or from the controller to verify tokens.

Network Applications, Orchestration, and Services

DLUX UI	A JavaScript-based stateless user interface that provides a consistent and user-friendly interface to interact with OpenDaylight projects and base controller. DLUX is a web-based interface that provides easy access to a model of the network controlled by this OpenDaylight controller.
VTN Controller	Provides API of VTN for users.
OpenStack Neutron	Neutron is a subsystem of OpenStack that allows for model-based integration of the network via APIs (in support of the core Infrastructure as a Service [IaaS] capabilities).
SDNi wrapper	Responsible for sharing and collecting information to/from federated controllers.
Distributed denial-of-service (DDoS) protection	Instructs an OpenFlow controller to program virtual and physical switches to be OpenFlow counters that collect statistics on network traffic. The application learns baseline traffic patterns and then watches for anomalies indicative of a network-level DDoS attack. If the application detects an attack, it instructs the OpenFlow controller to send suspect flows to specialized mitigation appliances to filter out malicious traffic.

5.4   REST

REpresentational State Transfer (REST) is an architectural style used to define APIs. This has become a standard way of constructing northbound APIs for SDN controllers. A REST API, or an API that is **RESTful** (adheres to the constraints of REST) is not a protocol, language, or established standard. It is essentially six constraints that an API must follow to be RESTful. The objective of these constraints is to maximize the scalability and independence/interoperability of software interactions, and to provide for a simple means of constructing APIs.

REST Constraints

REST assumes that the concepts of web-based access are used for interaction between the application and the service that are on either side of the API. REST does not define the specifics of the API but imposes constraints on the nature of the interaction between application and service. The six REST constraints are as follows:

- Client-server

- Stateless

- Cache

- Uniform interface

- Layered system

- Code on demand

The sections that follow cover these constraints in more detail.

Client-Server Constraint

This simple constraint dictates that interaction between application and server is in the client-server request/response style. The principle defined for this constraint is the separation of user interface concerns from data storage concerns. This separation allows client and server components to evolve independently and supports the portability of server-side functions to multiple platforms.

Stateless Constraint

The stateless constraint dictates that each request from a client to a server must contain all the information necessary to understand the request and cannot take advantage of any stored context on the server. Similarly, each response from the server must contain all the desired information for that request. One consequence is that any "memory" of a transaction is maintained in a session state kept entirely on the client.

Because the server does not retain any record of the client state, the result is a more efficient SDN controller. Another consequence is that if the client and server reside on different machines, and therefore communicate via a protocol, that protocol need not be connection oriented.

REST typically runs over Hypertext Transfer Protocol (HTTP), which is a stateless protocol.

Cache Constraint

The cache constraint requires that the data within a response to a request be implicitly or explicitly labeled as cacheable or noncacheable. If a response is cacheable, then a client cache is given the right to reuse that response data for later, equivalent requests. That is, the client is given permission to remember this data because the data is not likely to change on the server side. Therefore, subsequent requests for the same data can be handled locally at the client, reducing communication overhead between client and server, and reducing the server's processing burden.

Uniform Interface Constraint

REST emphasizes a uniform interface between components, regardless of the specific client-server application API implemented using REST. This enables controller services to evolve independently and provides the ability for an SDN controller provider to use software components from various vendors to implement the controller.

To obtain a uniform interface, REST defines four interface constraints:

- **Identification of resources:** Individual resources are identified using a resource identifier (for example, a URI).

- **Manipulation of resources through representations:** Resources are represented in a format like JSON, XML, or HTML.

- **Self-descriptive messages:** Each message has enough information to describe how the message is to be processed.

- **Hypermedia as the engine of the application state:** A client needs no prior knowledge of how to interact with a server, because the API is not fixed but dynamically provided by the server.

The REST style emphasizes that interactions between clients and services is enhanced by having a limited number of operations (verbs). Flexibility is provided by assigning resources (nouns) their own unique **Uniform Resource Identifier (URI)**. Because each verb has a specific meaning (GET, POST, PUT, and DELETE), REST avoids ambiguity.

Uniform Resource Identifier (URI)

A compact sequence of characters that identifies an abstract or physical resource. The URI specification (RFC 3986) defines a syntax for encoding arbitrary naming or addressing schemes and provides a list of such schemes. The URL (Uniform Resource Locator) is a type of URI in which an access protocol is designated and a specific Internet address is provided.

The benefit of this constraint, for an SDN environment is that different applications, perhaps written in different languages, can invoke the same controller service via a REST API.

Layered System Constraint

The layered system constraint simply means that a given function is organized in layers, with each layer only having direct interaction with the layers immediately above and below. This is a fairly standard architecture approach for protocol architectures, OS design, and system services design.

Code-on-Demand Constraint

REST allows client functionality to be extended by downloading and executing code in the form of applets or scripts. This simplifies clients by reducing the number of features required to be pre-implemented. Allowing features to be downloaded after deployment improves system extensibility.

Example REST API

To get a feel for the structure of a REST API, it is useful to look at an example. In this section, we discuss a REST API for the northbound interface of the Ryu SDN network operating system. The particular API switch manager service function in Ryu is designed to provide access to OpenFlow switches.

Each function that can be performed by the switch manager on behalf of an application is assigned a URI. For example, consider the function to get a description of all the entries in the group table of a particular switch. The URI for this function for this switch is as follows:

/stats/group/<*dpid*>

where stats (statistic) refers to the set of APIs for retrieving and updating switch statistics and parameters, group is the name of the function, and <*dpid*> (data path ID) is the unique identifier of the switch. To invoke the function for switch 1, the application issues the following command to the switch manager across the REST API:

GET http://localhost:8080/stats/groupdesc/1

The **localhost** portion of this command indicates that the application is running on the same server as the Ryu NOS. If the application were remote, the URI would be a URL that provides remote access via HTTP and the web. The switch manager responds to this command with a message whose message body includes the dpid then a sequence of blocks of values, one for each group defined in the switch dpid. The values are as follows:

- **type:** All, select, fast failover, or indirect (see Section 4.2).

- **group_id:** Identifier of an entry in the group table.

- **buckets:** A structured field consisting of the following subfields:

  - **weight:** Relative weight of bucket (only for select type).

  - **watch_port:** Port whose state affects whether this bucket is live (only required for fast failover groups).

  - **watch_group:** Group whose state affects whether this bucket is live (only required for fast failover groups).

  - **actions:** A list, possibly null, of actions.

The buckets portion of the message body is repeated, once for each group table entry.

Table 5.2 lists all the API functions for retrieving switch statistics and parameters that use the GET message type. There are also several functions that use the POST message type, in which the request message body includes a list of parameters that must be matched.

TABLE 5.2 Ryu REST APIs for Retrieving Switch Statistics Using GET

Request Type	Response Message Body Attributes
Get all switches	Data path ID
Get switch description	Data path ID, manufacturer description, hardware description, software description, serial number, human readable description of data path.
Get all flow stats of switch	Data path ID, length of this entry, table ID, time flow alive in seconds, time flow alive in nanoseconds, priority, number of seconds idle before expiration, number of seconds before expiration, flags, cookie, packet count, byte count, fields to match, actions
Get aggregate flow stats of switch	Data path ID, packet count, byte count, number of flows
Get port stats	Receive packet count, transmit packet count, receive byte count, transmit byte count, dropped receive packet count, dropped transmit packet count, receive error count, transmit error count, frame alignment error count, receive packet overrun count, CRC error count, collision count, time port alive in seconds, time port alive in nanoseconds
Get ports description	Data path ID, port number, Ethernet address, port name. config flags, state flag, current features, advertised features, supported features, features advertised by peer, current bit rate, max bitrate

Request Type	Response Message Body Attributes
Get queues stats	Data path ID, port number, queue ID, transmit byte count, transmit packet count, packet overrun count, time queue alive in seconds, time queue alive in nanoseconds
Get groups stats	Data path ID, length of this entry, group ID, number of flows or groups that forward to this group, packet count, byte count
Get group description	Data path ID, type, group ID, buckets (weight, watch_port, watch_group, actions)
Get group features	Data path ID, types, capabilities, max number of groups, actions supported
Get meters stats	Data path ID, meter ID, length of this entry, number of flows, input packet count, input byte count, time meter alive in seconds, time meter alive in nanoseconds, meter band (packet count, byte count)
Get meter configuration	Data path ID, flags, meter ID, bands (type, rate, burst size)
Get meter features	Data path ID, max number of meters, band types, capabilities, max bands per meter, max color value

The switch manager API also provides functions for updating switch parameters. These all use the POST message type. In this case, the request message body includes the parameters and their values to be updated. Table 5.3 lists the update API functions.

TABLE 5.3   Ryu REST APIs for Update Switch Statistics Filtered by Fields Using POST

Request Type	Request Message Body Attributes
Add flow entry	Data path ID, cookie, cookie mask, table ID, idle timeout, hard timeout, priority, buffer id, flags, fields to match, actions
Modify matching flow entries	Data path ID, cookie, cookie mask, table ID, idle timeout, hard timeout, priority, buffer id, flags, fields to match, actions
Delete matching flow entries	Data path ID, cookie, cookie mask, table ID, idle timeout, hard timeout, priority, buffer id, flags, fields to match, actions
Delete all flow entries	Data path ID
Add group entry	Data path ID, type, group ID, buckets (weight, watch_port, watch_group, actions)
Modify group entry	Data path ID, type, group ID, buckets (weight, watch_port, watch_group, actions)
Delete group entry	Data path ID, group id
Add meter entry	Data path ID, flags, meter ID, bands (type, rate, burst size)
Modify meter entry	Data path ID, flags, meter ID, bands (type, rate, burst size)
Delete meter entry	Data path ID, meter ID

5.5   Cooperation and Coordination Among Controllers

In addition to northbound and southbound interfaces, a typical SDN controller will have an east/westbound interface that enables communication with other SDN controllers and other networks. As yet, there has been no significant progress on open source or standardized east/west protocols or interfaces. This section surveys key design issues related to the east/westbound interface.

Centralized Versus Distributed Controllers

A key architectural design decision is whether a single centralized controller or a distributed set of controllers will be used to control the data plane switches. A centralized controller is a single server that manages all the data plane switches in the network.

In a large enterprise network, the deployment of a single controller to manage all network devices would prove unwieldy or undesirable. A more likely scenario is that the operator of a large enterprise or carrier network divides the whole network into a number of nonoverlapping SDN domains, also called SDN islands (Figure 5.10), managed by distributed controllers. Reasons for using SDN domains include those in the list that follows.

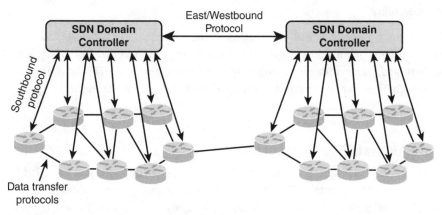

FIGURE 5.10   SDN Domain Structure

- **Scalability**: The number of devices an SDN controller can feasibly manage is limited. Therefore, a reasonably large network may need to deploy multiple SDN controllers.

- **Reliability**: The use of multiple controllers avoids the risk of a single point of failure.

■ **Privacy**: A carrier may choose to implement different privacy policies in different SDN domains. For example, an SDN domain may be dedicated to a set of customers who implement their own highly customized privacy policies, requiring that some networking information in this domain (for example, network topology) should not be disclosed to an external entity.

■ **Incremental deployment**: A carrier's network may consist of portions of legacy and nonlegacy infrastructure. Dividing the network into multiple individually manageable SDN domains allows for flexible incremental deployment.

Distributed controllers may be collocated in a small area, or widely dispersed, or a combination of the two. Closely placed controllers offer high throughput and are appropriate for data centers, whereas dispersed controllers accommodate multilocation networks.

Typically, controllers are distributed horizontally. That is, each controller governs a nonoverlapping subset of the data plane switches. A vertical architecture is also possible, in which control tasks are distributed to different controllers depending on criteria such as network view and locality requirements.

In a distributed architecture, a protocol is needed for communication among the controllers. In principle, a proprietary protocol could be used for this purpose, although an open or standard protocol would clearly be preferable for purposes of interoperability.

high-availability (HA) cluster

A multiple-computer architecture consisting of redundant network nodes that deliver a secondary or backup service when the primary service fails. Such clusters build redundancy into their computing environments to eliminate single points of failure, and they can incorporate multiple network connections, redundant data storage volumes, doubled-up power supplies, and other backup components and capabilities.

The functions associated with the east/westbound interface for a distributed architecture include maintaining either a partitioned or replicated database of network topology and parameters, and monitoring/notification functions. The latter function includes checking whether a controller is alive and coordinating changes in assignment of switches to controllers.

High-Availability Clusters

Within a single domain, the controller function can be implemented on a **high-availability (HA) cluster**. Typically, there would be two or more nodes that share a single IP address that is used by external systems (both north and southbound) to access the cluster. An example is the IBM SDN for Virtual Environments product, which uses two nodes. Each node is considered a peer of the other node in the cluster for data replication and sharing of the external IP address. When HA is running, the primary node is responsible for answering all traffic that is sent to the cluster's external IP address and holds a read/write copy of the configuration data. Meanwhile, the second node operates as a standby, with a read-only copy of the configuration data, which is kept current with the primary's copy. The secondary node monitors the state of the external IP. If the secondary node determines that the primary node is no longer answering the external IP, it triggers a failover, changing its mode to that of primary node. It assumes the responsibility for answering the external IP and changes its copy of configuration data to be read/write. If the old primary reestablishes connectivity, there is an automatic recovery process trigger to convert the old primary to secondary status so that configuration changes that are made during the failover period are not lost.

ODL Helium has HA built in, and Cisco XNC and the Open Network controller have HA features (up to five in a cluster).

Federated SDN Networks

The distributed SDN architecture discussed in the preceding paragraphs refers to a system of SDN domains that are all part of a single enterprise network. The domains may be collocated or on separate sites. In either case, the management of all the data plane switches is under the control of a single network management function.

It is also possible for SDN networks that are owned and managed by different organizations to cooperate using east/westbound protocols. Figure 5.11 is an example of the potential for inter-SDN controller cooperation.

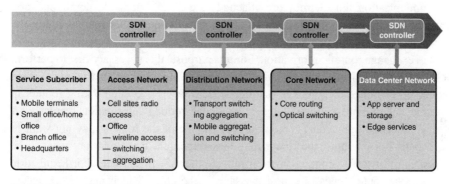

FIGURE 5.11   Federation of SDN Controllers [GUPT14]

In this configuration, we have a number of service subscribers to a data center network providing cloud-based services. Typically, as was illustrated previously in Figure 1.3, subscribers are connected to the service network through a hierarchy of access, distribution, and core networks. These intermediate networks may all be operated by the data center network, or they may involve other organizations. In the latter case, if all the networks implement SDN, they need to share common conventions for share control plane parameters, such as quality of service (QoS), policy information, and routing information.

Border Gateway Protocol

exterior router
protocol (ERP)

A generic term
for a protocol that
distributes routing
information to
collaborating routers
that connect auton-
omous systems.

Before proceeding further with our discussion, it will be useful to provide an overview of the Border Gateway Protocol (BGP). BGP was developed for use in conjunction with internets that use the TCP/IP suite, although the concepts are applicable to any internet. BGP has become the preferred **exterior router protocol (ERP)** for the Internet.

BGP enables routers, called gateways in the standard, in different autonomous systems to cooperate in the exchange of routing information. The protocol operates in terms of messages, which are sent over TCP connections. The current version of BGP is known as BGP-4.

Three functional procedures are involved in BGP:

- Neighbor acquisition
- Neighbor reachability
- Network reachability

Two routers are considered to be neighbors if they are attached to the same network or communication link. If they are attached to the same network, communication between the neighbor routers might require a path through other routers within the shared network. If the two routers are in different autonomous systems, they may want to exchange routing information. For this purpose, it is necessary first to perform **neighbor acquisition**. The term *neighbor* refers to two routers that share the same network. In essence, neighbor acquisition occurs when two neighboring routers in different autonomous systems agree to exchange routing information regularly. A formal acquisition procedure is needed because one of the routers may not want to participate. For example, the router may be overburdened and may not want to be responsible for traffic coming in from outside the AS. In the neighbor acquisition process, one router sends a request message to the other, which may either accept or refuse the offer. The protocol does not address the issue of how one router knows the address or even the existence of another router, nor how it decides that it needs to exchange routing information with that particular router. These issues must be dealt with at configuration time or by active intervention of a network manager.

To perform neighbor acquisition, one router sends an Open message to another. If the target router accepts the request, it returns a Keepalive message in response.

Once a neighbor relationship is established, the **neighbor reachability** procedure is used to maintain the relationship. Each partner needs to be assured that the other partner still exists and is still engaged in the neighbor relationship. For this purpose, the two routers periodically issue Keepalive messages to each other.

The final procedure specified by BGP is **network reachability**. Each router maintains a database of the networks that it can reach and the preferred route for reaching each network. Whenever a change is made to this database, the router issues an Update message that is broadcast to all other routers for which it has a neighbor relationship. Because the Update message is broadcast, all BGP routers can build up and maintain their routing information.

Routing and QoS Between Domains

For routing outside a controller's domain, the controller establishes a BGP connection with each neighboring router. Figure 5.12 illustrates a configuration with two SDN domains that are linked only through a non-SDN AS.

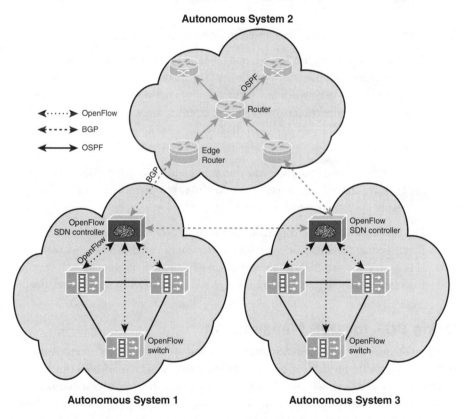

FIGURE 5.12 Heterogeneous Autonomous Systems with OpenFlow and Non-OpenFlow Domains

Within the non-SDN AS, OSPF is used for interior routing. OSPF is not needed in an SDN domain; rather, the necessary routing information is reported from each data plane switch to the centralized controller using a southbound protocol (in this case, OpenFlow). Between each SDN domain and the AS, BGP is used to exchange information, such as the following:

- **Reachability update:** Exchange of reachability information facilitates inter-SDN domain routing. This allows a single flow to traverse multiple SDNs and each controller can select the most appropriate path in the network.

- **Flow setup, tear-down, and update requests:** Controllers coordinate flow setup requests, which contain information such as path requirements, QoS, and so on, across multiple SDN domains.

- **Capability Update:** Controllers exchange information on network-related capabilities such as bandwidth, QoS and so on, in addition to system and software capabilities available inside the domain.

Several additional points are worth observing with respect to Figure 5.12:

- The figure depicts each AS as a cloud containing interconnected routers and, in the case of an SDN domain, a controller. The cloud represents an internet, so that the connection between any two routers is a network within the internet. Similarly, the connection between two adjacent autonomous systems is a network, which may be part of one of the two adjacent autonomous systems, or a separate network.

- For an SDN domain, the BGP function is implemented in the SDN controller rather than a data plane router. This is because the controller is responsible for managing the topology and making routing decisions.

- The figure shows a BGP connection between autonomous systems 1 and 3. It may be that these networks are not directly connected by a single network. However, if the two SDN domains are part of a single SDN system, or if they are federated, it may be desirable to exchange additional SDN-related information.

Using BGP for QoS Management

A common practice for inter-AS interconnection is a best-effort interconnection only. That is, traffic forwarding between autonomous systems is without traffic class differentiation and without any forwarding guarantee. It is common for network providers to reset any IP packet traffic class markings to zero, the best-effort marking, at the AS ingress router, which eliminates any traffic differentiation. Some providers perform higher-layer classification at the ingress to guess the forwarding requirements and to match on their AS internal QoS forwarding policy. There is no standardized set of classes, no standardized marking (class encoding), and no standardized forwarding behavior, that cross-domain traffic could rely on. However RFC 4594 (*Configuration Guidelines for DiffServ Service Classes*, August 2006) provides a set of "best practices" related to this parameters. QoS policy decisions are taken by network providers independently and in an uncoordinated fashion. This general statement does not cover existing individual agreements, which do offer quality-based interconnection with strict QoS guarantees. However, such service level agreement (SLA)-based agreements are of bilateral or multilateral nature and do not offer a means for a general "better than best effort" interconnection.

IETF is currently at work on a standardized scheme for QoS marking using BGP (*BGP Extended Community for QoS Marking*, draft-knoll-idr-qos-attribute-12, July 10, 2015). Meanwhile, SDN providers have implemented their own capabilities using the extensible nature of BGP. In either case, the interaction between SDN controllers in different domains using BGP would involve the steps illustrated in Figure 5.13 and described in the list that follows.

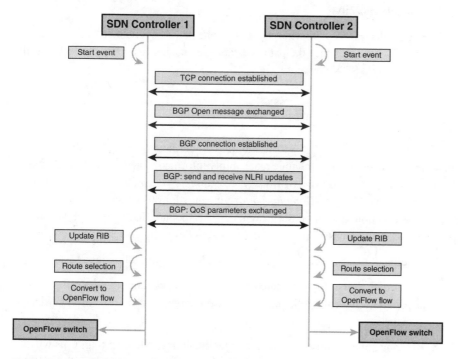

FIGURE 5.13   East-West Connection Establishment, Route, and Flow Setup

1. The SDN controller must be configured with BGP capability and with information about the location of neighboring BGP entices.

2. BGP is triggered by a start or activation event within the controller.

3. The BGP entity in the controller attempts to establish a TCP connection with each neighboring BGP entity.

4. Once a TCP connection is established, the controller's BGP entity exchanges Open messages with the neighbor. Capability information is exchanged with using the Open messages.

5. The exchange completes with the establishment of a BGP connection.

6. Update messages are used to exchange NLRI (network layer reachability information), indicating what networks are reachable via this entity. Reachability information is used in the selection of the most appropriate data path between SDN controllers. Information obtained through NLRI parameter is used to update the controller's Routing Information Base (RIB). This in turn enables the controller to set the appropriate flow information in the data plane switches.

7. The Update message can also be used to exchange QoS information, such as available capacity.

8. Route selection is done when more than one path is available based on BGP process decision. Once the path is established packets can traverse successfully between two SDN domains.

IETF SDNi

IETF has developed a draft specification that defines common requirements to coordinate flow setup and exchange reachability information across multiple domains, referred to as SDNi (*SDNi: A Message Exchange Protocol for Software Defined Networks across Multiple Domains*, draft-yin-sdn-sdni-00.txt, June 27, 2012). The SDNi specification does not define an east/westbound SDN protocol but rather provides some of the basic principles to be used in developing such a protocol.

SDNi functionality, as defined in the document, includes the following:

- Coordinate flow setup originated by applications, containing information such as path requirement, QoS, and service level agreements across multiple SDN domains.

- Exchange reachability information to facilitate inter-SDN routing. This will allow a single flow to traverse multiple SDNs and have each controller select the most appropriate path when multiple such paths are available.

SDNi depends on the types of available resources and capabilities available and managed by the different controllers in each domain. Therefore, it is important to implement SDNi in a descriptive and open manner so that new capabilities offered by different types of controllers will be supported. Because SDN in essence allows for innovation, it is important that data exchanged between controllers will be dynamic in nature; that is, there should be some metadata exchange that will allow SDNi to exchange information about unknown capabilities.

The message types for SDNi tentatively include the following:

- Reachability update

- Flow setup/teardown/update request (including application capability requirement such as QoS, data rate, latency, and so on)

- Capability update (including network-related capabilities, such as data rate and QoS, and system and software capabilities available inside the domain)

OpenDaylight SNDi

Included in the OpenDaylight architecture is an SDNi capability for connecting multiple OpenDaylight federated controllers in a network and sharing topology information among them. This capability appears to be compatible with the IETF specification for an SDNi function. The SDNi application deployable on an OpenDaylight controller consists of three components, as illustrated in Figure 5.14 and described in the list that follows.

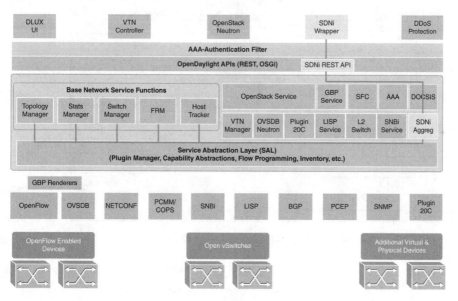

FIGURE 5.14 SDNi Components in OpenDaylight Structure (Helium)

- **SDNi aggregator:** Northbound SDNi plug-in acts as an aggregator for collecting network information such as topology, statistics, and host identifiers. This plug-in can evolve to meet the needs for network data requested to be shared across federated SDN controllers.

- **SDNi REST API:** SDNi REST APIs fetch the aggregated information from the northbound plug-in (SDNi aggregator).

- **SDNi wrapper:** SDNi BGP wrapper is responsible for the sharing and collecting information to/from federated controllers.

Figure 5.15 shows the interrelationship of the components, with a more detailed look at the SDNi wrapper. The SDNi aggregator collects statistics and parameters from the base network service functions, on behalf of requests via the REST API. The heart of the wrapper is an OpenDaylight implementation of the Border Gateway Protocol (BGP). BGP is an ERP suitable for exchanging routing information between routers that connect SDN domains.

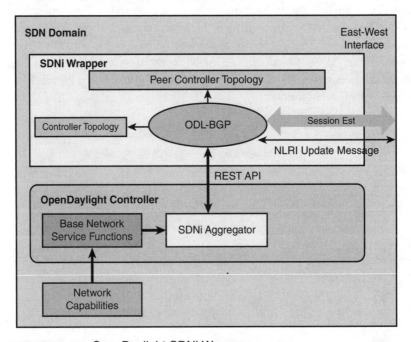

FIGURE 5.15   OpenDaylight SDNi Wrapper

5.6 Key Terms

After completing this chapter, you should be able to define the following terms.

Border Gateway Protocol (BGP)
centralized controller
distributed controller
east/westbound interface
exterior router protocol (ERP)
interior router protocol (IRP)
neighbor acquisition
neighbor reachability
network operating system (NOS)
network reachability
northbound interface
Open Service Gateway Initiative (OSGi)

OpenDaylight
OpenFlow
REpresentational State Transfer (REST)
RESTful
routing
Ryu
SDN control plane
SDNi
service abstraction layer (SAL)
southbound interface
Uniform Resource Identifier (URI)

5.7 References

GUPT14: Gupta, D., and Jahan, R. *Inter-SDN Controller Communication: Using Border Gateway Protocol.* Tata Consultancy Services White Paper, 2014. http://www.tcs.com.

KREU15: Kreutz, D., et al. "Software-Defined Networking: A Comprehensive Survey." *Proceedings of the IEEE*, January 2015.

Chapter | 6

SDN Application Plane

Life in the modern world is coming to depend more and more upon technical means of communication. Without such technical aids the modern city-state could not exist, for it is only by means of them that trade and business can proceed; that goods and services can be distributed where needed; that railways can run on schedule; that law and order are maintained; that education is possible. Communication renders true social life practicable, for communication means organization.

—On Human Communication, Colin Cherry

Chapter Objectives

After studying this chapter, you should be able to

- Present an overview of the SDN application plane architecture.
- Define the network services abstraction layers.
- List and explain three forms of abstraction in SDN.
- List and describe six major application areas of interest for SDN.

The power of the software-defined networking (SDN) approach to networking is in the support it provides for network applications to monitor and manage network behavior. The SDN control plane provides the functions and services that facilitate rapid development and deployment of network applications.

While the SDN data and control planes are well defined, there is much less agreement on the nature and scope of the application plane. At minimum, the application plane includes a number of network applications—that is, applications that specifically deal with network management and control. There is no agreed-upon set of such applications or even categories of such applications. Further, the application layer may include general-purpose network abstraction tools and services that might also be viewed as part of the functionality of the control plane.

With these limitations in mind, this chapter provides an overview of the SDN application plane. Section 6.1 begins with an overview of the SDN application plane architecture. Section 6.2 looks at a key component of that architecture, the network services abstraction layer. The remaining sections look at six major application areas that can be supported by SDN. These sections also describe a number of specific examples. The examples were chosen to give the reader a feel for the range of applications that can benefit from an SDN infrastructure.

6.1   SDN Application Plane Architecture

The application plane contains applications and services that define, monitor, and control network resources and behavior. These applications interact with the SDN control plane via application-control interfaces, for the SDN control layer to automatically customize the behavior and the properties of network resources. The programming of an SDN application makes use of the abstracted view of network resources provided by the SDN control layer by means of information and data models exposed via the application-control interface.

This section provides an overview of application plane functionality, depicted in Figure 6.1. The elements in this figure are analyzed through a bottom-up approach, and subsequent sections provide detail on specific application areas.

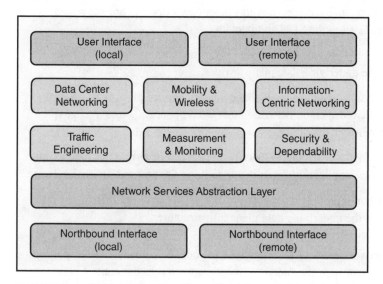

FIGURE 6.1   SDN Application Plane Functions and Interfaces

Northbound Interface

As described in Chapter 5, "SDN Control Plane," the northbound interface enables applications to access control plane functions and services without needing to know the details of the underlying network switches. Typically, the northbound interface provides an abstract view of network resources controlled by the software in the SDN control plane.

Figure 6.1 indicates that the northbound interface can be a local or remote interface. For a local interface, the SDN applications are running on the same server as the control plane software (controller network operating system). Alternatively, the applications could be run on remote systems and the northbound interface is a protocol or application programming interface (API) that connects the applications to the controller network operating system (NOS) running on central server. Both architectures are likely to be implemented.

An example of a northbound interface is the REST API for the Ryu SDN network operating system, described in Section 5.4.

Network Services Abstraction Layer

RFC 7426 defines a network services abstraction layer between the control and application planes and describes it as a layer that provides service abstractions that can be used by applications and services. Several functional concepts are suggested by the placement of this layer in the SDN architecture:

- This layer could provide an abstract view of network resources that hides the details of the underlying data plane devices.

- This layer could provide a generalized view of control plane functionality, so that applications could be written that would operate across a range of controller network operating systems.

- This functionality is similar to that of a hypervisor or virtual machine monitor that decouples applications from the underlying OS and underlying hardware.

- This layer could provide a network virtualization capability that allows different views of the underlying data plane infrastructure.

Arguably, the network services abstraction layer could be considered to be part of the northbound interface, with the functionality incorporated in the control plane or the application plane.

A wide range of schemes have been developed that roughly fall into this layer, and a full treatment is beyond our scope. Section 6.2 provides several examples for a better understanding.

Network Applications

There are many network applications that could be implemented for an SDN. Different published surveys of SDN have come up with different lists and even different general categories of SDN-based network applications. Figure 6.1 includes six categories that encompass the majority of SDN applications. Later sections of this chapter provide an overview of each area.

User Interface

The user interface enables a user to configure parameters in SDN applications and to interact with applications that support user interaction. Again, there are two possible interfaces. A user that is collocated with the SDN application server (which may or may not include the control plane) can use the server's keyboard/display. More typically, the user would log on to the application server over a network or communications facility.

6.2 Network Services Abstraction Layer

In the context of the discussion, **abstraction** refers to the amount detail about lower levels of the model that is visible to higher levels. More abstraction means less detail; less abstraction means more detail. An **abstraction layer** is a mechanism that translates a high-level request into the low-level commands required to perform the request. An API is one such mechanism. It shields the implementation details of a lower level of abstraction from software at a higher level. A network abstraction represents the basic properties or characteristics of network entities (such as switches, links, ports, and flows) is such a way that network programs can focus on the desired functionality without having to program the detailed actions.

Abstractions in SDN

Scott Shenker, an Open Networking Foundation (ONF) board member and OpenFlow researcher, indicates that SDN can be defined by three fundamental abstractions [SHEN11]: forwarding, distribution, and specification, as illustrated in Figure 6.2 and described further in the sections that follow.

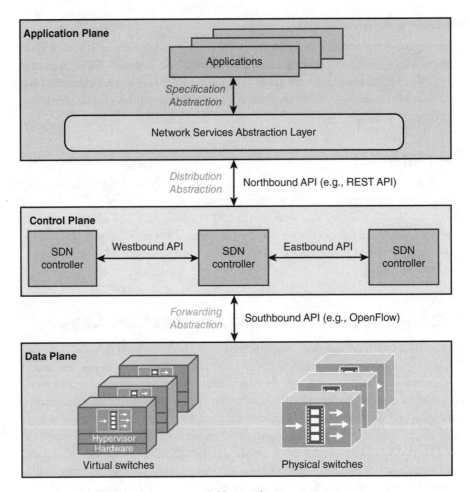

FIGURE 6.2   SDN Architecture and Abstractions

Forwarding Abstraction

← *See Sections
4.1, "SDN
Data
Plane," 4.2,
"OpenFlow
Logical
Network
Device"*

The forwarding abstraction allows a control program to specify data plane forwarding behavior while hiding details of the underlying switching hardware. This abstraction supports the data plane forwarding function. By abstracting away from the forwarding hardware, it provides flexibility and vender neutrality.

The OpenFlow API is an example of a forwarding abstraction.

Distribution Abstraction

This abstraction arises in the context of distributed controllers. A cooperating set of distributed controllers maintains a state description of the network and routes through the networks. The distributed state of the entire network may involve partitioned data sets, with controller instances exchanging routing information, or a replicated data set, so that the controllers must cooperate to maintain a consistent view of the global network.

This abstraction aims at hiding complex distributed mechanisms (used today in many networks) and separating state management from protocol design and implementation. It allows providing a single coherent global view of the network through an annotated network graph accessible for control via an API. An implementation of such an abstraction is an NOS, such as OpenDaylight or Ryu.

Specification Abstraction

The distribution abstraction provides a global view of the network as if there is a single central controller, even if multiple cooperating controllers are used. The specification abstraction then provides an abstract view of the global network. This view provides just enough detail for the application to specify goals, such as routing or security policy, without providing the information needed to implement the goals. The presentation by Shenker [SHEN11] summarizes these abstractions as follows:

- **Forwarding interface:** An abstract forwarding model that shields higher layers from forwarding hardware.

- **Distribution interface:** A global network view that shields higher layers from state dissemination/collection.

- **Specification interface:** An abstract network view that shields application program from details of physical network.

Figure 6.3 is a simple example of a specification abstraction. The physical network is a collection of interconnected SDN data plane switches. The abstract view is a single virtual switch. The physical network may consist of a single SDN domain. Ports on edge switches that connect to other domains and to hosts are mapped into ports on the virtual switch. At the application level, a module can be executed to learn the media access control (MAC) address of hosts. When a previously unknown host sends a packet, the application module can associate that address with the input port and direct future traffic direct to this host to this port. Similarly, if a packet arrives at one of the virtual switch ports with an unknown destination address, the module floods that packet to all output ports. The abstraction layer translates these actions into actions on the entire physical network, performing the internal forwarding with the domain.

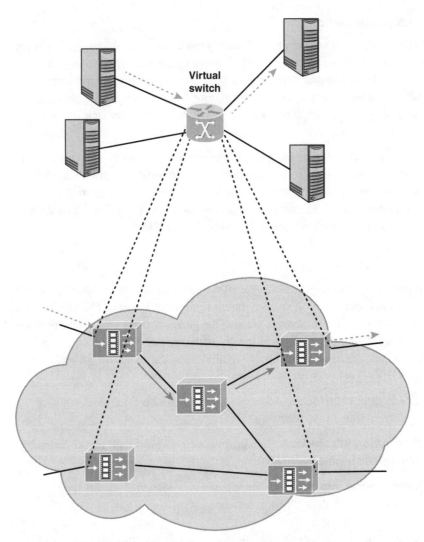

FIGURE 6.3   Virtualization of a Switching Fabric for MAC Learning

Frenetic

An example of a network services abstraction layer is the programming language Frenetic. Frenetic enables networks operators to program the network as a whole instead of manually configuring individual network elements. Frenetic was designed to solve challenges with the use of OpenFlow-based models by working with an abstraction at the network level as opposed to OpenFlow, which directly goes down to the network element level.

Frenetic includes an embedded query language that provides effective abstractions for reading network state. This language is similar to SQL and includes segments for selecting, filtering, splitting, merging and aggregating the streams of packets. Another special feature of this language is that it enables the queries to be composed with forwarding policies. A compiler produces the control messages needed to query and tabulate the counters on switches.

Frenetic consists of two levels of abstraction, as illustrated in Figure 6.4. The upper level, which is the Frenetic source-level API, provides a set of operators for manipulating streams of network traffic. The query language provides means for reading the state of the network, merging different queries, and expressing high-level predicates for classifying, filtering, transforming, and aggregating the packet streams traversing the network. The lower level of abstraction is provided by a run-time system that operates in the SDN controller. It translates high-level policies and queries into low-level flow rules and then issues the needed OpenFlow commands to install these rules on the switches.

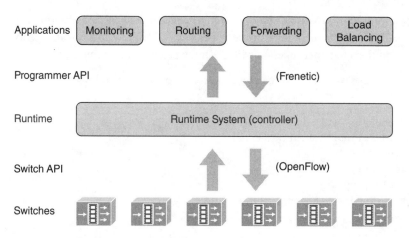

FIGURE 6.4 Frenetic Architecture

To get some idea of the two levels of abstraction, consider a simple example, from a paper by Foster in the February 2013 *IEEE Communications Magazine* [FOST13]. The program combines forwarding functionality with monitoring web traffic functionality. Consider the following Python program, which executes at the run-time level, to control OpenFlow switches:

```
def switch_join(s):
    pat1 = {inport:1}
    pat2web = {inport:2, srcport:80}
    pat2 = {inport:2}
    install(s, pat1, DEFAULT, [fwd(2)])
    install(s, pat2web, HIGH, [fwd(1)])
    install(s, pat2, DEFAULT, [fwd(1)])
```

```
        query_stats(s, pat2web)
def stats_in(s, xid, pat, pkts, bytes):
    print bytes
    sleep(30)
    query_stats(s, pat)
```

When a switch joins the network, the program installs three forwarding rules in the switch for three types of traffic: traffic arriving on port 1, web traffic arriving on port 2, and other traffic arriving on port 2. The second rule has HIGH priority and so takes precedence over the third rule, which has default priority. The call to `query_stats` generates a request for the counters associated with the `pat2web` rule. When the controller receives the reply, it invokes the `stats_in` handler. This function prints the statistics polled on the previous iteration of the loop, waits 30 seconds, and then issues a request to the switch for statistics matching the same rule.

The way the program is written, the logic for forwarding and web monitoring are intertwined. This reflects the nature of the underlying OpenFlow functionality. Any changes or additions to either function will affect the program in a complex way.

With Frenetic, these two functions can be expressed separately, as follows:

```
def repeater():
    rules=[Rule(inport:1, [fwd(2)])
           Rule(inport:2, [fwd(1)])]
    register(rules)
def web monitor():
    q = (Select(bytes) *
      Where(inport=2 & srcport=80) *
      Every(30))
    q >> Print()
def main():
    repeater()
    monitor()
```

With this code, it would be easy to change the monitor program or swap it out for another monitor program without touching the repeater code, and similarly for the changes to the repeater program. Importantly, the responsibility for installing specific OpenFlow rules that realize both components simultaneously is delegated to the run-time system. For this example, the run-time system would generate the same rules as the manually constructed rules in the switch join function listed above.

6.3   Traffic Engineering

Traffic engineering is a method for dynamically analyzing, regulating, and predicting the behavior of data flowing in networks with the aim of performance optimization to meet service level agreements (SLAs). Traffic engineering involves establishing routing and forwarding policies based on QoS requirements. With SDN, the task of traffic engineering should be considerably simplified compared with a non-SDN network. SDN offers a uniform global view of heterogeneous equipment and powerful tools for configuring and managing network switches.

This is an area of great activity in the development of SDN applications. The SDN survey paper by Kreutz in the January 2015 *Proceedings of the IEEE* [KREU15] lists the following traffic engineering functions that have been implemented as SDN applications:

- On-demand virtual private networks

- Load balancing

- Energy-aware routing

- Quality of service (QoS) for broadband access networks

- Scheduling/optimization

- Traffic engineering with minimal overhead

- Dynamic QoS routing for multimedia apps

- Fast recovery through fast-failover groups

- QoS policy management framework

- QoS enforcement

- QoS over heterogeneous networks

- Multiple packet schedulers

- Queue management for QoS enforcement

- Divide and spread forwarding tables

traffic engineering
That aspect of network engineering dealing with the issues of performance evaluation and performance optimization of operational networks. Traffic engineering encompasses the application of technology and scientific principles to the measurement, characterization, modeling, and control of network traffic.

PolicyCop

An instructive example of a traffic engineering SDN application is PolicyCop [BARI13], which is an automated QoS policy enforcement framework. It leverages the programmability offered by SDN and OpenFlow for

- Dynamic traffic steering

- Flexible Flow level control

■ Dynamic traffic classes

■ Custom flow aggregation levels

Key features of PolicyCop are that it monitors the network to detect policy violations (based on a QoS SLA) and reconfigures the network to reinforce the violated policy.

As shown in Figure 6.5, PolicyCop consists of eleven software modules and two databases, installed in both the application plane and the control plane. PolicyCop uses the control plane of SDNs to monitor the compliance with QoS policies and can automatically adjust the control plane rules and flow tables in the data plane based on the dynamic network traffic statistics.

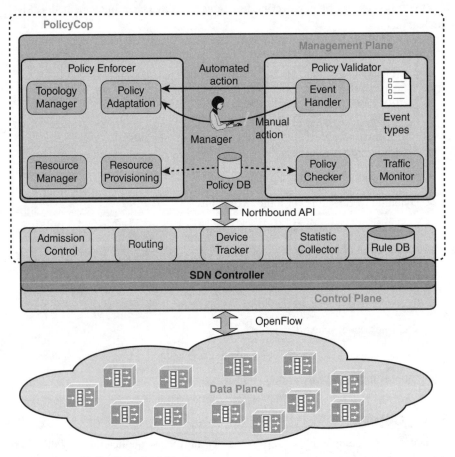

FIGURE 6.5   PolicyCop Architecture

In the control plane, PolicyCop relies on four modules and a database for storing control rules, described as follows:

- **Admission Control:** Accepts or rejects requests from the resource provisioning module for reserving network resources, such as queues, flow-table entries, and capacity.

- **Routing:** Determines path availability based on the control rules in the rule database.

- **Device Tracker:** Tracks the up/down status of network switches and their ports.

- **Statistics Collection:** Uses a mix of passive and active monitoring techniques to measure different network metrics.

- **Rule Database:** The application plane translates high-level network-wide policies to control rules and stores them in the rule database.

A RESTful northbound interface connects these control plane modules to the application plane modules, which are organized into two components: a policy validator that monitors the network to detect policy violations, and a policy enforcer that adapts control plane rules based on network conditions and high-level policies. Both modules rely on a policy database, which contains QoS policy rules entered by a network manager. The modules are as follows:

- **Traffic Monitor:** Collects the active policies from policy database, and determines appropriate monitoring interval, network segments, and metrics to be monitored.

- **Policy Checker:** Checks for policy violations, using input from the policy database and the Traffic Monitor.

- **Event Handler:** Examines violation events and, depending on event type, either automatically invokes the policy enforcer or sends an action request to the network manager.

- **Topology Manager:** Maintains a global view of the network, based on input from the device tracker.

- **Resource Manager:** Keeps track of currently allocated resources using admission control and statistics collection.

- **Policy Adaptation:** Consists of a set of actions, one for each type of policy violation. Table 6.1 shows the general functionality of some of the policy adaptation actions. The actions are pluggable components that can be specified by the network manager.

- **Resource Provisioning:** This module either allocates more resources or releases existing ones or both based on the violation event.

TABLE 6.1   Functionality of Some Example Policy Adaptation Actions (PAAs)

SLA Parameter	PAA Functionality
Packet loss	Modify queue configuration or reroute to a better path
Throughput	Modify rate limiters to throttle misbehaving flows
Latency	Schedule flow through a new path with less congestion and suitable delay
Jitter	Reroute flow through a less congested path
Device failure	Reroute flows through a different path to bypass the failure

Figure 6.6 shows the process workflow in PolicyCop.

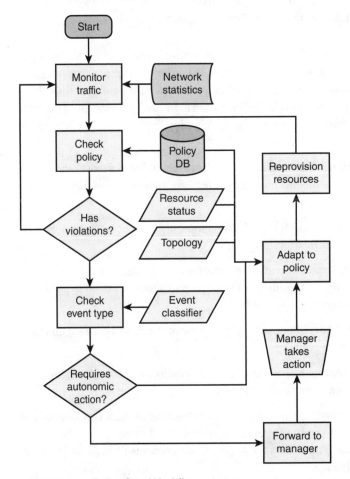

FIGURE 6.6   PolicyCop Workflow

6.4 Measurement and Monitoring

The area of measurement and monitoring applications can roughly be divided into two categories: applications that provide new functionality for other networking services, and applications that add value to OpenFlow-based SDNs.

An example of the first category is in the area of broadband home connections. If the connection is to an SDN-based network, new functions can be added to the measurement of home network traffic and demand, allowing the system to react to changing conditions. The second category typically involves using different kinds of sampling and estimation techniques to reduce the burden of the control plane in the collection of data plane statistics.

6.5 Security

Applications in this area have one of two goals:

- **Address security concerns related to the use of SDN:** SDN involves a three-layer architecture (application, control, data) and new approaches to distributed control and encapsulating data. All of this introduces the potential for new vectors for attack. Threats can occur at any of the three layers or in the communication between layers. SDN applications are needed to provide for the secure use of SDN itself.

- **Use the functionality of SDN to improve network security:** Although SDN presents new security challenges for network designers and managers, it also provides a platform for implementing consistent, centrally managed security policies and mechanisms for the network. SDN allows the development of SDN security controllers and SDN security applications that can provision and orchestrate security services and mechanisms.

This section provides an example of an SDN security application the illustrates the second goal. We examine the topic of SDN security in detail in Chapter 16, "Security."

OpenDaylight DDoS Application

In 2014, Radware, a provider of application delivery and application security solutions for virtual and cloud data centers, announced its contribution to the OpenDaylight Project with Defense4All, an open SDN security application integrated into OpenDaylight. Defense4All offers carriers and cloud providers **distributed denial of service (DDoS)** detection and mitigation as a native network service. Using the OpenDaylight SDN Controller that programs SDN-enabled networks to become part of the DoS/DDoS protection service itself, Defense4All enables operators to provision a DoS/DDoS protection service per virtual network segment or per customer.

distributed denial of service (DDoS)

An attack in which multiple systems are used to flood servers or network devices or links with traffic in an attempt to overwhelm its available resources (bandwidth, memory, processing power, and so on), making it unavailable to respond to legitimate users.

Defense4All uses a common technique for defending against DDoS attacks, which consists of the following elements:

- Collection of traffic statistics and learning of statistics behavior of protected objects during peacetime. The normal traffic baselines of the protected objects are built from these collected statistics.

- Detection of DDoS attack patterns as traffic anomalies deviating from normal baselines.

- Diversion of suspicious traffic from its normal path to attack mitigation systems (AMSs) for traffic scrubbing, selective source blockage, and so on. Clean traffic exiting out of scrubbing centers is re-injected back into the packet's original destination.

Figure 6.7 shows the overall context of the Defense4All application. The underlying SDN network consists of a number of data plane switches that support traffic among client and server devices. Defense4All operates as an application that interacts with the controller over an OpenDaylight controller (ODC) northbound API. Defense4All supports a user interface for network managers that can either be a command line interface or a RESTful API. Finally, Defense4All has an API to communicate with one or more AMSs.

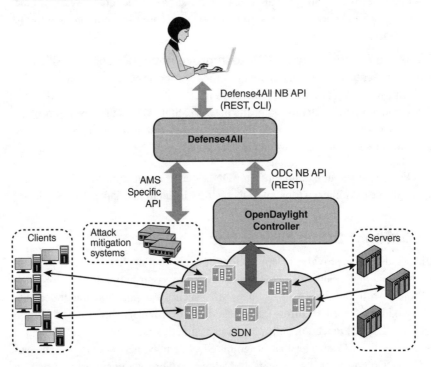

FIGURE 6.7   OpenDaylight DDoS Application

Administrators can configure Defense4All to protect certain networks and servers, known as protected networks (PNs) and protected objects (POs). The application instructs the controller to install traffic counting flows for each protocol of each configured PO in every network location through which traffic of the subject PO flows.

Defense4All then monitors traffic of all configured POs, summarizing readings, rates, and averages from all relevant network locations. If it detects a deviation from normal learned traffic behavior in a protocol (such as TCP, UDP, ICMP, or the rest of the traffic) of a particular PO, Defense4All declares an attack against that protocol in the subject PO. Specifically, Defese4All continuously calculates traffic averages for real time traffic it measured using OpenFlow; when real time traffic deviates by 80% from average then an attack is assumed.

To mitigate a detected attack, Defense4All performs the following procedure:

1. It validates that the AMS device is alive and selects a live connection to it. Currently, Defense4All is configured to work with Radware's AMS, known as DefensePro.

2. It configures the AMS with a security policy and normal rates of the attacked traffic. This provides the AMS with the information needed to enforce a mitigation policy until traffic returns to normal rates.

3. It starts monitoring and logging syslogs arriving from the AMS for the subject traffic. As long as Defense4All continues receiving syslog attack notifications from the AMS regarding this attack, Defense4All continues to divert traffic to the AMS, even if the flow counters for this PO do not indicate any more attacks.

4. It maps the selected physical AMS connection to the relevant PO link. This typically involves changing link definitions on a virtual network, using OpenFlow.

5. It installs higher-priority flow table entries so that the attack traffic flow is redirected to the AMS and re-injects traffic from the AMS back to the normal traffic flow route. When Defense4All decides that the attack is over (no attack indication from either flow table counters or from the AMS), it reverts the previous actions: It stops monitoring for syslogs about the subject traffic, it removes the traffic diversion flow table entries, and it removes the security configuration from the AMS. Defense4All then returns to peacetime monitoring.

Figure 6.8 shows the principal software components of Defense4All. The overall application structure, referred to as a framework, contains the modules described in the list that follows.

- **Web (REST) Server:** Interface to network manager.

- **Framework Main:** Mechanism to start, stop, or reset the framework.

- **Framework REST Service:** Responds to user requests received through the web (REST) server.

- **Framework Management Point:** Coordinates and invokes control and configuration commands.

- **Defense4All Application:** Described subsequently.

- **Common Classes and Utilities:** A library of convenient classes and utilities from which any framework or SDN application module can benefit.

- **Repository Services:** One of the key elements in the framework philosophy is decoupling the compute state from the compute logic. All durable states are stored in a set of repositories that can be then replicated, cached, and distributed, with no awareness of the compute logic (framework or application).

- **Logging and Flight Recorder Services:** The logging service uses logs error, warning, trace, or informational messages. These logs are mainly for Defense4All developers. The Flight Recorder records events and metrics during run time from Java applications.

- **Health Tracker:** Holds aggregated run-time indicators of the operational health of Defense4All and acts in response to severe functional or performance deteriorations.

- **Cluster Manager**: Responsible for managing coordination with other Defense4All entities operating in a cluster mode.

The Defense4All Application module consists of the following elements.

- **DF App Root:** The root module of the application.

- **DF Rest Service:** Responds to Defense4All application REST requests.

- **DF Management Point:** The point to drive control and configuration commands. DFMgmtPoint in turn invokes methods against other relevant modules in the right order.

- **ODL Reps:** A pluggable module set for different versions of the ODC. Comprises two functions in two submodules: stats collection for and traffic diversion of relevant traffic.

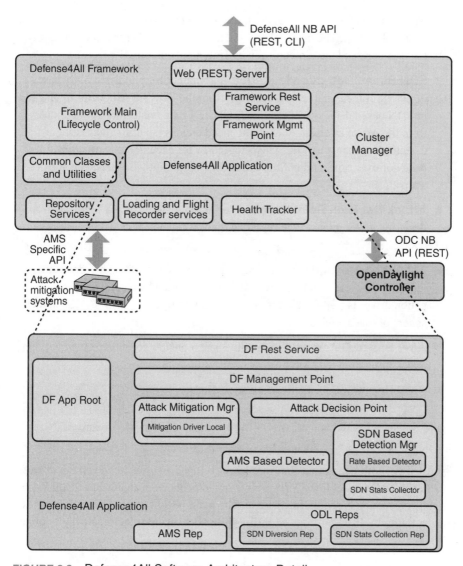

FIGURE 6.8 Defense4All Software Architecture Detail

■ **SDN Stats Collector:** Responsible for setting "counters" for every PN
  at specified network locations (physical or logical). A counter is a set of
  OpenFlow flow entries in ODC-enabled network switches and routers. The
  module periodically collects statistics from those counters and feeds them to
  the SDNBasedDetectionMgr. The module uses the SDNStatsCollectionRep to
  both set the counters and read latest statistics from those counters. A stat report
  consists of read time, counter specification, PN label, and a list of trafficData
  information, where each trafficData element contains the latest bytes and

packet values for flow entries configured for <protocol,port,direction> in the counter location. The protocol can be {tcp,udp,icmp,other ip}, the port is any Layer 4 port, and the direction can be {inbound, outbound}.

- **SDN Based Detection Manager:** A container for pluggable SDN-based detectors. It feeds stat reports received from the SDNStatsCollector to plugged-in SDN based detectors. It also feeds all SDN based detectors notifications from the AttackDecisionPoint about ended attacks (so as to allow reset of detection mechanisms). Each detector learns for each PN its normal traffic behavior over time, and notifies AttackDecisionPoint when it detects traffic anomalies.

- **Attack Decision Point:** Responsible for maintaining attack lifecycle, from declaring a new attack, to terminating diversion when an attack is considered over.

- **Mitigation Manager:** A container for pluggable mitigation drivers. It maintains the lifecycle of each mitigation being executed by an AMS. Each mitigation driver is responsible for driving attack mitigations using AMSs in their sphere of management.

- **AMS Based Detector:** This module is responsible for monitoring/querying attack mitigation by AMSs.

- **AMS Rep:** Controls the interface to AMSs.

Figure 6.8 suggests the complexity of even a relatively straightforward SDN application.

Finally, it is worth noting that Radware has developed a commercial version of Defese4All, named DefenseFlow. DefenseFlow implements more sophisticated algorithms for attack detection based on fuzzy logic. The main benefit is that DefenseFlow has a greater ability to distinguish attack traffic from abnormal but legitimate high volume of traffic.

6.6 Data Center Networking

So far we've discussed three areas of SDN applications: traffic engineering, measurement and monitoring, and security. The provided examples of these applications suggest the broad range of use cases for them, in many different kinds of networks. The remaining three applications areas (data center networking, mobility and wireless, and information-centric networking) have use cases in specific types of networks.

Cloud computing, big data, large enterprise networks, and even in many cases, smaller enterprise networks, depend strongly on highly scalable and efficient data centers.

[KREU15] lists the following as key requirements for data centers: high and flexible **cross-section bandwidth** and low latency, QoS based on the application requirements, high levels of resilience, intelligent resource utilization to reduce energy consumption and improve overall efficiency, and agility in provisioning network resources (for example, by means of network virtualization and orchestration with computing and storage).

With traditional network architectures, many of these requirements are difficult to satisfy because of the complexity and inflexibility of the network. SDN offers the promise of substantial improvement in the ability to rapidly modify data center network configurations, to flexibly respond to user needs, and to ensure efficient operation of the network.

The remainder of this subsection, examines two example data center SDN applications.

Big Data over SDN

A paper by Wang, et al., in the Proceedings of HotSDN'12 [WANG12], reports on an approach to use SDN to optimize data center networking for big data applications. The approach leverages the capabilities of SDN to provide application-aware networking. It also exploits characteristics of structured big data applications as well as recent trends in dynamically reconfigurable optical circuits. With respect to structured big data applications, many of these applications process data according to well-defined computation patterns, and also have a centralized management structure that makes it possible to leverage application-level information to optimize the network. That is, knowing the anticipated computation patterns of the big data application, it is possible to intelligently deploy the data across the big data servers and, more significantly, react to changing application patterns by using SDN to reconfigure flows in the network.

Compared to electronic switches, optical switches have the advantages of greater data rates with reduced cabling complexity and energy consumption. A number of projects have demonstrated how to collect network-level traffic data and intelligently allocate optical circuits between endpoints (for example, top-of-rack switches) to improve application performance. However, circuit utilization and application performance can be inadequate unless there is a true application-level view of traffic demands and dependencies. Combining an understanding of the big data computation patterns with the dynamic capabilities of SDN, efficient data center networking configurations can be used to support the increasing big data demands.

Figure 6.9 shows a simple hybrid electrical and optical data center network, in which OpenFlow-enabled top-of-rack (ToR) switches are connected to two aggregation switches: an Ethernet switch and an optical circuit switch (OCS). All the switches are controlled by a SDN controller that manages physical connectivity among ToR

---

cross-section bandwidth

For a network, this is the maximum bidirectional data rate that can pass between two parts of the network if it is divided into two equal halves. Also referred to as bisection bandwidth.

switches over optical circuits by configuring the optical switch. It can also manage the forwarding at ToR switches using OpenFlow rules.

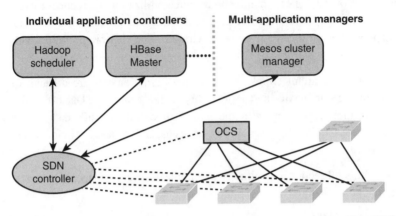

FIGURE 6.9   Integrated Network Control for Big Data Applications [WANG12]

The SDN controller is also connected to the Hadoop scheduler, which forms queues of jobs to be scheduled and the HBase Master controller of a relational database holding data for the big data applications. In addition, the SDN controller connects to a Mesos cluster manager. Mesos is an open source software package that provides scheduling and resource allocation services across distributed applications.

The SDN controller makes available network topology and traffic information to the Mesos cluster manager. In turn, the SDN controller accepts traffic demand request from Mesos managers.

With the organization of Figure 6.8, it is possible to set up a scheme whereby the traffic demands of big data applications are used to dynamically manage the network, using the SDN controller to manage this task.

Cloud Networking over SDN

Cloud Network as a Service (CloudNaaS) is a cloud networking system that exploits OpenFlow SDN capabilities to provide a greater degree of control over cloud network functions by the cloud customer [BENS11]. CloudNaaS enables users to deploy applications that include a number of network functions, such as virtual network isolation, custom addressing, service differentiation, and flexible interposition of various middleboxes. CloudNaaS primitives are directly implemented within the cloud infrastructure itself using high-speed programmable network elements, making CloudNaaS highly efficient.

Figure 6.10 illustrates the principal sequence of events in the CloudNaaS operation, as described in the list that follows.

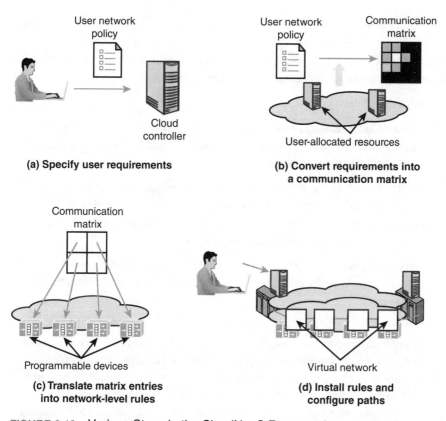

FIGURE 6.10   Various Steps in the CloudNaaS Framework

a. A cloud customer uses a simple policy language to specify network services required by the customer applications. These policy statements are issued to a cloud controller server operated by the cloud service provider.

b. The cloud controller maps the network policy into a communication matrix that defines desired communication patterns and network services. The matrix is used to determine the optimal placement of virtual machines (VMs) on cloud servers such that the cloud can satisfy the largest number of global policies in an efficient manner. This is done based on the knowledge of other customers' requirements and their current levels of activity.

c. The logical communication matrix is translated into network-level directives for data plane forwarding elements. The customer's VM instances are deployed by creating and placing the specified number of VMs.

   d. The network-level directives are installed into the network devices via OpenFlow.

The abstract network model seen by the customer consists of VMs and virtual network segments that connect VMs together. Policy language constructs identify the set of VMs that comprise an application and define various functions and capabilities attached to virtual network segments. The main constructs are as follows:

- **address:** Specify a customer-visible custom address for a VM.

- **group:** Create a logical group of one or more VMs. Grouping VMs with similar functions makes it possible for modifications to apply across the entire group without requiring changing the service attached to individual VMs.

- **middlebox:** Name and initialize a new virtual middlebox by specifying its type and a configuration file. The list of available middleboxes and their configuration syntax is supplied by the cloud provider. Examples include intrusion detection and audit compliance systems.

- **networkservice:** Specify capabilities to attach to a virtual network segment, such as Layer 2 broadcast domain, link QoS, and list of middleboxes that must be traversed.

- **virtualnet:** Virtual network segments connect groups of VMs and are associated with network services. A virtual network can span one or two groups. With a single group, the service applies to traffic between all pairs of VMs in the group. With a pair of groups, the service is applied between any VM in the first group and any VM in the second group. Virtual networks can also connect to some predefined groups, such as EXTERNAL, which indicates all endpoints outside of the cloud.

Infrastructure as a Service (IaaS)

A cloud service that provides the customer access to the underlying cloud infrastructure. IaaS offers the customer virtual machines, storage, networks, and other fundamental computing resources so that the customer can deploy and run arbitrary software, which may include operating systems and applications.

Figure 6.11 provides an overview of the architecture of CloudNaaS. Its two main components are a cloud controller and a network controller. The cloud controller provides a base **Infrastructure as a Service (IaaS)** service for managing VM instances. The user can communicate standard IaaS requests, such as setting up VMs and storage. In addition, the network policy constructs enable the user to define the virtual network capabilities for the VMs. The cloud controller manages a software programmable virtual switch on each physical server in the cloud that supports network services for tenant applications, including the management of the user-defined virtual network segments. The cloud controller constructs the communication matrix and transmits this to the network controller.

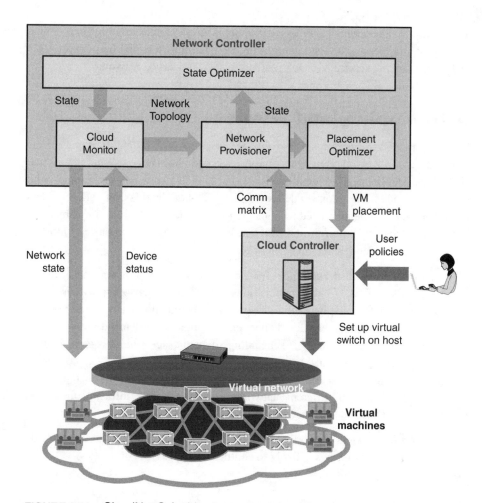

FIGURE 6.11 CloudNaaS Architecture

The network controller uses the communication matrix to configure data plane physical and virtual switches. It generates virtual networks between VMs and provides VM placement directives to the cloud controller. It monitors the traffic and performance on the cloud data plane switches and makes changes to the network state as needed to optimize use of resources to meet tenant requirements. The controller invokes the placement optimizer to determine the best location to place VMs within the cloud (and reports it to the cloud controller for provisioning). The controller then uses the network provisioner module to generate the set of configuration commands for each of the programmable devices in the network and configures them accordingly to instantiate the tenant's virtual network segment.

Thus, CloudNaaS provides the cloud customer with the ability to go beyond simple requesting a processing and storage resource, to defining a virtual network of VMs and controlling the service and QoS requirements of the virtual network.

6.7   Mobility and Wireless

In addition to all the traditional performance, security, and reliability requirements of wired networks, wireless networks impose a broad range of new requirements and challenges. Mobile users are continuously generating demands for new services with high quality and efficient content delivery independent of location. Network providers must deal with problems related to managing the available spectrum, implementing handover mechanisms, performing efficient load balancing, responding to QoS and QoE requirements, and maintaining security.

SDN can provide much-needed tools for the mobile network provider and in recent years a number of SDN-based applications for wireless network providers have been designed. [KREU15] lists the following SDN application areas, among others: seamless mobility through efficient handovers, creation of on-demand virtual access points, load balancing, downlink scheduling, dynamic spectrum usage, enhanced intercell interference coordination, per client / base station resource block allocations, simplified administration, easy management of heterogeneous network technologies, interoperability between different networks, shared wireless infrastructures, and management of QoS and access control policies.

SDN support for wireless network providers is an area of intense activity, and a wide range of application offerings is likely to continue to appear.

6.8   Information-Centric Networking

Information-centric networking (ICN), also known as content-centric networking, has received significant attention in recent years, mainly driven by the fact that distributing and manipulating information has become the major function of the Internet today. Unlike the traditional host-centric networking paradigm where information is obtained by contacting specified named hosts, ICN is aimed at providing native network primitives for efficient information retrieval by directly naming and operating on information objects.

With ICN, a distinction exists between location and identity, thus decoupling information for its sources. The essence of this approach is that information sources can place, and information users can find, information anywhere in the network, because the information is named, addressed, and matched independently of its location. In ICN, instead of specifying a source-destination host pair for communication, a piece of information itself is named. In ICN, after a request is sent, the network is responsible for locating the best source that can provide the desired information. Routing of information requests thus seeks to find the best source for the information, based on a location-independent name.

Deploying ICN on traditional networks is challenging, because existing routing equipment would need to be updated or replace with ICN-enabled routing devices. Further, ICN shifts the delivery model from host to user to content to user. This creates a need for a clear separation between the task of information demand and supply, and the task of forwarding. SDN has the potential to provide the necessary technology for deploying ICN because it provides for programmability of the forwarding elements and a separation of control and data planes.

A number of projects have proposed using SDN capabilities to implement ICNs. There is no consensus approach to achieving this coupling of SDN and ICN. Suggested approaches include substantial enhancements/modifications to the OpenFlow protocol, developing a mapping of names into IP addresses using a hash function, using the IP option header as a name field, and using an abstraction layer between an OpenFlow (OF) switch and an ICN router, so that the layer, OF switch, and ICN router function as a single programmable ICN router.

The remainder of this section briefly introduces this last approach [NGUY13, NGUY14]. This approach is designed to provide OF switches with ICN functionality, without having to modify the OF switches. The approach is built on an open protocol specification and a software reference implementation of ICN known as CCNx. Before looking at the abstraction layer approach, a brief background on CCNx is needed.

CCNx

CCNx is being developed by the Palo Alto Research Center (PARC) as an open source project, and a number of implementations have been experimentally deployed.

Communication in CCN is via two packet types: **Interest packets** and **Content packets**. A consumer requests content by sending an Interest packet. Any CCN node that receives the Interest and has named data that satisfies the Interest responds with a Content packet (also known as a Content). Content satisfies an Interest if the name in the Interest packet matches the name in the Content Object packet. If a CCN node receives an Interest, and does not already have a copy of the requested Content, it may forward the Interest toward a source for the content. The CCN node has forwarding tables that determine which direction to send the Interest. A provider receiving an Interest for which it has matching named content replies with a Content packet. Any intermediate node can optionally choose to cache the Content Object, and it can respond with a cached copy of the Content Object the next time it receives an Interest packet with the same name.

CCNx

The basic operation of a CCN node is similar to an IP node. CCN nodes receive and send packets over faces. A **face** is a connection point to an application, or another CCN node, or some other kind of channel. A face may have attributes that indicate expected latency and bandwidth, broadcast or multicast capability, or other useful features. A CCN node has three main data structures:

- **Content Store:** Holds a table of previously seen (and optionally cached) Content packets.

- **Forwarding Information Base (FIB):** Used to forward Interest packets toward potential data sources.

- **Pending Interest Table (PIT):** Used to keep track of Interests forwarded upstream by that CCN node toward the content source so that Content packets later received can be sent back to their requestors.

The details of how content sources become known and how routes are set up through the CCN network are beyond our scope. Briefly, content providers advertise names of content and routes are established through the CCN network by cooperation among the CCN nodes.

ICN relies substantially on in-network caching—that is, to cache content on the path from content providers to requesters. This **on-path caching** achieves good overall performance but is not optimal as content may be replicated on routers, thus reducing the total volume of content that can be cached. To overcome this limitation, **off-path caching** can be used, which allocates content to well-defined off-path caches within the network and deflects the traffic off the optimal path toward these caches that are spread across the network. Off-path caching improves the global hit ratio by efficiently utilizing the network-wide available caching capacity and permits to reduce egress links' bandwidth usage.

Use of an Abstraction Layer

The central design issue with using an SDN switch (in particular an OF switch) to function as an ICN router is that the OF switch forwards on the basis of fields in the IP packet, especially the destination IP address, and an ICN router forwards on the basis of a content name. In essence, the proposed approach hashes the name inside the fields with an OF switch can process.

Figure 6.12 shows the overall architecture of the approach. To link a CCNx node software module with an OF switch, an abstraction layer, called the wrapper, is used. The wrapper pairs a switch interface to a CCNx face, decodes and hashes content names in CCN messages into fields that an OF switch can process (for example, IP addresses, port numbers). The large naming space offered by these fields limits the probability of having collisions between two different content names. The forwarding tables in the OF switch are set to forward based on the contents of the hashed fields. The switch does not "know" that the contents of these fields are no longer legitimate IP addresses, TCP port numbers, and so forth. It forwards as always, based on the values found in the relevant fields of incoming IP packets.

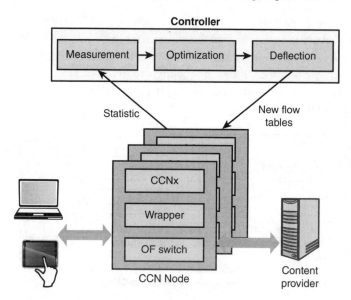

FIGURE 6.12   ICN Wrapper Approach

The abstraction layer solves the problem of how to provide CCN functionality using current OF switches. For efficient operation, two additional challenges need to be addressed: how to measure the popularity of content accurately and without a large overhead, and how to build and optimize routing tables to perform deflection. To address these issues, the architecture calls for three new modules in the SDN controller:

- **Measurement:** Content popularity can be inferred directly from OF flow statistics. The measurement module periodically queries and processes statistics from ingress OF switches to return the list of most popular content.

- **Optimization:** Uses the list of most popular contents as an input for the optimization algorithm. The objective is to minimize the sum of the delays over deflected contents under the following constraints: (1) each popular content is cached at exactly one node, (2) caching contents at a node does not exceed node's capacity, and (3) caching should not cause link congestion.

- **Deflection:** Uses the optimization results to build a mapping, for every content, between the content name (by means of addresses and ports computed from the content name hash) and an outgoing interface toward the node where the content is cached (for example, ip.destination = hash(content name), action = forward to interface 1).

Finally, mappings are installed on switches' flow tables using the OF protocol such that subsequent Interest packets can be forwarded to appropriate caches.

Figure 6.13 shows the flow of packets. The OpenFlow switch forwards every packet it receives from other ports to the wrapper, and the wrapper forwards it to the CCNx module. The OpenFlow switch needs to help the wrapper identify the switch source port of the packet. To achieve this, the OF switch is configured to set the ToS value of all packets it receives to the corresponding incoming port value and then forward all of them to the wrapper's port.

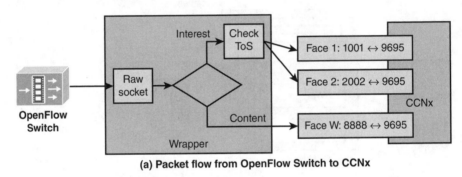

(a) Packet flow from OpenFlow Switch to CCNx

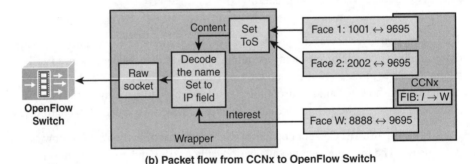

(b) Packet flow from CCNx to OpenFlow Switch

FIGURE 6.13 Packet Flow Between CCNx and OpenFlow Switch

The wrapper maps a face of CCNx to an interface (that is, port) of OpenFlow switches using ToS value. Face W is a special face between wrapper and the CCNx module. W receives every Content packet from the wrapper and is used to send every Interest packet from CCNx to the wrapper.

Part a of Figure 6.13 shows how incoming packets from the OF switch are handled by the wrapper. For an Interest packet, the wrapper extracts the face value from the

ToS field and forwards the packet to the corresponding CCNx face. If the CCNx node holds a copy of the requested content, it composes a Content packet and returns it back to the incoming face. Otherwise, it forwards this Interest to face W and updates its PIT accordingly. Upon Content packet arrival from the OF switch, the wrapper forwards it directly to face W.

Part b of Figure 6.13 shows the operation of the wrapper on packets received from the CCNx module. For content packets, it sets the ToS field accordingly, specifying the output port. Then, for any packet, it decodes the packet to extract the content name related to the packet. The name is hashed and the source IP address of the packet is set to correspond to the hashed value. Finally, the wrapper forwards the packets to OF switches. Content packets are returned to their corresponding incoming face. Interest packets have the ToS value set to zero so they are forwarded to next hop by the OF switch.

Thus, the use of the wrapper abstraction layer provides basic ICN functionality plus deflection functionality without needing to modify the CCNx module or the OpenFlow switch.

6.9 Key Terms

After completing this chapter, you should be able to define the following terms.

abstraction	information-centric networking (ICN)
abstraction layer	Infrastructure as a Service (IaaS)
CloudNaaS	measurement and monitoring
content-centric networking (CCN)	network services abstraction layer
cross-section bandwidth	off-path caching
distributed denial of service (DDoS)	on-path caching
distribution abstraction	PolicyCop
forwarding abstraction	specification abstraction
Frenetic	traffic engineering

PART III

Virtualization

The basic idea is that the several components in any complex system will perform particular subfunctions that contribute to the overall function.

—*The Sciences of the Artificial*, Herbert Simon

Interest in, and work on, network functions virtualization (NFV) began later than the corresponding software-defined network (SDN) effort. However, NFV and a broader conception of virtual networking have come to play a role of equal importance to that of SDN in modern networking. Part III is devoted to a broad and thorough presentation of NFV concepts, technology, and applications, and a discussion of network virtualization. Chapter 7 begins by introducing the concept of virtual machine and then looks of the use of virtual machine technology to develop NFV-based networking environments. Chapter 8 is a detailed looks at the functionality of NFV elements and also relates NFV to SDN. Chapter 9 looks at traditional concepts of virtual networks, and then at the more modern approach to network virtualization, and finally introduces the concept of software defined infrastructure.

Chapter 7

Network Functions Virtualization: Concepts and Architecture

It has been found useful in many installations to use an operating system to simulate the existence of several machines on a single physical set of hardware. The IBM VM/370 operating system is one example. This technique allows an installation to multiprogram several different operating systems (or different versions of the same operating system) on a single physical machine. The dynamic-address-translation hardware allows such a simulator to be efficient enough to be used, in many cases, in production mode.

—Architecture of the IBM System/370, *Communications of the ACM*, January 1978,
Richard Case and Adris Padegs

Chapter Objectives

After studying this chapter, you should be able to

- Understand the concept of virtual machine.
- Explain the difference between Type 1 and Type 2 hypervisors.
- List and explain the key benefits of NFV.
- List and explain the key requirements for NFV.
- Present an overview of the NFV architecture.

This chapter and the succeeding two chapters focus on the application of **virtualization** for modern networking. Virtualization encompasses a variety of technologies for managing computing resources, providing a software translation layer, known as an abstraction layer, between the software and the physical hardware. Virtualization turns physical resources into logical, or virtual, resources. Virtualization enables users, applications, and management software operating above the abstraction layer to manage and use resources without needing to be aware of the physical details of the underlying resources. In this chapter and the next, we focus on the use of virtual machine (VM) technology as a basis for the new concept of network functions virtualization (NFV). Chapter 9, "Network Virtualization," deals with virtual networks and the concept of network virtualization.

virtualization

A variety of technologies for managing computer resources by providing an abstraction layer between the software and the physical hardware. These technologies effectively emulate or simulate a hardware platform, such as a server, storage device, or network resource, in software.

7.1 Background and Motivation for NFV

NFV originated from discussions among major network operators and carriers about how to improve network operations in the high-volume multimedia era. These discussions resulted in the publication of the original NFV white paper, *Network Functions Virtualization: An Introduction, Benefits, Enablers, Challenges & Call for Action* [ISGN12]. In this white paper, the group listed as the overall objective of NFV is leveraging standard IT virtualization technology to consolidate many network equipment types onto industry standard high-volume servers, switches, and storage, which could be located in data centers, network nodes, and in the end-user premises.

The white paper highlights that the source of the need for this new approach is that networks include a large and growing variety of proprietary hardware appliances, leading to the following negative consequences:

- New network services may require additional different types of hardware appliances, and finding the space and power to accommodate these boxes is becoming increasingly difficult.

- New hardware means additional capital expenditures.

- Once new types of hardware appliances are acquired, operators are faced with the rarity of skills necessary to design, integrate, and operate increasingly complex hardware-based appliances.

- Hardware-based appliances rapidly reach end of life, requiring much of the procure-design-integrate-deploy cycle to be repeated with little or no revenue benefit.

- As technology and services innovation accelerates to meet the demands of an increasingly network-centric IT environment, the need for an increasing variety of hardware platforms inhibits the introduction of new revenue-earning network services.

The NFV approach moves away from dependence on a variety of hardware platforms to the use of a small number of standardized platform types, with virtualization techniques used to provide the needed network functionality. In the white paper, the group expresses the belief that the NFV approach is applicable to any data plane packet processing and control plane function in fixed and mobile network infrastructures.

In addition to providing a way to overcome the problems cited in the preceding list, NFV provides a number of other benefits. These are best examined in Section 7.4, after an introduction to VM technology and NFV concepts, in Sections 7.2 and 7.3, respectively.

7.2   Virtual Machines

hardware virtualization

The use of software to partition a computer's resources into separate and isolated entities called virtual machines. It enables multiple copies of the same or different operating system to execute on the computer and prevents applications from different VMs from interfering with each other.

Traditionally, applications have run directly on an operating system (OS) on a personal computer (PC) or on a server. Each PC or server would run only one OS at a time. Therefore, application vendors had to rewrite parts of its applications for each OS/platform they would run on and support, which increased time to market for new features/functions, increased the likelihood of defects, increased quality testing efforts, and usually led to increased price. To support multiple operating systems, application vendors needed to create, manage, and support multiple hardware and operating system infrastructures, a costly and resource-intensive process. One effective strategy for dealing with this problem is known as **hardware virtualization**. Virtualization technology enables a single PC or server to simultaneously run multiple operating systems or multiple sessions of a single OS. A machine running virtualization software can host numerous applications, including those that run on different operating systems, on a single hardware platform. In essence, the host operating system can support a number of **virtual machines (VMs)**, each of which has the characteristics of a particular OS and, in some versions of virtualization, the characteristics of a particular hardware platform.

virtual machine (VM)

One instance of an operating system along with one or more applications running in an isolated partition within the computer.

Virtualization is not a new technology. During the 1970s, IBM mainframe systems offered the first capabilities that would allow programs to use only a portion of a system's resources. Various forms of that ability have been available on platforms since that time. Virtualization came into mainstream computing in the early 2000s when the technology was commercially available on x86 servers. Organizations were suffering from a surfeit of servers because of a Microsoft Windows-driven "one application, one server" strategy. Moore's Law drove rapid hardware improvements outpacing software's ability, and most of these servers were vastly underutilized, often consuming less than 5 percent of the available resources in each server. In addition, this overabundance of servers filled data centers and consumed vast amounts of power and cooling, thereby straining a corporation's ability to manage and maintain their infrastructure. Virtualization helped relieve this stress.

The Virtual Machine Monitor

The solution that enables virtualization is a **virtual machine monitor (VMM)**, or commonly known today as a **hypervisor**. This software sits between the hardware and the VMs acting as a resource broker (see Figure 7.1). Simply put, the hypervisor allows multiple VMs to safely coexist on a single physical server host and share that host's resources. The number of guests that can exist on a single host is measured as a **consolidation ratio**. For example, a host that is supporting six VMs is said to have a consolidation ration of 6 to 1, also written as 6:1 (see Figure 7.2). The initial hypervisors in the commercial space could provide consolidation ratios of between 4:1 and 12:1, but even at the low end, if a company virtualized all of their servers, they could remove 75 percent of the servers from their data centers. More important, they could remove the cost as well, which often ran into the millions or tens of millions of dollars annually. With fewer physical servers, less power and less cooling was needed. Also this leads to fewer cables, fewer network switches, and less floor space. Server consolidation became, and continues to be, a tremendously valuable way to solve a costly and wasteful problem. Today, more virtual servers are deployed in the world than physical servers, and virtual server deployment continues to accelerate.

virtual machine monitor (VMM)

A system program that provides a VM environment. Also called a hypervisor.

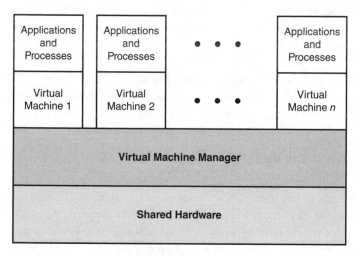

FIGURE 7.1   Virtual Machine Concept

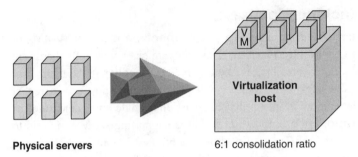

Physical servers   6:1 consolidation ratio

FIGURE 7.2   Virtual Machine Consolidation

The VM approach is a common way for businesses and individuals to deal with legacy applications and to optimize their hardware usage by maximizing the various kinds of applications that a single computer can handle. Commercial hypervisor offerings by companies such as VMware and Microsoft are widely used, with millions of copies having been sold. A key aspect of server virtualization is that, in addition to the capability of running multiple VMs on one machine, VMs can be viewed as network resources. Server virtualization masks server resources, including the number and identity of individual physical servers, processors, and operating systems, from server users. This makes it possible to partition a single host into multiple independent servers, conserving hardware resources. It also makes it possible to quickly migrate a server from one machine to another for load balancing or for dynamic switchover in the case of machine failure. Server virtualization has become a central element in dealing with big data applications and in implementing cloud computing infrastructures.

Architectural Approaches

Virtualization is all about abstraction. Much like an operating system abstracts the disk I/O commands from a user through the use of program layers and interfaces, virtualization abstracts the physical hardware from the VMs it supports. As noted already, virtual machine monitor, or hypervisor, is the software that provides this abstraction. It acts as a broker, or traffic cop, acting as a proxy for the guests (VMs) as they request and consume resources of the physical host.

A VM is a software construct that mimics the characteristics of a physical server. It is configured with some number of processors, some amount of RAM, storage resources, and connectivity through the network ports. Once that VM is created, it can be powered on like a physical server, loaded with an operating system and applications, and used in the manner of a physical server. Unlike a physical server, this virtual server sees only the resources it has been configured with, not all the resources of the physical host itself. This isolation allows a host machine to run many VMs, each running the same or different copies of an operating system, sharing RAM, storage, and network bandwidth, without problems. An operating system in a VM accesses the resource that is presented to it by the hypervisor. The hypervisor facilitates the translation of I/O from the VM to the physical server devices, and back again to the correct VM. To achieve this, certain privileged instructions that a "native" operating system would be executing on its host's hardware now trigger a hardware trap and are run by the hypervisor as a proxy for the VM. This creates some performance degradation in the virtualization process though over time both hardware and software improvements have minimalized this overhead.

VMs are made up of files. A typical VM can consist of just a few files. There is a configuration file that describes the attributes of the VM. It contains the server definition, how many virtual processors (vCPUs) are allocated to this VM, how much RAM is allocated, which I/O devices the VM has access to, how many network interface cards (NICs) are in the virtual server, and more. It also describes the storage that the VM can access. Often that storage is presented as virtual disks that exist as additional files in the physical file system. When a VM is powered on, or instantiated, additional files are created for logging, for memory paging, and other functions. That a VM consists of files makes certain functions in a virtual environment much simpler and quicker than in a physical environment. Since the earliest days of computers, backing up data has been a critical function. Because VMs are already files, copying them produces not only a backup of the data but also a copy of the entire server, including the operating system, applications, and the hardware configuration itself.

To create a copy of a physical server, additional hardware needs to be acquired, installed, configured, loaded with an operating system, applications, and data, and then patched to the latest revisions, before being turned over to the users. This provisioning can take weeks or even months depending on the processes in places. Because a VM consists of files, by duplicating those files, in a virtual environment there is a perfect copy of the server available in a matter of minutes. There are a few configuration changes to make (server name and IP address to name two), but administrators routinely stand up new VMs in minutes or hours, as opposed to months.

Another method to rapidly provision new VMs is through the use of templates. A template provides a standardized group of hardware and software settings that can be used to create new VMs configured with those settings. Creating a new VM from a template consists of providing unique identifiers for the new VM and having the provisioning software build a VM from the template and adding in the configuration changes as part of the deployment.

In addition to consolidation and rapid provisioning, virtual environments have become the new model for data center infrastructures for many reasons. One of these is increased availability. VM hosts are clustered together to form pools of computer resources. Multiple VMs are hosted on each of these servers and in the case of a physical server failure, the VMs on the failed host can be quickly and automatically restarted on another host in the cluster. Compared with providing this type of availability for a physical server, virtual environments can provide higher availability at significantly lower cost and less complexity. For servers that require greater availability, fault tolerance is available in some solutions through the use of shadowed VMs in running lockstep to ensure that no transactions are lost in the event of a physical server failure, again without increased complexity. One of the most compelling features of virtual environments is the capability to move a running VM from one physical host to another, without interruption, degradation, or impacting the users of that VM. vMotion, as it is known in a VMware environment, or Live Migration, as it is known in others, is used for a number of crucial tasks. From an availability standpoint, moving VMs from one host to another without incurring downtime allows administrators to perform work on the physical hosts without impacting operations. Maintenance can be performed on a weekday morning instead of during scheduled downtime on a weekend. New servers can be added to the environment and older servers removed without impacting the applications. In addition to these manually initiated migrations, migrations can be automated depending on resource usage. If a VM starts to consume more resources than normal, other VMs can be automatically relocated to hosts in the cluster where resources are available, ensuring adequate performance for all the VMs and better overall performance. These are simple examples that only scratch the surface of what virtual environments offer.

As mentioned earlier, the hypervisor sits between the hardware and the VMs. There are two types of hypervisors, distinguished by whether there is another operating system between the hypervisor and the host. A Type 1 hypervisor (see part a of Figure 7.3) is loaded as a thin software layer directly into a physical server, much like an operating system is loaded. Once it is installed and configured, usually within a matter of minutes, the server can then support VMs as guests. In mature environments, where virtualization hosts are clustered together for increased availability and load balancing, a hypervisor can be staged on a new host, the new host can be joined to an existing cluster, and VMs can be moved to the new host without any interruption of service. Some examples of Type 1 hypervisors are VMware ESXi, Microsoft Hyper-V, and the various open source Xen variants. This idea that the hypervisor is loaded onto the "bare metal" of a server is usually a difficult concept for people to understand. They are more comfortable with a solution that works as a traditional application, program code that is loaded on top of a Microsoft Windows or UNIX/Linux operating system environment. This is exactly how a Type 2 hypervisor (see part b of Figure 7.3) is deployed. Some examples of Type 2 hypervisors are VMware Workstation and Oracle VM Virtual Box.

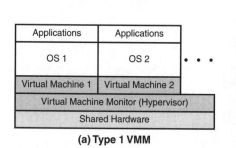

FIGURE 7.3   Type 1 and Type 2 Virtual Machine Monitors

There are some important differences between the Type 1 and the Type 2 hypervisors. A Type 1 hypervisor is deployed on a physical host and can directly control the physical resources of that host, whereas a Type 2 hypervisor has an operating system between itself and those resources and relies on the operating system to handle all the hardware interactions on the hypervisor's behalf. Typically, Type 1 hypervisors perform better than Type 2 because Type 1 hypervisors do not have that extra layer. Because a Type 1 hypervisor doesn't compete for resources with an operating system, there are more resources available on the host, and by extension, more VMs can be hosted on a virtualization server using a Type 1 hypervisor. Type 1 hypervisors are also considered to be more secure than the Type 2 hypervisors. VMs on a Type 1 hypervisor make resource requests that are handled external to that guest, and they cannot affect other VMs or the hypervisor by which they are supported. This is not necessarily true for VMs on a Type 2 hypervisor and a malicious guest could potentially affect more than itself. A Type 1 hypervisor implementation would not require the cost of a host operating system, though a true cost comparison would be a more complicated discussion. Type 2 hypervisors allow a user to take advantage of virtualization without needing to dedicate a server to only that function. Developers who need to run multiple environments as part of their process, in addition to taking advantage of the personal productive workspace that a PC operating system provides, can do both with a Type 2 hypervisor installed as an application on their Linux or Windows desktop. The VMs that are created and used can be migrated or copied from one hypervisor environment to another, reducing deployment time and increasing the accuracy of what is deployed, reducing the time to market of a project.

Container Virtualization

A relatively recent approach to virtualization is known as **container virtualization**. In this approach, software, known as a virtualization **container**, runs on top of the host OS kernel and provides an execution environment for applications (Figure 7.4). Unlike hypervisor-based VMs, containers do not aim to emulate physical servers. Instead, all containerized applications on a host share a common OS kernel. This

container

Hardware or software that provides an execution environment for software.

container virtualization

A technique where the underlying operating environment of an application is virtualized. This will commonly be the operating system kernel, and the result is an isolated container in which the application can run.

eliminates the resources needed to run a separate OS for each application and can greatly reduce overhead.

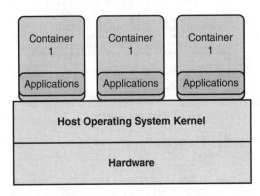

FIGURE 7.4   Container Virtualization

Because the containers execute on the same kernel, thus sharing most of the base OS, containers are much smaller and lighter weight compared to a hypervisor/guest OS VM arrangement. Accordingly, an OS can have many containers running on top of it, compared to the limited number of hypervisors and guest operating systems that can be supported.

7.3   NFV Concepts

Chapter 2, "Requirements and Technology," defined network functions virtualization (NFV) as the virtualization of network functions by implementing these functions in software and running them on VMs. NFV is a significant departure from traditional approaches to the design, deployment, and management of networking services. NFV decouples network functions, such as Network Address Translation (NAT), firewalling, intrusion detection, Domain Name Service (DNS), and caching, from proprietary hardware appliances so that they can run in software on VMs. NFV builds on standard VM technologies, extending their use into the networking domain.

Virtual machine technology, as discussed in Section 7.2, enables migration of dedicated application and database servers to **commercial off-the-shelf (COTS)** x86 servers. The same technology can be applied to network-based devices, including the following:

- **Network function devices:** Such as switches, routers, network access points, customer premises equipment (CPE), and deep packet inspectors (for **deep packet inspection**).

- **Network-related compute devices:** Such as firewalls, intrusion detection systems, and network management systems.

commercial off-the-shelf (COTS)

Item that is commercially available, leased, licensed, or sold to the general public and that requires no special modification or maintenance over the life-cycle of the product to meet the needs of the procuring agency.

deep packet inspection

Analyzing network traffic to discover the type of application that sent the data. To prioritize traffic or filter out unwanted data, deep packet inspection can differentiate data, such as video, audio, chat, Voice over IP (VoIP), e-mail, and web. Inspecting the packets all the way up to the application layer, it can be used to analyze anything within the packet that is not encrypted. For example, it can determine not only that the packets contain the contents of a web page but also which website the page is from.

- **Network-attached storage:** File and database servers attached to the network.

In traditional networks, all devices are deployed on proprietary/closed platforms. All network elements are enclosed boxes, and hardware cannot be shared. Each device requires additional hardware for increased capacity, but this hardware is idle when the system is running below capacity. With NFV, however, network elements are independent applications that are flexibly deployed on a unified platform comprising standard servers, storage devices, and switches. In this way, software and hardware are decoupled, and capacity for each application is increased or decreased by adding or reducing virtual resources (see Figure 7.5).

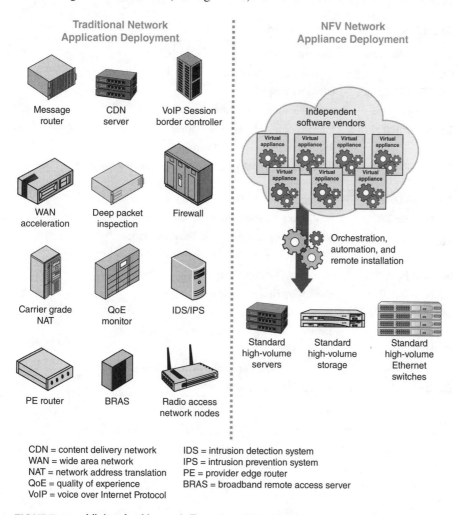

CDN = content delivery network
WAN = wide area network
NAT = network address translation
QoE = quality of experience
VoIP = voice over Internet Protocol

IDS = intrusion detection system
IPS = intrusion prevention system
PE = provider edge router
BRAS = broadband remote access server

FIGURE 7.5 Vision for Network Functions Visualization

NFV ISG

By broad consensus, the Network Functions Virtualization Industry Standards Group (ISG NFV), created as part of the European Telecommunications Standards Institute (ETSI), has the lead and indeed almost the sole role in creating NFV standards. ISG NFV was established in 2012 by seven major telecommunications network operators. Its membership has since grown to include network equipment vendors, network technology companies, other IT companies, and service providers such as cloud service providers.

ISG NFV published the first batch of specifications in October 2013, and subsequently updated most of those in late 2014 and early 2015. Table 7.1 shows the complete list of specifications as of early 2015. Table 7.2 provides definitions for a number of terms that are used in the ISG NFV documents and the NFV literature in general.

TABLE 7.1 ISG NFV Specifications

Standard Number	Standard Title
GS NFV 002	Architectural Framework
GS NFV-INF 001	Infrastructure Overview
GS NFV-INF 003	Infrastructure; Computer Domain
GS NFV-INF 004	Infrastructure; Hypervisor Domain
GS NFV-INF 005	Infrastructure; Network Domain
GS NFV-INF 007	Infrastructure; Methodology to Describe Interfaces and Abstractions
GS NFV-MAN 001	Management and Orchestration
GS NFV-SEC 001	NFV Security; Problem Statement
GS NFV-SEC 003	NFV Security; Security and Trust Guidance
GS NFV-PER 001	NFV Performance & Portability Best Practices
GS NFV-PER 002	Proofs of Concept; Framework
GS NFV-REL 001	Resiliency Requirements
GS NFV-INF 010	Service Quality Metrics
GS NFV 003	Terminology for Main Concepts in NFV
GS NFV 001	Use Cases
GS NFV-SWA 001	Virtual Network Functions Architecture
GS NFV 004	Virtualization Requirements

TABLE 7.2 NFV Terminology

Term	Definition
Compute domain	Domain within the NFVI that includes servers and storage.
Infrastructure network domain (IND)	Domain within the NFVI that includes all networking that interconnects compute/storage infrastructure.
Network function (NF)	A functional block within a network infrastructure that has well-defined external interfaces and well-defined functional behavior. Typically, this is a physical network node or other physical appliance.
Network functions virtualization (NFV)	The principle of separating network functions from the hardware they run on by using virtual hardware abstraction.
Network functions virtualization infrastructure (NFVI)	The totality of all hardware and software components that build up the environment in which virtual network functions (VNFs) are deployed. The NFVI can span across several locations (that is, multiple points of presence [N-PoPs]). The network providing connectivity between these locations is considered to be part of the NFVI.
NFVI-Node	Physical devices deployed and managed as a single entity, providing the NFVI functions required to support the execution environment for VNFs.
NFVI-PoP	An N-PoP where a network function is or could be deployed as a VNF.
Network forwarding path	Ordered list of connection points forming a chain of NFs, along with policies associated with the list.
Network point of presence (N-PoP)	A location where a network function is implemented as either a physical network function (PNF) or a VNF.
Network service	A composition of network functions that is defined by its functional and behavioral specification.
Physical network function (PNF)	An implementation of a NF via a tightly coupled software and hardware system. This is typically a proprietary system.
Virtual machine (VM)	A virtualized computation environment that behaves very much like a physical computer/server.
Virtual network	A topological component used to affect routing of specific characteristic information. The virtual network is bounded by its set of permissible network interfaces. In the NFVI architecture, a virtual network routes information among the network interfaces of VM instances and physical network interfaces, providing the necessary connectivity.
Virtualized network function (VNF)	An implementation of an NF that can be deployed on an NFVI.
VNF forwarding graph (VNF FG)	Graph of logical links connecting VNF nodes for the purpose of describing traffic flow between these network functions.
VNF set	Collection of VNFs with unspecified connectivity between them.

Simple Example of the Use of NFV

This section considers a simple example from the NFV Architectural Framework document. Part a of Figure 7.6 shows a physical realization of a network service. At a top level, the network service consists of endpoints connected by a forwarding graph of network functional blocks, called network functions (NFs). Examples of NFs are firewalls, load balancers, and wireless network access points. In the Architectural Framework, NFs are viewed as distinct physical nodes. The endpoints are beyond the scope of the NFV specifications and include all customer-owned devices. So, in the figure, endpoint A could be a smartphone and endpoint B a content delivery network (CDN) server.

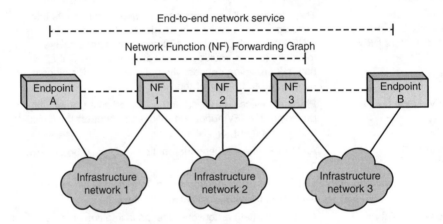

(a) Graph representation of an end-to-end network service

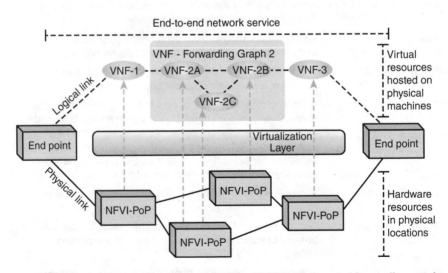

(b) Example of an end-to-end network service with VNFs and nested forwarding graphs

FIGURE 7.6   A Simple NFV Configuration Example

Part a of Figure 7.6 highlights the network functions that are relevant to the service provider and customer. The interconnections among the NFs and endpoints are depicted by dashed lines, representing logical links. These logical links are supported by physical paths through infrastructure networks (wired or wireless).

Part b of Figure 7.6 illustrates a virtualized network service configuration that could be implemented on the physical configuration of part a of Figure 7.6. VNF-1 provides network access for endpoint A, and VNF-2 provides network access for B. The figure also depicts the case of a nested VNF forwarding graph (VNF-FG-2) constructed from other VNFs (that is, VNF-2A, VNF-2B and VNF-2C). All of these VNFs run as VMs on physical machines, called points of presence (PoPs). This configuration illustrates several important points. First, VNF-FG-2 consists of three VNFs even though ultimately all the traffic transiting VNF-FG-2 is between VNF-1 and VNF-3. The reason for this is that three separate and distinct network functions are being performed. For example, it may be that some traffic flows need to be subjected to a traffic policing or shaping function, which could be performed by VNF-2C. So, some flows would be routed through VNF-2C, while others would bypass this network function.

A second observation is that two of the VMs in VNF-FG-2 are hosted on the same physical machine. Because these two VMs perform different functions, they need to be distinct at the virtual resource level but can be supported by the same physical machine. But this is not required, and a network management function may at some point decide to migrate one of the VMs to another physical machine, for reasons of performance. This movement is transparent at the virtual resource level.

NFV Principles

As suggested by Figure 7.6, the VNFs are the building blocks used to create end-to-end network services. Three key NFV principles are involved in creating practical network services:

- **Service chaining:** VNFs are modular and each VNF provides limited functionality on its own. For a given traffic flow within a given application, the service provider steers the flow through multiple VNFs to achieve the desired network functionality. This is referred to as service chaining.

- **Management and orchestration (MANO):** This involves deploying and managing the lifecycle of VNF instances. Examples include VNF instance creation, VNF service chaining, monitoring, relocation, shutdown, and billing. MANO also manages the NFV infrastructure elements.

- **Distributed architecture:** A VNF may be made up of one or more VNF components (VNFC), each of which implements a subset of the VNF's functionality. Each VNFC may be deployed in one or multiple instances. These instances may be deployed on separate, distributed hosts to provide scalability and redundancy.

High-Level NFV Framework

Figure 7.7 shows a high-level view of the NFV framework defined by ISG NFV. This framework supports the implementation of network functions as software-only VNFs. We use this to provide an overview of the NFV architecture, which is examined in more detail in Chapter 8, "NFV Functionality."

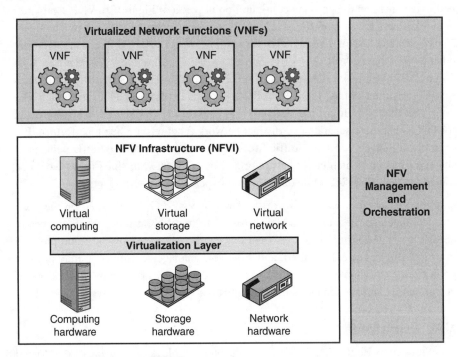

FIGURE 7.7   High-Level NFV Framework

The NFV framework consists of three domains of operation:

- **Virtualized network functions:** The collection of VNFs, implemented in software, that run over the NFVI.

- **NFV infrastructure (NFVI):** The NFVI performs a virtualization function on the three main categories of devices in the network service environment: computer devices, storage devices, and network devices.

- **NFV management and orchestration:** Encompasses the orchestration and lifecycle management of physical/software resources that support the infrastructure virtualization, and the lifecycle management of VNFs. NFV management and orchestration focuses on all virtualization-specific management tasks necessary in the NFV framework.

The ISG NFV Architectural Framework document specifies that in the deployment, operation, management and orchestration of VNFs, two types of relations between VNFs are supported:

- **VNF forwarding graph (VNF FG):** Covers the case where network connectivity between VNFs is specified, such as a chain of VNFs on the path to a web server tier (for example, firewall, network address translator, load balancer).

- **VNF set:** Covers the case where the connectivity between VNFs is not specified, such as a web server pool.

7.4   NFV Benefits and Requirements

Having considered on overview of NFV concepts, we can now summarize key benefits of NFV and requirements for successful implementation.

NFV Benefits

If NFV is implemented efficiently and effectively, it can provide a number of benefits compared to traditional networking approaches. The following are the most important potential benefits:

- Reduced **CapEx**, by using commodity servers and switches, consolidating equipment, exploiting economies of scale, and supporting pay-as-you grow models to eliminate wasteful overprovisioning. This is perhaps the main driver for NFV.

- Reduced **OpEx**, in terms of power consumption and space usage, by using commodity servers and switches, consolidating equipment, and exploiting economies of scale, and reduced network management and control expenses. Reduced CapeX and OpEx are perhaps the main drivers for NFV.

- The ability to innovate and roll out services quickly, reducing the time to deploy new networking services to support changing business requirements, seize new market opportunities, and improve return on investment of new services. Also lowers the risks associated with rolling out new services, allowing providers to easily trial and evolve services to determine what best meets the needs of customers.

- Ease of interoperability because of standardized and open interfaces.

- Use of a single platform for different applications, users and tenants. This allows network operators to share resources across services and across different customer bases.

capital expenditure (CapEx)

A business expense incurred to create future benefits. A CapEx is incurred when a business spends money either to buy fixed assets or to add to the value of an existing asset with a useful life that extends beyond the tax year.

operational expenditure (OpEx)

Refers to business expenses incurred in the course of ordinary business, such as maintenance and operation of equipment.

- Provided agility and flexibility, by quickly scaling up or down services to address changing demands.

- Targeted service introduction based on geography or customer sets is possible. Services can be rapidly scaled up/down as required.

- A wide variety of ecosystems and encourages openness. It opens the virtual appliance market to pure software entrants, small players and academia, encouraging more innovation to bring new services and new revenue streams quickly at much lower risk.

NFV Requirements

To deliver these benefits, NFV must be designed and implemented to meet a number of requirements and technical challenges, including the following [ISGN12]:

- **Portability/interoperability:** The capability to load and execute VNFs provided by different vendors on a variety of standardized hardware platforms. The challenge is to define a unified interface that clearly decouples the software instances from the underlying hardware, as represented by VMs and their hypervisors.

- **Performance trade-off:** Because the NFV approach is based on industry standard hardware (that is, avoiding any proprietary hardware such as acceleration engines), a probable decrease in performance has to be taken into account. The challenge is how to keep the performance degradation as small as possible by using appropriate hypervisors and modern software technologies, so that the effects on latency, throughput, and processing overhead are minimized.

- **Migration and coexistence with respect to legacy equipment:** The NFV architecture must support a migration path from today's proprietary physical network appliance-based solutions to more open standards-based virtual network appliance solutions. In other words, NFV must work in a hybrid network composed of classical physical network appliances and virtual network appliances. Virtual appliances must therefore use existing northbound Interfaces (for management and control) and interwork with physical appliances implementing the same functions.

- **Management and orchestration:** A consistent management and orchestration architecture is required. NFV presents an opportunity, through the flexibility afforded by software network appliances operating in an open and standardized infrastructure, to rapidly align management and orchestration northbound interfaces to well defined standards and abstract specifications.

- **Automation:** NFV will scale only if all the functions can be automated. Automation of process is paramount to success.

- **Security and resilience:** The security, resilience, and availability of their networks should not be impaired when VNFs are introduced.

- **Network stability:** Ensuring stability of the network is not impacted when managing and orchestrating a large number of virtual appliances between different hardware vendors and hypervisors. This is particularly important when, for example, virtual functions are relocated, or during reconfiguration events (for example, because of hardware and software failures) or because of cyber-attack.

- **Simplicity:** Ensuring that virtualized network platforms will be simpler to operate than those that exist today. A significant focus for network operators is simplification of the plethora of complex network platforms and support systems that have evolved over decades of network technology evolution, while maintaining continuity to support important revenue generating services.

- **Integration:** Network operators need to be able to "mix and match" servers from different vendors, hypervisors from different vendors, and virtual appliances from different vendors without incurring significant integration costs and avoiding lock-in. The ecosystem must offer integration services and maintenance and third-party support; it must be possible to resolve integration issues between several parties. The ecosystem will require mechanisms to validate new NFV products.

7.5 NFV Reference Architecture

Figure 7.7 provided a high-level view of the NFV framework. Figure 7.8 shows a more detailed look at the ISG NFV reference architectural framework. You can view this architecture as consisting of four major blocks:

- **NFV infrastructure (NFVI):** Comprises the hardware and software resources that create the environment in which VNFs are deployed. NFVI virtualizes physical computing, storage, and networking and places them into resource pools.

- **VNF/EMS:** The collection of VNFs implemented in software to run on virtual computing, storage, and networking resources, together with a collection of element management systems (EMS) that manage the VNFs.

- **NFV management and orchestration (NFV-MANO):** Framework for the management and orchestration of all resources in the NFV environment. This includes computing, networking, storage, and VM resources.

- **OSS/BSS:** Operational and business support systems implemented by the VNF service provider.

It is also useful to view the architecture as consisting of three layers. The NFVI together with the virtualized infrastructure manager provide and manage the virtual resource environment and its underlying physical resources. The VNF layer provides the software implementation of network functions, together with element management systems and one or more VNF managers. Finally, there is a management, orchestration, and control layer consisting of OSS/BSS and the NFV orchestrator.

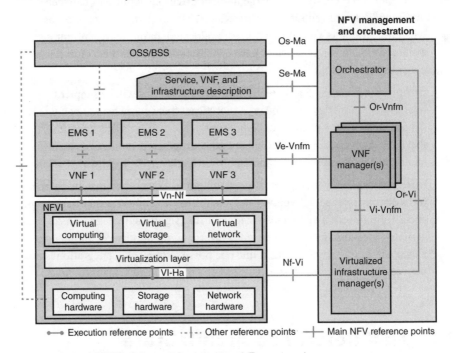

FIGURE 7.8   NFV Reference Architectural Framework

NFV Management and Orchestration

The NFV management and orchestration facility includes the following functional blocks:

- **NFV orchestrator:** Responsible for installing and configuring new network services (NS) and virtual network function (VNF) packages, NS lifecycle management, global resource management, and validation and authorization of NFVI resource requests.

- **VNF manager:** Oversees lifecycle management of VNF instances.

- **Virtualized infrastructure manager:** Controls and manages the interaction of a VNF with computing, storage, and network resources under its authority, in addition to their virtualization.

Reference Points

Figure 7.8 also defines a number of reference points that constitute interfaces between functional blocks. The main (named) reference points and execution reference points are shown by solid lines and are in the scope of NFV. These are potential targets for standardization. The dashed line reference points are available in present deployments but might need extensions for handling network function virtualization. The dotted reference points are not a focus of NFV at present.

The main reference points include the following considerations:

- **Vi-Ha:** Marks interfaces to the physical hardware. A well-defined interface specification will facilitate for operators sharing physical resources for different purposes, reassigning resources for different purposes, evolving software and hardware independently, and obtaining software and hardware component from different vendors.

- **Vn-Nf:** These interfaces are APIs used by VNFs to execute on the virtual infrastructure. Application developers, whether migrating existing network functions or developing new VNFs, require a consistent interface the provides functionality and the ability to specify performance, reliability, and scalability requirements.

- **Nf-Vi:** Marks interfaces between the NFVI and the virtualized infrastructure manager (VIM). This interface can facilitate specification of the capabilities that the NFVI provides for the VIM. The VIM must be able to manage all the NFVI virtual resources, including allocation, monitoring of system utilization, and fault management.

- **Or-Vnfm:** This reference point is used for sending configuration information to the VNF manager and collecting state information of the VNFs necessary for network service lifecycle management.

- **Vi-Vnfm:** Used for resource allocation requests by the VNF manager and the exchange of resource configuration and state information.

- **Or-Vi:** Used for resource allocation requests by the NFV orchestrator and the exchange of resource configuration and state information.

- **Os-Ma:** Used for interaction between the orchestrator and the OSS/BSS systems.

- **Ve-Vnfm:** Used for requests for VNF lifecycle management and exchange of configuration and state information.

- **Se-Ma:** Interface between the orchestrator and a data set that provides information regarding the VNF deployment template, VNF forwarding graph, service-related information, and NFV infrastructure information models.

Implementation

As with SDN, success for NFV requires standards at appropriate interface reference points and open source software for commonly used functions. For several years, ISG NFV is working on standards for the various interfaces and components of NFV. In September of 2014, the Linux Foundation announced the Open Platform for NFV (OPNFV) project. OPNFV aims to be a carrier-grade, integrated platform that introduces new products and services to the industry more quickly. The key objectives of OPNFV are as follows:

Open Platform for NFV (OPNFV)

- Develop an integrated and tested open source platform that can be used to investigate and demonstrate core NFV functionality.

- Secure proactive participation of leading end users to validate that OPNFV releases address participating operators' needs.

- Influence and contribute to the relevant open source projects that will be adopted in the OPNFV reference platform.

- Establish an open ecosystem for NFV solutions based on open standards and open source software.

- Promote OPNFV as the preferred open reference platform to avoid unnecessary and costly duplication of effort.

OPNFV and ISG NFV are independent initiatives but it is likely that they will work closely together to assure that OPNFV implementations remain within the standardized environment defined by ISG NFV.

The initial scope of OPNFV will be on building NFVI, VIM, and including application programmable interfaces (APIs) to other NFV elements, which together form the basic infrastructure required for VNFs and MANO components. This scope is highlighted in Figure 7.9 as consisting of NFVI and VMI. With this platform as a common base, vendors can add value by developing VNF software packages and associated VNF manager and orchestrator software.

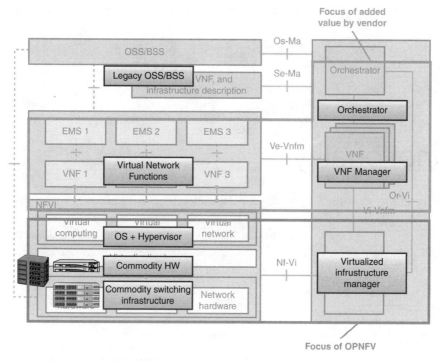

FIGURE 7.9   NFV Implementation

7.6 Key Terms

After completing this chapter, you should be able to define the following terms.

business support system (BSS)

capital expenditure (CapEx)

commercial off-the-shelf (COTS)

consolidation ratio

hardware virtualization

hypervisor

hypervisor domain

infrastructure-based virtual network

L2 virtual network

network functions virtualization (NFV)

Open Platform for NFV (OPNFV)

operational expenditure (OpEx)

point of presence (PoP)

scale down

scale in

Type 1 hypervisor

Type 2 hypervisor

virtual machine (VM)

virtual machine monitor (VMM)

7.7 References

ISGN12: ISG NFV. Network Functions Virtualization: An Introduction, Benefits, Enablers, Challenges & Call for Action. ISG NFV White Paper, October 2012.

Chapter 8

NFV Functionality

The world has arrived at an age of cheap, complex devices of great reliability; and something is bound to come of it.

— "As We May Think," Vannevar Bush, *The Atlantic*, July 1945

Chapter Objectives

After studying this chapter, you should be able to

- Explain the elements of the NFV infrastructure and their interrelationships.
- Understand key design issues related to virtualized network functions.
- Explain the purpose of and operation of NFV management and orchestration.
- Present an overview of important NFV use cases.
- Discuss the relationship between SDN and NFV.

This chapter concludes our discussion of network functions virtualization (NFV).

8.1 NFV Infrastructure

The heart of the NFV architecture is a collection of resources and functions known as
the NFV infrastructure (NFVI). The NFVI encompasses three domains, as illustrated
in Figure 8.1 and described in the list that follows.

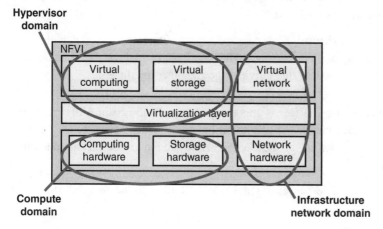

FIGURE 8.1   NFV Domains

- **Compute domain:** Provides commercial off-the-shelf (COTS) high-volume
  servers and storage.

- **Hypervisor domain:** Mediates the resources of the compute domain to the
  VMs of the software appliances, providing an abstraction of the hardware.

- **Infrastructure network domain (IND):** Comprises all the generic high volume switches interconnected into a network that can be configured to supply
  infrastructure network services.

Container Interface

Before proceeding with a discussion of NFVI, we need to clarify the concept of
container interface as used in the Network Functions Virtualization Industry
Standards Group (ISG NFV) documents. Unfortunately, the European Telecommunications Standards Institute (ETSI) documents use the term *container* in a different
sense than that of container virtualization. The NFV Infrastructure document states
that *container interface* should not be confused with *container* as used in the context
of container virtualization as an alternative to full VMs. Further, the Infrastructure
document states that some virtual network functions (VNFs) may be designed for
hypervisor virtualization and other VNFs may be designed for container virtualization.
With this clarification, the following examines the container interface concept.

The ETSI documents make a distinction between a functional block interface and a container interface, as follows:

- **Functional block interface:** An interface between two blocks of software that perform separate (perhaps identical) functions. The interface allows communication between the two blocks. The two functional blocks may or may not be on the same physical host.

- **Container interface:** An execution environment on a host system within which a functional block executes. The functional block is on the same physical host as the container that provides the container interface.

The concept of container interface is important because, in discussing VMs and VNFs within the NFV architecture, and how these functional blocks interact, it is easy to lose sight of the fact that all of these virtualized functions must execute on actual physical hosts.

Figure 8.2 relates container and functional block interfaces to the domain structure of NFVI.

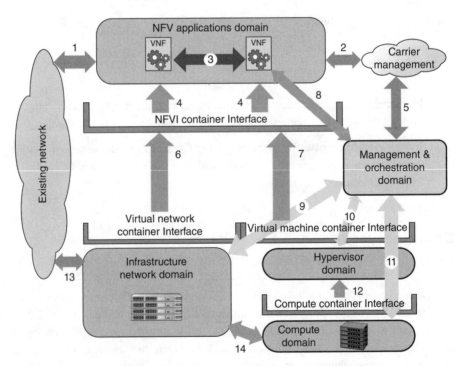

FIGURE 8.2   General Domain Architecture and Associated Interfaces

The ETSI NFVI Architecture Overview document makes the following points concerning this figure:

- The architecture of the VNFs is separated from the architecture hosting the VNFs (that is, the NFVI).

- The architecture of the VNFs may be divided into a number of domains with consequences for the NFVI and vice versa.

- Given the current technology and industrial structure, compute (including storage), hypervisors, and infrastructure networking are already largely separate domains and are maintained as separate domains within the NFVI.

- Management and orchestration tends to be sufficiently distinct from the NFVI as to warrant being defined as its own domain; however, the boundary between the two is often only loosely defined with functions such as element management functions in an area of overlap.

- The interface between the VNF domains and the NFVI is a container interface and not a functional block interface.

- The management and orchestration functions are also likely to be hosted in the NFVI (as VMs) and therefore also likely to sit on a container interface.

Figure 8.2 gives insight into the deployment of NFV. The user view of a network of interconnected VNFs is of a virtualized network in which the physical and lower level logical details are transparent. But the VNFs and logical links between VNFs are hosted on an NFVI container, which in turn is hosted on VM and VM containers running on physical hosts. Therefore, if we view the VNF architecture as having three layers (physical resource, virtualization, application), all three layers are present on a single physical host. Of course, functionality may be distributed across multiple computer and switch hosts, but all application software ultimately runs on the same physical host as the virtualization software. This is in contrast to software-defined networking (SDN), where by design the data plane functions and the control plane functions are on separate physical hosts. Application plane SDN functions may execute on the same host as the control plane functions but may also execute remotely on another host.

Table 8.1 describes the interfaces labeled in Figure 8.2; the numbers in the second column of the table correspond to the numbered arrows in the figure. Interfaces 4, 6, 7, and 12 are container interfaces, so that components on both side of the interface are executing on the same host. Interfaces 3, 8, 9, 10, 11, and 14 are functional block interfaces and, in most cases, the functional blocks on the two sides of the interface execute on different hosts. However, in some cases, some of the management and orchestration software may be hosted on a system that also hosts other NFVI components. Figure 8.2 also shows interfaces 1, 2, 5, and 13 to existing networks that have not implemented NFV. The NFV documents anticipate that typically NFV will be introduced over time into an enterprise facility, so that interaction with non-NFV network is necessary.

TABLE 8.1   Inter-Domain Interfaces Arising from Domain Architecture

Interface Type	#	Description
NFVI container interfaces	4	Primary interface provided by the infrastructure to host VNFs. The applications may be distributed and the infrastructure provides virtual connectivity that interconnects the distributed components of an application.
VNF interconnect interfaces	3	Interfaces between VNFs. The specification of these interfaces does not include, and is transparent to, the way the infrastructure provides the connectivity service between the hosted functional blocks, however distributed.
VNF management and orchestration interface	8	Interface that allows the VNFs to request different resources of the infrastructure (for example, request new infrastructure connectivity services, allocate more compute resources, or activate/deactivate other VM components of the application).
Infrastructure container interfaces	6	Virtual network container interface: Interface to the connectivity services provided by the infrastructure. This container interface makes the infrastructure appear to NFV applications as instances of these connectivity services.
	7	Virtual machine container interface: Primary hosting interface on which VNF VMs run.
	12	Compute container interface: Primary hosting interface on which the hypervisor runs.
Infrastructure interconnect interfaces	9	Management and orchestration interface with the infrastructure network domain.
	10	Management and orchestration interface with the hypervisor domain.
	11	Management and orchestration interface with the compute domain.
	14	Network interconnect between the compute equipment and the infrastructure network equipment.
Legacy interconnect interfaces	1	Interface between the VNF and the existing network. This is likely to be higher layers of protocol only as all protocols provided by the infrastructure are transparent to the VNFs.
	2	Management of VNFs by existing management systems.
	5	Management of NFV infrastructure by existing management systems.
	13	Interface between the infrastructure network and the existing network. This is likely to be lower layers of protocol only because all protocols provided by VNFs are transparent to the infrastructure.

Deployment of NFVI Containers

A single compute or network host can host multiple virtual machines (VMs), each of which can host a single VNF. The single VNF hosted on a VM is referred to as a VNF component (VNFC). A network function may be virtualized by a single VNFC, or multiple VNFCs may be combined to form a single VNF. Part a of Figure 8.3 shows the organization of VNFCs on a single compute node. The compute container interface hosts a hypervisor, which in turn can host multiple VMs, each hosting a VNFC.

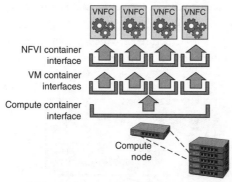

(a) A single compute platform supporting multiple VNFCs

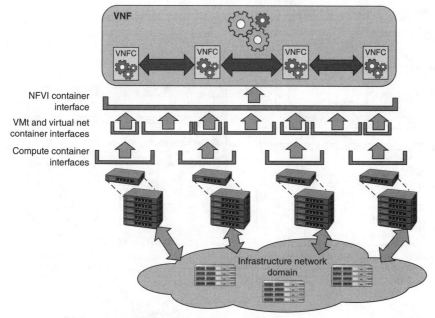

(b) A composed, distributed VNF hosted across multiple compute platforms

FIGURE 8.3 Deployment of NVFI Containers

When a VNF is composed of multiple VNFCs, it is not necessary that all the VNFCs execute in the same host. As shown in part b of Figure 8.3, the VNFCs can be distributed across multiple compute nodes interconnected by network hosts forming the infrastructure network domain.

Logical Structure of NFVI Domains

The ISG NFV standards documents lay out the logical structure of the NFVI domains and their interconnections. The specifics of the actual implementation of the elements of this architecture will evolve in both open source and proprietary implementation efforts. The NFVI domain logical structure provides a framework for such development and identifies the interfaces between the main components, as shown in Figure 8.4.

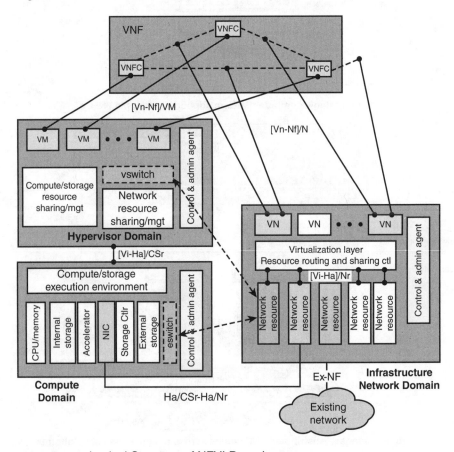

FIGURE 8.4   Logical Structure of NFVI Domains

Compute Domain

The principal elements in a typical compute domain may include the following:

- **CPU/memory:** A COTS processor, with main memory, that executes the code of the VNFC.

- **Internal storage:** Nonvolatile storage housed in the same physical structure as the processor, such as flash memory.

- **Accelerator:** Accelerator functions for security, networking, and packet processing may also be included.

- **External storage with storage controller:** Access to secondary memory devices.

- **Network interface card (NIC):** Provides the physical interconnection with the infrastructure network domain, which is labeled Ha/CSr-Ha/Nr and corresponds to interface 14 of Figure 8.2.

- **Control and admin agent:** Connects to the virtualized infrastructure manager (VIM); see Figure 7.8 in Chapter 7, "Network Functions Virtualization: Concepts and Architecture."

- **Eswitch:** Server embedded switch. The eswitch function, described in the following section, is implemented in the compute domain. However, functionally it forms an integral part of the infrastructure network domain.

- **Compute/storage execution environment:** This is the execution environment presented to the hypervisor software by the server or storage device ([VI-Ha]/CSr, interface 12 of Figure 8.2).

network interface card

An adapter circuit board installed in a computer to provide a physical connection to a network.

Eswitch

To understand the functionality of the eswitch, first note that, broadly speaking, VNFs deal with two different kinds of workloads:

- **Control plane workloads:** Concerned with signaling and control plane protocols such as BGP. Typically, these workloads are more processor rather than I/O intensive and do not place a significant burden on the I/O system.

- **Data plane workloads:** Concerned with the routing, switching, relaying or processing of network traffic payloads. Such workloads can require high I/O throughput.

In a virtualized environment such as NFV, all VNF network traffic would go through a virtual switch in the hypervisor domain, which invokes a layer of software between virtualized VNF software and host networking hardware. This can create a significant performance penalty. The purpose of the eswitch is to bypass the virtualization software and provide the VNF with a direct memory access (DMA) path to the NIC. The eswitch approach accelerates packet processing without any processor overhead.

NFVI Implementation Using Compute Domain Nodes

As suggested by Figure 8.3, a VNF consists of one or more logically connected VNFCs. The VNFCs run as software on hypervisor domain containers that in turn run on hardware in the compute domain. Although virtual links and networks are defined through the infrastructure network domain, the actual implementation of network functions at the VNF level consists of software on compute domain nodes. The IND interfaces with the compute domain and not directly with the hypervisor domain or the VNFs. Again, this latter point is illustrated in Figure 8.3.

Before proceeding, we need to define the term *node*, which is used often in the ISG NFV documents. The documents define an **NFVI-Node** as collection of physical devices deployed and managed as a single entity, providing the NFVI functions required to support the execution environment for VNFs. NFVI nodes are in the compute domain and encompass the following types of compute domain nodes:

- **Compute node:** A functional entity which is capable of executing a generic computational instruction set (each instruction be being fully atomic and de-terministic) in such a way that the execution cycle time is of the order of units to tens of nanoseconds irrespective of what specific state is required for cycle execution. In practical terms, this defines a compute node in terms of memory access time. A distributed system cannot meet this requirement as the time taken to access state stored in remote memory cannot meet this requirement.

- **Gateway node:** A single identifiable, addressable, and manageable element within an NFVI-Node that implements gateway functions. Gateway functions provide the interconnection between NFVI-PoPs and the transport networks. They also connect virtual networks to existing network components. A gateway may process packets going between different networks, such as removing headers and adding headers. A gateway may operate at the transport level, dealing with IP and data-link packets, or at the application level.

- **Storage node:** A single identifiable, addressable, and manageable element within an NFVI-Node that provides storage resource using compute, storage, and networking functions. Storage may be physically implemented in a variety of ways. It could, for example be implemented as a component within a compute node. An alternative approach is to implement storage nodes independent of the compute nodes as physical nodes within the NFVI-Node. An example of such a storage node may be a physical device accessible via a remote storage technology, such as Network File System (NFS) and Fibre Channel.

- **Network node:** A single identifiable, addressable, and manageable element within an NFVI-Node that provides networking (switching/routing) resources using compute, storage, and network forwarding functions.

A compute domain within an NFVI node will often be deployed as a number of interconnected physical devices. Physical compute domain nodes may include a number of physical resources, such as a multicore processor, memory subsystems, and NICs. An interconnected set of these nodes comprise one NFVI-Node and constitutes one NFVI point of presence (NFVI-PoP). An NFV provider might maintain a number of NFVI-PoPs at distributed locations, providing service to a variety of users, each of whom could implement their VNF software on compute domain nodes at various NFVI-PoP locations.

Table 8.2 lists some deployment scenarios suggested in the ISG NFV Compute Domain document. The scenarios include the following:

- **Monolithic operator:** One organization owns and houses the hardware equipment and deploys and operates the VNFs and the hypervisors they run on. A private cloud or a data center are examples of this deployment model.

- **Network operator hosting virtual network operators:** Based on the monolithic operator scenario, with the addition that the monolithic operator host other virtual network operators within the same facility. A hybrid cloud is an example of this deployment model.

- **Hosted network operator:** An IT services organization (for example, HP, Fujitsu) operates the compute hardware, infrastructure network, and hypervisors on which a separate network operator (for example, BT, Verizon) runs VNFs. These are physically secured by the IT services organization.

- **Hosted communications providers:** Similar to the hosted network operator scenario, but in this case multiple communications providers are hosted. A community cloud is an example of this deployment model.

- **Hosted communications and application providers:** Similar to the previous scenario. In addition to host network and communications providers, servers in a data center facility are offered to the public for deploying virtualized applications. A public cloud is an example of this deployment model.

- **Managed network service on customer premises:** Similar to the monolithic operator scenario. In this case, the NFV provider's equipment is housed on the customer's premises. One example of this model is a remotely managed gateway in a residential or enterprise location. Another example is remotely managed networking equipment such as firewalls or virtual private network gateways.

■ **Managed network service on customer equipment:** Similar to the monolithic operator scenario. In this case, the equipment is housed on the customer's premises on customer equipment. This scenario could be used for managing an enterprise network. A private cloud could also be deployed in this fashion.

TABLE 8.2 Some Realistic Deployment Scenarios

Deployment Scenario	Building	Host Hardware	Hypervisor	Guest VNF
Monolithic operator	N	N	N	N
Network operator hosting virtual network operators	N	N	N	N, N1, N2
Hosted network operator	H	H	H	N
Hosted communications providers	H	H	H	N1, N2, N3
Hosted communications and application providers	H	H	H	N1, N2, N3, P
Managed network service on customer premises	C	N	N	N
Managed network service on customer equipment	C	C	N	N

NOTE

The different letters represent different companies or organizations, and are chosen to represent different roles (for example, H = hosting provider, N = network operator, P = public, C = customer). The numbered network operators (N1, N2, and so on) represent multiple individual hosted network operators.

→ *See Chapter 13, "Cloud Computing"* See the discussion on the National Institute of Standards and Technology (NIST) cloud computing models for a definition of the four cloud types referenced in the preceding list.

Hypervisor Domain

The hypervisor domain is a software environment that abstracts hardware and implements services, such as starting a VM, terminating a VM, acting on policies, scaling, live migration, and high availability. The principal elements in the hypervisor domain are the following:

- **Compute/storage resource sharing/management:** Manages these resources and provides virtualized resource access for VMs.

- **Network resource sharing/management:** Manages these resources and provides virtualized resource access for VMs.

- **Virtual machine management and API:** This provides the execution environment of a single VNFC instance ([Vn-Nf]/VM, interface 7 of Figure 8.2).

- **Control and admin agent:** Connects to the virtualized infrastructure manager (VIM); see Figure 7.8.

- **Vswitch:** The vswitch function, described in the next paragraph, is implemented in the hypervisor domain. However, functionally it forms an integral part of the infrastructure network domain.

The vswitch is an Ethernet switch implemented by the hypervisor that interconnects virtual NICs of VMs with each other and with the NIC of the compute node. If two VNFs are on the same physical server, they would be connected through the same vswitch. If two VNFs are on different servers, the connection passes through the first vswitch to the NIC and then to an external switch. This switch forwards the connection to the NIC of the desired server. Finally, this NIC forwards it to its internal vswitch and then to the destination VNF.

Infrastructure Network Domain

The infrastructure network domain (IND) performs a number of roles. It provides

- The communication channel between the VNFCs of a distributed VNF

- The communications channel between different VNFs

- The communication channel between VNFs and their orchestration and management

- The communication channel between components of the NFVI and their orchestration and management

- The means of remote deployment of VNFCs

- The means of interconnection with the existing carrier network

Figure 8.2 illustrates key reference points defined for the IND. As already mentioned, Ha/CSr-Ha/Nr defines the interface between the IND and the servers/storage of the compute domain, connecting the NIC in the compute domain to a network resource in the infrastructure network domain. Ex-Nf is the reference point between any existing/nonvirtualized network (interface 13 of Figure 8.2). Reference point [VI-HA]/Nr is the interface between the hardware network resources of the IND and the virtualization layer. The virtualization layer provides container interfaces for virtual network entities. The [Vn-Nf]/N reference point (interface 7 of Figure 8.2) is the virtual network (VN) container interface (for example, a link or a LAN) for carrying communication between VNFC instances. Note that a single VN can support communication between more than a single pairing of VNFC instances (for example, a LAN).

There is an important distinction to be made between the virtualization function provided by the hypervisor domain and that provided by the infrastructure network domain. Virtualization in the hypervisor domain uses VM technology to create an execution environment for individual VNFCs. Virtualization in IND creates virtual networks for interconnecting VNFCs with each other and with network nodes outside the NFV ecosystem. These latter types of nodes are called physical network functions (PNFs).

Virtual Networks

Before proceeding, we need to clarify how the term *virtual network* is used in the ISG NFV documents. In general terms, a virtual network is an abstraction of physical network resources as seen by some upper software layer. Virtual network technology enables a network provider to support multiple virtual networks that are isolated from one another. Users of a single virtual network are not aware of the details of the underlying physical network or of the other virtual network traffic sharing the physical network resources. Two common approaches for creating virtual networks are (1) protocol-based methods that define virtual networks based on fields in protocol headers, and (2) virtual-machine-based methods, in which networks are created among a set of VMs by the hypervisor. The NFVI network virtualization combines both these forms.

L2 Versus L3 Virtual Networks

Protocol-based virtual networks can be classified by whether they are defined at protocol Layer 2 (L2), which is typically the LAN media access control (MAC) layer, or Layer 3 (L3), which is typically the Internet Protocol (IP). With an L2 VN, a virtual LAN is identified by a field in the MAC header, such as the MAC address or a virtual LAN ID field inserted into the header. So, for example, within a data center, all the servers and end systems connected to a single Ethernet switch could support virtual LANs among the connected devices. Now suppose there are IP routers connecting segments of the data center, as illustrated in Figure 8.5. Normally, an IP router will strip off the MAC header of incoming Ethernet frames and insert a new MAC header when forwarding the packet to the next network. The L2 VN could be extended across this router only if the router had additional capability to support the L2 VN, such as being able to reinsert the virtual LAN ID field in the outgoing MAC frame. Similarly, if an enterprise had two data centers connected by a router and a dedicated line, that router would need the L2 VN capability to extend a VN.

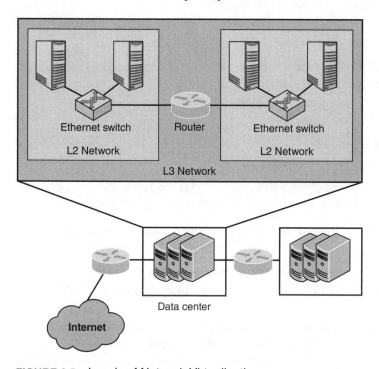

FIGURE 8.5   Levels of Network Virtualization

An L3 VN makes use of one or more fields in the IP header. A good example of this is the virtual private network (VPN) defined using IPsec. Packets traveling on a VPN are encapsulated in a new outer IP header and the data are encrypted so that VPN traffic is isolated and protected as it transits third-party network such as the Internet.

Chapter 9, "Network Virtualization," covers virtual LANs and VPNs in more detail.

NFVI Virtual Network Alternatives

ISG NFV defines a virtual network as the network construct that provides network connectivity to one or more VNFs that are hosted on the NFVI. Therefore, the concept of a virtual network that extends beyond the NFV infrastructure is not currently addressed. In NFV, a virtual network is a network among VNFs.

The Network Domain document indicates that three approaches are envisioned for providing a virtual network service:

- Infrastructure-based VNs

■ Layered VNs using virtual overlays

■ Layered VNs using virtual partitioning

A facility can use one or a combination of these approaches.

The **infrastructure-Based VN** uses the native networking functions of the NFVI compute and networking components. The address space is partitioned so that VNF membership in a VN is defined by IP address. The IND document gives the following example of an L3 infrastructure-based VN:

■ Each VNF is assigned its own unique IP address that does not overlap with any other address of elements within the NFVI.

■ Logical partitioning of the VNFs into their VNs is achieved by managing access control lists in the L3 forwarding function in each compute node.

■ The L3 forwarding between VNFs and the physical fabric can then be handled by the L3 forwarding information base running on the hosting compute node.

■ Control plane solutions, such as Border Gateway Protocol (BGP), can be used to advertise reachability of the VNFs to other compute hosts.

The other two approaches are referred to as *layered virtual network approaches*. These approaches allow overlapping address spaces. That is, a VNF may participate in more than one VN using the same IP address. The virtualization layer of the IND essentially creates private topologies on the underlying NFVI network fabric, using either virtual overlays or virtual partitioning.

The **virtual overlay VN** uses the concept of an overlay network. In essence, an overlay network is a logical network that is built on the top of another network. Nodes in the overlay network can be thought of as being connected by virtual or logical links, each of which corresponds to a path, perhaps through many physical links in the underlying network. However, overlay networks do not have the ability to control the routing between two overlay network nodes. In the NFV context, the overlay networks are the VNs used by the VNFs and the underlay network consists of the infrastructure network resources. These overlay networks are normally created by edge nodes which have a dual personality, participating in both the creation of the virtual networks and also acting as infrastructure network resources. In contrast, the core nodes of the infrastructure network only participate in the infrastructure network and have no overlay awareness. The L2 and L3 virtual networks discussed earlier fit into this category.

The virtual partitioning VN approach directly integrates VNs, called virtual network partitions in this context, into the infrastructure network on an end-to-end basis. Discrete virtual topologies are built in both the edge and core nodes of the infrastructure network for each virtual network. This can consist of per virtual network forwarding tables, logical links and even control planes on an end-to-end basis across the infrastructure network.

8.2 Virtualized Network Functions

A VNF is a virtualized implementation of a traditional network function. Table 8.3 contains examples of functions that could be virtualized.

TABLE 8.3   Potential Network Functions to Be Virtualized

Network Element	Function
Switching elements	Broadband network gateways, carrier grade Network Address Translation (NAT), routers
Mobile network nodes	Home location register/home subscriber server, gateway, General Packet Radio Service (GPRS) Protocol support node, radio network controller, various node B functions
Customer premises equipment	Home routers, set-top boxes
Tunneling gateway elements	IPsec / Secure Sockets Layer (SSL) virtual private network gateways
Traffic analysis	Deep packet inspection (DPI), quality of experience (QoE) measurement
Assurance	Service assurance, service level agreement (SLA) monitoring, testing and diagnostics
Signaling	Session border controllers, IP multimedia subsystem (IMS) components
Control plane / access functions	AAA (authentication, authorization, and accounting) servers, policy control and charging platforms, Dynamic Host Configuration Protocol (DHCP) servers
Application optimization	Content delivery networks, cache servers, load balancers, accelerators
Security	Firewalls, virus scanners, intrusion detection systems, spam protection

VNF Interfaces

As discussed earlier, a VNF consists of one or more VNF components (VNFCs). The VNFCs of a single VNF are connected internal to the VNF. This internal structure is not visible to other VNFs or to the VNF user.

Figure 8.6 shows the interfaces relevant to a discussion of VNFs as described in the list that follows.

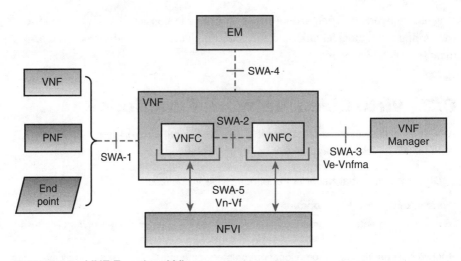

FIGURE 8.6   VNF Functional View

- **SWA-1:** This interface enables communication between a VNF and other VNFs, PNFs, and endpoints. Note that the interface is to the VNF as a whole and not to individual VNFCs. SWA-1 interfaces are logical interfaces that primarily make use of the network connectivity services available at the SWA-5 interface.

- **SWA-2:** This interface enables communications between VNFCs within a VNF. This interface is vendor specific and therefore not a subject for standardization. This interface may also make use of the network connectivity services available at the SWA-5 interface. However, if two VNFCs within a VNF are deployed on the same host, other technologies may be used to minimize latency and enhance throughput, as described below.

- **SWA-3:** This is the interface to the VNF manager within the NFV management and orchestration module. The VNF manager is responsible for lifecycle management (creation, scaling, termination, and so on). The interface typically is implemented as a network connection using IP.

- **SWA-4:** This is the interface for runtime management of the VNF by the element manager.

- **SWA-5:** This interface describes the execution environment for a deployable instance of a VNF. Each VNFC maps to a virtualized container interface to a VM.

VNFC to VNFC Communication

As mentioned earlier, the internal structure of a VNF, in terms of multiple VNFCs, is not exposed externally. The VNF appears as a single functional system in the network it supports. However, internal connectivity between VNFCs within the same VNF or across co-located VNFs needs to be specified by the VNF provider, supported by the NFVI, and managed by the VNF manager. The VNF Architecture document describes a number of architecture design models that are intended to provide desired performance and quality of service (QoS), such as access to storage or compute resources. One of the most important of these design models relates to communication between VNFCs.

Figure 8.7, from the ETSI VNF Architecture document, illustrates six scenarios using different network technologies to support communication between VNFCs:

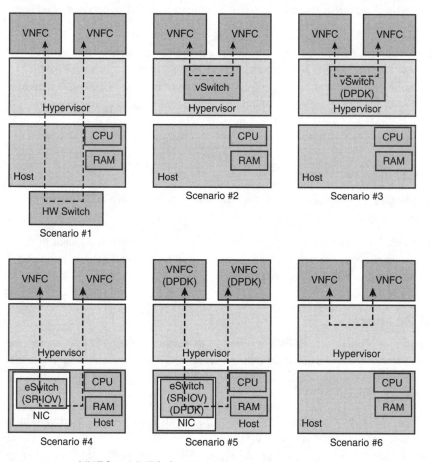

FIGURE 8.7   VNFC to VNFC Communication

1. Communication through a hardware switch. In this case, the VMs supporting the VNFCs bypass the hypervisor to directly access the physical NIC. This provides enhanced performance for VNFCs on different physical hosts.

2. Communication through the vswitch in the hypervisor. This is the basic method of communication between co-located VNFCs but does not provide the QoS or performance that may be required for some VNFs.

3. Greater performance can be achieved by using appropriate data processing acceleration libraries and drivers compatible with the CPU being used. The library is called from the vswitch. An example of a suitable commercial product is the Data Plane Development Kit (DPDK), which is a set of data plane libraries and network interface controller drivers for fast packet processing on Intel architecture platforms. Scenario 3 assumes a Type 1 hypervisor (see Figure 7.3).

4. Communication through an embedded switch (eswitch) deployed in the NIC with Single Root I/O Virtualization (SR-IOV). SR-IOV is a PCI-SIG specification that defines a method to split a device into multiple PCI express requester IDs (virtual functions) in a fashion that allows an I/O memory management unit (MMU) to distinguish different traffic streams and apply memory and interrupt translations so that these traffic streams can be delivered directly to the appropriate VM, and in a way that prevents nonprivileged traffic flows from impacting other VMs.

5. Embedded switch deployed in the NIC hardware with SR-IOV, and with data plane acceleration software deployed in the VNFC.

6. A serial bus connects directly two VNFCs that have extreme workloads or very low-latency requirements. This is essentially an I/O channel means of communication rather than a NIC means.

VNF Scaling

scale up

Expand capability by adding additional physical or virtual machines.

An important property of VNFs is referred to as elasticity, which simply means the ability to **scale up**/down or **scale out**/in. Every VNF has associated with it an elasticity parameter of no elasticity, scale up/down only, scale out/in only, or both scale up/down and scale out/in.

scale out

Expand the capability of a single physical machine or VM.

A VNF is scaled by scaling one or more of its constituent VNFCs. Scale out/in is implemented by adding/removing VNFC instances that belong to the VNF being scaled. Scale up/down is implemented by adding/removing resources from existing VNFC instances that belong to the VNF being scaled.

8.3 NFV Management and Orchestration[1]

The NFV management and orchestration (MANO) component of NFV has as its primary function the management and orchestration of an NFV environment. This task, by itself, is complex. Further complicating MANO functionality is its need to interoperate with and cooperate with existing operations support systems (OSS) and business support systems (BSS) in providing management functionality for customers whose networking environment consists of a mixture of physical and virtual elements.

Figure 8.8, from the ETSI MANO document, shows the basic structure of NFV-MANO and its key interfaces. As can be seen, there are five management blocks: three within NFV-MANO, EMS associated with VNFs, and OSS/BSS. These two latter blocks are not part of MANO but do exchange information with MANO for the purpose of the overall management of a customer's networking environment.

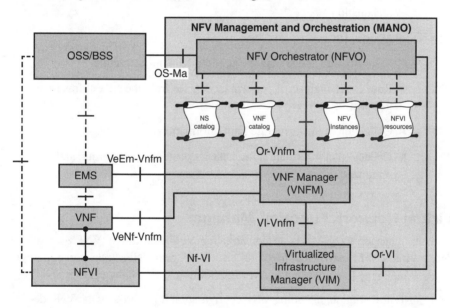

FIGURE 8.8 The NFV-MANO Architectural Framework with Reference Points

Virtualized Infrastructure Manager

Virtualized infrastructure management (VIM) comprises the functions that are used to control and manage the interaction of a VNF with computing, storage, and network resources under its authority, as well as their virtualization. A single instance of a VIM is responsible for controlling and managing the NFVI compute, storage, and network resources, usually within one operator's infrastructure domain. This domain could

---

1 Some of the material in this section is based on [KHAN15].

consist of all resources within an NFVI-PoP, resources across multiple NFVI-PoPs, or a subset of resources within an NFVI-PoP. To deal with the overall networking environment, multiple VIMs within a single MANO may be needed.

A VIM performs the following:

- **Resource management, in charge of the**

    - Inventory of software (for example, hypervisors), computing, storage and network resources dedicated to NFV infrastructure.

    - Allocation of virtualization enablers, for example, VMs onto hypervisors, compute resources, storage, and relevant network connectivity

    - Management of infrastructure resource and allocation, for example, increase resources to VMs, improve energy efficiency, and resource reclamation

- **Operations, for**

    - Visibility into and management of the NFV infrastructure

    - Root cause analysis of performance issues from the NFV infrastructure perspective

    - Collection of infrastructure fault information

    - Collection of information for capacity planning, monitoring, and optimization

Virtual Network Function Manager

A VNF manager (VNFM) is responsible for VNFs. Multiple VNFMs may be deployed; a VNFM may be deployed for each VNF, or a VNFM may serve multiple VNFs. Among the functions that a VNFM performs are the following:

- VNF instantiation, including VNF configuration if required by the VNF deployment template (for example, VNF initial configuration with IP addresses before completion of the VNF instantiation operation)

- VNF instantiation feasibility checking, if required

- VNF instance software update/upgrade

- VNF instance modification

- VNF instance scaling out/in and up/down

- VNF instance-related collection of NFVI performance measurement results and faults/events information, and correlation to VNF instance-related events/faults

- VNF instance assisted or automated healing

- VNF instance termination

- VNF lifecycle management change notification

- Management of the integrity of the VNF instance through its lifecycle

- Overall coordination and adaptation role for configuration and event reporting between the VIM and the EM

NFV Orchestrator

The NFV orchestrator (NFVO) is responsible for resource orchestration and network service orchestration.

Resource orchestration manages and coordinates the resources under the management of different VIMs. NFVO coordinates, authorizes, releases and engages NFVI resources among different PoPs or within one PoP. This does so by engaging with the VIMs directly through their northbound APIs instead of engaging with the NFVI resources directly.

Network services orchestration manages/coordinates the creation of an end-to-end service that involves VNFs from different VNFMs domains. Service orchestration does this in the following way:

- It creates end-to-end service between different VNFs. It achieves this by coordinating with the respective VNFMs so that it does not need to talk to VNFs directly. An example is creating a service between the base station VNFs of one vendor and core node VNFs of another vendor.

- It can instantiate VNFMs, where applicable.

- It does the topology management of the network services instances (also called VNF forwarding graphs).

Repositories

Associated with NFVO are four repositories of information needed for the management and orchestration functions:

- **Network services catalog:** List of the usable network services. A deployment template for a network service in terms of VNFs and description of their connectivity through virtual links is stored in NS catalog for future use.

- **VNF catalog:** Database of all usable VNF descriptors. A VNF descriptor (VNFD) describes a VNF in terms of its deployment and operational behavior requirements. It is primarily used by VNFM in the process of VNF instantiation and lifecycle management of a VNF instance. The information provided in the VNFD is also used by the NFVO to manage and orchestrate network services and virtualized resources on NFVI.

- **NFV instances:** List containing details about network services instances and related VNF instances.

- **NFVI resources:** List of NFVI resources utilized for the purpose of establishing NFV services.

Element Management

The element management is responsible for fault, configuration, accounting, performance, and security (FCAPS) management functionality for a VNF. These management functions are also the responsibility of the VNFM. But EM can do it through a proprietary interface with the VNF in contrast to VNFM. However, EM needs to make sure that it exchanges information with VNFM through open reference point (VeEm-Vnfm). The EM may be aware of virtualization and collaborate with VNFM to perform those functions that require exchange of information regarding the NFVI resources associated with VNF. EM functions include the following:

- Configuration for the network functions provided by the VNF

- Fault management for the network functions provided by the VNF

- Accounting for the usage of VNF functions

- Collecting performance measurement results for the functions provided by the VNF

- Security management for the VNF functions

OSS/BSS

The OSS/BSS are the combination of the operator's other operations and business support functions that are not otherwise explicitly captured in the present architectural framework, but are expected to have information exchanges with functional blocks in the NFV-MANO architectural framework. OSS/BSS functions may provide management and orchestration of legacy systems and may have full end-to-end visibility of services provided by legacy network functions in an operator's network.

In principle, it would be possible to extend the functionalities of existing OSS/BSS to manage VNFs and NFVI directly, but that may be a proprietary implementation of a vendor. Because NFV is an open platform, managing NFV entities through open interfaces (as that in MANO) makes more sense. The existing OSS/BBS, however, can add value to the NFV MANO by offering additional functions if they are not supported by a certain implementation of NFV MANO. This is done through an open reference point (Os-Ma) between NFV MANO and existing OSS/BSS.

8.4 NFV Use Cases

ISG NFV has developed a representative set of service models and high-level use cases that may be addressed by NFV. These use cases are intended to drive further development of standards and products for network-wide implementation. The Use Cases document identifies and describes a first set of service models and high-level use cases that represent, in the view of NFV ISG member companies, important service models and initial fields of application for NFV, and that span the scope of technical challenges being addressed by the NFV ISG.

There are currently nine use cases, which can be divided into the categories of architectural use cases and service-oriented use cases, as described in Table 8.4.

TABLE 8.4 ETSI NFV Use Cases

Use Case	Description
Architectural Use Cases	
Network Functions Virtualization Infrastructure as a Service (NFVIaaS)	Provides an approach to mapping the cloud computing service models Infrastructure as a Service (IaaS) and Network as a Service (NaaS) as elements with the NFVI when it is provided as a service
Virtual Network Function as a Service (VNFaaS)	Application of virtualization to the enterprise to enable a lower-cost model in which the operator provides services and the enterprise consumes the resources it requires
Virtual Network Platform as a Service (VNPaaS)	Similar to VNFaaS, but in this use case the enterprise has the opportunity to host and introduce VNF instances on their own
VNF Forwarding Graphs	Building end-to-end services by composition
Service-Oriented Use Cases	
Virtualization of Mobile Core Network and IMS	Encompasses virtualization of the mobile packet core and IMS
Virtualization of the Mobile Base Station	Encompasses virtualization of the mobile RAN onto standard servers
Virtualization of the Home Environment	Encompasses virtualization of CPE, such as set-top boxes residential gateways
Virtualization of CDNs (vCDN)	Encompasses virtualization of content delivery networks (CDNs) to enable a more scalable and lower cost off-peak operational model
Fixed Access NFV	Encompasses virtualization of fixed network access infrastructure to optimize deployment costs and enable co-location with wireless access nodes

Architectural Use Cases

The four architectural use cases focus on providing general-purpose services and applications based on the NFVI architecture.

NFVI as a Service

NFVIaaS is a scenario in which a service provider implements and deploys an NFVI that may be used to support VNFs both by the NFVIaaS provider and by other network service providers. For the NFVIaaS provider, this service provides for economies of scale. The infrastructure is sized to support the provider's own needs for deploying VNFs and extra capacity that can be sold to other providers. The NFVIaaS customer can offer services using the NFVI of another service provider. The NFVIaaS customer has flexibility in rapidly deploying VNFs, either for new services or to scale out existing services. Cloud computing providers may find this service particularly attractive.

Figure 8.9 provides an example [ONF14]. Service provider X offers a virtualized load balancing service. Some of carrier X's customers need load balancing services at locations where X does not maintain NFVI, but where service provider Z does. NFVIaaS offers a means for carrier Z to lease NFV infrastructure (computer, network, hypervisors, and so on) to service provider X, which gives the latter access to infrastructure that would otherwise be prohibitively expensive to obtain. Through leasing, such capacity is available on demand, and can be scaled as needed.

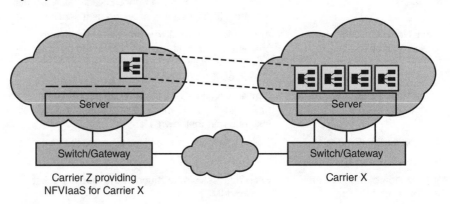

FIGURE 8.9   NFVIaaS Example

VNF as a Service

Whereas NFVIaaS is similar to the cloud model of Infrastructure as a Service (IaaS), VNFaaS corresponds to the cloud model of Software as a Service (SaaS). NFVIaaS provides the virtualization infrastructure to enable a network service provider to develop and deploy VNFs with reduced cost and time compared to implementing the NFVI and the VNFs. With VNFaaS, a provider develops VNFs that are then available off the shelf to customers. This model is well suited to virtualizing customer premises equipment such as routers and firewalls.

Virtual Network Platform as a Service

VNPaaS is similar to an NFVIaaS that includes VNFs as components of the virtual network infrastructure. The primary differences are the programmability and development tools of the VNPaaS that allow the subscriber to create and configure custom ETSI NFV-compliant VNFs to augment the catalog of VNFs offered by the service provider. This allows all the third-party and custom VNFs to be orchestrated via the VNF FG.

VNF Forwarding Graphs

VNF FG allows virtual appliances to be chained together in a flexible manner. This technique is called **service chaining**. For example, a flow may pass through a network monitoring VNF, a load-balancing VNF, and finally a firewall VNF in passing from one endpoint to another. The VNF FG use case is based on an information model that describes the VNFs and physical entities to the appropriate management/orchestration systems used by the service provider. The model describes the characteristics of the entities including the NFV infrastructure requirements of each VNF and all the required connections among VNFs and between VNFs and the physical network included in the IaaS service. To ensure the required performance and resiliency of the end-to-end service, the information model must be able to specify the capacity, performance and resiliency requirements of each VNF in the graph. To meet SLAs, the management and orchestration system will need to monitor the nodes and linkages included in the service graph. In theory, a VNF FG can span the facilities of multiple network service providers.

Service-Oriented Use Cases

These use cases focus on the provision of services to end customers, in which the underlying infrastructure is transparent.

Virtualization of Mobile Core Network and IP Multimedia Subsystem

Mobile cellular networks have evolved to contain a variety of interconnected network function elements, typically involving a large variety of proprietary hardware appliances. NFV aims at reducing the network complexity and related operational issues by leveraging standard IT virtualization technologies to consolidate different types of network equipment onto industry standard high-volume servers, switches, and storage, located in NFVI-PoPs.

Virtualization of Mobile Base Station

The focus of this use case is radio access network (RAN) equipment in mobile networks. RAN is the part of a telecommunications system that implements a wireless technology to access the core network of the mobile network service provider. At minimum, it involves hardware on the customer premises or in the mobile device and equipment forming a base station for access to the mobile network. There is the possibility that a number of RAN functions can be virtualized as VNFs running on industry standard infrastructure.

Virtualization of the Home Environment

This use case deals with network provider equipment located as customer premises equipment (CPE) in a residential location. These CPE devices mark the operator/service provider presence at the customer premises and usually include a residential gateway (RGW) for Internet and Voice over IP (VoIP) services (for example, a modem/router for digital subscriber line [DSL] or cable), and a set-top box (STB) for media services normally supporting local storage for personal video recording (PVR) services. NFV technologies become ideal candidates to support this concentration of computation workload from formerly dispersed functions with minimal cost and improved time to market, while new services can be introduced as required on a grow-as-you-need basis. Further, the VNFs can reside on services in the network service provider's PoP. This greatly simplifies the electronics environment of the home, reducing end user and operator capital expenditure (CapEx).

Virtualization of CDNs

Delivery of content, especially of video, is one of the major challenges of all operator networks because of the massive growing amount of traffic to be delivered to end customers of the network. The growth of video traffic is driven by the shift from broadcast to unicast delivery via IP, by the variety of devices used for video consumption and by increasing quality of video delivered via IP networks in resolution and frame rate.

Complementary to the growth of today's video traffic, the requirements on quality are also evolving: Internet actors are more and more in position to provide both live and on-demand content services to Internet end users, with similar quality constraints as for traditional TV service of network operators.

Some Internet service providers (ISPs) are deploying proprietary Content Delivery Network (CDN) cache nodes in their networks to improve delivery of video and other high-bandwidth services to their customers. Cache nodes typically run on dedicated appliances running on custom or industry standard server platforms. Both CDN cache nodes and CDN control nodes can potentially be virtualized. The benefits of CDN virtualization are similar to those gained in other NFV use cases, such as VNFaaS.

Fixed Access Network Functions Virtualization

NFV offers the potential to virtualize remote functions in the hybrid fiber/copper access network and passive optical network (PON) fiber to the home and hybrid fiber/wireless access networks. This use case has the potential for cost savings by moving complex processing closer to the network. An additional benefit is that virtualization supports multiple tenancy, in which more than one organizational entity can either be allocated, or given direct control of, a dedicated partition of a virtual access node. Finally, virtualizing broadband access nodes can enable synergies to be exploited by the co-location of wireless access nodes in a common NFV platform framework (that is, common NFVI-PoPs), thereby improving the deployment economics and reducing the overall energy consumption of the combined solution.

An indication of the relative importance of the various use cases is found in a survey of 176 network professionals from a range of industries, reported in *2015 Guide to SDN and NFV* [METZ14] and conducted in late 2014. The survey respondents were asked to indicate the two use cases that they think will gain the most traction in the market over the next two years. Table 8.5 shows their responses. The data in Table 8.5 indicates that although IT organizations have interest in a number of the ETSI-defined use cases, by a wide margin they are most interested in the NFVIaaS use case.

TABLE 8.5 Interest in ETSI NFV Use Cases

Use Case	Percentage of Respondents
Network Functions Virtualization Infrastructure as a Service	51 percent
Virtual Network Function as a Service (VNFaaS)	37 percent
Virtualization of Mobile Core Networks and IMS	32 percent
Virtual Network Platform as a Service (VNPaaS)	22 percent
Fixed Access Network Functions Virtualization	13 percent
Virtualization of CDNs (vCDN)	12 percent
Virtualization of Mobile base station	11 percent
Virtualization of the Home Environment	4 percent
VNF Forwarding Graphs	1 percent

8.5 SDN and NFV

Over the past few years, the hottest topics in networking have been SDN and NFV. Separate standards bodies are pursuing the two technologies, and a large, growing number of providers have announced or are working on products in the two fields. Each technology can be implemented and deployed separately, but there is clearly a potential for added value by the coordinated use of both technologies. It is likely that over time, SDN and NFV will tightly interoperate to provide a broad, unified software-based networking approach to abstract and programmatically control network equipment and network-based resources.

The relationship between SDN and NFV is perhaps viewed as SDN functioning as an enabler of NFV. A major challenge with NFV is to best enable the user to configure a network so that VNFs running on servers are connected to the network at the appropriate place, with the appropriate connectivity to other VNFs, and with desired QoS. With SDN, users and orchestration software can dynamically configure the network and the distribution and connectivity of VNFs. Without SDN, NFV requires much more manual intervention, especially when resources beyond the scope of NFVI are part of the environment.

The *Kemp Technologies Blog* [MCMU14] gives the example of load balancing where load balancer services are implemented as VNF entities. If demand for load-balancing capacity increases, a network orchestration layer can rapidly spin up new load-balancing instances and also adjust the network switching infrastructure to accommodate the changed traffic patterns. In turn, the load-balancing VNF entity can interact with the SDN controller to assess network performance and capacity and use this additional information to balance traffic better, or even to request provisioning of additional VNF resources.

Some of the ways that ETSI believes that NFV and SDN complement each other include the following:

- The SDN controller fits well into the broader concept of a network controller in an NFVI network domain.

- SDN can play a significant role in the orchestration of the NFVI resources, both physical and virtual, enabling functionality such as provisioning, configuration of network connectivity, bandwidth allocation, automation of operations, monitoring, security, and policy control.

- SDN can provide the network virtualization required to support multitenant NFVIs.

- Forwarding graphs can be implemented using the SDN controller to provide automated provisioning of service chains, while ensuring strong and consistent implementation of security and other policies.

- The SDN controller can be run as a VNF, possibly as part of a service chain including other VNFs. For example, applications and services originally developed to run on the SDN controller could also be implemented as separate VNFs.

Figure 8.10, from the ETSI VNF Architecture document, indicates the potential relationship between SDN and NFV. The arrows can be described as follows:

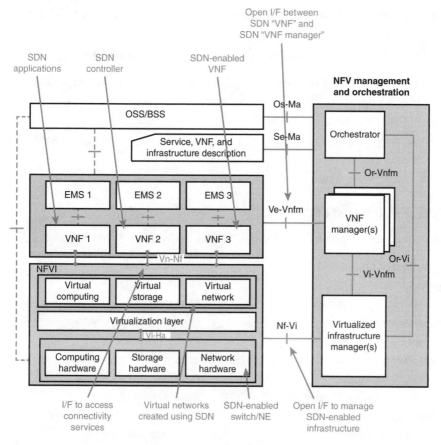

FIGURE 8.10   Mapping of SDN Components with NFV Architecture

- SDN enabled switch/NEs include physical switches, hypervisor virtual switches, and embedded switches on the NICs.

- Virtual networks created using an infrastructure network SDN controller provide connectivity services between VNFC instances.

- SDN controller can be virtualized, running as a VNF with its EM and VNF manager. Note that there may be SDN controllers for the physical infrastructure, the virtual infrastructure, and the virtual and physical network functions. As such, some of these SDN controllers may reside in the NFVI or management and orchestration (MANO) functional blocks (not shown in figure).

- SDN enabled VNF includes any VNF that may be under the control of an SDN controller (for example, virtual router, virtual firewall).

- SDN applications, for example service chaining applications, can be VNF themselves.

- Nf-Vi interface allows management of the SDN enabled infrastructure.

- Ve-Vnfm interface is used between the SDN VNF (SDN controller VNF, SDN network functions VNF, SDN applications VNF) and their respective VNF Manager for lifecycle management.

- Vn-Nf allows SDN VNFs to access connectivity services between VNFC interfaces.

8.6 Key Terms

After completing this chapter, you should be able to define the following terms.

compute domain	NFV infrastructure (NFVI)
compute node	NFV orchestrator
container	NFVI domain
container interface	operations support system
content delivery network (CDN)	reference points
deep packet inspection	scale out
element management	scale up
element management system (EMS)	service chaining
forwarding graph (FG)	storage node
functional block interface	virtual network
gateway node	virtual overlay
hypervisor	virtual partition
hypervisor domain	virtualized infrastructure manager
infrastructure network domain (IND)	virtualization
L3 virtual network	virtualization container
layered virtual network	virtualized network function (VNF)
network interface card	VNF manager
network node	vswitch
NFV management and orchestration (MANO)	

8.7 References

KHAN15: Khan, F. *A Beginner's Guide to NFV Management & Orchestration (MANO)*. Telecom Lighthouse. April 9, 2015. http://www.telecomlighthouse. com.

MCMU14: McMullin, M. "SDN is from Mars, NFV is from Venus." *Kemp Technologies Blog*, November 20, 2014. http://kemptechnologies.com/blog/ sdn-mars-nfv-venus.

METZ14a: Metzler, J. *The 2015 Guide to SDN and NFV*. Webtorials, December 2014.

ONF14: Open Networking Foundation. *OpenFlow-Enabled SDN and Network Functions Virtualization*. ONF white paper, February 17, 2014.

Network Virtualization

In recent years a strong and significant partnership has grown up between computers and communication systems. On the one hand, computers are being used to effect far-reaching improvements in communication systems, while on the other, communication systems are being used to increase and extend the utility of computers.

—What Can Be Automated?
The Computer Science and Engineering Research Study, National Science Foundation, 1980

Chapter Objectives

After studying this chapter, you should be able to

- Understand the concept of a virtual LAN and the three ways of defining a VLAN.
- Present an overview of the IEEE 802.1Q standards.
- Explain how OpenFlow supports VLANs.
- Understand the concept of a virtual private network.
- Define network virtualization.
- Understand the operation of OpenDaylight's Virtual Tenant Network.
- Summarize the concepts of software-defined infrastructure.
- Discuss software-defined storage.

Mechanisms for defining virtual networks have been in use for many years. Virtual networks have two important benefits:

- They enable the user to construct and manage networks independent of the underlying physical network and with assurance of isolation from other virtual networks using the same physical network.
- They enable network providers to efficiently use network resources to support a wide range of user requirements.

The chapter begins with a discussion of two well-established and widely used virtual network techniques: virtual LANs (VLANs) and virtual private networks (VPNs). The chapter then introduces the more general and broader concept of network virtualization. After exploring a simple example, you will learn about the network virtualization architecture and the benefits of this approach. The chapter also looks at OpenDaylight's Virtual Tenant Network, which is a VLAN-based capability, but which exhibits many of the features of network virtualization. Finally, the chapter introduces the concept of software-defined infrastructure, which encompasses many of the concepts of software-defined network (SDN), network functions virtualization (NFV), and network virtualization.

9.1 Virtual LANs

Figure 9.1 shows a relatively common type of hierarchical LAN configuration. In this example, the devices on the LAN are organized into four segments, each served by a LAN switch. The **LAN switch** is a store-and-forward packet-forwarding device used to interconnect a number of end systems to form a LAN segment. The switch can forward a **media access control (MAC) frame** from a source-attached device to a destination-attached device. It can also broadcast a frame from a source-attached device to all other attached devices. Multiples switches can be interconnected so that multiple LAN segments form a larger LAN. A LAN switch can also connect to a transmission link or a router or other network device to provide connectivity to the Internet or other WANs.

Traditionally, a LAN switch operated exclusively at the MAC level. Contemporary LAN switches generally provide greater functionality, including multilayer awareness (Layers 3, 4, application), quality of service (QoS) support, and trunking for wide-area networking.

The three lower groups in Figure 9.1 might correspond to different departments, which are physically separated, and the upper group could correspond to a centralized server farm that is used by all the departments.

Consider the transmission of a single MAC frame from workstation X. Suppose the destination MAC address in the frame is workstation Y. This frame is transmitted from X to the local switch, which then directs the frame along the link to Y. If X transmits a frame addressed to Z or W, its local switch forwards the MAC frame through the appropriate switches to the intended destination. All these are examples of **unicast addressing**, in which the destination address in the MAC frame designates a unique destination. A MAC frame may also contain a **broadcast address**, in which case the destination MAC address indicates that all devices on the LAN should receive a copy of the frame. Thus, if X transmits a frame with a broadcast destination address, all the devices on all the switches in Figure 9.1 receive a copy of the frame. The total collection of devices that receive broadcast frames from each other is referred to as a **broadcast domain**.

LAN switch

A packet-forwarding network device for (1) interconnecting end systems in a local area to form a local-area network (LAN) segment, (2) connecting with other LAN switches to for a larger LAN, and (3) providing connection to routers and other network devices for wide-area network (WAN) connectivity.

media access control (MAC) frame

A group of bits that includes source and destination addresses and other protocol control information plus, optionally, data. It is the basic unit of transmission on Ethernet and Wi-Fi LANs.

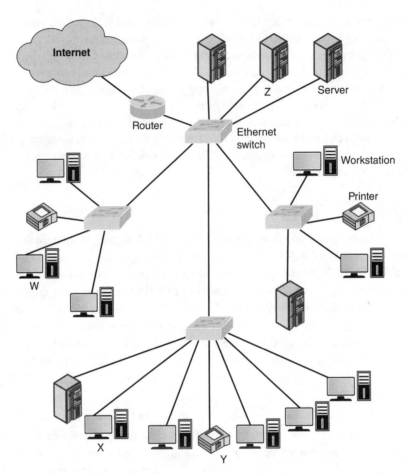

FIGURE 9.1   A LAN Configuration

In many situations, a broadcast frame is used for a purpose, such as network management or the transmission of some type of alert, with a relatively local significance. Thus, in Figure 9.1, if a broadcast frame has information that is useful only to a particular department, transmission capacity is wasted on the other portions of the LAN and on the other switches.

One simple approach to improving efficiency is to physically partition the LAN into separate broadcast domains, as shown in Figure 9.2. We now have four separate LANs connected by a router. In this case, a broadcast frame from X is transmitted only to the other devices directly connected to the same switch as X. An IP packet from X intended for Z is handled as follows. The IP layer at X determines that the next hop to the destination is via router V. This information is handed down to X's MAC layer, which prepares a MAC frame with a destination MAC address of router V. When V receives the frame, it strips off the MAC header, determines the destination, and

encapsulates the IP packet in a MAC frame with a destination MAC address of Z. This
frame is then sent to the appropriate Ethernet switch for delivery.

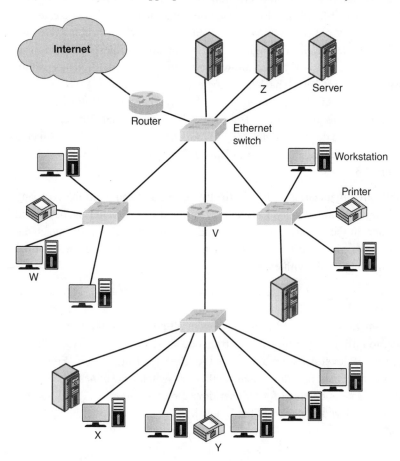

FIGURE 9.2   A Partitioned LAN

The drawback to this approach is that the traffic pattern may not correspond to the
physical distribution of devices. For example, some departmental workstations may
generate a lot of traffic with one of the central servers. Further, as the networks
expand, more routers are needed to separate users into broadcast domains and provide
connectivity among broadcast domains. Routers introduce more latency than switches
because the router must process more of the packet to determine destinations and
route the data to the appropriate end node.

The Use of Virtual LANs

virtual local-area network (VLAN)

A virtual network abstraction on top of a physical packet-switched network. A VLAN is essentially a broadcast domain for a specified set of switches. These switches are required to be aware of the existence of VLANs and configured accordingly, to perform switching of packets between devices belonging to the same VLAN.

A more effective alternative is the creation of VLANs. In essence, a **virtual local-area network (VLAN)** is a logical subgroup within a LAN that is created by software rather than by physically moving and separating devices. It combines user stations and network devices into a single broadcast domain regardless of the physical LAN segment they are attached to and allows traffic to flow more efficiently within populations of mutual interest. The VLAN logic is implemented in LAN switches and functions at the MAC layer. Because the objective is to isolate traffic within the VLAN, a router is required to link from one VLAN to another. Routers can be implemented as separate devices, so that traffic from one VLAN to another is directed to a router, or the router logic can be implemented as part of the LAN switch, as shown in Figure 9.3.

VLANs enable any organization to be physically dispersed throughout the company while maintaining its group identity. For example, accounting personnel can be located on the shop floor, in the research and development center, in the cash disbursement office, and in the corporate offices, while all members reside on the same virtual network, sharing traffic only with each other.

Figure 9.3 shows five defined VLANs. A transmission from workstation X to server Z is within the same VLAN, so it is efficiently switched at the MAC level. A broadcast MAC frame from X is transmitted to all devices in all portions of the same VLAN. But a transmission from X to printer Y goes from one VLAN to another. Accordingly, router logic at the IP level is required to move the IP packet from X to Y. Figure 9.3 shows that logic integrated into the switch, so that the switch determines whether the incoming MAC frame is destined for another device on the same VLAN. If not, the switch routes the enclosed IP packet at the IP level.

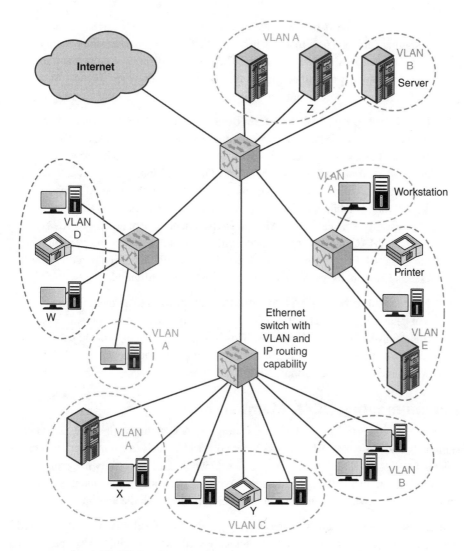

FIGURE 9.3 A VLAN Configuration

Defining VLANs

A VLAN is a broadcast domain consisting of a group of end stations, perhaps on multiple physical LAN segments, that are not constrained by their physical location and can communicate as if they were on a common LAN. Some means is therefore needed for defining VLAN membership. A number of different approaches have been used for defining membership, including the following:

- **Membership by port group**: Each switch in the LAN configuration contains two types of ports: a trunk port, which connects two switches; and an end port, which connects the switch to an end system. A VLAN can be defined by assigning each end port to a specific VLAN. This approach has the advantage that it is relatively easy to configure. The principle disadvantage is that the network manager must reconfigure VLAN membership when an end system moves from one port to another.

- **Membership by MAC address**: Because MAC layer addresses are hard-wired into the workstation's network interface card (NIC), VLANs based on MAC addresses enable network managers to move a workstation to a different physical location on the network and have that workstation automatically retain its VLAN membership. The main problem with this method is that VLAN membership must be assigned initially. In networks with thousands of users, this is no easy task. Also, in environments where notebook PCs are used, the MAC address is associated with the docking station and not with the notebook PC. Consequently, when a notebook PC is moved to a different docking station, its VLAN membership must be reconfigured.

- **Membership based on protocol information**: VLAN membership can be assigned based on IP address, transport protocol information, or even higher-layer protocol information. This is a quite flexible approach, but it does require switches to examine portions of the MAC frame above the MAC layer, which may have a performance impact.

Communicating VLAN Membership

Switches must have a way of understanding VLAN membership (that is, which stations belong to which VLAN) when network traffic arrives from other switches; otherwise, VLANs would be limited to a single switch. One possibility is to configure the information manually or with some type of network management signaling protocol, so that switches can associate incoming frames with the appropriate VLAN.

A more common approach is frame tagging, in which a header is typically inserted into each frame on interswitch trunks to uniquely identify to which VLAN a particular MAC-layer frame belongs. The **IEEE 802** committee has developed a standard for frame tagging, **IEEE 802.1Q**, which we examine next.

IEEE 802.1Q VLAN Standard

The IEEE 802.1Q standard, last updated in 2014, defines the operation of VLAN bridges and switches that permits the definition, operation, and administration of VLAN topologies within a bridged/switched LAN infrastructure. In this section, we concentrate on the application of this standard to **802.3** LANs.

Recall that a VLAN is an administratively configured broadcast domain, consisting of a subset of end stations attached to a LAN. A VLAN is not limited to one switch but can span multiple interconnected switches. In that case, traffic between switches must indicate VLAN membership. This is accomplished in 802.1Q by inserting a tag with a VLAN identifier (VID) with a value in the range from 1 to 4094. Each VLAN in a LAN configuration is assigned a globally unique VID. By assigning the same VID to end systems on many switches, one or more VLAN broadcast domains can be extended across a large network.

Figure 9.4 shows the position and content of the 802.1 tag, referred to as Tag Control Information (TCI). The presence of the two-octet TCI field is indicated by inserting a Length/Type field in the 802.3 MAC frame with a value of 8100 hex. The TCI consists of three subfields, as described in the list that follows.

IEEE 802

A committee of the Institute of Electrical and Electronics Engineers (IEEE) responsible for developing standards for local and metropolitan area networks (LANs).

IEEE 802.1

An IEEE 802 working group responsible for developing standards in the following areas: 802 LAN/MAN architecture, internetworking among 802 LANs, MANs and other WANs, 802 security, 802 overall network management.

IEEE 802.3

An IEEE 802 working group responsible for developing standards for Ethernet local-area networks (LANs).

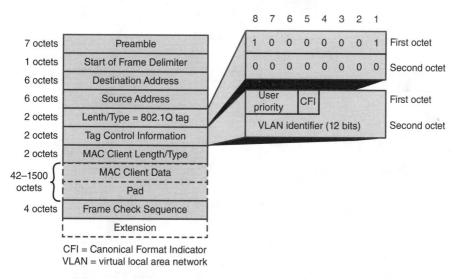

CFI = Canonical Format Indicator
VLAN = virtual local area network

FIGURE 9.4   Tagged IEEE 802.3 MAC Frame Format

- **User priority (3 bits):** The priority level for this frame.
- **Canonical format indicator (1 bit):** Is always set to 0 for Ethernet switches. CFI is used for compatibility between Ethernet type networks and Token Ring type networks. If a frame received at an Ethernet port has a CFI set to 1, that frame should not be forwarded as it is to an untagged port.

■ **VLAN identifier (12 bits):** The identification of the VLAN. Of the 4096 possible VIDs, a VID of 0 is used to identify that the TCI contains only a priority
value, and 4095 (0xFFF) is reserved, so the maximum possible number of
VLAN configurations is 4094.

Figure 9.5 illustrates a LAN configuration that includes three switches that implement
802.1Q and one "legacy" switch that does not. In this case, all the end systems of the
legacy device must belong to the same VLAN. The MAC frames that traverse trunks
between VLAN-aware switches include the 802.1Q TCI tag. This tag is stripped off
before a frame is forwarded to a legacy switch. For end systems connected to a VLAN-
aware switch, the MAC frame may or may not include the TCI tag, depending on the
implementation. The important point is that the TCI tag is used between VLAN-aware
switches so that appropriate routing and frame handling can be performed.

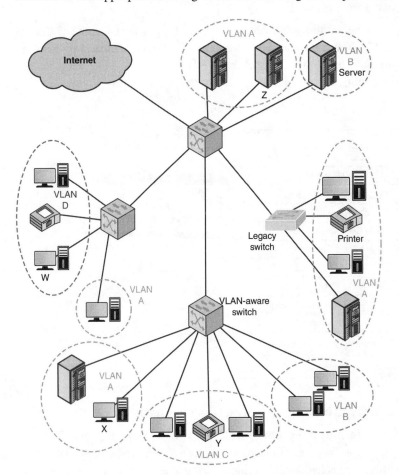

FIGURE 9.5   A VLAN Configuration with 802.1Q and Legacy Switches

Nested VLANs

The original 802.1Q specification allowed for a single VLAN tag field to be inserted into an Ethernet MAC frame. More recent versions of the standard allow for the insertion of two VLAN tag fields, allowing the definition of multiple sub-VLANs within a single VLAN. This additional flexibility might be useful in some complex configurations.

For example, a single VLAN level suffices for an Ethernet configuration entirely on a single premises. However, it is not uncommon for an enterprise to make use of a network service provider to interconnect multiple LAN locations, and to use metropolitan area Ethernet links to connect to the provider. Multiple customers of the service provider may wish to use the 802.1Q tagging facility across the service provider network (SPN).

One possible approach is for the customer's VLANs to be visible to the service provider. In that case, the service provider could support a total of only 4094 VLANs for all its customers. Instead, the service provider inserts a second VLAN tag into Ethernet frames. For example, consider two customers with multiple sites, both of which use the same SPN (see part a of Figure 9.6). Customer A has configured VLANs 1 to 100 at their sites, and similarly Customer B has configured VLANs 1 to 50 at their sites. The tagged data frames belonging to the customers must be kept separate while they traverse the service provider's network. The customer's data frame can be identified and kept separate by associating another VLAN for that customer's traffic. This results in the tagged customer data frame being tagged again with a VLAN tag, when it traverses the SPN (see part b of Figure 9.6). The additional tag is removed at the edge of the SPN when the data enters the customer's network again. Packed VLAN tagging is known as VLAN stacking or as Q-in-Q.

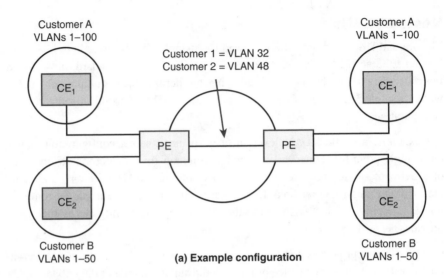

(a) Example configuration

Original Ethernet Frame

Preamble/SFD	Destination MAC address	Source MAC address	T/L	Data/Pad	FCS

Single 802.1Q tag

Preamble/SFD	Destination MAC address	Source MAC address	VLAN tag	T/L	Data/Pad	FCS

Two Q-in-Q tags

Preamble/SFD	Destination MAC address	Source MAC address	VLAN tag	VLAN tag	T/L	Data/Pad	FCS

(b) Position of tags in Ethernet frame

FIGURE 9.6   Use of Stacked VLAN Tags

9.2 OpenFlow VLAN Support

A traditional 802.1Q VLAN requires that the network switches have a complete knowledge of the VLAN mapping. This knowledge may be manually configured or acquired automatically. Another drawback is related to the choice of one of three ways of defining group membership (port group, MAC address, protocol information). The network administrator must evaluate the trade-offs according to the type of network they wish to deploy and choose one of the possible approaches. It would be difficult to deploy a more flexible definition of a VLAN or even a custom definition (for example, use a combination of IP addresses and ports) with traditional networking devices. Reconfiguring VLANs is also a daunting task for administrators: Multiple switches and routers have to be reconfigured whenever VMs are relocated.

SDN, and in particular OpenFlow, allows for much more flexible management and control of VLANs. It should be clear how OpenFlow can set up flow table entries for forwarding based on one or both VLAN tags, and how tags can be added, modified, and removed.

9.3 Virtual Private Networks

In today's distributed computing environment, the **virtual private network (VPN)** offers an attractive solution to network managers. A VPN is a private network that is configured within a public network (a carrier's network or the Internet) to take advantage of the economies of scale and management facilities of large networks. VPNs are widely used by enterprises to create WANs that span large geographic areas, to provide site-to-site connections to branch offices, and to allow mobile users to dial up their company LANs. From the point of view of the provider, the public network facility is shared by many customers, with the traffic of each customer segregated from other traffic. Traffic designated as VPN traffic can only go from a VPN source to a destination in the same VPN. It is often the case that encryption and authentication facilities are provided for the VPN.

A typical scenario for an enterprise that uses VPNs is the following. At each corporate site, one or more LANs link workstations, servers, and databases. The LANs are under the control of the enterprise and can be configured and tuned for cost-effective performance. VPNs over the Internet or some other public network can be used to interconnect sites, providing a cost savings over the use of a private network and offloading the WAN management task to the public network provider. That same public network provides an access path for telecommuters and other mobile employees to log on to corporate systems from remote sites.

The subject of VPNs is extraordinarily complex and this section can only provide a concise overview of the two most common technologies for creating VPNs: **IP security (IPsec)** and Multiprotocol Label Switching (MPLS).

IPsec VPNs

Use of a shared network, such as the Internet or a public carrier network, as part of an enterprise network architecture exposes corporate traffic to eavesdropping and provides an entry point for unauthorized users. To counter this problem, IPsec can be used to construct VPNs. The principal feature of IPsec that enables it to support these varied applications is that it can encrypt/authenticate traffic at the IP level. Therefore, all distributed applications, including remote logon, client/server, e-mail, file transfer, web access, and so on, can be secured.

Part a of Figure 9.7 shows the packet format for an IPsec option known as tunnel mode. Tunnel mode makes use of the combined authentication/encryption function

IP security (IPsec)

Suite of protocols for securing IP communications at the network layer by authenticating/ encrypting each IP packet in a data stream. IPsec also includes protocols for cryptographic key management.

IPsec called Encapsulating Security Payload (ESP), and a key exchange function. For VPNs, both authentication and encryption are generally desired, because it is important both to (1) ensure that unauthorized users do not penetrate the VPN, and (2) ensure that eavesdroppers on the Internet cannot read messages sent over the VPN.

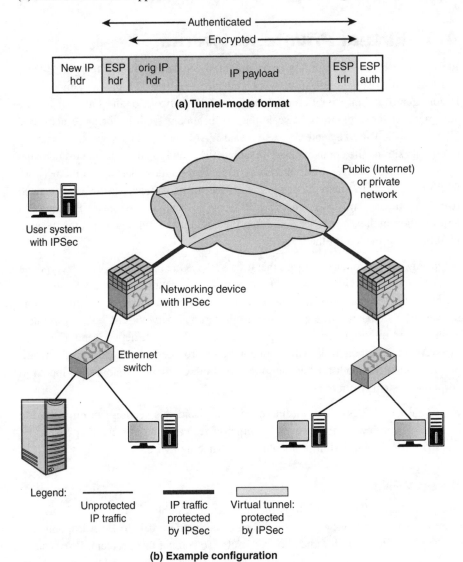

(a) Tunnel-mode format

(b) Example configuration

FIGURE 9.7   An IPsec VPN Scenario

Part b of Figure 9.7 is a typical scenario of IPsec usage. An organization maintains LANs at dispersed locations. Nonsecure IP traffic is conducted on each LAN. For traffic offsite, through some sort of private or public WAN, IPsec protocols are used.

These protocols operate in networking devices, such as a router or firewall, that connect each LAN to the outside world. The IPsec networking device will typically encrypt all traffic going into the WAN, and decrypt and authenticate traffic coming from the WAN; these operations are transparent to workstations and servers on the LAN. Secure transmission is also possible with individual users who connect to the WAN. Such user workstations must implement the IPsec protocols to provide security.

Using IPsec to construct a VPN has the following benefits:

- When IPsec is implemented in a firewall or router, it provides strong security that can be applied to all traffic crossing the perimeter. Traffic within a company or workgroup does not incur the overhead of security-related processing.

- IPsec in a firewall is resistant to bypass if all traffic from the outside must use IP and the firewall is the only means of entrance from the Internet into the organization.

- IPsec is below the transport layer (TCP, UDP) and so is transparent to applications. There is no need to change software on a user or server system when IPsec is implemented in the firewall or router. Even if IPsec is implemented in end systems, upper-layer software, including applications, is not affected.

- IPsec can be transparent to end users. There is no need to train users on security mechanisms, issue keying material on a per-user basis, or revoke keying material when users leave the organization.

- IPsec can provide security for individual users if needed. This is useful for offsite workers and for setting up a secure virtual subnetwork within an organization for sensitive applications.

MPLS VPNs

An alternative, and popular, means of constructing VPNs is using MPLS. This discussion begins with a brief summary of MPLS, followed by a an overview of two of the most common approaches to VPN implementation using MPLS: the Layer 2 VPN (L2VPN) and the Layer 3 VPN (L3VPN).

MPLS Overview

Multiprotocol Label Switching (MPLS) is a set of Internet Engineering Task Force (IETF) specifications for including routing and traffic engineering information in packets. MPLS comprises a number of interrelated protocols, which can be referred to as the MPLS protocol suite. It can be used in IP networks but also in other types of packet-switching networks. MPLS is used to ensure that all packets in a particular flow take the same route over a backbone. Deployed by many telecommunication companies and service providers, MPLS delivers the QoS required to support real-time voice and video as well as service level agreements (SLAs) that guarantee bandwidth.

In essence, MPLS is an efficient technique for forwarding and routing packets. MPLS was designed with IP networks in mind, but the technology can be used without IP to construct a network with any link-level protocol. In an ordinary packet-switching network, packet switches must examine various fields within the packet header to determine destination, route, QoS, and any traffic management functions (such as discard or delay) that may be supported. Similarly, in an IP-based network, routers examine a number of fields in the IP header to determine these functions. In an MPLS network, a fixed-length label encapsulates an IP packet or a data link frame. The MPLS label contains all the information needed by an MPLS-enabled router to perform routing, delivery, QoS, and traffic management functions. Unlike IP, MPLS is connection oriented.

An MPLS network or internet consists of a set of nodes, called **label-switching routers (LSRs)** capable of switching and routing packets on the basis of a label appended to each packet. Labels define a flow of packets between two endpoints or, in the case of multicast, between a source endpoint and a multicast group of destination endpoints. For each distinct flow, called a **forwarding equivalence class (FEC)**, a specific path through the network of LSRs is defined, called a **label-switched path (LSP)**. In essence, an FEC represents a group of packets that share the same transport requirements. All packets in an FEC receive the same treatment en route to the destination. These packets follow the same path and receive the same QoS treatment at each hop. In contrast to forwarding in ordinary IP networks, the assignment of a particular packet to a particular FEC is done just once, when the packet enters the network of MPLS routers.

The list that follows, based on RFC 4026, *Provider Provisioned Virtual Private Network Terminology*, defines key VPN terms used in the following discussion:

- **Attachment circuit (AC):** In a Layer 2 VPN, the CE is attached to PE via an AC. The AC may be a physical or logical link.
- **Customer edge (CE):** A device or set of devices on the customer premises that attaches to a provider-provisioned VPN.
- **Layer 2 VPN (L2VPN):** An L2VPN interconnects sets of hosts and routers based on Layer 2 addresses.
- **Layer 3 VPN (L3VPN):** An L3VPN interconnects sets of hosts and routers based on Layer 3 addresses.
- **Packet-switched network (PSN):** A network through which the tunnels supporting the VPN services are set up.
- **Provider edge (PE):** A device or set of devices at the edge of the provider network with the functionality that is needed to interface with the customer.

- **Tunnel:** Connectivity through a PSN that is used to send traffic across the network from one PE to another. The tunnel provides a means to transport packets from one PE to another. Separation of one customer's traffic from another customer's traffic is done based on tunnel multiplexers

- **Tunnel multiplexer:** An entity that is sent with the packets traversing the tunnel to make it possible to decide which instance of a service a packet belongs to and from which sender it was received. In an MPLS network, the tunnel multiplexor is formatted as an MPLS label.

- **Virtual channel (VC):** A VC is transported within a tunnel and identified by its tunnel multiplexer. In an MPLS-enabled IP network, a VC label is an MPLS label used to identify traffic within a tunnel that belongs to a particular VPN; that is, the VC label is the tunnel multiplexer in networks that use MPLS labels.

- **Virtual private network (VPN):** A generic term that covers the use of public or private networks to create groups of users that are separated from other network users and that may communicate among them as if they were on a private network.

Layer 2 MPLS VPN

With a Layer 2 MPLS VPN, there is mutual transparency between the customer network and the provider network. In effect, the customer requests a mesh of unicast LSPs among customer switches that attach to the provider network. Each LSP is viewed as a Layer 2 circuit by the customer. In an L2VPN, the provider's equipment forwards customer data based on information in the Layer 2 headers, such as an Ethernet MAC address.

Figure 9.8 depicts key elements in an L2VPN. Customers connect to the provider by means of a Layer 2 device, such as an Ethernet switch; the customer device that connects to the MPLS network is generally referred to as a customer edge (CE) device. The MPLS edge router is referred to as a provider edge (PE) device. The link between the CE and the PE operates at the link layer (for example, Ethernet), and is referred to as an attachment circuit (AC). The MPLS network then sets up an LSP that acts as a tunnel between two edge routers (that is, two PEs) that attach to two networks of the same enterprise. This tunnel can carry multiple virtual channels (VCs) using label stacking. In a manner very similar to VLAN stacking, the use of multiple MPLS labels enables the nesting of VCs.

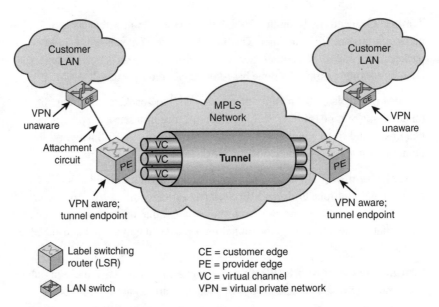

FIGURE 9.8   MPLS Layer 2 VPN Concepts

When a link-layer frame arrives at the PE from the CE, the PE creates an MPLS packet. The PE pushes a label that corresponds to the VC assigned to this frame. Then the PE pushes a second label onto the label stack for this packet that corresponds to the tunnel between the source and destination PE for this VC. The packet is then routed across the LSP associated with this tunnel, using the top label for label switched routing. At the destination edge, the destination PE pops the tunnel label and examines the VC label. This tells the PE how to construct a link-layer frame to deliver the payload across to the destination CE.

If the payload of the MPLS packet is an Ethernet frame, the destination PE needs to be able to infer from the VC label the outgoing interface, and perhaps the VLAN identifier. This process is unidirectional, and will be repeated independently for bidirectional operation.

The VCs in the tunnel can all belong to a single enterprise, or it is possible for a single tunnel to manage VCs from multiple enterprises. In any case, from the point of view of the customer, a VC is a dedicated link-layer point-to-point channel. If multiple VCs connect a PE to a CE, this is logically the multiplexing of multiple link-layer channels between the customer and the provider.

Layer 3 MPLS VPN

Whereas L2VPNs are constructed based on link-level addresses (for example, MAC addresses), L3VPNs are based on VPN routes between CEs based on IP addresses.

As with an L2VPN, an MPLS-based L3VPN typically uses a stack of two labels. The inner label identifies a specific VPN instance; the outer label identifies a tunnel or route through the MPLS provider network. The tunnel label is associated with an LSP and is used for label swapping and forwarding. At the egress PE, the tunnel label is stripped off, and the VPN label is used to direct the packet to the proper CE and to the proper logical flow at that CE.

For an L3VPN, the CE implements IP and is thus a router. The CE routers advertise their networks to the provider. The provider network can then use an enhanced version of Border Gateway Protocol (BGP) to establish VPNs between CEs. Inside the provider network, MPLS tools are used to establish routes between edge PEs supporting a VPN. Thus, the provider's routers participate in the customer's L3 routing function.

9.4   Network Virtualization

This section looks at the important area of network virtualization. One immediate difficulty is that this term is defined differently in a number of academic and industry publications. So we begin by defining some terms, based on definitions in ITU-T Y.3011 (*Framework of Network Virtualization for Future Networks*, January 2012):

- **Physical resource:** In the context of networking, physical resources include the following: network devices, such as routers, switches, and firewalls; and communication links, including wire and wireless. Hosts such as cloud servers may also be considered as physical network resources.

- **Logical resource:** An independently manageable partition of a physical resource, which inherits the same characteristics as the physical resource and whose capability is bound to the capability of the physical resource. An example is a named partition of disk memory.

- **Virtual resource:** An abstraction of a physical or logical resource, which may have different characteristics from the physical or logical resource and whose capability may be not bound to the capability of the physical or logical resource. As examples, virtual machines (VMs) may be moved dynamically, VPN topologies can be altered dynamically, and access control restrictions may be imposed on a resource.

- **Virtual network:** A network composed of multiple virtual resources (that is, a collection of virtual nodes and virtual links) that is logically isolated from other virtual networks. Y.3011 refers to a virtual network as a logically isolated network partition (LINP).

- **Network virtualization (NV):** A technology that enables the creation of logically isolated virtual networks over shared physical networks so that heterogeneous collections of multiple virtual networks can simultaneously coexist over the shared physical networks. This includes the aggregation of multiple resources in a provider and appearing as a single resource.

NV is a far broader concept than VPNs, which only provide traffic isolation, or VLANs, which provide a basic form of topology management. NV implies full administrative control for customizing virtual networks both in terms of the physical resources used and the functionalities provided by the virtual networks.

The virtual network presents an abstracted network view whose virtual resources provide users with services similar to those provided by physical networks. Because the virtual resources are software defined, the manager or administrator of a virtual network potentially has a great deal of flexibility in altering topologies, moving resources, and changing the properties and service of various resources. In addition, virtual network users can include not only users of services or applications but also service providers. For example, a cloud service provider can quickly add new services or expanded coverage by leasing virtual networks as needed.

A Simplified Example

To get some feel for the concepts involved in network virtualization, we begin with a simplified example. Figure 9.9, adapted from the ebook *Software Defined Networking—A Definitive Guide* [KUMA13], shows a network consisting of three servers and five switches. One server is a trusted platform with a secure operating system that hosts firewall software. All the servers run a hypervisor (virtual machine monitor) enabling them to support multiple VMs. The resources for one enterprise (Enterprise 1) are hosted across the servers and consist of three VMs (VM1a, VM1b, and VM1c) on physical server 1, two VMs (VM1d and VM1e) on physical server 2, and firewall 1 on physical server 3. The virtual switches are used to set up any desired connectivity between the VMs across the servers through the physical switches. The physical switches provide the connectivity between the physical servers. Each enterprise network is layered as a separate virtual network on top of the physical network. Thus, the virtual network for Enterprise 1 is indicated in Figure 9.9 by a dashed circle and labeled VN1. The labeled circle VN2 indicates another virtual network.

This example illustrates three layers of abstraction (see Figure 9.10). At the bottom are the physical resources, managed across one or more administrative domains. The servers are logically partitioned to support multiple VMs. This includes, at least, a partitioning of memory, but may also include a partitioning of the pool of I/O and communications ports and even of the processors or cores of the server. There is then an abstraction function that maps these physical and logical resources into virtual resources. This type of abstraction could be enabled by SDN and NFV functionality, and is managed by software at the virtual resource level.

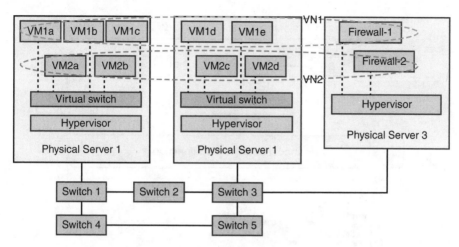

FIGURE 9.9 Simple Network with Virtual Machines Assigned to Different Administrative Groups

Another abstraction function is used to create network views organized as distinct virtual networks. Each virtual network is managed by a separate virtual network management function.

Because resources are defined in software, network virtualization provides a great deal of flexibility, as this example suggests. The manager of virtual network 1 may specify certain QoS requirements for traffic between VMs attached to switch 1 and VMs attached to switch 2, and may specify firewall rules for traffic external to the virtual network. These specification must ultimately be translated into forwarding rules configured on the physical switches and filtering rules on the physical firewall. Because it is all done in software and without the need for the virtual network manager to understand the physical topology and physical suite of servers, changes are easily implemented.

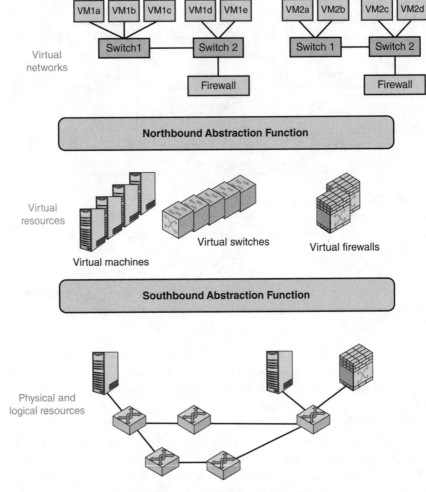

FIGURE 9.10 Levels of Abstraction for Network Virtualization

Network Virtualization Architecture

An excellent overview of the many elements that contribute to an NV environment is provided by the conceptual architecture defined in Y.3011 and shown in Figure 9.11. The architecture depicts NV as consisting of four levels:

- Physical resources
- Virtual resources
- Virtual networks
- Services

A single physical resource can be shared among multiple virtual resources. In turn, each LINP (virtual network) consists of multiple virtual resources and provides a set of services to users.

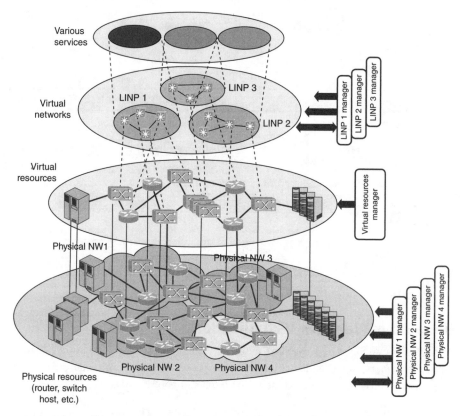

FIGURE 9.11 Conceptual Architecture of Network Virtualization (Y.3011)

Various management and control functions are performed at each level, not necessarily by the same provider. There are management functions associated with each physical network and its associated resources. A virtual resource manager (VRM) manages a pool of virtual resources created from the physical resources. A VRM interacts with physical network managers (PNMs) to obtain resource commitments. The VRM constructs LINPs, and an LINP manager is allocated to each LINP.

Figure 9.12 provides another view of the NV architectural elements. Physical resource management manages physical resources and may create multiple logical resources that have the same characteristics as physical resources. Physical and logical resources are available to the virtual resource management at the interface between physical and virtual layers. The virtual resource management abstracts from the physical and logical resources to create virtual resources. It can also construct a virtual resource that combines other virtual resources. Virtual network management can build VNs on multiple virtual resources that are provided by the virtual resource management. Once a VN is created, the VN management starts to manage its own VN.

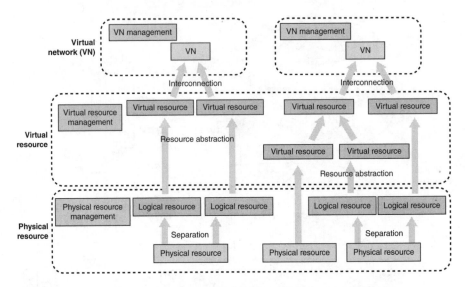

FIGURE 9.12   Network Virtualization Resource Hierarchical Model

Benefits of Network Virtualization

A 2014 survey [SDNC14] by SDxCentral of 220 organizations, including network service providers, small and medium-size businesses (SMB), large enterprises, and cloud service providers, reported the following benefits of NV (see Figure 9.13):

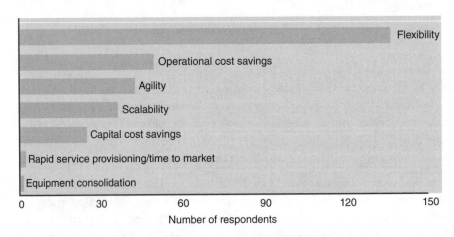

FIGURE 9.13   Reported Benefits of Network Virtualization

- **Flexibility:** NV enables the network to be quickly moved, provisioned, and scaled to meet the ever-changing needs of virtualized compute and storage infrastructures.

- **Operational cost savings:** Virtualization of the infrastructure streamlines the operational processes and equipment used to manage the network. Similarly, base software can be unified and more easily supported, with a single unified infrastructure to manage services. This unified infrastructure also allows for automation and orchestration within and between different services and components. From a single set of management components, administrators can coordinate resource availability and automate the procedures necessary to make services available, reducing the need for human operators to manage the process and reducing the potential for error.

- **Agility:** Modifications to the network's topology or how traffic is handled can be tried in different ways, without needing to modify the existing physical networks.

- **Scalability:** A virtual network can be rapidly scaled to respond to shifting demands by adding or removing physical resources from the pool of available resources.

- **Capital cost savings:** A virtualized deployment can reduce the number of devices needed, providing capital as well as operational costs savings.

- **Rapid service provisioning/time to market:** Physical resources can be allocated to virtual networks on demand, so that within an enterprise resources can be quickly shifted as demand by different users or applications changes. From a user perspective, resources can be acquired and released to minimize utilization demand on the system. New services require minimal training and can be deployed with minimal disruption to the network infrastructure.

- **Equipment consolidation:** NV enables the more efficient use of network resources, thus allowing for consolidating equipment purchases to fewer, more off-the-shelf products.

9.5 OpenDaylight's Virtual Tenant Network

Virtual Tenant Network (VTN) is an OpenDaylight (ODL) plug-in developed by NEC. It provides multitenant virtual networks on an SDN, using VLAN technology. The VTN abstraction functionality enables users to design and deploy a virtual network without knowing the physical network topology or bandwidth restrictions. VTN allows the users to define the network with a look and feel of a conventional

L2/L3 (LAN switch/IP router) network. Once the network is designed on VTN, it is automatically mapped onto the underlying physical network, and then configured on the individual switches leveraging the SDN control protocol.

VTN consists of two components (see Figure 5.6 in Chapter 5, "SDN Control Plane"):

- **VTN Manager:** An ODL controller plug-in that interacts with other modules to implement the components of the VTN model. It also provides a REST interface to configure VTN components in the controller.

- **VTN Coordinator:** An external application that provides a REST interface to users for VTN virtualization. It interacts with VTN Manager plug-in to implement the user configuration. It is also capable of multiple controller orchestration.

Table 9.1 shows the elements that are building blocks for constructing a virtual network. A virtual network is constructed using virtual nodes (vBridge, vRouter) and virtual interfaces and links. It is possible, by connecting the virtual interfaces made on virtual nodes via virtual links, to configure a network that has L2 and L3 transfer function.

TABLE 9.1   Virtual Tenant Network Elements

Name of Element		Description
Virtual node	vBridge	Logical representation of L2 switch function.
	vRouter	Logical representation of L3 router function. Only one vRouter can be defined in a VTN, and it can connect only to the vBridge.
	vTerminal	Logical representation of a virtual node that is connected to an interface mapped to a physical port that is the source or target of a redirect section attribute in a flow filter.
	vTunnel	Logical representation of Tunnel (consists of vTeps and vBypasses).
	vTep	Logical representation of tunnel endpoint (TEP).
	vBypass	Logical representation of connectivity between controlled networks.
Virtual interface	Interface	Representation of endpoint on the virtual node (VM, servers, vBridge, vRouter, and so on).
Virtual link	vLink	Logical representation of L1 connectivity between virtual interfaces.

The upper part of Figure 9.14 is a virtual network example. VRT is defined as the vRouter, and BR1 and BR2 are defined as vBridges. Interfaces of the vRouter and vBridges are connected using vLinks. Once a user of VTN Manager has defined a virtual network, the VTN Coordinator maps physical network resources to the constructed virtual network. Mapping identifies which virtual network each packet transmitted or received by an OpenFlow switch belongs to, as well as which interface in the OpenFlow switch transmits or receives that packet. There are two mapping methods:

- **Port mapping:** This mapping method is used to map a physical port as an interface of virtual node (vBridge/vTerminal). Port-map is enabled when the network topology is known in advance.

- **VLAN mapping:** This mapping method is used to map VLAN ID of VLAN tag in incoming Layer 2 frame with the vBridge. This mapping is used when the affiliated network and its VLAN tag are known. Whenever this mapping method is used, it is possible to reduce the number of commands to be set.

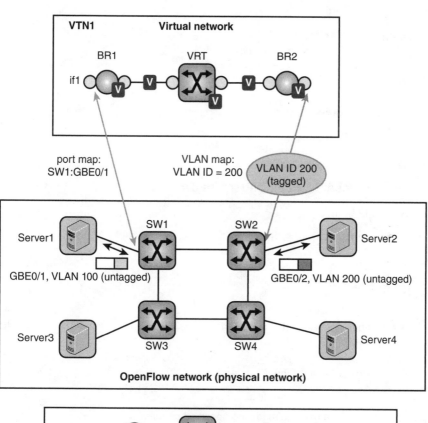

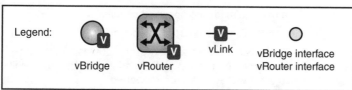

FIGURE 9.14 VTN Mapping Example

Figure 9.14 shows a mapping example. An interface of BR1 is mapped to a port on OpenFlow switch SW1. Packets received from that SW1 port are regarded as those from the corresponding interface of BR1. The interface if1 of vBridge (BR1) is mapped to the port GBE0/1 of switch1 using **port-map**. Packets received or transmitted by GBE0/1 of switch1 are considered as those from or to the interface if1 of vBridge. vBridge BR2 is mapped to VLAN 200 using **vlan-map**. Packets having the VLAN ID of 200 received or transmitted by the port of any switch in the network are mapped to the vBridge BR2.

VTN provides the capability to define and manage traffic flows across a virtual network. As with OpenFlow, flows are defined based on the value of various fields in packets. A flow can be defined using one or a combination of the following fields:

- Source MAC Address

- Destination MAC Address

- Ethernet Type

- VLAN Priority

- Source IP Address

- Destination IP Address

- IP Version

differentiated services codepoint (DSCP)

A 6-bit field in the IP header that is used to classify packets for differentiated services (a form of QoS traffic management).

- **Differentiated Services Codepoint (DSCP)**

- TCP/UDP Source Port

- TCP/UDP Destination Port

- ICMP Type

- ICMP Code

Table 9.2 outlines the types of Action that can be applied on packets that match the Flow Filter conditions.

TABLE 9.2   Virtual Tenant Flow Filter Actions

Action	Description
Pass	Pass packets matching specified conditions.
Drop	Drop packets matching specified conditions.
Redirect	Redirect packets to a specified virtual interface. Both transparent redirection (not changing MAC address) and router redirection (changing MAC address) are supported.
Priority	Set a priority for packets, using IP DSCP field.

Action	Description
Bandwidth	Set policing parameters. Set action based on threshold data rate statistics. Actions include pass, drop, and reduce priority.
Statistics	Collect statistics information.

Figure 9.15 shows the overall architecture of VTN. The VTN Manager is part of the OpenDaylight controller and uses base network service functions to learn the topology and statistics of the underlying network. A user or application creates virtual networks and specifies network behavior to the VTN Coordinator across a web or REST interface. The VTN Coordinator translates these commands into detailed instructions to the VTN Manager, which in turn uses OpenFlow to map virtual networks to the physical network infrastructure.

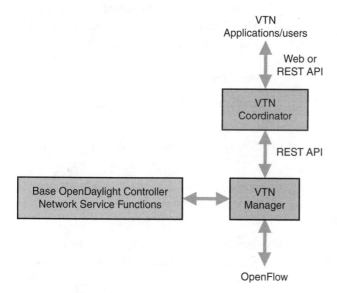

FIGURE 9.15   OpenDaylight VTN Architecture

9.6 Software-Defined Infrastructure

Recent years have seen explosive growth in the complexity of data centers, cloud computing facilities, and network infrastructures for enterprises and carriers. An emerging design philosophy to address the challenges of this complexity is software-defined infrastructure (SDI). With SDI, a data center or network infrastructure can autoconfigure itself at run time based on application/business requirements and operator constraints. Automation in SDIs enables infrastructure operators to achieve higher conformance to SLAs, avoid overprovisioning, and automate security and other network-related functions.

Another key characteristic of SDI is that it is highly application driven. Applications tend to change much more slowly than the ecosystem (hardware, system software, networks) that supports them. Individuals and enterprises stay with chosen applications for long periods of time, whereas they replace the hardware and other infrastructure elements at a fast pace. So, providers are at an advantage if the entire infrastructure is software defined and thus able to cope with rapid changes in infrastructure technology.

SDN and NFV are the key enabling technologies for SDI. SDN provides network control systems with the flexibility to steer and provision network resources dynamically. NFV virtualizes network functions as prepackaged software services that are easily deployable in a cloud or network infrastructure environment. So instead of hard-coding a service deployment and its network services, these can now be dynamically provisioned; traffic is then steered through the software services, significantly increasing the agility with which these are provisioned. Although SDN and NFV are necessary components of an SDI, they do not by themselves provide the intelligence that can generate or recommend the required configuration that can then be automatically implemented. Therefore, we can think of SDN and NFV as providing a platform for deploying SDI-enabling software.

A recent paper by Pott [POTT14] lists the following as some of the key features of an SDI offering:

data deduplication

The elimination of redundant data. It includes (1) compressing data by only storing changes to data, and (2) replacing duplicate copies of chunks of data or files with pointers to a single copy.

- Distributed storage resources with fully inline **data deduplication** and compression.

- Fully automated and integrated backups that are application aware, with autoconfiguring and autotesting. This new generation will be as close to "zero touch" as is possible.

- Fully automated and integrated disaster recovery that is application aware, with autoconfiguring and autotesting. This new generation will be as close to "zero touch" as is possible.

- Fully integrated hybrid cloud computing, with resources in the public cloud consumed as easily as local. The ability to move between multiple cloud providers, based on cost, data sovereignty requirements, or latency/locality needs. The providers that want to win the hybrid cloud portion of the exercise will build in awareness of privacy and security and allow administrators to easily select not only geolocal providers, but those known to have zero foreign legal attack surface, and they will clearly differentiate between them.

- WAN optimization technology.

- A hypervisor or hypervisor/container hybrid running on the metal.

- Management software to allow administrators to manage the hardware and the hypervisor.

- Adaptive monitoring software that will detect new applications and operating systems and automatically monitor them properly. Adaptive monitoring will not require manual configuration.

- Predictive analytics software that will determine when resources will exceed capacity, when hardware is likely to fail, or when licensing can no longer be worked around.

- Automation and load maximization software that will make sure the hardware and software components are used to their maximum capacity, given the existing hardware and existing licensing bounds.

- Orchestration software that will not only spin up groups of applications on demand or as needed, but will provide an "App Store"-like experience for selecting new workloads and getting them up and running on your local infra-structure in just a couple of clicks.

- Autobursting, as an adjunct of orchestration, will intelligently decide between hot-adding capacity to legacy workloads (CPU, RAM, and so on) or spinning up new instances of modern burstable applications to handle load. It would, of course, scale them back down when possible.

- Hybrid identity services that work across private infrastructure and public cloud spaces. They will not only manage identity but also provide complete user experience management solutions that work anywhere.

- Complete software-defined networking stack, including Layer 2 extension between data centers as well as the public and private cloud. This means that spinning up a workload will automatically configure networking, firewalls, intrusion detection, application layer gateways, mirroring, load balancing, content distribution network registration, certificates, and so forth.

- Chaos creation in the form of randomized automated testing for failure of all nonlegacy workloads and infrastructure elements to ensure that the network still meets requirements.

Software-Defined Storage

As mentioned, SDN and NFV are key elements of SDI. A third, equally important element is the emerging technology known as software-defined storage (SDS). SDS is a framework for managing a variety of storage systems in the data center that are traditionally not unified. SDS provides the ability to manage these storage assets to meet specific SLAs and to support a variety of applications. The dominant physical architecture for SDS is based on distributed storage, with storage devices distributed across a network.

Figure 9.16 illustrates the main elements of a typical SDS architecture. Physical storage consists of a number of magnetic and solid-state disk arrays, possibly from multiple vendors. Separate from this physical storage plane is a unified set of control software. This must include adaptation logic that can interface with a variety of vendor equipment and controlling and monitoring that equipment. On top of this adaptation layer are a number of basic storage services. An application interface provides an abstracted view of data storage so that applications need not be concerned with the location, attributes, or capacity of individual storage systems. There is also an administrative interface to enable the SDS administrator to manage the distributed storage suite.

SDS puts the emphasis on storage services instead of storage hardware. By decoupling the storage control software from the hardware, a storage resource can be used more efficiently and its administration simplified. For example, a storage administrator can use SLAs when deciding how to provision storage without needing to consider specific hardware attributes. In essence, resources are aggregated into storage pools assigned to users. Data services are applied to meet user or application requirements, and service levels are maintained. When additional resources are needed by an application, the storage control software automatically adds the resources. Conversely, resources are freed up when not in use. The storage control software automatically removes failed components and systems that fail.

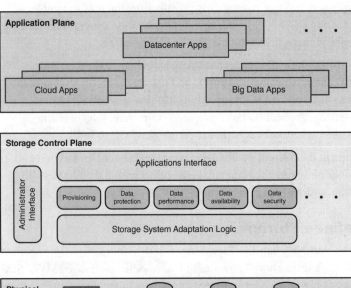

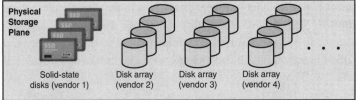

FIGURE 9.16   Software-Defined Storage Architecture

SDI Architecture

A number of companies, including IBM, Cisco, Intel, and HP, either have produced or are working on SDI offerings. There is no standardized specification for SDI, and there are numerous differences in the different initiatives. Nevertheless, the overall SDI architecture is quite similar among the different efforts. A typical example is the SDI architecture defined by Intel. This architecture is organized into three layers, as illustrated in Figure 9.17 and described in the list that follows.

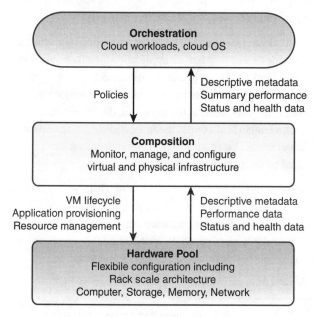

FIGURE 9.17   Intel's 3-Layer SDI Model

Orchestration: A policy engine that allows higher level frameworks to manage composition dynamically without interrupting ongoing operations.

Composition: A low-level layer of system software that continually and automatically manages the pool of hardware resources.

Hardware pool: An abstracted pool of modular hardware resources.

The orchestration layer drives the architecture. This layer is concerned with efficient configuration or resources while at the same time meeting application service requirements. Intel's initial focus appears to be on cloud providers, but other application areas, such as big data and other data center applications, lend themselves to the SDI approach. This layer continually monitors status data, enabling it to solve service issues faster and to continually optimize hardware resource assignment.

The composition layer is a control layer that manages VMs, storage, and network assets. In this architecture, the VM is seen as a dynamic federation of compute, storage, and network resources assembled to run an application instance. Although current VM technology provides a level of flexibility and cost savings over the use of nonvirtualized servers, there is still considerable inefficiency. Suppliers tend to size systems to meet the maximum demand that a VM might impose and hence overprovision so as to guarantee service. With software-defined allocation of resources, more flexibility is available in creating, provisioning, managing, moving, and retiring VMs. Similarly, SDS provides the opportunity to use storage more efficiently.

Composition enables the logical disaggregation of compute, network, and storage resources, so that each VM provides exactly what an application needs. Supporting this at the level of the hardware is Intel's rack scale architecture (RSA). RSA exploits extremely high data rate optical connection components to redesign the way computer rack systems are implemented. In an RSA design, the speed of the silicon interconnects means that individual components (processors, memory, storage, and network) no longer need to reside in the same box. Individual racks can be dedicated to each of the component classes and scaled to meet the demands of the data center.

Figure 9.18 provides another view of Intel's SDI architecture, which is in general terms typical of SDI architectures from other organizations. The resource pool consists of storage, network, and compute resources. From a hardware perspective, these can be deployed in an RSA. From a control perspective, SDS, SDN, and NFV technologies enable the management of these resources with an overall SDI framework.

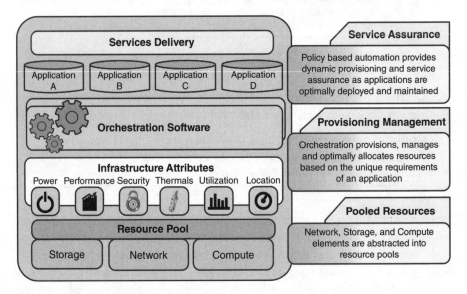

FIGURE 9.18   Intel's SDI Architecture

9.7 Key Terms

After completing this chapter, you should be able to define the following terms.

broadcast addressing	physical resource
broadcast domain	software-defined infrastructure (SDI)
data deduplication	software-defined storage (SDS)
differentiated services codepoint (DSCP)	unicast addressing
IEEE 802.3	virtual LAN (VLAN)
IP security (IPsec)	virtual network
LAN switch	virtual private network (VPN)
logical resource	virtual resource
MAC frame	Virtual Tenant Network (VTN)
network virtualization	

9.8 References

KUMA13: Kumar, R. Software Defined Networking—a Definitive Guide. Smashwords.com, 2013.

POTT14: Pott, T. "SDI Wars: WTF Is Software Defined Center Infrastructure?" *The Register*, October 17, 2014. http://www.theregister.co.uk/2014/10/17/sdi_wars_what_is_software_defined_infrastructure/

SDNC14: SDNCentral. SDNCentral Network Virtualization Report, 2014 Edition, 2014.

PART IV

Defining and Supporting User Needs

We are beginning to understand, or at least to appreciate, the cause of time delays and over-loading phenomena in communication systems handling competing users with different levels of importance. There is a basis for hope that one day we may be able to automate highly sophisticated priority systems. Such systems may even be so effective as to provide the operational equivalent of exercised judgment.

—On Distributed Communications, Introduction to Distributed Communications Networks, Report RM-3420-PR, Paul Baran, August 1964

Fundamental to the acceptance and success of any complex shared networking architecture is that it meets users expectations for performance. Traditionally, the means of defining expected performance, measuring it, providing it, and entering into well-defined agreements relating to it has been the concept of quality of service (QoS). QoS remains an essential ingredient in any network design. Chapter 10 provides an overview of QoS concepts and standards. Recently, QoS has been augmented with the concept of quality of experience (QoE), which is particularly relevant to interactive video and multimedia network traffic. Chapter 11 provides an overview of QoE and discusses a number of practical aspects of implementing QoE mechanisms. Chapter 12 looks further into the network design implications of the combined use of QoS and QoE.

Chapter 10

Quality of Service

In the schemes considered, precedence is determined moment-by-moment, automatically for all traffic in the network. Precedence is computed as a composite function of: (1) the ability of the network to accept additional traffic; (2) the "importance" of each user and the "utility" of his traffic; (3) the data rate of each input transmission medium or the transducer used; and (4) the tolerable delay time for delivery of the traffic.

—On Distributed Communications: Priority, Precedence, and Overload,
Rand Report RM-3638-PR, Paul Baran, August 1964

Chapter Objectives

After studying this chapter, you should be able to

- Describe the ITU-T QoS architectural framework.
- Summarize the key concepts of the Integrated Services Architecture.
- Compare and contrast elastic and inelastic traffic.
- Explain the concept of differentiated services.
- Understand the use of service level agreements.
- Describe IP performance metrics.
- Present an overview of OpenFlow QoS support.

The Internet and enterprise IP-based networks continue to see rapid growth in the volume and variety of data traffic. Cloud computing, big data, the pervasive use of mobile devices on enterprise networks, and the increasing use of video streaming all contribute to the increasing difficulty in maintaining satisfactory network performance. Two key tools in measuring the network performance that an enterprise desires to achieve are quality of service (QoS) and quality of experience (QoE). As is discussed in Chapter 2, "Requirements and Technology," QoS is the measurable end-to-end performance properties of a network service, which can be guaranteed in advance by a service level agreement (SLA) between a user and a service provider, so as to satisfy specific customer application requirements. QoE is a subjective measure of performance as reported by the user. Unlike QoS, which can be precisely measured, QoE relies on human opinion.

QoS and QoE enable the network manager to determine whether the network is meeting user needs and to diagnose problem areas that require adjustment to network management and network traffic control. This chapter looks in some detail at QoS. Chapter 11, "QoE: User Quality of Experience," and Chapter 12, "Network Design Implications of QoS and QoE," examine QoE, the relationship between QoS and QoE, and the design implications of a QoE/QoS architecture.

There is a strong need to be able to support a variety of traffic, with a variety of QoS requirements, on IP-based networks. This chapter begins with a look at an overall QoS architecture, which describes internetwork functions and services designed to meet this need. Next, the chapter looks at the Integrated Services Architecture (ISA), which provides a framework for current and future Internet services. We then examine the key concept of differentiated services. The chapter concludes with an introduction to the topics of SLAs and IP performance metrics.

You might find it useful at this point to review Section 2.1, "Types of Network and Internet Traffic," which reviews various types of traffic and their QoS requirements.

10.1 Background

Historically, the Internet and other IP-based networks provided a **best effort** delivery service. This means that the network attempts to allocate its resources with equal availability and priority to all traffic flows, with no regard for application priorities, traffic patterns and load, and customer requirements. To protect the network from congestion collapse and to guarantee that some flows do not crowd out other flows, congestion control mechanisms were introduced, which tended to throttle traffic that consumed excessive resources.

One of the most important congestion control techniques, introduced early on and still in wide use, is the TCP congestion control mechanism. TCP congestion control has become increasingly complex and sophisticated, but it is worth briefly summarizing the principles involved here. For each TCP connection between two end systems across a network, in each direction, a concept known as sliding window is used. TCP segments on a connection are numbered sequentially. The sending and receiving TCP entities maintain a window, or buffer, that defines the range of sequence numbered segments that may be transmitted. As segments arrive and are processed by the receiver, the receiver returns an acknowledgment indicating which segments have been received and implicitly indicated to the sender that the window of sequence numbers has advanced to allow more segments to be sent. Various algorithms are used by the sender to deduce the amount of congestion on a connection based on the round-trip delay for acknowledgments plus whether an acknowledgment is even received for a particular segment.

best effort

A network or Internet delivery technique that does not guarantee delivery of data and treats all packets equally. All packets are forwarded on a first-come, first-served basis. Preferential treatment based on priority or other concerns is not provided.

As congestion is detected, the sending TCP entity reduces its transmission of segments to help ease congestion on the intervening network.

TCP can work well if all the TCP connections across an Internet conform to the congestion control mechanism. The scheme is less effective if some connections, on behalf of "selfish" applications, ignore the congestion control rules and attempt to send segments as rapidly as possible.

Although TCP congestion control and other network congestion control techniques can reduce the risk of excessive congestion, these techniques do not directly address QoS requirements. As the intensity and variety of traffic increased, various QoS mechanisms were developed, including Integrated Services Architecture (ISA) and differentiated services (DiffServ), accompanied by service level agreements (SLAs) so that the service provided to various customers was tunable and somewhat predictable. These mechanisms and services serve two purposes:

- Allocate network resources efficiently so as to maximize effective capacity

- Enable networks to offer different levels of QoS to customers on the basis of customer requirements

In this more sophisticated environment, the term *best effort* refers not to the network service as a whole but to a class of traffic treated in best effort fashion. All packets in the best effort traffic class are transmitted with no guarantee regarding the speed with which the packets will be transmitted to the recipient or that the data will even be delivered entirely. Typically, in a network that provides multiple levels of service, best effort is the classification for the lowest priority traffic. However, for some applications, a class of traffic known as *lower than best effort*, or *lower effort* (LE), may be used. LE classification permits a network operator to strictly limit the effect of LE traffic on best effort/normal or all other network traffic. This classification may be suitable for background data transfer applications (such as file sharing and update fetching) or traffic that could be delayed to off-peak times.

10.2   QoS Architectural Framework

Before looking at the Internet standards that deal with provision of QoS in the Internet and private internetworks, it is useful to consider an overall architectural framework that relates the various elements that go into QoS provision. Such a framework has been developed by the Telecommunication Standardization Sector of the International Telecommunication Union (ITU-T) as part of its Y series of Recommendations.[1]

---

1   The Y series, titled *Global Information Infrastructure, Internet Protocol Aspects and Next-Generation Networks*, contains a number of very useful documents dealing with QoS, congestion control, and traffic management.

Recommendation Y.1291, *An Architectural Framework for Support of Quality of Service in Packet Networks*, gives a "big picture" overview of the mechanisms and services that comprise a QoS facility.

The Y.1291 framework consists of a set of generic network mechanisms for controlling the network service response to a service request, which can be specific to a network element, or for signaling between network elements, or for controlling and administering traffic across a network. Figure 10.1 shows the relationship among these elements, which are organized into three planes: data, control, and management. This architectural framework is an excellent overview of QoS functions and their relationships and provides a useful basis for summarizing QoS.

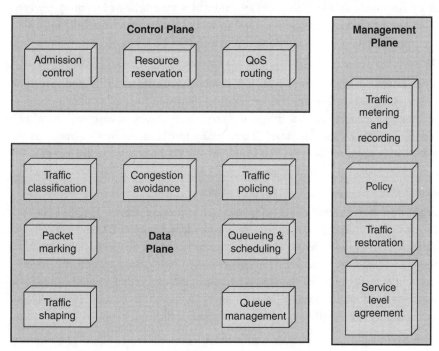

FIGURE 10.1 Architectural Framework for QoS Support

Data Plane

The data plane includes those mechanisms that operate directly on flows of data. The following discussion briefly describes each mechanism in turn.

Traffic classification refers to the assignment of packets to a traffic class by the ingress router at the ingress edge of the network. Typically, the classification entity looks at multiple fields of a packet, such as source and destination address, application payload, and QoS markings, and determines the aggregate to which the packet belongs. This classification provides network elements a method to weigh the relative importance of one packet over another in a different class. All traffic assigned to a particular flow or other aggregate can be treated similarly. The flow label in the IPv6 header can be used for traffic classification. Other routers en route perform a classification function as well, but the classification does not change as the packets traverse the network.

Packet marking encompasses two distinct functions. First, packets may be marked by ingress edge nodes of a network to indicate some form of QoS that the packet should receive. An example is the Differentiated Services (DiffServ) field in the IPv4 and IPv6 packets and the Traffic Class field in MPLS labels. An ingress edge node can set the values in these fields to indicate a desired QoS. Such markings may be used by intermediate nodes to provide differential treatment to incoming packets. Second, packet marking can also be used to mark packets as nonconformant, either by the ingress node or intermediate nodes, which may be dropped later if congestion is experienced.

Traffic shaping controls the rate and volume of traffic entering and transiting the network on a per-flow basis. The entity responsible for traffic shaping buffers nonconformant packets until it brings the respective aggregate in compliance with the traffic limitations for this flow. The resulting traffic thus is not as bursty as the original and is more predictable. For example, Y.1221 recommends the use of leaky bucket/token bucket for traffic shaping. Typically, this is a function performed at the ingress edge.

Congestion avoidance deals with means for keeping the load of the network under its capacity such that it can operate at an acceptable performance level. The specific objectives are to avoid significant queuing delays and, especially, to avoid congestion collapse. A typical congestion avoidance scheme acts by senders reducing the amount of traffic entering the network upon an indication that network congestion is occurring (or about to occur). Unless there is an explicit indication, packet loss or timer expiration is normally regarded as an implicit indication of network congestion.

Traffic policing determines whether the traffic being presented is, on a hop-by-hop basis, compliant with prenegotiated policies or contracts. Nonconformant packets may be dropped, delayed, or labeled as nonconformant. As an example, ITU-T Recommendation Y.1221, *Traffic Control and Congestion Control in IP-Based Networks*, recommends the use of token bucket to characterize traffic for purposes of traffic policing.

Queuing and scheduling algorithms, also referred to as queuing discipline algorithms, determine which packet to send next and are used primarily to manage the allocation of transmission capacity among flows. Queuing discipline is discussed in Section 9.3.

Queue management algorithms manage the length of packet queues by dropping packets when necessary or appropriate. Active management of queues is concerned primarily with congestion avoidance. In the early days of the Internet, the queue management discipline was to drop any incoming packets when the queue was full, referred to as the **tail drop** technique. As pointed out in RFC 2309, *Recommendations on Queue Management and Congestion Avoidance in the Internet*, there are a number of drawbacks to tail drop, including the following:

1. There is no reaction to congestion until it is necessary to drop packets, whereas a more aggressive congestion avoidance technique would likely improve over-all network performance.

2. Queues tend to be close to full, which causes an increase in packet delay through a network and which can result in a large batch of drop packets for bursty traffic, necessitating many packet retransmissions.

3. Tail drop may allow a single connection or a few flows to monopolize queue space, preventing other connections from getting room in the queue.

One noteworthy example of queue management is random early detection (RED), defined in RFC 2309. RED drops incoming packets probabilistically based on an estimated average queue size. The probability for dropping increases as the estimated average queue size grows. There are a number of variants of RED that are in more common use than the original RED, with weighted RED (WRED) perhaps the most commonly implemented. WRED prevents network congestion by detecting and slowing flows (according to service class) before congestion occurs. WRED drops selected packets, which alerts the TCP sender to reduce its transmission rate. Weights are assigned to service classes, resulting in low priority flows being slowed more aggressively than high priority ones.

Control Plane

The control plane is concerned with creating and managing the pathways through which user data flows. It includes admission control, QoS routing, and resource reservation.

Admission control determines what user traffic may enter the network. This may be in part determined by the QoS requirements of a data flow compared to the current resource commitment within the network. But beyond balancing QoS requests with available capacity to determine whether to accept a request, there are other considerations in admission control. Network managers and service providers must be able to monitor, control, and enforce use of network resources and services based on policies derived from criteria such as the identity of users and applications, traffic/bandwidth requirements, security considerations, and time of day/week. RFC 2753, *A Framework for Policy-Based Admission Control*, discusses such policy-related issues.

QoS routing determines a network path that is likely to accommodate the requested QoS of a flow. This contrasts with the philosophy of the traditional routing protocols, which generally are looking for a least-cost path through the network. RFC 2386, *A Framework for QoS-Based Routing in the Internet*, provides an overview of the issues involved in QoS routing. This is an area of ongoing study. An example of a current implementation is Cisco's Performance Routing (PfR). PfR monitors network performance and selects the best path for each application based upon advanced criteria such as reachability, delay, jitter, and loss. PfR can evenly distribute traffic to maintain equivalent link utilization levels using an advanced load-balancing technique.

Resource reservation is a mechanism that reserves network resources on demand for delivering desired network performance to a requesting flow. An example of a protocol that uses this capability is the Resource Reservation Protocol (RSVP). However, this approach has been found to not scale well and is rarely used today.

Management Plane

The management plane contains mechanisms that affect both control plane and data plane mechanisms. The control plane deals with the operation, administration, and management aspects of the network. It includes SLAs, traffic restoration, traffic metering and recording, and policy.

A **service level agreement (SLA)** typically represents the agreement between a customer and a provider of a service that specifies the level of availability, serviceability, performance, operation, or other attributes of the service. SLAs are discussed in Section 10.5.

Traffic metering and recording concerns monitoring the dynamic properties of a traffic stream using performance metrics such as data rate and packet loss rate. It involves observing traffic characteristics at a given network point and collecting and storing the traffic information for analysis and further action. Depending on the conformance level, a meter can invoke necessary treatment (for example, dropping or shaping) for the packet stream. Section 10.6 discusses the types of metrics that are used in this function.

Traffic restoration refers to the network response to failures. This encompasses a number of protocol layers and techniques.

Policy is a category that refers to a set of rules for administering, managing, and controlling access to network resources. They can be specific to the needs of the service provider or reflect the agreement between the customer and service provider, which may include reliability and availability requirements over a period of time and other QoS requirements.

10.3 Integrated Services Architecture

To define the requirements for QoS-based service, the IETF developed a suite of standards under the general umbrella of the Integrated Services Architecture (ISA). ISA, intended to provide QoS transport over IP-based internets, is defined in overall terms in RFC 1633, while a number of other documents fill in the details. ISA as such is not implemented in any current products. However, the architectural principles are in wide use, and ISA provides a convenient structure for discussing a number of QoS mechanisms.

ISA Approach

The purpose of ISA is to enable the provision of QoS support over IP-based internets. The central design issue for ISA is how to share the available capacity in times of congestion.

For an IP-based Internet that provides only a best effort service, the tools for controlling congestion and providing service are limited. In essence, routers have two mechanisms to work with:

- **Routing algorithm**: Some routing protocols in use in internets allow routes to be selected to minimize delay. Routers exchange information to get a picture of the delays throughout the Internet. Minimum-delay routing helps to balance loads, thus decreasing local congestion, and helps to reduce delays seen by individual TCP connections. Interface data rate may also be used as a metric.

- **Packet discard**: When a router's buffer overflows, it discards packets. Typically, the most recent packet is discarded. The effect of lost packets on a TCP connection is that the sending TCP entity backs off and reduces its load, thus helping to alleviate Internet congestion.

These tools have worked reasonably well. However, as the discussion in Section 2.1 (Types of Network and Internet Traffic) shows, such techniques are inadequate for the variety of traffic now coming to internets.

In ISA, each IP packet can be associated with a flow. A flow is a distinguishable stream of related IP packets that results from a single user activity and requires the same QoS. For example, a flow might consist of traffic on one transport connection in one direction or one video stream distinguishable by the ISA. A flow differs from a TCP connection in two respects: A flow is unidirectional, and there can be more than one recipient of a flow (multicast). Typically, an IP packet is identified as a member of a flow on the basis of source and destination IP addresses and port numbers, and protocol type. The flow identifier in the IPv6 header is not necessarily equivalent to an ISA flow, but in future the IPv6 flow identifier could be used in ISA.

ISA makes use of the following functions to manage congestion and provide QoS transport:

- **Admission control**: For QoS transport (other than default best effort transport), ISA requires that a reservation be made for a new flow. If the routers collectively determine that there are insufficient resources to guarantee the requested QoS, the flow is not admitted. The protocol RSVP is used to make reservations.

- **Routing algorithm**: The routing decision may be based on a variety of QoS parameters, not just minimum delay.

- **Queuing discipline**: A vital element of the ISA is an effective queuing policy that takes into account the differing requirements of different flows.

- **Discard policy**: A discard policy determines which packets to drop when a buffer is full and new packets arrive. A discard policy can be an important element in managing congestion and meeting QoS guarantees.

ISA Components

Figure 10.2 is a general depiction of the implementation architecture for ISA within a router. Below the thick horizontal line are the forwarding functions of the router; these are executed for each packet and therefore must be highly optimized. The remaining functions, above the line, are background functions that create data structures used by the forwarding functions. Thus, the lower portion of Figure 10.2 corresponds roughly to the data plane of Figure 10.1, and the upper portion corresponds to the control plane.

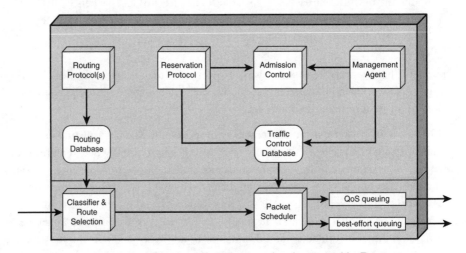

FIGURE 10.2   Integrated Services Architecture Implemented in Router

The principal background functions are as follows:

- **Reservation protocol**: This protocol reserves resources for a new flow at a given level of QoS. It is used among routers and between routers and end systems. The reservation protocol is responsible for maintaining flow-specific state information at the end systems and at the routers along the path of the flow. RSVP is used for this purpose. The reservation protocol updates the traffic control database used by the packet scheduler to determine the service provided for packets of each flow.

- **Admission control**: When a new flow is requested, the reservation protocol invokes the admission control function. This function determines if sufficient resources are available for this flow at the requested QoS. This determination is based on the current level of commitment to other reservations or on the current load on the network.

- **Management agent**: A network management agent can modify the traffic control database and to direct the admission control module to set admission control policies.

- **Routing protocol**: The routing protocol is responsible for maintaining a routing database that gives the next hop to be taken for each destination address and each flow.

These background functions support the main task of the router, which is the forwarding of packets. The two principal functional areas that accomplish forwarding are the following:

- **Classifier and route selection**: For the purposes of forwarding and traffic control, incoming packets must be mapped into classes. A class may correspond to a single flow or to a set of flows with the same QoS requirements. For example, the packets of all video flows or the packets of all flows attributable to a particular organization may be treated identically for purposes of resource allocation and queuing discipline. The selection of class is based on fields in the IP header. Based on the packet's class and its destination IP address, this function determines the next-hop address for this packet.

- **Packet scheduler**: This function manages one or more queues for each output port. It determines the order in which queued packets are transmitted and the selection of packets for discard, if necessary. Decisions are made based on a packet's class, the contents of the traffic control database, and current and past activity on this outgoing port. Part of the packet scheduler's task is that of policing, which is the function of determining whether the packet traffic in a given flow exceeds the requested capacity and, if so, deciding how to treat the excess packets.

ISA Services

ISA service for a flow of packets is defined on two levels. First, a number of general categories of service are provided, each of which provides a certain general type of service guarantees. Second, within each category, the service for a particular flow is specified by the values of certain parameters; together, these values are referred to as a traffic specification (TSpec). Three categories of service are defined:

- Guaranteed

- Controlled load

- Best effort

An application can request a reservation for a flow for a guaranteed or controlled load QoS, with a TSpec that defines the exact amount of service required. If the reservation is accepted, the TSpec is part of the contract between the data flow and the service. The service agrees to provide the requested QoS as long as the flow's data traffic continues to be described accurately by the TSpec. Packets that are not part of a reserved flow are by default given a best effort delivery service.

Guaranteed Service

The key elements of the guaranteed service are as follows:

- The service provides assured capacity, or data rate.

- There is a specified upper bound on the queuing delay through the network. This must be added to the propagation delay, or latency, to arrive at the bound on total delay through the network.

- There are no queuing losses. That is, no packets are lost because of buffer overflow; packets may be lost because of failures in the network or changes in routing paths.

With this service, an application provides a characterization of its expected traffic profile, and the service determines the end-to-end delay that it can guarantee.

One category of applications for this service is those that need an upper bound on delay so that a delay buffer can be used for real-time playback of incoming data, and that do not tolerate packet losses because of the degradation in the quality of the output. Another example is applications with hard real-time deadlines.

The guaranteed service is the most demanding service provided by ISA. Because the delay bound is firm, the delay has to be set at a large value to cover rare cases of long queuing delays.

Controlled Load

The key elements of the controlled load service are as follows:

- The service tightly approximates the behavior visible to applications receiving best effort service under unloaded conditions.

- There is no specified upper bound on the queuing delay through the network. However, the service ensures that a very high percentage of the packets do not experience delays that greatly exceed the minimum transit delay (that is, the delay due to propagation time plus router processing time with no queuing delays).

- A very high percentage of transmitted packets will be successfully delivered (that is, almost no queuing loss).

As was mentioned, the risk in an internet that provides QoS for real-time applications is that best effort traffic is crowded out. This is because best effort types of applications are assigned a low priority and their traffic is throttled in the face of congestion and delays. The controlled load service guarantees that the network will set aside sufficient resources so that an application that receives this service will see a network that responds as if these real-time applications were not present and competing for resources.

The controlled service is useful for applications that have been referred to as adaptive real-time applications. Such applications do not require an *a priori* upper bound on the delay through the network. Rather, the receiver measures the jitter experienced by incoming packets and sets the playback point to the minimum delay that still produces a sufficiently low loss rate. (For example, video can be adaptive by dropping a frame or delaying the output stream slightly; voice can be adaptive by adjusting silent periods.)

Queuing Discipline

An important component of an ISA implementation is the queuing discipline used at the routers. The simplest approach that can be used by a router is a first-in, first-out (FIFO) queuing discipline at each output port. A single queue is maintained at each output port. When a new packet arrives and is routed to an output port, it is placed at the end of the queue. As long as the queue is not empty, the router transmits packets from the queue, taking the oldest remaining packet next.

There are several drawbacks to the FIFO queuing discipline:

- No special treatment is given to packets from flows that are of higher priority or are more delay sensitive. If a number of packets from different flows are ready to be forwarded, they are handled strictly in FIFO order.

- If a number of smaller packets are queued behind a long packet, FIFO queuing results in a larger average delay per packet than if the shorter packets were transmitted before the longer packet. In general, flows of larger packets get better service.

- A selfish TCP connection, which ignores the TCP congestion control rules, can crowd out conforming connections. If congestion occurs and one TCP connection fails to back off, other connections along the same path segment must back off more than they would otherwise have to do.

To overcome the drawbacks of FIFO queuing, a number of more complex routing algorithms have been implemented in routers. These algorithms involve the use of multiple queues at each output port and some method of prioritizing the traffic to provide better service. Typical of the networking industry are the routers from Cisco which, in addition to FIFO, include the following queuing approaches outlined in the Cisco *Internetworking Technology Handbook* [CISC15]:

- Priority queuing (PQ)

- Custom queuing (CQ)

- Flow-based weighted fair queuing (WFQ)

- Class-based weighted fair queuing (CBWFQ)

For **priority queuing**, each packet is assigned a priority level, and there is one queue for each priority level. In the Cisco implementation, four levels are used: high, medium, normal, and low. Packets not otherwise classified are assigned to the normal priority. PQ can flexibly prioritize according to network protocol, incoming interface, packet size, source/destination address, or other parameters. The queuing discipline gives absolute preference based on priority. Thus, if there are packets waiting in multiple queues, the router dispatches packets on a FIFO basis from the highest-priority queue that is not empty. Only after that queue is empty are packets dispatched from the next lower priority queue. When new packets arrive in a higher priority queue, they immediately take precedence over any packets already waiting in lower priority queues. PQ is useful for assuring that mission-critical application traffic is handled as well as possible, but it risks crowding out lower priority traffic for very long periods of time.

Custom queuing is designed to allow various applications or organizations to share the network among applications with specific minimum throughput or latency requirements. For CQ, there are multiple queues, with each having a configured byte count. The queues are serviced in round-robin fashion. As each queue is visited, a number of packets are dispatched up to the configured byte count. By providing different byte counts for different queues, traffic on each queue is guaranteed a minimum fraction of the overall capacity. Application or protocol traffic can then be assigned to the desired queue.

The remaining queuing algorithms on the preceding list are based on a mechanism known as fair queuing. With simple fair queuing, each incoming packet is placed in the queue for its flow. The queues are serviced in round-robin fashion, taking one packet from each nonempty queue in turn. Empty queues are skipped over. This scheme is fair in that each busy flow gets to send exactly one packet per cycle. Further, this is a form of load balancing among the various flows. There is no advantage in being greedy. A greedy flow finds that its queues become long, increasing its delays, whereas other flows are unaffected by this behavior.

The term *weighted fair queuing* (WFQ) is used in the literature to refer to a class of scheduling algorithms that use multiple queues to support capacity allocation and delay bounds. Some WFQ schemes take into account the amount of traffic through each queue and gives busier queues more capacity without completely shutting out less busy queues. WFQ may also take into account the amount of service requested by each traffic flow and adjust the queuing discipline accordingly.

Flow-based WFQ, which Cisco simply refers to as WFQ, creates flows based on a number of characteristics in a packet, including source and destination addresses, socket numbers, and session identifiers. The flows are assigned different weights to based on IP precedent bits to provide greater service for certain queues.

Class-based WFQ (CBWFQ) allows a network administrator to create minimum guaranteed bandwidth classes. Instead of providing a queue for each individual flow, a class is defined that consists of one or more flows. Each class can be guaranteed a minimum amount of bandwidth.

10.4 Differentiated Services

The differentiated services (DiffServ) architecture (RFC 2475) is designed to provide a simple, easy-to-implement, low-overhead tool to support a range of network services that are differentiated on the basis of performance.

Several key characteristics of DiffServ contribute to its efficiency and ease of deployment:

- IP packets are labeled for differing QoS treatment using the existing IPv4 or IPv6 DSField. Thus, no change is required to IP.

- A service level specification (SLS) is established between the service provider (Internet domain) and the customer prior to the use of DiffServ. This avoids the need to incorporate DiffServ mechanisms in applications. Therefore, existing applications need not be modified to use DiffServ. The SLS is a set of parameters and their values that together define the service offered to a traffic stream by a DiffServ domain.

■ A traffic conditioning specification (TCS) is a part of the SLS that specifies traffic classifier rules and any corresponding traffic profiles and metering, marking, discarding/shaping rules which are to apply to the traffic stream.

■ DiffServ provides a built-in aggregation mechanism. All traffic with the same DiffServ octet is treated the same by the network service. For example, multiple voice connections are not handled individually but in the aggregate. This provides for good scaling to larger networks and traffic loads.

■ DiffServ is implemented in individual routers by queuing and forwarding packets based on the DiffServ octet. Routers deal with each packet individually and do not have to save state information on packet flows.

Today, DiffServ is the most widely accepted QoS mechanism in enterprise networks.

Although DiffServ is intended to provide a simple service based on relatively simple mechanisms, the set of RFCs related to DiffServ is relatively complex. Table 10.1 summarizes some of the key terms from these specifications.

TABLE 10.1   Terminology for Differentiated Services

Term	Definition
Behavior aggregate	A set of packets with the same DiffServ codepoint crossing a link in a particular direction.
Classifier	Selects packets based on the DSField (BA classifier) or on multiple fields within the packet header (MF classifier).
DiffServ boundary node	A DiffServ node that connects one DiffServ domain to a node in another domain
DSField	The 6 most significant bits of the (former) IPv4 TOS octet or the (former) IPv6 Traffic Class octet.
DiffServ codepoint	A value that is encoded in the DSField.
DiffServ domain	A contiguous (connected) set of nodes, capable of implementing differentiated services, that operate with a common set of service provisioning policies and per-hop behavior definitions.
DiffServ interior node	A DiffServ node that is not a DiffServ boundary node.
DiffServ node	A node that supports differentiated services. Typically, a DiffServ node is a router. A host system that provides differentiated services for applications in the host is also a DiffServ node.
Dropping	The process of discarding packets based on specified rules; also called policing.

Marking	The process of setting the DiffServ codepoint in a packet. Packets may be marked on initiation and may be re-marked by an en route DiffServ node.
Metering	The process of measuring the temporal properties (for example, rate) of a packet stream selected by a classifier. The instantaneous state of that process may affect marking, shaping, and dropping functions.
Per-hop behavior (PHB)	The externally observable forwarding behavior applied at a node to a behavior aggregate.
Service level agreement (SLA)	A service contract between a customer and a service provider that specifies the forwarding service a customer should receive.
Shaping	The process of delaying packets within a packet stream to cause it to conform to some defined traffic profile.
Traffic conditioning	Control functions performed to enforce rules specified in a TCA, including metering, marking, shaping, and dropping.
Traffic conditioning agreement (TCA)	An agreement specifying classifying rules and traffic conditioning rules that are to apply to packets selected by the classifier.

Services

The DiffServ type of service is provided within a DiffServ domain, which is defined as a contiguous portion of the Internet over which a consistent set of DiffServ policies are administered. Typically, a DiffServ domain would be under the control of one administrative entity. The services provided across a DiffServ domain are defined in an SLA, which is a service contract between a customer and the service provider that specifies the forwarding service that the customer should receive for various classes of packets. A customer may be a user organization or another DiffServ domain. Once the SLA is established, the customer submits packets with the DiffServ octet marked to indicate the packet class. The service provider must ensure that the customer gets at least the agreed QoS for each packet class. To provide that QoS, the service provider must configure the appropriate forwarding policies at each router (based on DiffServ octet value) and must measure the performance being provided for each class on an ongoing basis.

If a customer submits packets intended for destinations within the DiffServ domain, the DiffServ domain is expected to provide the agreed service. If the destination is beyond the customer's DiffServ domain, the DiffServ domain will attempt to forward the packets through other domains, requesting the most appropriate service to match the requested service.

A DiffServ framework document lists the following detailed performance parameters that might be included in an SLA:

- Detailed service performance parameters such as expected throughput, drop probability, and latency.

- Constraints on the ingress and egress points at which the service is provided, indicating the scope of the service.

- Traffic profiles that must be adhered to for the requested service to be provided, such as token bucket parameters.

- Disposition of traffic submitted in excess of the specified profile.

The framework document also gives some examples of services that might be provided:

- Traffic offered at service level A will be delivered with low latency.

- Traffic offered at service level B will be delivered with low loss.

- 90 percent of in-profile traffic delivered at service level C will experience no more than 50 ms latency.

- 95 percent of in-profile traffic delivered at service level D will be delivered.

- Traffic offered at service level E will be allotted twice the bandwidth of traffic delivered at service level F.

- Traffic with drop precedence X has a higher probability of delivery than traffic with drop precedence Y.

The first two examples are qualitative and are valid only in comparison to other traffic, such as default traffic that gets a best effort service. The next two examples are quantitative and provide a specific guarantee that can be verified by measurement on the actual service without comparison to any other services offered at the same time. The final two examples are a mixture of quantitative and qualitative.

DiffServ Field

Packets are labeled for service handling by means of the 6-bit DSField in the IPv4 header or the IPv6 header (Figure 10.3). The value of the DSField, referred to as the **DiffServ codepoint (DSCP),** is the label used to classify packets for differentiated services.

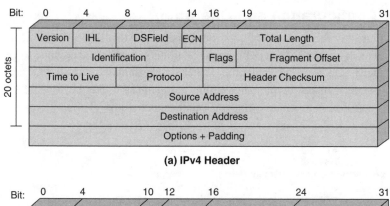

(a) IPv4 Header

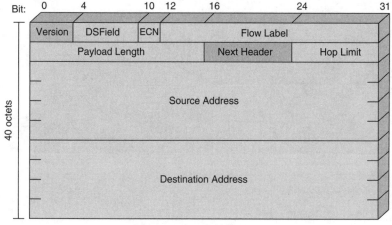

(b) IPv6 Header

DSField = Differentiated services field
ECN = Explicit congestion notification field

Note: The 8-bit DSField/ECN fields were formerly known as the Type of Service field in the IPv4 header and the Traffic Class field in the IPv6 header.

FIGURE 10.3   IP Headers

With a 6-bit codepoint, there are in principle 64 different classes of traffic that could be defined. These 64 codepoints are allocated across three pools of codepoints, as follows:

- Codepoints of the form xxxxx0, where x is either 0 or 1, are reserved for assignment as standards.

- Codepoints of the form xxxx11 are reserved for experimental or local use.

- Codepoints of the form xxxx01 are also reserved for experimental or local use but may be allocated for future standards action as needed.

DiffServ Configuration and Operation

Figure 10.4 illustrates the type of configuration envisioned in the DiffServ documents. A DiffServ domain consists of a set of contiguous routers; that is, it is possible to get from any router in the domain to any other router in the domain by a path that does not include routers outside the domain. Within a domain, the interpretation of DS codepoints is uniform, so that a uniform, consistent service is provided.

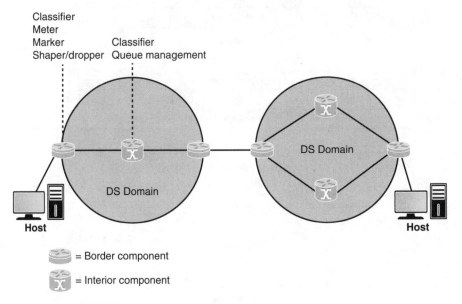

Classifier
Meter
Marker
Shaper/dropper   Classifier
Queue management

DS Domain

DS Domain

Host

Host

= Border component

= Interior component

FIGURE 10.4   DS Domains

Routers in a DiffServ domain are either boundary nodes or interior nodes. Typically, the interior nodes implement simple mechanisms for handling packets based on their DS codepoint values. This includes queuing discipline to give preferential treatment depending on codepoint value, and packet dropping rules to dictate which packets should be dropped first in the event of buffer saturation. The DiffServ specifications refer to the forwarding treatment provided at a router as per-hop behavior (PHB). This PHB must be available at all routers, and typically PHB is the only part of DiffServ implemented in interior routers.

The boundary nodes include PHB mechanisms but more sophisticated traffic conditioning mechanisms are also required to provide the desired service. Therefore, interior routers have minimal functionality and minimal overhead in providing the DiffServ service; most of the complexity is in the boundary nodes. The boundary node function can also be provided by a host system attached to the domain, on behalf of the applications at that host system.

The traffic conditioning function consists of five elements:

- **Classifier**: Separates submitted packets into different classes. This is the foundation of providing differentiated services. A classifier may separate traffic only on the basis of the DS codepoint (behavior aggregate classifier) or based on multiple fields within the packet header or even the packet payload (multifield classifier).

- **Meter**: Measures submitted traffic for conformance to a profile. The meter determines whether a given packet stream class is within or exceeds the service level guaranteed for that class.

- **Marker**: Re-marks packets with a different codepoint as needed. This may be done for packets that exceed the profile; for example, if a given throughput is guaranteed for a particular service class, any packets in that class that exceed the throughput in some defined time interval may be re-marked for best effort handling. Also, re-marking may be required at the boundary between two DiffServ domains. For example, if a given traffic class is to receive the highest supported priority, and this is a value of 3 in one domain and 7 in the next domain, packets with a priority 3 value traversing the first domain are re-marked as priority 7 when entering the second domain.

- **Shaper**: Delays packets as necessary so that the packet stream in a given class does not exceed the traffic rate specified in the profile for that class.

- **Dropper**: Drops packets when the rate of packets of a given class exceeds that specified in the profile for that class.

Figure 10.5 illustrates the relationship between the elements of traffic conditioning. After a flow is classified, its resource consumption must be measured. The metering function measures the volume of packets over a particular time interval to determine a flow's compliance with the traffic agreement. If the host is bursty, a simple data rate or packet rate may not be sufficient to capture the desired traffic characteristics. A **token bucket** scheme is an example of a way to define a traffic profile to take into account both packet rate and burstiness.

If a traffic flow exceeds some profile, several approaches can be taken. Individual packets in excess of the profile may be re-marked for lower-quality handling and allowed to pass into the DiffServ domain. A traffic shaper may absorb a burst of packets in a buffer and pace the packets over a longer period. A dropper may drop packets if the buffer used for pacing becomes saturated.

token bucket

A data flow control mechanism that adds tokens in periodical time intervals into a buffer (bucket) and allows a data packet to leave the sender only if there are at least as many tokens in the bucket as the packet length of the data packet. This strategy allows precise control of the time interval between two data packets in the network.

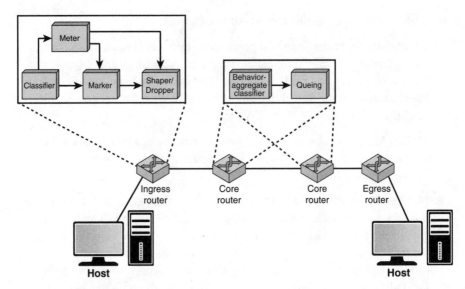

FIGURE 10.5   DS Functions

Per-Hop Behavior

DiffServ is a general architecture that can be used to implement a variety of services. As part of the DS standardization effort, specific types of PHB need to be defined, which can be associated with specific differentiated services. Three fundamental forwarding behaviors have been defined and characterized for general use, plus a "legacy" forwarding behavior class has been defined. The four behavior classes are as follows:

- Default forwarding (DF) for elastic traffic

- Assured forwarding (AF) for general QoS requirements

- Expedited forwarding (EF) for real-time (inelastic) traffic

- Class selector for historical codepoint definitions and PHB requirements

Figure 10.6 shows the DSCP encodings corresponding to the four classes. The remainder of this section discusses each class in turn.

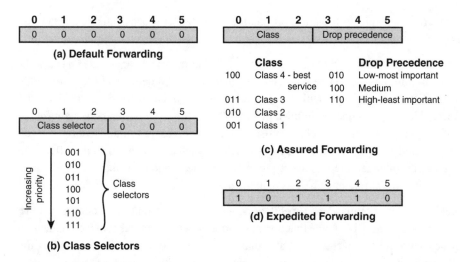

FIGURE 10.6   DiffServ Forwarding Behavior Classes and Corresponding DSField Encoding

Default Forwarding PHB

The default class, referred to as default forwarding (DF), is the best effort forwarding behavior in existing routers. Such packets are forwarded in the order that they are received as soon as link capacity becomes available. If other higher-priority packets in other DiffServ classes are available for transmission, the latter are given preference over best effort default packets. Application traffic in the Internet that uses default forwarding is expected to be elastic in nature. The sender of traffic is expected to adjust its transmission rate in response to changes in available rate, loss, or delay.

Expedited Forwarding PHB

RFC 3246 defines the expedited forwarding (EF) PHB as a building block for low-loss, low-delay, and low-jitter end-to-end services through DiffServ domains. In essence, such a service should appear to the endpoints as providing close to the performance of a point-to-point connection or leased line.

In an internet or packet-switching network, a low-loss, low-delay, and low-jitter service is difficult to achieve. By its nature, an internet involves queues at each node, or router, where packets are buffered waiting to use a shared output link. It is the queuing behavior at each node that results in loss, delays, and jitter. Therefore, unless the internet is grossly oversized to eliminate all queuing effects, care must be taken in handling traffic for EF PHB to ensure that queuing effects do not result in loss, delay, or jitter above a given threshold. RFC 3246 declares that the intent of the EF PHB is to provide a PHB in which suitably marked packets usually encounter short or empty queues. The relative absence of queuing effects minimizes delay and jitter.

Furthermore, if queues remain short relative to the buffer space available, packet loss is also kept to a minimum.

The EF PHB is designed to configure nodes so that the traffic aggregate[2] has a well-defined minimum departure rate. (*Well-defined* means "independent of the dynamic state of the node," in particular, independent of the intensity of other traffic at the node.) The general concept outlined in RFC 3246 is this: The border nodes control the traffic aggregate to limit its characteristics (rate, burstiness) to some predefined level. Interior nodes must treat the incoming traffic in such a way that queuing effects do not appear. In general terms, the requirement on interior nodes is that the aggregate's maximum arrival rate must be less than the aggregate's minimum departure rate.

RFC 3246 does not mandate a specific queuing policy at the interior nodes to achieve the EF PHB. The RFC notes that a simple priority scheme could achieve the desired effect, with the EF traffic given absolute priority over other traffic. So long as the EF traffic itself did not overwhelm an interior node, this scheme would result in acceptable queuing delays for the EF PHB. However, the risk of a simple priority scheme is that packet flows for other PHB traffic would be disrupted. Therefore, some more sophisticated queuing policy might be warranted.

Assured Forwarding PHB

The assured forwarding (AF) PHB is designed to provide a service superior to best effort but one that does not require the reservation of resources within an Internet and does not require the use of detailed discrimination among flows from different users. The concept behind the AF PHB was first introduced in a paper by Clark and Fang [CLAR98] and is referred to as explicit allocation. The AF PHB is more complex than explicit allocation, but it is useful to first highlight the key elements of the explicit allocation scheme:

- Users are offered the choice of a number of classes of service for their traffic. Each class describes a different traffic profile in terms of an aggregate data rate and burstiness.

- Traffic from a user within a given class is monitored at a boundary node. Each packet in a traffic flow is marked out or in based on whether it does or does not exceed the traffic profile.

- Inside the network, there is no separation of traffic from different users or even traffic from different classes. Instead, all traffic is treated as a single pool of packets, with the only distinction being whether each packet has been marked in or out.

---

2   The term *traffic aggregate* refers to the flow of packets associated with a particular service for a particular user.

- When congestion occurs, the interior nodes implement a dropping scheme in which out packets are dropped before in packets.

- Different users will see different levels of service because they will have different quantities of in packets in the service queues.

The advantage of this approach is its simplicity. Very little work is required by the internal nodes. Marking of the traffic at the boundary nodes based on traffic profiles provides different levels of service to different classes.

The AF PHB defined in RFC 2597 expands on the preceding approach in the following ways:

- Four AF classes are defined, allowing the definition of four distinct traffic profiles. A user may select one or more of these classes to satisfy requirements.

- Within each class, packets are marked by the customer or by the service provider with one of three drop precedence values. In case of congestion, the drop precedence of a packet determines the relative importance of the packet within the AF class. A congested DiffServ node tries to protect packets with a lower drop precedence value from being lost by preferably discarding packets with a higher drop precedence value.

This approach is still simpler to implement than any sort of resource reservation scheme but provides considerable flexibility. Within an interior DiffServ node, traffic from the four classes can be treated separately, with different amounts of resources (buffer space, data rate) assigned to the four classes. Within each class, packets are handled based on drop precedence. Therefore, as RFC 2597 points out, the level of forwarding assurance of an IP packet depends on the following:

- How many forwarding resources have been allocated to the AF class to which the packet belongs.

- The current load of the AF class.

- In case of congestion within the class, the drop precedence of the packet.

RFC 2597 does not mandate any mechanisms at the interior nodes to manage the AF traffic. It does reference the RED algorithm as a possible way of managing congestion.

Part c of Figure 10.6 shows the recommended codepoints for AF PHB in the DSField.

Class Selector PHB

Codepoints of the form xxx000 are reserved to provide backward compatibility with the IPv4 precedence service. The IPv4 type of service (TOS) field, which has been replaced by the DSField and ECN field (Figure 10.3a), includes two subfields: a 3-bit precedence subfield and a 4-bit TOS subfield. These subfields serve complementary functions. The TOS subfield provides guidance to the IP entity (in the source or router) on selecting the next hop for this datagram, and the precedence subfield provides guidance about the relative allocation of router resources for this datagram.

The precedence field is set to indicate the degree of urgency or priority to be associated with a datagram. If a router supports the precedence subfield, there are three approaches to responding:

- **Route selection**: A particular route may be selected if the router has a smaller queue for that route or if the next hop on that route supports network precedence or priority (for example, a Token Ring network supports priority).

- **Network service**: If the network on the next hop supports precedence, that service is invoked.

- **Queuing discipline**: A router may use precedence to affect how queues are handled. For example, a router may give preferential treatment in queues to datagrams with higher precedence.

RFC 1812, *Requirements for IP Version 4 Routers*, provides recommendations for queuing discipline that fall into two categories:

- Queue service:

  Routers *should* implement precedence-ordered queue service. Precedence-ordered queue service means that when a packet is selected for output on a (logical) link, the packet of highest precedence that has been queued for that link is sent.

  Any router *may* implement other policy-based throughput management procedures that result in other than strict precedence ordering, but it *must* be configurable to suppress them (that is, use strict ordering).

- Congestion control. When a router receives a packet beyond its storage capacity, it must discard it or some other packet or packets:

  A router *may* discard the packet it has just received; this is the simplest but not the best policy.

  Ideally, the router should select a packet from one of the sessions most heavily abusing the link, given that the applicable QoS policy permits this. A recommended policy in datagram environments using FIFO queues is to discard a packet randomly selected from the queue. An equivalent algorithm in routers using fair queues is to discard from the longest queue. A router *may* use these algorithms to determine which packet to discard.

If precedence-ordered queue service is implemented and enabled, the router *must not* discard a packet whose IP precedence is higher than that of a packet that is not discarded.

A router *may* protect packets whose IP headers request the maximize reliability TOS, except where doing so would be in violation of the previous rule.

A router *may* protect fragmented IP packets, on the theory that dropping a fragment of a datagram may increase congestion by causing all fragments of the datagram to be retransmitted by the source.

To help prevent routing perturbations or disruption of management functions, the router may protect packets used for routing control, link control, or network management from being discarded. Dedicated routers (that is, routers that are not also general purpose hosts, terminal servers, and so on) can achieve an approximation of this rule by protecting packets whose source or destination is the router itself.

The class selector PHB should provide a service that at minimum is equivalent to that of the IPv4 precedence functionality.

10.5 Service Level Agreements

A service level agreement (SLA) is a contract between a network provider and a customer that defines specific aspects of the service that is to be provided. The definition is formal and typically defines quantitative thresholds that must be met. An SLA typically includes the following information:

- **A description of the nature of service to be provided**: A basic service would be IP-based network connectivity of enterprise locations plus access to the Internet. The service may include additional functions such as web hosting, maintenance of domain name servers, and operation and maintenance tasks.

- **The expected performance level of the service**: The SLA defines a number of metrics, such as delay, reliability, and availability, with numerical thresholds.

- **The process for monitoring and reporting the service level:** This describes how performance levels are measured and reported.

Figure 10.7 shows a typical configuration that lends itself to an SLA. In this case, a network service provider maintains an IP-based network. A customer has a number of private networks (for example, LANs) at various sites. Customer networks are connected to the provider via access routers at the access points. The SLA dictates service and performance levels for traffic between access routers across the provider network. In addition, the provider network links to the Internet and thus provides Internet access for the enterprise. For example, for the standard SLA provided by Cogent Communications for its backbone networks includes the following items:

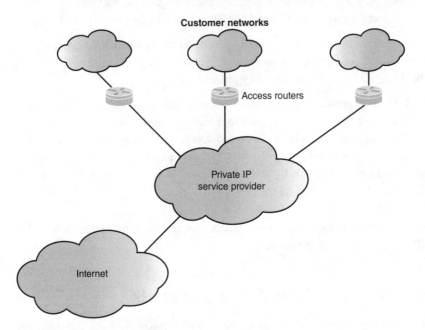

FIGURE 10.7   Typical Framework for Service Level Agreement

- **Availability**: 100 percent availability.

- **Latency (delay):** Monthly average network latency for packets carried over the Cogent Network between backbone hubs for the following regions is as specified here:

  Intra-North America: 45 milliseconds or less

  Intra-Europe: 35 milliseconds or less

  New York to London (transatlantic): 85 milliseconds or less

  Los Angeles to Tokyo (transpacific): 120 milliseconds or less

  Network latency (or round-trip time) is defined as the average time taken for an IP packet to make a round-trip between backbone hubs within the regions specified above on the Cogent Network. Cogent monitors aggregate latency within the Cogent Network by monitoring round-trip times between a sampling of backbone hubs on an ongoing basis.

- Network packet delivery (reliability): Average monthly packet loss no greater than 0.1 percent (or successful delivery of 99.9 percent of packets). Packet loss is defined as the percentage of packets that are dropped between backbone hubs on the Cogent Network.

An SLA can be defined for the overall network service. In addition, SLAs can be defined for specific end-to-end services available across the carrier's network, such as a virtual private network, or differentiated services.

10.6   IP Performance Metrics

The IP Performance Metrics Working Group (IPPM) is chartered by IETF to develop standard metrics that relate to the quality, performance, and reliability of Internet data delivery. Two trends dictate the need for such a standardized measurement scheme:

- The Internet has grown and continues to grow at a dramatic rate. Its topology is increasingly complex. As its capacity has grown, the load on the Internet has grown at an even faster rate. Similarly, private internets, such as corporate intranets and extranets, have exhibited similar growth in complexity, capacity, and load. The sheer scale of these networks makes it difficult to determine quality, performance, and reliability characteristics.

- The Internet serves a large and growing number of commercial and personal users across an expanding spectrum of applications. Similarly, private networks are growing in terms of user base and range of applications. Some of these applications are sensitive to particular QoS parameters, leading users to require accurate and understandable performance metrics.

A standardized and effective set of metrics enables users and service providers to have an accurate common understanding of the performance of the Internet and private internets. Measurement data is useful for a variety of purposes, including the following:

- Supporting capacity planning and troubleshooting of large complex internets.
- Encouraging competition by providing uniform comparison metrics across service providers.
- Supporting Internet research in such areas as protocol design, congestion control, and QoS.
- Verification of SLAs.

Table 10.2 lists the metrics that have been defined in RFCs at the time of this writing. Section a of Table 10.2 lists those metrics which result in a value estimated based on a sampling technique.

TABLE 10.2 IP Performance Metrics

(a) Sampled Metrics

Metric Name	Singleton Definition	Statistical Definitions
One-way delay	Delay = dT, where Src transmits first bit of packet at T and Dst received last bit of packet at T + dT	Percentile, median, minimum, inverse percentile
Round-trip delay	Delay = dT, where Src transmits first bit of packet at T and Src received last bit of packet immediately returned by Dst at T + dT	Percentile, median, minimum, inverse percentile
One-way loss	Packet loss = 0 (signifying successful transmission and reception of packet); = 1 (signifying packet loss)	Average
One-way loss pattern	Loss distance: Pattern showing the distance between successive packet losses in terms of the sequence of packets Loss period: Pattern showing the number of bursty losses (losses involving consecutive packets)	Number or rate of loss distances below a defined threshold, number of loss periods, pattern of period lengths, pattern of interloss period lengths
Packet delay variation	Packet delay variation (pdv) for a pair of packets with a stream of packets = difference between the one-way-delay of the selected packets	Percentile, inverse percentile, jitter, peak-to-peak pdv

(b) Other Metrics

Metric	General Definition	Metrics
Connectivity	Ability to deliver a packet over a transport connection.	One-way instantaneous connectivity, two-way instantaneous connectivity, one-way interval connectivity, two-way interval connectivity, two-way temporal connectivity
Bulk transfer capacity	Long-term average data rate (bps) over a single congestion-aware transport connection.	BTC = (Data sent) / (Elapsed time)

Src = IP address of a host

Dst = IP address of a host

These metrics are defined in three stages:

■ **Singleton metric**: The most elementary, or atomic, quantity that can be measured for a given performance metric. For example, for a delay metric, a singleton metric is the delay experienced by a single packet.

- **Sample metric**: A collection of singleton measurements taken during a given time period. For example, for a delay metric, a sample metric is the set of delay values for all the measurements taken during a one-hour period.

- **Statistical metric**: A value derived from a given sample metric by computing some statistic of the values defined by the singleton metric on the sample. For example, the mean of all the one-way delay values on a sample might be defined as a statistical metric.

The measurement technique can be either active or passive. **Active techniques** require injecting packets into the network for the sole purpose of measurement. There are several drawbacks to this approach. The load on the network is increased. This, in turn, can affect the desired result. For example, on a heavily loaded network, the injection of measurement packets can increase network delay, so that the measured delay is greater than it would be without the measurement traffic. In addition, an active measurement policy can be abused for denial-of-service attacks disguised as legitimate measurement activity. **Passive techniques** observe and extract metrics from existing traffic. This approach can expose the contents of Internet traffic to unintended recipients, creating security and privacy concerns. So far, the metrics defined by the IPPM working group are all active.

For the sample metrics, the simplest technique is to take measurements at fixed time intervals, known as periodic sampling. There are several problems with this approach. First, if the traffic on the network exhibits periodic behavior, with a period that is an integer multiple of the sampling period (or vice versa), correlation effects may result in inaccurate values.

Also, the act of measurement can perturb what is being measured (for example, injecting measurement traffic into a network alters the congestion level of the network), and repeated periodic perturbations can drive a network into a state of synchronization, greatly magnifying what might individually be minor effects. Accordingly, RFC 2330, *Framework for IP Performance Metrics*, recommends Poisson sampling. This method uses a Poisson distribution to generate random time intervals with the desired mean value.

Most of the statistical metrics listed in part a of Table 10.2 are self-explanatory. The percentile metric is defined as follows: The xth percentile is a value y such that $x\%$ of measurements $\geq y$. The inverse percentile of x for a set of measurements is the percentage of all values $\leq x$.

Figure 10.8 illustrates the packet delay variation metric. This metric is used to measure jitter, or variability, in the delay of packets traversing the network. The singleton metric is defined by selecting two packet measurements and measuring the difference in the two delays. The statistical measures make use of the absolute values of the delays.

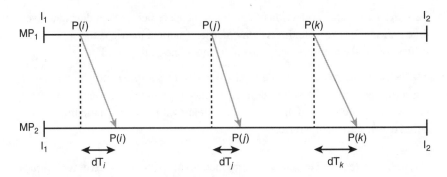

I_1, I_2 = times that mark that beginning and ending of the interval
   in which the packet stream from which the singleton
   measurement is taken occurs.
MP_1, MP_2 = source and destination measurement points
$P(i)$ = ith measured packet in a stream of packets
dT_i = one-way delay for $P(i)$

FIGURE 10.8   Model for Defining Packet Delay Variation

Section b of Table 10.2 lists two metrics that are not defined statistically. Connectivity deals with the issue of whether a transport-level connection is maintained by the network. The current specification (RFC 2678) does not detail specific sample and statistical metrics but provides a framework within which such metrics could be defined. Connectivity is determined by the ability to deliver a packet across a connection within a specified time limit. The other metric, bulk transfer capacity, is similarly specified (RFC 3148) without sample and statistical metrics but begins to address the issue of measuring the transfer capacity of a network service with the implementation of various congestion control mechanisms.

10.7   OpenFlow QoS Support

OpenFlow offers two tools for implementing QoS in data plane switches. The sections that follow examine each of these in turn.

Queue Structures

An OpenFlow switch provides limited QoS support through a simple queuing mechanism. One or more queues can be associated with a port. Queues support the ability to provide minimum data rate guarantees and maximum data rate limits. Queue configuration takes place outside the OpenFlow protocol, either through a command-line tool or through an external dedicated configuration protocol.

A data structure defines each queue. The data structure includes a unique identifier, port this queue is attached to, minimum data rate guaranteed, and maximum data rate.

Counters associated with each queue capture the number of transmitted bytes and packets, number of packets dropped because of overrun, and the elapsed time the queue has been installed in the switch.

The OpenFlow Set-Queue action is used to map a flow entry to an already configured port. Thus, when an arriving packet matches a flow table entry, the packet is directed to a given queue on a given port.

The behavior of the queue is determined beyond the scope of OpenFlow. Thus, although OpenFlow provides a way to define queues, direct packet flows to specific queues, and monitor traffic on each queue, any QoS feature must be implemented outside of OpenFlow.

Meters

A meter is a switch element that can measure and control the rate of packets or bytes. Associated with each meter is a set of one or more bands. If the packet or byte rate exceeds a predefined threshold, the meter triggers the band. The band may drop the packet, in which case it is called a **rate limiter**. Other QoS and policing mechanisms can be designed using meter bands. Each meter is defined by an entry in the meter table for a switch. Each meter has a unique identifier. Meters are not attached to a queue or a port; rather, a meter can be invoked by an instruction from a flow table entry. Multiple flow entries can point to the same meter.

With that brief overview, let's look at the details of meters. A meter measures the rate of packets assigned to it and enables controlling the rate of those packets. The meter measures and controls the rate of the aggregate of all flow entries to which it is attached. Multiple meters can be used in the same table, but in an exclusive way (disjoint set of flow entries). Multiple meters can be used on the same set of packets by using them in successive flow tables.

Figure 10.9 shows the structure of a meter table entry and how it is related to a flow table entry.

A flow table entry may include a `meter` instruction with a `meter_id` as an argument. Any packet that matches that flow entry is directed to the corresponding meter. Within the meter table, each entry consists of three main fields:

- **Meter identifier:** A 32-bit unsigned integer uniquely identifying the meter.

- **Meter bands:** An unordered list of one or more meter bands, where each meter band specifies the rate of the band and the way to process the packet.

- **Counters:** Updated when packets are processed by a meter. These are aggregate counters. That is, the counters count the total traffic of all flows, and do not break the traffic down by flow.

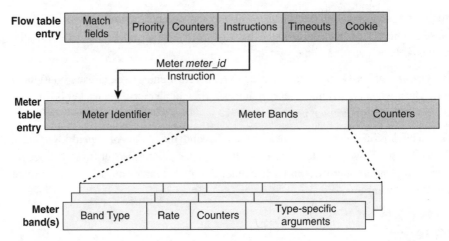

FIGURE 10.9   OpenFlow QoS-Related Formats

Each band has the following structure:

- **Band type:** `drop` or `dscp remark`.

- **Rate:** Used by the meter to select the meter band, defines the lowest rate at which the band can apply.

- **Counters:** Updated when packets are processed by a meter band.

- **Type specific arguments:** Some band types may have optional arguments. Currently, the only optional argument is for the `dscp remark` band type, specifying the amount of drop in precedence.

The meter triggers a meter band if the packet rate or byte rate passing through the meter exceed a predefined threshold. A band of type drop drops packets when the band's rate is exceeded. This can be used to define a rate limiter band. A band of type `dscp remark` increases the drop precedence in the DS codepoint field in the IP header of the packet. This can be used to define a simple DiffServ policer.

Figure 10.10, from the *OpenFlow Switch Specification* (Version 1.5.1, March 2015), illustrates the use of OpenFlow to set, modify, and match on DSCPs. The figure shows three flow tables in one switch. Multiple flow entries in one flow table may use the same meter. Different entries in the same flow table may point to different meters, and a flow entry need not use a meter. By using different meters in a flow table, disjoint set of flow entries can be metered independently. Packets may go through multiple meters when using meters in successive flow tables, at each flow table the matching flow entry may direct it to one meter. The black arrowed lines indicate the progress of one flow through the flow tables. Figure 10.10 shows how multiple meters can be used for a given flow as the flow passes through the network, with the DCSP value changing based on traffic conditions observed by the meters.

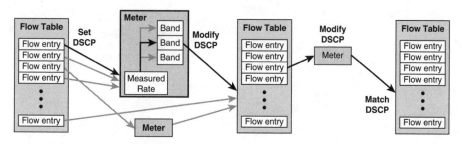

FIGURE 10.10 DSCP Metering

10.8 Key Terms

After completing this chapter, you should be able to define the following terms.

best effort	IP performance metrics
differentiated services	jitter
DS codepoint	OpenFlow meter
elastic traffic	quality of service (QoS)
inelastic traffic	service level agreements (SLA)
Integrated Services Architecture (ISA)	

10.9 References

CISC15: Cisco Systems. *Internetworking Technology Handbook.* July 2015. http://docwiki.cisco.com/wiki/Internetworking_Technology_Handbook

CLAR98: Clark, D., and Fang, W. "Explicit Allocation of Best-Effort Packet Delivery Service." *IEEE/ACM Transactions on Networking*, August 1998.

Chapter 11

QoE: User Quality of Experience

By Florence Agboma
British Sky Broadcasting

It is, of course, important to distinguish between the objective and subjective views, but we cannot pretend the latter are of no concern. Dismissal of subjective matters as being scientifically indecent springs from an excessive zeal for detachment. The objective view, which is predominant in the physical sciences and in strict behaviorist psychology, comes from regarding the observer as being "in" the world, which is out there around him and he can see it "through" his eyes. The subjective view comes from regarding the world as being in the mind of the observer, reality as mental experience.

—*On Human Communication*, Colin Cherry, 1957

Chapter Objectives

After studying this chapter, you should be able to

- Explain the motivations for QoE.
- Define QoE.
- Explain the factors that could influence QoE.
- Present an overview of how QoE can be measured, including a discussion of the differences between subjective and objective assessment.
- Discuss the various application areas of QoE.

This chapter discusses quality of experience (QoE) by providing background information and motivations for its emergence and use. It also discusses the key features of QoE and the factors influencing it. The primary focus is that of QoE within the context of multimedia communication systems, given that bad network performance often highly affects the user's experience.

11.1   Why QoE?

Before the advent of the public Internet, video content delivery was a monopoly of content publishers who delivered their products and services over closed video delivery systems built and managed by cable and satellite TV operators. The operators owned and operated the entire distribution chain as well as the video reception devices (set-top boxes) in the home. These closed networks and devices were under the full control of these operators and were designed, deployed, provisioned, and optimized specifically to deliver high-quality video to consumers.

Figure 11.1 shows an abstraction of the typical satellite TV end-to-end delivery chain. In practice, however, such content delivery and distribution chains are made up of very complex integrations of applications and systems.

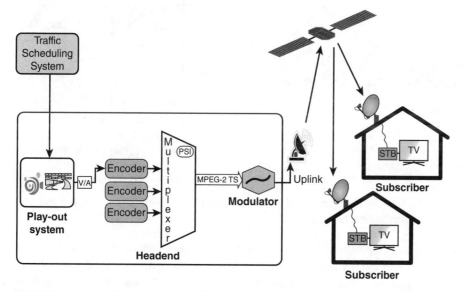

FIGURE 11.1   An Abstraction of a Content Distribution Network Using a Typical Satellite TV Distribution Network

As the illustration shows, the traffic (which in broadcasting means "program material") scheduling system provides audio and video (A/V) content via the play-out system to be encoded and aggregated into a single MPEG transport stream (TS). Together with the program specific information (PSI), the transport stream is transmitted to the subscriber's set-top box (STB) via a satellite.

Online Video Content Delivery

Video delivery over the Internet takes a different approach. Because numerous subnetworks and devices that constitute the Internet are situated in varied geographical locations, video streams reach the user by traversing through uncharted territories, as illustrated in Figure 11.2. With this arrangement, the guaranteeing of a good network performance is often a very challenging task.

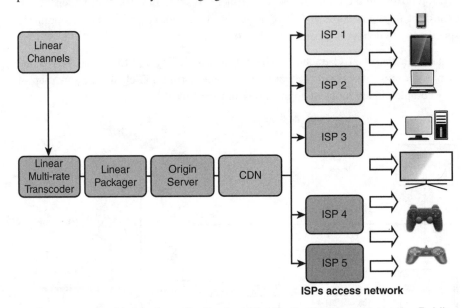

FIGURE 11.2   An Abstraction of a Content Distribution Network Using the Public Internet Distribution Network

Internet service providers (ISPs) do not own the entire content distribution network, and the risk of quality degradations is high. The access network may consist of coax, copper, fiber, or wireless (fixed and mobile) technology. Issues such as packet delay, jitter, and loss may plague such networks.

The growth and expansion of the Internet over the past couple of decades has led to an equally huge growth in the availability of network-enabled video streaming services. Giant technological strides have also been made in the development of network access devices.

With the current popularity of these services, providers need to ensure that user experiences are comparable to what the users would consider to be their reference standards. Users' standards are often influenced by the typically high video quality experience with the older technology, that is, those offered by the cable and satellite TV operators. User expectations can also be influenced by capabilities that currently can only be adequately offered by broadcast TV. These capabilities include the following:

- **Trick mode** functionalities, which are features of video streaming systems that mimic visual feedback given during fast-forward and rewind operations.

Trick mode

A playback feature in any mode other than forward playback at the recorded speed of the audio/video content (1x). Examples include fast-forward, slow motion, reverse, and random access.

- **Contextual** experiences across multiple screens, which includes the ability to pause viewing on one screen and switch to another, thus letting users take the video experience with them on the go.

To manage user experiences for online services, quality of service (QoS) frameworks became the adopted set of technologies and tools employed in managing network traffic in the delivery systems that provide these services. The aim of QoS is to manage the performance of networks and to provide performance guarantees to network traffic. QoS enables the measurement of network parameters, and the detection of changing network conditions (for example, congestion, availability of bandwidth), with the aim to implement stabilization strategies such as resource management and traffic prioritization.

There is now a growing realization, however, that QoS processes by themselves are not fully adequate in providing performance guarantees, because they do not take into account the user perception of network performance and service quality. It is this realization that has led to the emerging discipline of QoE.

The proliferation of different types of access devices further highlights the importance of QoE frameworks. As an illustration, the QoE for a user watching a news clip on a PDA will most likely differ from another user watching that same news clip on a 3G mobile phone. This is because the two terminals come with different display screens, bandwidth capabilities, frame rates, codecs, and processing power. Therefore, delivering multimedia content or services to these two terminal types, without carefully thinking about the users' quality expectations or requirements for these terminal types, might lead to service overprovisioning and network resource wastage.

Informally, QoE refers to the user perception of a particular service. QoE needs to be one of the central metrics employed during the design and management of networks, content delivery systems, and other engineering processes. This is because it refers to a measure of the end-to-end performance at the service level from the user's perspective as measured at the end user devices.

Contextual

Any situational property to describe the end user's environment in terms of physical, temporal, social, task, economic, and technical characteristics. The physical context describes the characteristics of location and space, including movements within and transitions between locations. Temporal context describes the characteristics of time of day, duration, and frequency of use of the system/service. The social context describes the characteristics of service usage; that is, is the end user alone or with other persons? The economic context refers to the characteristics of costs and subscription type.

 See Section 11.4, "Definition of Quality of Experience"

11.2   Service Failures Due to Inadequate QoE Considerations

The stereoscopic 3D TV service is often cited as a prime example of a service that was a spectacular commercial failure because it had very poor QoE ratings.

In 2010, broadcasters such as Disney, Foxtel, BBC, and Sky began actively making 3D content delivery available as a service to their customers as a premium service experience. Indeed, each of these broadcasters rolled out their own dedicated 3D television channels. Within five years, all of them except Sky had to terminate their operations.

A number of factors contributed to the failure of these services. The first was the general unavailability of "wow video content" (that is, content that users are most likely to find exciting or take much interest in). The second was the need to wear special 3D glasses even when using these services in a home environment. Third, because broadcasters were initially in a rush to deploy the 3D TV technology, content was produced by inexperienced creators using inadequate systems and tools. This resulted in a great deal of poorly produced 3D content, which may have alienated the early subscribers.

11.3   QoE-Related Standardization Projects

Because the field of QoE has been growing rapidly, a number of projects have been initiated to address issues relating to best practices and standards. These projects have been aimed at preventing commercial failures like the one described in the Section 11.2. Table 11.1 summarizes the prominent ones amongst these project initiatives, two of which are described in the paragraphs that follow.

TABLE 11.1   QoE Initiatives and Projects

Organization	Mission	QoE-Related effort
QUALINET	A multidisciplinary consortium for QoE research	A common terminology for QoE framework
Eureka Celtic	A collaborative industry-driven European research in the area of telecommunications	Quality of Experience Estimators in Networks (QuEEN) agent to estimate QoE for generic services
International Telecommunication Union— Telecommunication Standardization Sector (ITU-T)	United Nations agency that produces recommendations with a view to standardizing telecommunications on a worldwide basis	QoE standardization IPTV QoE requirements

Organization	Mission	QoE-Related effort
IEEE Standards Association (IEEE-SA)	A standards-setting body within IEEE, develops consensus standards through an open process that engages industry and brings together a broad stakeholder community	Standard for Network-Adaptive Quality of Experience (QoE)

The Video Quality Experts Group (VQEG) is currently working on draft ITU recommendations for 3D video quality assessments for home entertainment systems (http://www.its.bldrdoc.gov/vqeg/projects/3dtv/3dtv.aspx). The VQEG is also working on producing reference documentation regarding the features that can impact 3D TV viewing experience, as well as ways in which they can be minimized. Examples of these features are crosstalk, visual discomfort, and visual fatigue.

Video Quality Experts Group (VQEG)

Another initiative is by the Quality of Experience Estimators in Networks (QuEEN) project [ETSI14], which is a multi-organizational and multinational initiative aimed at addressing issues relating to online services such as voice, video, and IPTV. These are areas where service and network providers seek to differentiate their service offerings, in terms of QoE and lower churn rates, from their competitors.

QuEEN developed an operational framework by categorizing the factors that may have an influence on QoE into well-defined layers. This provided an insight into how each layer could be associated with a quality value. The process of the QoE estimation employed the use of a software agent that integrated with each of the layers, and also with software systems that attempt to model how a human subject would give approval ratings based on the values of these parameters. The agent had the capability of aggregating data from various probes across the network.

The QuEEN agent was at the core of the layered model. It enabled the flexible deployments of QoE estimators in a large-scale distributed environment. The three-year QuEEN project, which concluded in 2014, produced some impressive results. The QuEEN approach of using software QoE agents has been standardized in different ETSI and ITU standards. It is envisaged that this will encourage the development of new ways of using QoE, as well as new methods in QoE management.

11.4 Definition of Quality of Experience

There are a number of different, although similar, definitions of QoE. The nature of QoE, which turns out to vary from person to person, is difficult to grasp in a quantitative way. QoE requires a multidisciplinary approach, encompassing communication networks, cognitive processes, multimedia signal processing, and social psychology, focused on understanding the user perception of quality.

Researchers working within these various disciplines often use their own specialist language and terminology in describing identical concepts. Thus, studying and interpreting literature from a given discipline is usually not a trivial exercise for researchers from other disciplines. As a consequence, there is the lack of a consensus of how to measure or describe QoE and the wide range of factors that influence it.

A first step toward a multidisciplinary approach to QoE involves specifying a common terminology framework.

Work toward drawing up this common framework was begun in 2012 by the European Network on Quality of Experience in Multimedia Systems and Services (QUALINET) [MOLL12]. This is a group of researchers and industry experts whose main objectives were to foster discussions about the formal definitions of QoE and its related concepts.

The definitions of quality, experience, and quality of experience presented in this section are based on the ones provided in the QUALINET's white paper of definitions [MOLL12].

Definition of Quality

Quality is the resulting verdict produced by a user after he/she has carried a "comparison and judgment" process on an observable occurrence or event.

This process comprises the following key sequential steps:

Perception

The conscious processing of sensory information by the human sensory organs.

- **Perception** of the event
- Reflection on the perception
- Description of the perception
- Evaluation and description of the result or outcome

Thus, quality is evaluated in terms of the degree to which the user's needs have been fulfilled within the context of the event. The result of this evaluation is usually referred to as the quality score (or rating) if it is presented with reference to a scale.

Definition of Experience

Experience is an individual's description of a stream of perceptions, and his/her interpretation of one or multiple events. An experience might result from an encounter with a system, service, or an artifact.

It is important to note that the description of an experience need not necessarily result in a judgment of its quality.

Quality Formation Process

As shown in Figure 11.3, there are two distinct subprocess paths to the formation of a quality score: the perception path and the reference path.

The reference path reflects the temporal and contextual nature of the quality formation process. This path is influenced by memories of former experienced qualities, as indicated by the arrow from experienced quality to the reference path.

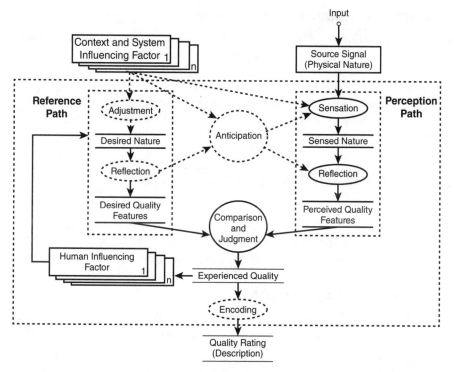

FIGURE 11.3   A Schematic Illustration of the Quality Formation Process from an Individual Point of View. Source: [MOLL12]

The perception path is characterized by the physical input signal, which is to be assessed, reaching the sensory organs of the observer. This physical event is processed through low-level perceptual processes into a perceived feature within the constraints of the reference path. This perceived feature undergoes a reflection process, which interprets these sensory features through **cognitive** processing. At this point, the perceived concepts can be described and potentially quantified to become perceived quality features.

Cognitive

The mental processes of perception, memory, judgment and reasoning.

The quality features resulting from the reference and perception paths are then translated into the experienced quality on behalf of the comparison and judgment

Event

An observable occurrence.

process. This experienced quality is delimited in time, space, and character, and thus can be called a quality **event**. The relevant information about the event can only be obtained on a descriptive level from the user.

The final step of the quality formation lies in some kind of comparison of the expected and experienced features. In this particular case, the output of the quality formation process corresponds to the quality of experiencing.

Definition of Quality of Experience

Combining the concepts and definitions from the preceding sections, the definition of QoE that reflects broad industry and academic consensus is as follows:

> Quality of experience (QoE) is the degree of delight or annoyance of the user of an application or service. It results from the fulfillment of his or her expectations with respect to the utility/enjoyment of the application or service in the light of the user's personality and current state.

11.5   QoE Strategies in Practice

Key findings from QoE-related projects show that for many services, multiple QoS parameters contribute toward the overall user's perception of quality. This has resulted in the emergence of the concept of the QoE/QoS layered approach in which the requirements of the users drive network-dimensioning strategies.

The QoE/QoS Layered Model

The QoE/QoS layered approach does not ignore the QoS aspect of the network, but instead, user and service level perspectives are complementary, as shown in Figure 11.4.

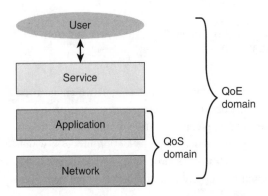

FIGURE 11.4   QoE/QoS Layered Model with the Domains of Interest for the Frameworks

Note that because there is an overlap between the QoE and QoS domains, there is a considerable amount of information sharing/feedback between the frameworks.

The levels in the layered approach are as follows:

- **User**: The user interacts with the service. It is their degree of delight or annoyance from using the service that is to be measured. Being linked to human perception, QoE is hard to describe in a quantitative way, and it varies from person to person. The complexities of QoE at the user level stem from the differences between individual user characteristics, of which some might be time-varying, whereas others are of a relatively stable nature. Examples could include gender, age, attitudes, prior experience, expectations, socio-economic status, cultural background, educational level, and so on. Therefore, it becomes a challenge to derive unified QoE metrics for all users and their contexts. The current practice in any QoE measurement is to identify and control for the relatively stable characteristics of a user in a way that is satisfactory to at least a large proportion of the potential user group.

- **Service**: The service level provides a virtual level where the user's experience of the overall performance of the service can be measured. It is the interface where the user interacts with the service (for example, the visual display to the user). It is also where tolerance thresholds are measured. As an illustration, the QoE measures from the user perspective for streaming applications could be startup time, audio/visual quality, channel change delay, and buffering interruptions. However, the QoE measures for web browsing applications could be page load waiting times.

- **Application-level QoS (AQoS)**: AQoS deals with the control of application-specific parameters such as content resolution, bit rate, frame rate, color depth, codec type, layering strategy, and sampling rate. The network capacity often dictates the bandwidth that will be allocated to a service for transmission. Because of this fixed underlying resource, some parameters at the application level are usually adjusted and controlled to achieve a desired quality level. For example, for an audio service, a sampling rate of 96 kHz might allow for more information to be audibly perceived as compared to a 48-kHz rate. But this larger sampling rate comes with the expense of generating bigger audio file sizes. This is because the sampling rate is the number of times an analog sound signal is measured per second. Each of these measurements (or samples) is stored or transmitted as a digital value.

As another example, for video services, there is a huge variety in device screen sizes (each featuring varied aspect ratios) from which to choose. The one common feature in this array of equipment is that they are all capable of rescaling video images. For a given bit rate, there might be a trade-off between lower resolution images that are slightly blurred and with fewer digital artifacts (visual anomalies) versus higher resolution images that provide sharper images but possibly having more artifacts. The bit rate usually provides an indication of the quality of a video (or audio) file. This is because it represents the number of bits used in encoding each second of a file. Most compression standards use block-based and motion compensation coding schemes and as a result, additional compression artifacts are added to the decoded video.

- **Network-level QoS (NQoS)**: This level is concerned with the low-level network parameters such as service coverage, bandwidth, delay, throughput, and packet loss. There are a number of ways in which network-level QoS parameters impact QoE. One such way is via network delay, which impacts QoE especially for interactive services. For instance, the interactive nature of web browsing that requires multiple retrieval events within a certain window of time might be affected by delay variations of the network. Voice over IP (VoIP) services might have stringent response-time demands, whereas e-mail services might tolerate much longer delays.

The different distribution methods of streaming video over the network also affect QoE in different ways. For instance, HTTP-based adaptive streaming, which uses TCP, reacts to bandwidth constraints and CPU capacity in either of the following ways:

- Switching to streaming using other available bit rate encodings, depending on available resources

- Frame freeze (rebuffering) occurring because of incoming packet starvation in the player buffer

The bit rate switches and rebuffering have an adverse effect on QoE.

UDP streaming, however, uses multicast to replicate the streams throughout the network. Quite often a resilient coding scheme and a flow control mechanism are implemented to maintain the viewing experience despite the effects of bad network conditions.

Summarizing and Merging the QoE/QoS Layers

The preceding discussion suggests that the effect of QoE could be an attribute of only the application layer or a combination of both the application and network layers. Although the trade-offs between quality and network capacity may begin with application-level QoS because of network capacity considerations, an understanding of the user requirements at the service level (that is, in terms QoE measures) would enable a better choice of application-level QoS parameters to be mapped onto the network-level QoS parameters. A scenario that aims at controlling QoE using QoS parameters as actuators is discussed in Section 11.8.

11.6   Factors Influencing QoE

QoE must be studied and addressed by taking into account both technical and nontechnical factors. Many factors contribute to producing a good QoE. Here, the key factors are as follows:

- **User demographics**: The context of demographics herein refers to the relatively stable characteristics of a user that might have an indirect influence on perception, and intimately affects other technical factors to determine QoE. In a landmark project [QUIN12] studying the adoption of HD voice telephony, the different user groups produced significantly different quality ratings. The grouping of users was based on demographic characteristics such as their attitudes toward adoption of new technologies, socio-demographic information, socioeconomic status, and prior knowledge. Cultural background is another user demographic factor that might also have an influence on perception because of cultural attitude to quality.

- **Type of device**: Different device types possess different characteristics that may impact on QoE. An application designed to run on more than one device type, for example on a connected TV device such as Roku and on an iOS device such as an iPhone, may not deliver the same QoE on every device.

- **Content:** Content types can range from interactive content specifically curated according to personal interests, to content that is produced for linear TV transmission. Studies have suggested that people tend to watch video on-demand (VoD) content with a higher level of engagement than its competing alternative, linear TV. This may be because users will make an active decision to watch specific VoD content, and as a result, give their full attention to it. One could infer that for VoD users might be less tolerant of any quality degradations because of their high level of engagement.

- **Connection type:** The type of connection used to access the service influences users' expectations and their QoEs. Users have been found to have lower expectations when using 3G connections in contrast to a wire line connection even when the two connection types were identical in terms of their technical conditions. Users have also been found to lower their expectations considerably, and are more tolerant to visual impairments, on small devices.

- **Media (audio-visual) quality:** This is a significant factor affecting QoE, as it is the part of a service that is most noticeable by the user. The overall audio and video quality appears to be content dependent. For less-complex scenes (for example, head and shoulder content), audio quality is slightly more important than video quality. In contrast, for high-motion content, video quality tends to be significantly more important than audio quality.

- **Network:** Content delivery via the Internet is highly susceptible to the effects of delays, jitter, packet loss, and available bandwidth. Delay variation results in the user experiencing frame freeze and the lack of lip synchronization between what is heard (audio) and what is seen (video). Although video content can be delivered using a number of Internet protocols, not all of them are reliable. However, content delivery is guaranteed using TCP/IP. Nevertheless, bad network conditions degrade QoE because of increased rebuffering and increased interruptions in playback. Rebuffering interruptions in IP video playback is seen to be the worst degradation on user QoE and should be avoided at the cost of startup delay. On the same note, QoE for a given startup delay strongly depends on the application context and the user expectations. In spite of the different QoE factors that are concerned with the network, reliability and a strong wireless signal are crucial for consuming TV-like services.

- **Usability:** Another QoE factor is the amount of effort that is required to use the service. The service design must render good quality without a great deal of technical input from the user.

- **Cost:** The long-established practice of judging quality by price implies that expectations are price dependent. If the tariff for a certain service quality is high, users may be highly sensitive to any quality degradations.

11.7 Measurements of QoE

QoE measurement techniques evolved through the adaptation and application of psychophysics methods during the early stages of television systems. This section introduces three QoE measurement methods: subjective assessment, objective assessment, and end-user device analytics.

Subjective Assessment

For subjective assessment of QoE, experiments are carefully designed to a high level of control (such as in a controlled laboratory, field tests, or crowdsourcing environments) so that the validity and reliability of the results can be trusted. It might be useful to consult expert advice during the initial design of the subjective experiment, because the topics of experimental design, experimental execution, and statistical analysis are complex. In general terms, a methodology to obtain subjective QoE data might consist of the following phases:

- **Characterize the service:** The task at this stage is to choose the QoE measures that affect user experience the most. As an example, for a multimedia conferencing service, the quality of the voice takes precedence over the quality of video. Also, the video quality required for such applications does not demand a very high frame rate, provided that audio-to-video synchronization is maintained. Therefore, the resolution of individual frames can be considerably lower than the case of other video streaming services, especially when the size of the screen is small (such as a mobile phone). So, in multimedia conferencing, the QoE measures might be prioritized as voice quality, audio-video synchronization, and image quality.

- **Design and define test matrix:** Once the service has been characterized, the QoS factors that affect the QoE measures can be identified. For instance, the video quality in streaming services might be directly affected by network parameters such as bandwidth, packet loss, and encoding parameters such as frame rate, resolution, and codec. The capability of the rendering device will also play a significant role in terms of screen size and processing power. However, testing such a large combination of parameters may not be feasible. This draft matrix could be reduced to more achievable test conditions by eliminating the combinations that have similar effects on QoE.

- **Specify test equipment and materials:** Subjective tests should be designed to specify test equipment that will allow the test matrix to be enforced in a controlled fashion. For instance, to assess the correlation between NQoS parameters and the perceived QoE in a streaming application, at least a client device and a streaming server separated by an emulated network are needed. If the objective is to evaluate how different device capabilities impact QoE, a video content is chosen to produce formats that can run in each of the client devices under scrutiny.

- **Identify sample population:** A representative sample population is identified, possibly covering different classes of users categorized by the user demographics that are of interest to the experimenter. Depending on the target environment for the subjective test, at least 24 test subjects has been suggested as the ideal number for a controlled environment (for example, a laboratory) and at least 35 test subjects for a public environment. Fewer subjects may be used for pilot studies to indicate trending. The use of crowdsourcing in the context of subjective assessment is still nascent, but it has the potential to further increase the size of the sample population and could reduce the completion time of the subjective test.

- **Subjective methods:** Several subjective assessment methodologies exist within the industry recommendations. However, in most of them, the typical recommendation is for each test subject to be presented with the test conditions under scrutiny along with a set of rating scales that allows the correlation of the users' responses with the actual QoS test conditions being tested. There are several rating scales, depending on the design of the experiment.

- **Analysis of results:** When the test subjects have rated all QoS test conditions, a post-screening process might be applied to the data to remove any erroneous data from a test subject that appears to have voted randomly. Depending on the design of the experiment, a variety of statistical approaches could be used to analyze results. The simplest and the most common quantification method is the mean opinion score (MOS), which is the average of the opinions collected for a particular QoS test condition. The results from subjective assessment experiments are used to quantify QoE, and to model the impacts of QoS factors. Subjective experiments require significant planning and design so as to produce reliable subjective MOS ratings. However, they are time-consuming, expensive to carry out, and are not feasible for real-time in-service monitoring. In such situations, the use of objective assessment is often desirable.

Objective Assessment

For objective assessment of QoE, computational algorithms provide estimates of audio, video, and audiovisual quality as perceived by the user. Each objective model targets a specific service type. The goal of any objective model is to find the optimum fit that strongly correlates with data obtained from subjective experiments. The following phases presented here should not be considered as exhaustive, but aim at illustrating a process of obtaining objective QoE data. A methodology to obtain objective QoE data might consist of the following phases:

- **Database of subjective data**: A starting point might be the collection of a group of subjective datasets as this could serve as benchmark for training and verifying the performance of the objective model. A typical example of one of these datasets might be the subjective QoE data generated from well-established subjective testing procedures, as discussed earlier. The selection of the subjective datasets should typically reflect the use cases of the objective model.

- **Preparation of objective data**: The data preparation for the objective model might typically include a combination of the same QoS test conditions as found in the subjective datasets, as well as other complex QoS conditions. A variety of preprocessing procedures might be applied to the video data prior to training, and refinement of the algorithm.

- **Objective methods**: There are various algorithms in existence that can provide estimates of audio, video, and audiovisual quality as perceived by the user. Some algorithms are specific to a perceived quality artifact, while others can provide estimates for a wider scope of quality artifacts. Examples of the perceived artifacts might include blurring, blockiness, unnatural motion, pausing, skipping, rebuffering, and imperfect error concealment after transmission errors.

- **Verification of results**: After the objective algorithm has processed all QoS test conditions, the predicted values might benefit from a post-screening process to remove any outliers; this is the same concept applied to the subjective datasets. The predicted values from the objective algorithm might be in a different scale as compared to the subjective QoE datasets. The predicted values might be transformed to the same scale as obtained in the subjective experiments (for example, into the mean opinion scores) to enable like-for-like comparisons, and also so that an optimum fit between the predicted QoE values and subjective QoE data can be obtained.

■ **Validation of objective model**: The objective data analysis might be evaluated with respect to its prediction accuracy, consistency, and linearity by using a different subjective dataset. It is worth noting that the performance of the model might depend on the training datasets and the verification procedures. The Video Quality Experts Group (VQEG) validates the performance of objective perceptual models so that they can become ITU recommendations and standards for objective quality models for both television and multimedia applications.

End-User Device Analytics

End-user device analytics is yet another alternative method of QoE measurement. Real-time data such as the connection time, bytes sent, and average playback rate are collected by the video player application for each video viewing session and fed back to a server module where the data is pre-aggregated and then turned into actionable QoE measures. Some of the metrics reported for per-user and aggregate viewing sessions include startup delay, rebuffering delays, average bit rates, and the frequency of bit rate switches.

Operators may be inclined to associate viewer engagement levels with their QoE because good QoEs usually make viewers less likely to abandon a viewing session. The definition of viewer engagement may have different meanings for different operators and context. First of all, operators might like to know which viewer engagement metrics affect QoE the most to guide the design of the delivery infrastructures. Second, they might also like to quickly identify and resolve service outages, and other quality issues. A minute of encoder glitch could replicate throughout the ISPs, and the various delivery infrastructures, and affect all their customers. Operators might like to know the scale of this impact, and how it affects users' engagement. Finally, they would like to understand their customers' demographics (connection methods, type of device, bit rates of the consumed asset) within a demographic region so that resources can be strategically dimensioned.

QoE enthusiasts advocate QoE measurement to be a multidisciplinary approach that seeks to explain its findings, building on general laws of perception, sociology, and user psychology. With the use of end-user device analytics as a means of QoE measurement, there are many variables that cannot be accounted for (for example, why a user exits a service). A lack of interest in watching the content might result in a user exiting a service, and not necessarily because of poor QoE.

One method of tackling these unexplained variables is to use the fraction of video viewed as a measure of engagement because this can be measured objectively. The data that appears to belong to early quitters can then be systematically removed from any analyses to obtain a clearer understanding of how the QoE measures impact viewer engagement.

Summarizing the QoE Measurement Methods

The mean opinion score (MOS) appears to be the de facto standard metric for QoE. The possible reasons could be its long-term establishment in telephony networks, and perhaps its widespread acceptance on the merits that it can be easily understood. There are different types of MOS values and different test methodologies to produce them. See ITU-T Recommendation P 913, *Methods for the Subjective Assessment of Video Quality, Audio Quality and Audiovisual Quality of Internet Video and Distribution Quality Television in Any Environment*, 2014, for more details. Table 11.2 shows the five-point absolute category rating MOS scale that is commonly used

TABLE 11.2   Five Point MOS Rating Scale

Score	Label
5	Excellent
4	Good
3	Fair
2	Poor
1	Bad

The MOS value is the average opinion for the group of users, for a given QoS test condition. It is not necessarily the opinion score for an individual user, because different users have different opinions. Additional information such as statistical uncertainty in terms of confidence intervals is usually encouraged. The MOS is considered to be characteristic of only the experiment and the group of test subjects from which it was derived.

MOS has to be interpreted within context. First of all, the MOS value obtained for a particular QoS test condition, in a subjective experiment, may depend on the range of the QoS test conditions used in the experiment. This might be due to test subjects recalibrating their use of the rating scale to the conditions in the experiment. An appropriately designed experiment whereby there is a practice period at the start of the experiment, and the test conditions include the best and worst conditions, minimizes the effects of the aforementioned behavior.

Direct comparisons of MOS scores obtained from separate experiments are generally not meaningful. They are only meaningful if the experiments have been specially designed to enable such comparisons. Data from such specially configured experiments must be studied and shown that their MOS comparisons are statistically valid. Biases in the rating scale interpretation might exist because of differences in the test subject profiles (for example, age and technology exposure, test environment, and the presentation order of the test conditions).

It is possible that different objective models that have been trained and optimized using different subjective contexts will predict nonidentical MOS values for the same QoS conditions. Objective models are usually developed and optimized for a specific scope of quality features. As a consequence, comparisons between MOS predictions and thresholds can only be reliably made if the thresholds are chosen in the context of the MOS model.

Objective assessment seems to offer real-time QoE measurements, but end-user device analytics as a method of QoE measurement appears to be an alternative approach. Currently, there is the lack of a reference methodology for end-user device analytics as a method of QoE measurement, analogous to mean opinion scores found in subjective assessments and objective assessments.

A limiting factor to this development might be the restricted rights governing service providers on the usage of their databases. This makes it challenging for researchers, service providers, and delivery infrastructure designers to develop better delivery infrastructures.

Subjective experiments are probably still the most accurate way to measure QoE, and also the only way to obtain reliable ground truth data used in benchmarking objective QoE models.

11.8 Applications of QoE

The practical applications of QoE can be grouped into two areas based on the main usage.

- **Service QoE monitoring:** Service monitoring allows the support teams (for example, service provider and network operator) to continually monitor the quality experienced by the end users of the service. A service alert message might be sent to the support teams when QoE falls below a certain threshold value, as this will allow the support teams to quickly identify and resolve service outages and other QoE issues.

  Depending on the use case of the service being monitored, such monitoring tools might be located at any one node, or at all nodes, within the content delivery ecosystem. The nodes could be at the headend incoming feeds, distribution networks, and at endpoints locations. This approach might introduce high monitoring overheads for a per-user scenario.

- **QoE-centric network management:** The ability to control and optimize the user experience when QoE degradation issues arise is the holy grail of QoE network management. Given the multidimensional aspect of the overall QoE (such as the network-level conditions of the subnetworks, application-level QoS, device capability, and user demographics), a typical challenge lies in providing actionable QoE information feedback to the network or service provider.

    Two approaches in which QoE-centric network management can be exploited are as follows:

    - In the first approach, a set of QoS measurement values together with the appropriate assumptions, are used in computing the expected QoE for a user.

    - In the second approach, which is somewhat the opposite of the first, a target QoE for a user together with the appropriate assumptions is used to produce estimates of the required QoS values.

The first approach can be taken by a service provider, who can provide a range of QoS offerings with an outline of the QoE that the customer might reasonably expect.

The second approach can be taken by a customer who defines the required QoE, and then determines what level of service will meet that need.

Figure 11.5 illustrates a scenario where the user can make a selection from a range of services, including the required level of service (SLA). By contrast to the purely QoS-based management, the SLA here is not expressed in terms of raw network parameters. Instead, the user indicates a QoE target; it is the service provider that maps this QoE target together with the type of service selected, onto QoS demands.

For instance, in the case of multimedia streaming service, the user may simply choose between two QoE levels (high or low). The service provider selects the appropriate quality prediction model and management strategy (for example, minimize network resource consumption) and forwards a QoS request to the operator. It is possible that the network cannot sustain the required level of QoS, making it impossible to deliver the requested QoE. This situation leads to a signal back to the user, prompting a reduced set of services/QoE values.

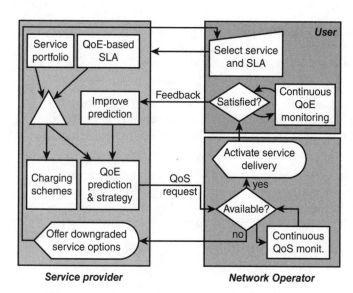

FIGURE 11.5   QoE-Centric Network Management

Assuming that the network can support the service, delivery can be activated. During service operation, two monitoring and control loops run concurrently: one at network level and the other at service level. The latter allows the user to switch to a different level of QoE (for example, to get a cheaper service or to request higher quality). If the user generates no explicit feedback, this means that the user is satisfied, which confirms that the quality prediction model is working. In this way, the quality prediction model continues to be redefined during service delivery, allowing it to evolve as user needs and devices change over time.

11.9   Key Terms

After completing this chapter, you should be able to define the following terms.

trick mode	contextual	quality of experience
cognitive	perception	Event
QoE measurement	subjective assessment	Objective assessment

11.10   References

ETSI14: ETSI TS 103 294 V1.1.1 Speech and Multimedia Transmission Quality (STQ); Quality of Experience; A Monitoring Architecture (2014-12).

MOLL12: Moller, S., Callet, P., and Perkis, A. "Qualinet White Paper on Definitions on Quality of Experienced," European Network on Quality of Experience in Multimedia Systems and Services (COST Action IC 1003) (2012).

QUIN12: M.R.Quintero, M., and Raake, A. "Is Taking into Account the Subjects' Degree of Knowledge and Expertise Enough When Rating Quality?" Fourth International Workshop on Quality of Multimedia Experience (QoMEX), pp.194,199, 5[nd]7 July 2012.

Chapter | **12**

Network Design Implications of QoS and QoE

By Sofiene Jelassi

Assistant Professor, University of Monastir, Tunisia

But some amazing experience had disturbed his native composure and left its traces in his bristling hair, his flushed, angry cheeks, and his flurried, excited manner.

—*The Adventure of Wisteria Lodge*, Sir Arthur Conan Doyle

Chapter Objectives

After studying this chapter, you should be able to

- Translate metrics from QoS to QoE domain.
- Select the appropriate QoE/QoS mapping model for a given operational situation.
- Deploy QoE-centric monitoring solutions over a given infrastructure.
- Deploy QoE-aware applications over QoE-centric infrastructure.

This chapter concludes Part Four by bringing together the concepts of quality of service (QoS) and quality of experience (QoE) and discussing the practical implications of employing these two concepts.

The chapter is organized as follows; section 12.1 classifies existing **QoS/QoE mapping models** from practical perspectives. Section 12.2 enumerates few IP-oriented QoE/QoS mapping models used for video services. Section 12.3 discusses approaches that could be used to add QoE capability to networks and services. Sections 12.4 and 12.5 describe respectively QoE-centric monitoring and management solutions.

QoE/QoS mapping model

A function that transforms metrics from QoS to QoE domains.

12.1 Classification of QoE/QoS Mapping Models

Typically, mathematical models are used to define the empirical relationship between QoS and QoE. These models will be referred to hereafter as either *QoE/QoS mapping models* or *quality models*. They are derived using classical approaches that fit a model to a dataset, such as regression, artificial neural network, and Bayesian network. Today, a wide range of QoE/QoS mapping models are reported in the literature. They differ in term of their inputs, working modes, accuracy, and application areas. The application area of QoE/QoS mapping models depends mostly on their inputs. QoE/QoS mapping models can be classified according to their inputs into three categories:

- Black-box media-based models

- Glass-box parameter-based models

- Gray-box parameter-based models

The sections that follow describe these models.

Black-Box Media-Based QoS/QoE Mapping Models

Black-box media-based quality models rely on the analysis of media gathered at system entrance and exit. Hence, they account implicitly for the characteristics of examined media processing system. They are classified into two categories:

- **Double-sided or full-reference quality models:** They use as inputs the clean stimulus and the corresponding degraded stimulus (see part a of Figure 12-1). They compare the clean and degraded stimulus in a *perceptual domain* that accounts for psychophysics capability of human sensory system. The perceptual domain is a transformation of traditional physical temporal and frequency domains performed according to characteristics of users perceptions. Basically, the larger the perceptual distance, the greater the degradation level. This model needs to align clean and degraded stimulus because the comparison is made on per-block basis. The stimulus alignment should be realized autonomously, that is, without adding extra control information describing stimulus structure.

■ **One-sided or no-reference quality models**: They rely solely on the degraded stimulus to estimate the final QoE values. They parse the degraded stimulus to extract the observed distortions, which are dependent on the media type, for example, audio, image and video. As an example, artifacts extracted from audio stimulus include whistle, circuit noises, echoes, level saturation, clapping, interruptions, and pauses (see part b of Figure 11-1). The gathered distortions are adequately combined and transformed to compute the QoE values.

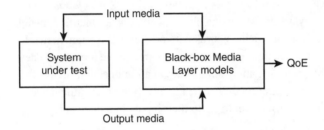

(a): Double-sided or full-reference quality models.

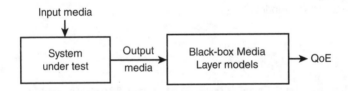

(b): One-sided or no-reference mapping models.

FIGURE 12.1   Black-Box Media-Based QoS/QoE Mapping Models

The main advantage of black-box quality models resides in their ability to measure QoE values using information gathered at the periphery of a given media processing system. Hence, they may be used in a generic fashion over different infrastructures and technologies. This sidesteps a complex and cumbersome measuring process of the underlying systems. Moreover, it enables enhancing unconditionally quality models, that is, independently of technical and ethical constraints related to the measurement processes. Furthermore, black-box quality models may easily operate on either per-user or per-content basis.

The main shortcoming of black-box quality models resides in the requirements to access the final representation of stimulus, which is often inaccessible in practice for privacy reasons. Moreover, full-reference quality models use clean stimulus as inputs that is often unavailable or hardly accessible at the system output. This issue may be sidestepped using no-reference quality models, but their unproved and instable performance confines their effectiveness.

The full-reference black-box quality models are widely used for onsite benchmarking, diagnosis, and tuning of network equipments, where clean stimulus is available. The no-reference quality models may be used for the same purposes, but their limited accuracy reduces their results credibility. The black-box quality models are used offline for the evaluation of application-layer components, such as codec, packet loss concealment (PLC), and buffering schemes. In addition, the no-reference black-box quality models may be used online for QoE monitoring.

Glass-Box Parameter-Based QoS/QoE Mapping Models

The glass-box parameter-based quality models quantify the QoE of a given service through the full characterization of the underlying transport network and edge devices. The set of considered characterization parameters and their combination rules are derived based on extensive subjective experiments and thorough statistical analysis. The glass-box parameter-based models may operate off line or on line according to the availability of characterization parameters at a given measurement instant. The characterization parameters include noise, packet loss, coding scheme, one-way delay, and delay jitter. The glass-box parameter-based models are generally less accurate and coarser than black-box media-based ones.

A well-known offline glass-box parameter-based model, named E-Model, has been defined by the ITU-T in Rec. G.107. E-Model aims at estimating QoE of voice calls transmitted over a planned transport infrastructure (*The E-Model, A Computational Model for Use in Transmission Planning*, 2007). The prevailing version of E-Model includes 21 basic characterization parameters. E-Model provides a single scalar value referred to as rating factor R that lies between 0 (worst quality) and 100 (excellent quality). In practice, any designed transport configurations that result in a rating factor below 60 should be avoided. In such a case, adequate actions should be undertaken to enhance QoE of voice calls. The basic characterization parameters are classified into simultaneous, equipment, and delay impairment factors, denoted respectively as I_s, I_e, and I_d. I_s quantifies the impairments that depends on characteristics of voice signals, such as quantification and compression. I_e quantifies the impairments caused by equipments, such as packet loss or interruption. I_d quantifies the impairment caused by delays and echoes. ITU-T Rec. G.107 gives the range values of each basic parameter and the mathematical expressions, which enable computing the value of each impairment factor. For simplification reasons, E-Model assumes that the perceived effects of impairment factors are additive on a psychological scale. Thus, the final rating score R is given by, $R = R_0 - I_s - I_e - I_d$, where R_0 refers to user satisfaction under no-distortion condition.

The offline glass-box parameter-based quality models are suitable for planning purposes. They enable a general overview pf QoE values of a voice transmission system at an early phase. However, for service monitoring and management, online models are needed. In such a case, the variable model parameters should be acquired at run time. This is especially suitable for IP-based services where control data, such as sequence number and time stamp, are included in each packet header. In such an environment, it is possible to extract static characterization parameters from signaling messages and variable ones from the received packets captured at the destination port. This means that parameters are acquired without acceding to the media content, which is preferable for privacy reasons. This class of models will be considered in more detail in Section 12.2.

Gray-Box QoS/QoE Mapping Models

The gray-box quality models combine advantages of black- and glass-box mapping models. They sample basic characterization parameters at system output in addition to some control data describing the structure of clean stimulus (see Figure 12.2). The control data may be sent in separate control packets or piggybacked inside transmitted media packets. Hence, perceptually important information about a given content can be considered by the quality models. Therefore, they can measure QoE value on per-content basis. Given its simplicity to deploy and its reasonable accuracy, this class of QoS/QoE mapping models is quickly proliferating.

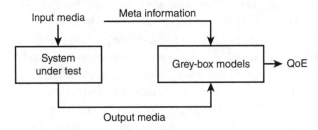

FIGURE 12.2   Gray-Box QoS/QoE Mapping Models

Typically, large telecom operators, such as Ericsson, Deutsch Telekom, and British Telecom, develop their propriety implementations of QoS/QoE mapping models and their companion software tools to acquire, record, and analyze measures that satisfy their specific needs. However, the majority of telecom operators delegate the task of assessment of their transport infrastructure, services, and equipments to specialized corporations, such as GL, OPTICOM, Telchemy, and HEAD Acoustics. In reality, QoS/QoE mapping models should be maintained and evolved to account for a new technology or usage context.

Tips for QoS/QoE Mapping Model Selection

The following checklist of five items can aid in the selection of a QoS/QoE mapping model:

- Which types of operations am I considering?

- Which parameters do I have? Can I access the signals, the contents, the packet payload or the header?

- Do I expect specifications and usage conditions to use a given mapping model?

- How much precision do I need?

- Do I have all inputs available for selected mapping models?

12.2   IP-Oriented Parameter-Based QoS/QoE Mapping Models

The area of measuring QoE of IP networks and applications is still in its infancy. However, the popularity of multimedia and user-friendly IP-based services puts QoE at the center of interest of today's ecosystem. In contrast to legacy content-oriented telecom systems (for example, public switched telephone network [PSTN], radio, and TV), IP networks carry clean media content from a server to a destination using a flow of media packets composed of a header and a payload. Therefore, parameters gathered at network layer, in addition to application layer, are easily accessible at run time on user devices. This enables measuring QoE at run time using online glass- or gray-box parameter-based quality models. The QoE over IP-based networks are time-varying in contrast to telecom networks, which are roughly time-invariant. This characteristic leads to considering instantaneous and overall QoE. The former refers to the observed QoE over a short time interval, on the order of 8 to 20 seconds. The latter refers to the overall QoE observed throughout a whole session in order of 1 to 3 minutes. The next sections give examples of online glass-box parameter-based quality models of IP-based video streaming applications.

Network Layer QoE/QoS Mapping Models for Video Services

The network layer QoS/QoE mapping models rely solely on NQoS metrics gathered from the TCP/IP stack except for the application layer (that is, transport, network, link, and physical layers). In a 2010 paper, Ketyko et al. proposed the following parameter-based quality model for estimating video streaming quality in 3G environment [KETY10]:

$$\overline{QoE} = 8.49 - 0.02 \cdot AL - 0.01 \cdot VL - 1.12 \cdot AJ + 0.04 \cdot RSSI \qquad \text{(Eqtn. 12.1)}$$

where AL and VL refer respectively to audio and video packet loss rates, AJ and VJ represent respectively audio and video packet jitter (VJ), and RSSI is the received signal strength indicator. A 2014 paper by Kim and Choi presented a two-stage QoE/QoS mapping model for IPTV over 3G networks [KIM14]. The first stage consists of combining a set of basic QoS parameters into one metric as follows:

$$QoS(L, U, J, D, B) = K \{W_L \cdot L + W_U \cdot U + W_J \cdot J + W_d \cdot D + W_b \cdot B\} \qquad \text{(Eqtn. 12.2)}$$

where L, U, J, D, and B refer, respectively, to packet loss, burst level, packet jitter, packet delay, and bandwidth. The constants K, W_J, W_u, W_J, W_d and W_b are predefined weighting coefficients, which depend on the type of the access network (that is, wired or wireless). The second stage consists of computing QoE value as following:

$$QoE(QoS(X)) = Q_r \, (1 - QoS \, (X))^{\, QoS(X) \times A/R} \qquad \text{(Eqtn. 12.3)}$$

where, X is a vector of parameters {L, U, J, D, B} and Q_r is a scalar limiting the range of the IPTV QoE obtained as a function of the display size/resolution of the screen. The constant A expresses the subscribed service class and R is a constant reflecting the structure of the video frames.

Application Layer QoE/QoS Mapping Models for Video Services

Besides NQoS parameters, application layer QoE/QoS mapping models use metrics gathered at application layers (AQoS). Moreover, they can account for the user behavior while interacting with a given video content. In a 2014 paper by Ma et al., the following parameter-based quality model is presented for video streaming application [MA14]:

$$QoE = 4023 - 0.0672 \, L_x - 0.742 \, (N_{QS} + N_{RE}) - 0.106 \, T_{mr} \qquad \text{(Eqtn. 12.4)}$$

where Lx refers to the start-up latency, that is, the waiting time before playing a video sequence, N_{QS} is the number of quality switches that count the number of times the video bit rate is changed during a session, N_{RE} is the number of rebuffering events, and T_{MR} is the mean rebuffering time. The following parameter-based quality models, reported in a 2009 paper by Khan et al., estimate QoE of a generic streamed content video over wireless networks using MPEG4 codec [KHAN14]:

$$\text{QoE}(FR, SBR, PER) = \frac{a_1 + a_2 \ FR + a_3 \cdot \ln(SBR)}{1 + a_4 \cdot PER + a_5 \cdot (PER)^2}$$

(Eqtn. 12.5)

where FR, SBR, and PER refer, respectively, to the frame rate sampled at the application level, sent bit rate, and packet error rate sampled at the network level. The coefficients a_1 to a_5 are used to calibrate the quality model. This model has been updated to account for three types of video content: slight movement, gentle walking, and rapid movement. The quality model is given by the following:

$$\text{QoE}(FR, SBR, BLER, CT) = a + \frac{b \cdot e^{FR} + c \cdot \ln(SBR) + CT \cdot (d + e \cdot \ln(SBR))}{1 + f \cdot (BLER) + g \cdot (BLER)^2}$$

(Eqtn. 12.6)

where a, b, c, d, e, f, g represent constants; CT is the content type of the video; and SBR and BLER refer respectively to the sent bit rate and the bit loss error rate. This model was developed for video streaming service transmitted over UMTS networks using H.264 video codec.

A QoE /QoS mapping model for IPTV was developed by Kuipers et al. [KUIP10], which accounts for the start-up latency and zapping time. The latter is defined as the change frequency of TV channels. The quality model in given by the following

$$\text{QoE}_{zapping} = a \cdot \ln(ZT) + b$$

(Eqtn. 12.7)

where $\text{QoE}_{zapping}$ is a one-dimension QoE component considering zapping behaviour, ZT is the zapping time expressed in seconds, and a and b are numeric constants that might be positive or negative. Finally, the following parameter-based quality models proposed by Hossfeld et al. [HOSS13] accounts for stalling events, which are defined as involuntary pauses in the rendered video streams. The quality model is given by the following:

$$\text{QoE} = 3.5e^{-(0.15 \cdot L + 0.19)}N + 1.5$$

(Eqtn. 12.8)

where L refers to average stalling duration and N is the number of stalling events.

12.3   Actionable QoE over IP-Based Networks

actionable QoE

A measure of QoE that may be used to undertake decisions.

This section introduces **actionable QoE,** which refers to all techniques and mechanisms enabling to concretely measure and utilize QoE metrics. Actionable QoE goes beyond QoE definition and measurement toward QoE exploitation. An actionable QoE solution strongly depends on the underlying system and services characteristics. Moreover, actionable QoE solution works over multiplane architectures that integrate data, control, and management planes. Basically, two solutions may be used to achieve actionable QoE:

- System-oriented actionable QoE solution

- Service-oriented actionable QoE solution

The System-Oriented Actionable QoE Solution

The system-oriented actionable QoE solutions account for QoE measures within the delivery infrastructure. In such a condition, services are engineered while assuming that underlying system is perfect; that is, no degradations are inserted. Figure 12.3 illustrates a nominal environment where system-oriented actionable QoE solution may be provided. As can be seen, actionable QoE solution requires (1) a QoS measurement module that gathers basic **key performance indicators** (KPIs) from the underlying system, (2) a QoE/QoS mapping model, and (3) a resource management module of controlled devices. Each service provider specifies a target QoE level that should be offered for its customers. The QoE/QoS mapping model should be selected in a way that guarantees (a) the availability of quality model input parameters and (b) conformity with service specifications and conditions. A signaling procedure may be executed to do that. The management procedure may be executed either before starting a service or during its delivery. It involves specifications of all configurable parameters provided by a given infrastructure, such as priority, marking threshold, traffic shaping, and so on. This should be realized using an autonomous decision system, including a policy that maps observed QoE measures to a course of actions executed by managed devices.

Key Performance Indicators (KPIs)

Quantifiable measurements, agreed to beforehand, that reflect the critical success factors of an organization.

This operational mode applies well for software-defined networking (SDN) where the network paths are managed by an SDN controller. In such a case, the measured QoE values are reported to the SDN controller, which uses them to define the behavior of SDN switches. The SDN controller should include a QoE policy and rules module that (1) checks whether the contracted QoE level is respected on a per-user/per-flow basis and (2) specifies SDN paths that should be used to forward users flows. The QoE policy and rules module should consider situations where services cross SDN-supported and -unsupported realms.

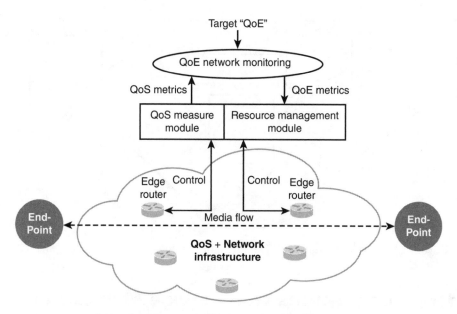

FIGURE 12.3   A Nominal Environment for Providing QoE-Centric Services

The Service-Oriented Actionable QoE Solution

The service-oriented actionable QoE solutions account for QoE values measured at endpoints and service level (see Figure 12.4). In such a situation, services are engineered to deal with the underlying system flaws to reach a specified QoE level. The services may change their behavior as a function of the current context and condition. The measurement module of KPI is installed on endpoints. The QoE/QoS mapping models may be deployed either on endpoints or specialized devices. The measured QoE values are sent to endpoints to configure different application modules at sender, proxy, and receiver entities.

The service-oriented actionable QoE solution involves multiple advantages. First, per-service, per-user, and per-content QoE monitoring and management solutions are performed to provide a given QoE level. Second, it provides more adaptation possibility because it precisely discerns capability and the role of each service component. Third, it reduces the communication overhead and balances computing loads. Finally, it enables component-level granularity treatment of QoE in addition to stream- and packet-level granularities. However, this solution cannot be applied to already running services and results in higher complexity in service design and engineering.

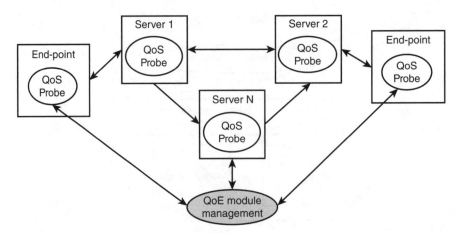

FIGURE 12.4   Service-Aware QoE Deployment Scheme

12.4   QoE Versus QoS Service Monitoring

Monitoring is a strategic function that should be supported by today's IT system. It returns indicators and provides clues regarding the system performance and its workload. Moreover, it enables detecting system dysfunction and defects as well as underperforming devices and applications so that the best course of actions may be undertaken. The monitoring solutions of current IT systems may be classified into the following four categories (see Figure 12-5):

- **Network monitoring:** Provides measures about performance of paths and links used to deliver media units. They are collected at packet processing devices (router and switch) and may operate on per-flow or per-packet bases. The path characterization metrics, such as throughput, packet loss, reorder and duplication, delay, and jitter, are calculated using atomic metrics extracted from packet header, such as sequence number and time stamps.

- **Infrastructure monitoring:** Provides measures about devices performance and resources state, such as memory, CPU, IO, load, and so on.

- **Platform monitoring:** Provides performance indicators about the computing center where back-end servers are running. They may work over a virtualized infrastructure where business application logics are deployed using virtual machines.

- **Service monitoring:** Provides measures about services performance. The metrics are dependent on each application, and may be realized from technical or perceptual perspectives.

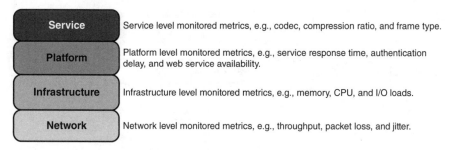

FIGURE 12.5   A Classification of Monitoring Solutions

Typically, the monitoring solution in a distributed system involves a variety of **probes** that measure the performance of a given element participating in the service delivery chain. They are distributed and deployed over the system following a particular policy. Moreover, it includes a reliable and scalable manager that remotely configures probe behavior, especially in terms of the frequency and content of measurement reports. Often, probes are built in a given managed device or component (for example, SNMP agent). They may be configured by the network or system administrators to fit specific environment requirements. Typically, probes send atomic and elementary metrics that are transformed by the manager into human-friendly metrics. The manager logs all measures following a specific representation and saves them at a specific location.

The monitoring solution should provide communication facility between the manager and the managed devices. The interaction between the manager and managed entities is conventionally realized using the connectionless User Datagram Protocol (UDP) through a couple of reserved ports. This has been evolved to work as a short-lived HTTP connection. The probes are defined as a RESTful service that may be called by the manager. Moreover, exchanged reports can be realized either in band or out of band. The first strategy shares the resource used for data delivery, but the second one uses a dedicated and autonomous devices and channels to perform monitoring tasks.

Figure 12.6 presents a typical configuration of an on-demand monitoring solution. The manager receives monitoring requests from customers expressed using specific syntax. Upon the receipt of a new monitoring request, the manager inquires with a Universal Description, Discovery, and Integration (UDDI) directory to get more information about the monitored service, such as location and properties. The monitoring solution, including a set of probes, is deployed over a given infrastructure. They register themselves automatically once a monitored component is activated in a preconfigured registrar. The registrar keeps traces and features of all active probes. They should be configured off line by the administrator to report metrics according to a given behavior during a service. The metrics generated by the probes may be aggregated and processed before sending them to the manager that performs data analytic procedure.

Probes

Probes gather information about different components of the delivery path. Often, this information relates to performance (for example, network QoS, server loads), but it can also relate to application specific factors (for example, codec, resolution), devices (for example, screen resolution, processing capacity), context (for example, ambient lighting, motion), or other factors.

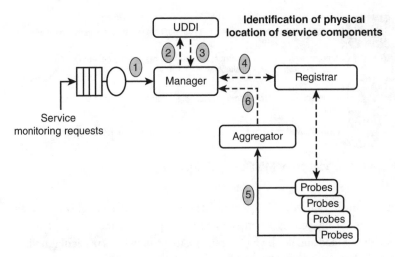

FIGURE 12.6   A Baseline and Generic Monitoring Solution

The traditional QoS metrics may be measured at network, infrastructure, platform, and service layers. However, QoE metrics may be only measured at the service layer, where it is possible to interact with final users. The next sections present recent technologies and trends in QoS and QoE monitoring solutions.

QoS Monitoring Solutions

The emerging QoS monitoring solutions are basically developed for data centers and clouds where virtualization technology is supported. Figure 12.7 shows a network- and infrastructure-level monitoring solution built for cloud-based IPTV service. The audiovisual content servers are placed on a cloud. The traffic sent from the content servers to IPTV devices is permanently monitored through a set of Vprobes deployed across the network. A Vprobe is an open-ended investigatory tool that is used in the cloud environment to inspect, record, and compute the state of the hypervisor as well as each virtual machine running service business logics. The flows of video packets are parsed at different measurement points. The information collected by Vprobes is used next to reconstruct service-level detailed records (SDRs). Each record contains the most relevant information of the complete session between an origin (server) and a destination (user). The critical parameters of the messages associated with an IPTV session are stored inside the SDRs.

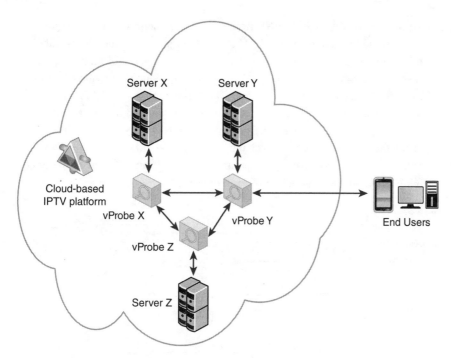

FIGURE 12.7   vProbes Approach in Cloud-Based IPTV Network

Amazon developed CloudWatch, which is a tied monitoring solution over Amazon cloud (http://aws.amazon.com/cloudwatch/). It can monitor cloud resources, such as CPU and memory utilization, in addition to client applications and services. The administrators can collect and track customized metrics that are dependent on each application. Amazon CloudWatch retrieves the monitored data, displays graphs, and sets alarms to help in resolving troubleshooting, performing spot trends, and taking automated courses of action based on the state of the cloud.

QoE Monitoring Solutions

The emerging QoE monitoring solutions extend and adapt QoS ones. As discussed before, the QoE monitoring solution strongly depends on QoE/QoS mapping models. Moreover, there is no one-size-fits-all solution for QoE monitoring, in opposition with QoS monitoring solutions.

The diagrams in Figure 12.8 show four configurations that can be used to monitor at run time the QoE values of IP-based video streaming services. The configurations differ in term of the measurement and mapping model locations. Each configuration is denoted using XY expression, where X refers to the measurement location and Y refers to the quality model location. They may take one of these values: N for network, C for client, and B for both:

A. **Static operation mode (NN):** Both the measurements of KPIs and QoE
are performed inside the network. The QoE/QoS mapping model is installed
on a device listening to the service delivery path (see part a of Figure 12.8).
The quality model uses collected KPIs, prior knowledge about video coding
schemes, and endpoint characteristics. The parameters of QoE/QoS mapping
models are extracted from decrypted information included in the transmitted media packets. The characteristics of endpoints can be acquired either by
polling them or by inspecting exchanged SDP (Session Description Protocol)
messages. The QoE measurement points may include an endpoint emulator enabling a realistic reconstruction of received streams.

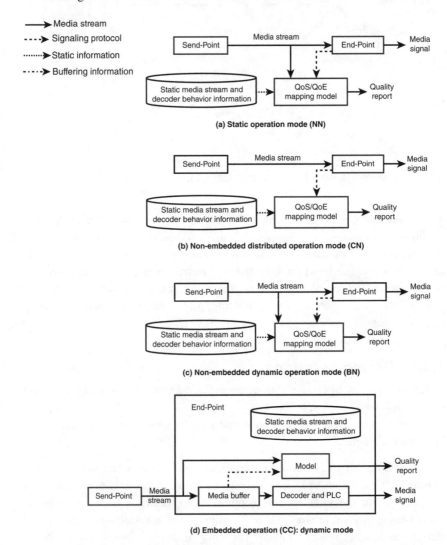

FIGURE 12.8   The Operational Working Modes of Quality Models in Networks

B. **Nonembedded dynamic operation (BN):** The measurement of KPIs is performed at both the network and the client, whereas QoE values are measured inside the network (see part c of Figure 12.8). The quality model uses gathered KPIs, prior knowledge about coding schemes, and information about the client obtained using a customized signaling protocols.

C. **Nonembedded distributed operation (CN):** The measurement of KPIs is performed at the client side, and these are sent periodically to the QoE/QoS mapping model located inside the network (see part b of Figure 12.8).

D. **Operation embedded (CC):** The measurement of KPIs and QoE is performed at the client side. The QoS/QoE mapping model is embedded inside the client (see part d of Figure 12.8). The measured QoE metrics may be reported to a centralized monitoring entity.

A standardized multidimensional QoE monitoring solution is defined in ETSI Technical Specification TS 103 294 (Speech and Multimedia Transmission Quality (STQ); Quality of Experience; A Monitoring Architecture, 2014). This solution used QoE agents deployed over devices that communicate with each other and with data-acquisition objects (or probes). The architecture of QoE-agent is based on a layered definition of APIs that enable convenient grouping of different factors that influence QoE. The six layers are defined as follows:

QoE agent
An entity residing at possibly many points along the service delivery path, which receive input from probes (network, infrastructure, and so on) and process that input with a QoE/QoS mapping model for the service in question.

- **Resource:** Composed of dimensions representing the characteristics and performance of the technical system(s) and network resources used to deliver the service. Examples of such factors include network QoS in terms of delay, jitter, loss, error rate, and throughput. Furthermore, system resources such as server processing capabilities and end user device capabilities (e.g. computational power, memory, screen resolution, user interface, battery lifetime, etc.) are included.

- **Application:** Composed of dimensions representing application/service configuration factors. Examples of such factors include media encoding, resolution, sample rate, frame rate, buffer sizes, SNR, etc. Content-related factors (e.g., specific temporal or spatial requirements, 2D/3D content, and color depth) also belong to this space.

- **Interface:** Represents the physical equipment and interface through which the user is interacting with the application (type of device, screen size, mouse, etc.).

- **Context:** Related to the physical context (e. g. geographical aspects, ambient light and noise, time of the day), the usage context (e.g. mobility/no-mobility or stress/no-stress), and the economic context (e.g. the cost that a user is paying for a service).

- **Human:** Represents all factors related to the perceptual characteristics of users (e.g. sensitivity to audio-visual stimulus, perception of durations, etc.).

- **User:** Users' factors that are not represented in the Human layer. These factors encompass all aspects of humans as users of services or applications (e.g., history and social characteristics, motivation, expectation, and level of expertise).

The strength of the QoE monitoring solution using these layers resides in its ability to monitor any service using customized QoS/QoE mapping models. The QoE agent is composed of the six major objects illustrated in Figure 12.9 and described in the list that follows.

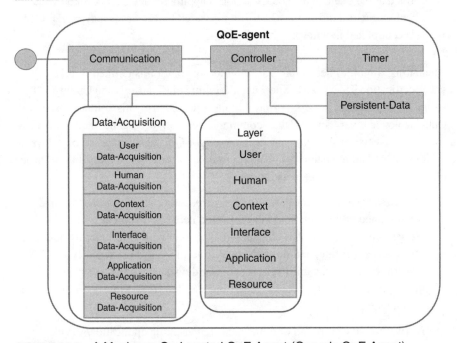

FIGURE 12.9   A Maximum Co-Located QoE Agent (Generic QoE Agent)

- The **Communication** object manages inter-QoE agent communications.

- The **Data-Acquisition** object implements all data-acquisition sublayers. It acquires atomic information necessary for the calculation of the internal parameters of a given QoE/QoS mapping model.

- The **Controller** object implements global QoE/QoS mapping models and handles external requests and commands, such as get and set operations.

- The **Layer** object is an interface object that implements different model layers, such as Application model, Context model, and User model.

- The **Persistent-Data** object stores the quality parameters for all layers.

- The **Timer** object is used as the internal time for the QoE agent.

The QoE agent must implement all layers of the ARCU model. However, they may be distributed over many physical devices. To do that, two types of QoE agents are introduced:

- A **master QoE agent** is a nondistributed entity implementing at least the User model sublayer, which contains at least a Layer object of type User. It must implement a Communication object, a Controller object, a Timer object, and a Persistent-Data object. It must also implement a Data-Acquisition object (see Figure 12.10).

- A **slave QoE Agent** is a nondistributed entity implementing a Data-Acquisition object / some Layer object, but no Layer object of type User. It must also implement a Communication object, a Controller object, and a Timer object.

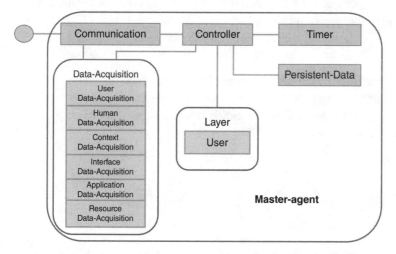

FIGURE 12.10   A Minimum Master Agent (With Only User Model)

The components of maximum and minimum master QoE agents are, respectively, illustrated in Figure 12.9 and Figure 12.10. The maximum master QoE agent includes all ACRU layers, whereas the minimum master QoE agent implements only the user layer. Figure 12.11 illustrates a slave QoE agent that implements only one layer of ACRU model other than the user layer.

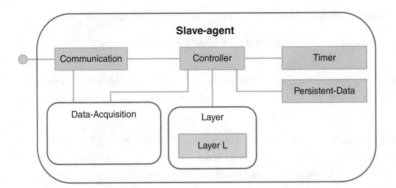

FIGURE 12.11   A Slave QoE Agent Implementing Only One Layer Model (Besides the User Layer)

The data-acquisition module is encapsulated into a probe agent specified as follows:

- **A probe agent of type L:** A nondistributed entity implementing the data-acquisition sublayer of type L and no Layer objects (see Figure 12.12). It must also implement a Communication object, a Controller object, and a Timer object.

- **A probe agent** is used when the type of the probe agent of type L is irrelevant or when the entity implements several sublayers of different types. It must also implement a Communication object, a Controller object, and a Timer object.

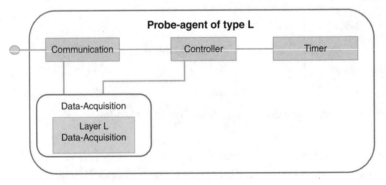

FIGURE 12.12   A Probe Agent of Type L

12.5 QoE-Based Network and Service Management

The quantified QoE values may be considered in networks and services management. This enables getting an optimal trade-off that maximizes QoE and minimizes consumption of resources. The major challenge resides in the translation of QoE metrics into a course of actions that definitely enhance encountered QoE and reduce resources consumptions. Unfortunately, there is no systematic approach for reaching such a goal. The following sections describe a number of applications that seek to undertake a set of actions as a function of measured QoE.

QoE-Based Management of VoIP Calls

The management of Voice over IP (VoIP) based on QoE has been extensively investigated in the literature. The goal is to maintain a constant QoE level during a whole packet voice session transmitted over time-varying quality IP networks. Typically, QoE measurement probes following one glass-box parameter-based model are installed on VoIP endpoints. They collect at run time atomic KPIs, which are transformed and given as inputs to a QoE/QoS mapping model. After a new measure of QoE values is received, a QoS controller adjusts the reconfigurable network parameters within a delivery path, such as queuing allocation and congestion thresholds. A simple policy consists of allocating more (respectively less) network resource if the QoE value is less (greater) than a targeted QoE value.

QoE-Based Host-Centric Vertical Handover

Mobile consumers over next-generation networks could be served at one moment by several overlapping heterogeneous wireless networks. In such a case, mobile users should choose the access network that will likely achieve good quality. The network selection/switching procedure can be performed either at the start or during the service. An internetwork hard handover occurs when users switch from one network to another because of specific reasons related to both consumers and providers. A handover could be managed in network- or host-centric way. In a traditional network-centric approach, the infrastructure monitored by providers decides when a handover is required through a set of control algorithms. In a host-centric approach, however, end nodes can perform a handover when quality of service becomes unsteady and unsatisfactory.

Figure 12.13 illustrates a likely envisaged scenario where the client could be served either by WiMAX or Wi-Fi systems. Appropriate equipment should be deployed and configured, such as outdoor and indoor units, server, router, and Wi-Fi and WiMAX access points to enable network handover. Throughout a vocal call, the client may switch from WiMAX system to Wi-Fi system, and vice versa.

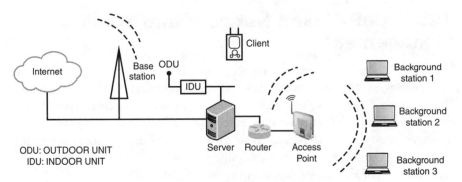

FIGURE 12.13   Network Selection Between Wi-Fi and WiMAX Based on Client and Link Quality [MURP007]

Murphy et al. argue that a host-centric network selection approach is more suitable to support delay-sensitive services [MURP07]. Indeed, in such a case, internetwork handover may be performed according to customized requirements specified by on a per-service and per-user basis. In general, for delay-sensitive services, a seamless network switching that reduces/cancels service interruptions network selection controller may be used.

To do that, it is possible to use message-based, multistreamed, multihomed, and reliable Stream Control Transmission Protocol (SCTP) transport protocol. In contrast to TCP, SCTP allows delivering out-of-order packets to applications, which is more suitable for delay-sensitive applications. The multihoming feature of SCTP enables a transparent handover over several heterogeneous overlapping wireless networks. One path with specified destination and source addresses plays the role of primary path. The remaining ones play the role of secondary paths. SCTP can monitor at run time delay and jitter on all active paths, and makes them available to the application. Heartbeat messages are sent over secondary paths to collect required measurements. The collected KPIs are mapped to QoE values using a suitable QoE/QoS mapping model. The path quality is compared at a regular interval, and the client decides whether a network switch is necessary according to its customized and internal policy.

QoE-Based Network-Centric Vertical Handover

This section covers a QoE-based network-centric internetwork handover scheme. The goal is to perform a handover between overlapping WLAN and GSM networks. This allows, on one hand, relatively exploiting the high capacity of a WLAN, and on the other hand, reducing the GSM network load and cost. Figure 12.14 shows a scenario where a mobile subscriber initiates a voice call to a landline PSTN subscriber using a WLAN as a last-wireless hop. Next, when the QoE of the voice call goes below a given critical threshold because of mobility or congestion, a handover is performed.

In such a case, the mobile subscriber is linked to the landline subscriber using the GSM infrastructure. The hands-free terminal is equipped with two wireless card interfaces to allow connection to WLAN and GSM networks. The mobile terminal sends adequate "quality reports" to a PBX that analyzes received feedbacks. Once an unsatisfied score is detected, the PBX instructs the mobile terminal to perform a handover. To do that seamlessly, a voice channel is opened using GSM infrastructure between the mobile terminal and PBX, which is responsible to relay received voice information toward the fixed subscriber.

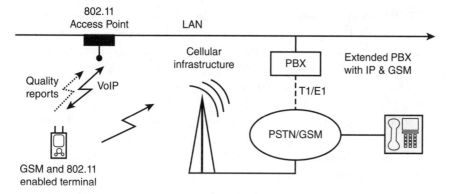

FIGURE 12.14   Handover Scenario Between WLAN and GSM Networks [MAES06]

The handovers are controlled using the following simplified additive quality models, installed at the private branch exchange (PBX), as reported by Marsh et al. [MARS06]:

$$\text{Handover score} = \text{Signal} + \text{Loss} + \text{Jitter} + \text{Report loss} \qquad \text{(Eqtn. 12.9)}$$

where, the handover scores vary from −100 to 100. The remaining variables are defined as follows:

- **Received signal strength indicator:** The signal-to-noise ratio is a good indicator about quality of service, especially over wireless Telecom networks. This metric may entail inaccurate estimates about quality over wireless data networks. In fact, over wireless telecom networks, high signal strength indicates that users sustain potentially a good QoE. This rule is inaccurate over wireless data networks where QoE could be poor in spite of high measured signal strength because of, for example, congestion-induced packet losses. The mobile terminal periodically records the received signal strength. The obtained value is scaled according to handover score defined by authors. Specifically, the measured received signal strengths are mapped to values varying from 0 to +90.

- **Delay jitter:** An increasing delay jitter is a good indicator of poor quality. According to a preliminary empirical study, a score of +10 and 0 is assigned to good and negligible jitter conditions, respectively. A score of −10 and −20 is assigned to poor and very poor jitter conditions, respectively.

- **Packet loss:** High packet loss rate indicates that users sustain undoubtedly a very poor quality. A decreasing score step of −10 is assigned to encountered packet loss ratio with an increasing step of 8 percent. A long bad period is accounted for by increasing properly the contribution of packet loss.

- **RTCP losses:** The mobile terminal will likely sustain reception problems when the monitoring node does not receive RTCP quality reports. Three or more consecutive losses of RTCP feedback are generally quite significant to reduce aggressively the overall handover score. A decreasing score step of −10 is assigned to each consecutively lost RTCP report.

A large positive score indicates a good QoE. The mobile users are allowed to specify the lower acceptable threshold score. As a consequence, a handover is performed only when the calculated handover score falls below the defined threshold. An increasing threshold results in the improvement of average quality at the expense of a higher communication cost, because the system will switch the voice session to GSM system earlier. Conversely, a decreasing threshold results in the reduction of communication cost at the expense of longer periods of degraded quality.

12.6   Key Terms

After completing this chapter, you should be able to define the following terms.

QoE/QoS model mapping	gray-box mapping model	QoE-based management
black-box mapping model	QoE-aware services	
glass-box mapping model	QoE-based monitoring	

12.7   References

HOSS13: Hossfeld, T., et al. " Internet Video Delivery in YouTube: From Traffic Measurements to Quality of Experience." Book chapter in *Data Traffic Monitoring and Analysis: From Measurement, Classification, and Anomaly Detection to Quality of Experience*, Lecture Notes in Computer Science, Volume 7754, 2013.

KETY10: Ketyko, I., De Moor, K., Joseph, W., and Martens, L. "Performing QoE-Measurements in an Actual 3G Network," IEEE International Symposium on Broadband Multimedia Systems and Broadcasting, March 2010.

KHAN09: Khan, A., Sun, L., and Ifeachor, E. "Content Clustering Based Video Quality Prediction Model for MPEG4 Video Streaming over Wireless Networks," *IEEE International Conference on Communications*, 2009.

KIM14: Kim, H., and Choi, S. "QoE Assessment Model for Multimedia Streaming Services Using QoS Parameters," *Multimedia Tools and Applications*, October 2014.

KUIP10: Kuipers, F. et al. "Techniques for Measuring Quality of Experience," 8th International Conference on Wired/Wireless Internet Communications, 2010.

MA14: Ma, H., Seo, B., and Zimmermann, R. "Dynamic Scheduling on Video Transcoding for MPEG DASH in the Cloud Environment," Proceedings of the 5th ACM Multimedia Systems Conference, March 2014.

MARS06: Marsh, I., Grönvall, B., and Hammer, F. "The Design and Implementation of a Quality-Based Handover Trigger," 5th International IFIP-TC6 Networking Conference, Coimbra, Portugal.

MURP07: Murphy, L. et al. "An Application-Quality-Based Mobility Management Scheme," Proceedings of 9th IFIP/IEEE International Conference on Mobile and Wireless Communications Networks, 2007.

PART V

Modern Network Architecture: Clouds and Fog

We have discussed a new large communication system, one markedly different from the present in both concept and equipment, and one which will mean a merging of two different technologies: computers and communications.

—On Distributed Communication: Summary Overview, Rand Report RM-3767-PR, Paul Baran, August 1964

The two dominant modern network architectures are cloud computing and the Internet of Things (IoT), sometimes referred to as fog computing. The technologies and applications discussed in the preceding sections all provide a foundation for cloud computing and IoT. Chapter 13 is a survey of cloud computing. The chapter begins with a definition of basic concepts, and then covers cloud services, deployment models, and architecture. The chapter then discusses the relationship between cloud computing and software-defined networking (SDN) and network functions virtualization (NFV). Chapter 14 and Chapter 15 provide a detailed look at IoT, with Chapter 14 providing coverage of the principal components of IoT-enabled things, while Chapter 15 examines IoT reference architectures and looks at three implementation examples.

Chapter 13

Cloud Computing

One can now picture a future investigator in his laboratory. His hands are free, and he is not anchored. As he moves about and observes, he photographs and comments. Time is automatically recorded to tie the two records together. If he goes into the field, he may be connected by radio to his recorder. As he ponders over his notes in the evening, he again talks his comments into the record. His typed record, as well as his photographs, may both be in miniature, so that he projects them for examination.

—"As We May Think," Vannevar Bush, *The Atlantic*, July 1945

Chapter Objectives

After studying this chapter, you should be able to

- Present an overview of cloud computing concepts.
- List and define the principal cloud services.
- List and define the cloud deployment models.
- Compare and contrast the NIST and ITU-T cloud computing reference architectures.
- Discuss the relevance of SDN and NFV to cloud computing.

Section 1.6 provided a brief overview of the concept of cloud computing, and Section 2.2 included a discussion of the requirements that cloud computing generates with respect to networking. This chapter begins with a more detailed look at the basic concepts of cloud computing. Next is a discussion of the principal types of services typically offered by cloud providers. The chapter then looks at various deployment models for cloud systems, followed by an examination of two cloud computing reference architectures, developed by NIST and ITU-T, respectively. A consideration of these two different models provides insight into the nature of cloud computing. Finally, the chapter discusses how SDN and NFV can support cloud computing deployment and operation.

13.1   Basic Concepts

There is an increasingly prominent trend in many organizations to move a substantial portion or even all information technology (IT) operations to an Internet-connected infrastructure known as enterprise cloud computing. At the same time, individual users of PCs and mobile devices are relying more and more on cloud computing services to backup data, synch devices, and share. NIST defines cloud computing, in NIST SP-800-145, *The NIST Definition of Cloud Computing*, as follows:

← *See Section 1.6, "Cloud Computing"*

> **Cloud computing:** A model for enabling ubiquitous, convenient, on-demand network access to a shared pool of configurable computing resources (for example, networks, servers, storage, applications, and services) that can be rapidly provisioned and released with minimal management effort or service provider interaction. This cloud model promotes availability and is composed of five essential characteristics, three service models, and four deployment models.

← *See Figure 1.7, Cloud Computing Context*

The definition refers to various models and characteristics, whose relationship is illustrated in Figure 13.1. The five essential characteristics were discussed in Chapter 1, "Elements of Modern Networking." This chapter covers the three service models and the four deployment models.

← *See Section 2.2, "Demand: Big Data, Cloud Computing, and Mobile Traffic"*

Basically, cloud computing provides economies of scale, professional network management, and professional security management. These features can be attractive to companies large and small, government agencies, and individual PC and mobile users. The individual or company only needs to pay for the storage capacity and services they use. The user, be it company or individual, does not have the hassle of setting up a database system, acquiring the hardware they need, doing maintenance, and backing up the data—all these are part of the cloud service.

← *See Figure 2.4, Cloud Network Model*

In theory, another big advantage of using cloud computing to store your data and share it with others is that the cloud provider takes care of security. Alas, the customer is not always protected. There have been a number of security failures among cloud providers. Evernote made headlines in early 2013 when it told all of its users to reset their passwords after an intrusion was discovered.

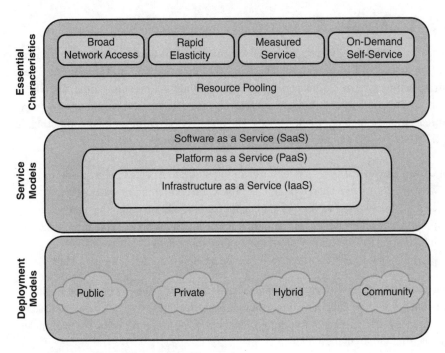

FIGURE 13.1   Cloud Computing Elements

Cloud networking refers to the networks and network management functionality that must be in place to enable cloud computing. Most cloud computing solutions rely on the Internet, but that is only a piece of the networking infrastructure. One example of cloud networking is the provisioning of high-performance/high-reliability networking between the provider and subscriber. In this case, some or all of the traffic between an enterprise and the cloud bypasses the Internet and uses dedicated private network facilities owned or leased by the cloud service provider. More generally, cloud networking refers to the collection of network capabilities required to access a cloud, including making use of specialized services over the Internet, linking enterprise data centers to a cloud, and using firewalls and other network security devices at critical points to enforce access security policies.

We can think of **cloud storage** as a subset of cloud computing. In essence, cloud storage consists of database storage and database applications hosted remotely on cloud servers. Cloud storage enables small businesses and individual users to take advantage of data storage that scales with their needs and to take advantage of a variety of database applications without having to buy, maintain, and manage the storage assets.

13.2   Cloud Services

This section looks at commonly defined cloud services, beginning with three service models defined by NIST:

- Software as a Service (SaaS)

- Platform as a Service (PaaS)

- Infrastructure as a Service (IaaS)

These can be viewed as nested service alternatives (see Figure 13.2) and are universally accepted as the basic service models for cloud computing. The section then examines other popular cloud service models.

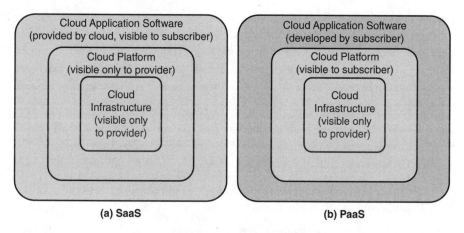

(a) SaaS   **(b) PaaS**

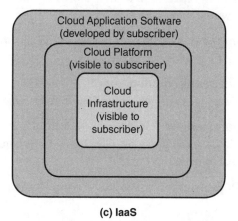

(c) IaaS

FIGURE 13.2   Cloud Service Models

Software as a Service

As the name implies, an **SaaS** cloud provides service to customers in the form of software, specifically application software running on and accessible in the cloud. SaaS follows the familiar model of web services, in this case applied to cloud resources. SaaS enables the customer to use the cloud provider's applications running on the provider's cloud infrastructure. The applications are accessible from various client devices through a simple interface such as a web browser. Instead of obtaining desktop and server licenses for software products it uses, an enterprise obtains the same functions from the cloud service. The use of SaaS avoids the complexity of software installation, maintenance, upgrades, and patches. Examples of services at this level are Google Gmail, Microsoft 365, Salesforce, Citrix GoToMeeting, and Cisco WebEx.

Common subscribers to SaaS are organizations that want to provide their employees with access to typical office productivity software, such as document management and e-mail. Individuals also commonly use the SaaS model to acquire cloud resources. Typically, subscribers use specific applications on demand. The cloud provider also usually offers data-related features such as automatic backup and data sharing between subscribers.

The following list, derived from an ongoing industry survey by OpenCrowd (http://cloudtaxonomy.opencrowd.com/taxonomy), describes example SaaS services. The numbers in parentheses refer to the number of vendors currently offering each service.

Cloud Taxonomy

- **Billing** (3): Application services to manage customer billing based on usage and subscriptions to products and services.

- **Collaboration** (18): Platforms providing tools that allow users to collaborate in workgroups, within enterprises, and across enterprises.

- **Content management** (7): Services for managing the production and access to content for Web-based applications.

- **Customer relationship management** (13): Platforms for CRM application that range from call center applications to sales force automation.

- **Document management** (6): Platforms of managing documents, document production workflows, and providing workspaces for groups or enterprises to find and access documents.

- **Education** (4): Provides online services to Educators and Educational institutions.

- **Enterprise resource planning** (8): ERP is an integrated computer-based system used to manage internal and external resources, including tangible assets, financial resources, materials, and human resources.

- **Financials** (11): Applications for managing financial processes for companies that range from expense processing and invoicing to tax management.

- **Healthcare** (10): Services for improving and managing people's health and healthcare management.

- **Human resources** (10): Software for managing human resources functions within companies.

- **IT services management** (5): Software that helps enterprises manage IT services delivery to services consumers and manage performance improvement.

- **Personal productivity** (5): Software that business users use on a daily basis in the normal course of business. The typical suite includes applications for word processing, spreadsheets, and presentations.

- **Project management** (12): Software packages for managing projects. Features of packages may specialize the offering for specific types of projects such as software development, construction, and so on.

- **Sales** (7): Applications that are specifically designed for sales functions such as pricing, commission tracking, and so on.

- **Security** (10): Hosted products for security services such as malware and virus scanning, single sign-on, and so on.

- **Social networks** (4): Platforms for creating and customizing social networking applications.

Platform as a Service

A **PaaS** cloud provides service to customers in the form of a platform on which the customer's applications can run. PaaS enables the customer to deploy onto the cloud infrastructure customer-created or -acquired applications. A PaaS cloud provides useful software building blocks, plus a number of development tools, such as programming language tools, runtime environments, and other tools that assist in deploying new applications. In effect, PaaS is an operating system in the cloud. PaaS is useful for an organization that wants to develop new or tailored applications while paying for the needed computing resources only as needed and only for as long as needed. AppEngine, Engine Yard, Heroku, Microsoft Azure, Force.com, and Apache Stratos are examples of PaaS.

The following list describes example PaaS services. The numbers in parentheses refer to the number of vendors currently offering each service:

- **Big data as a service** (19): These are cloud-based services for the analysis of large or complex data sets that require high scalability.

Platform as a Service (PaaS)

A group of capabilities offered via cloud computing in which the cloud service customer can deploy, manage, and run customer-created or customer-acquired applications using one or more programming languages and one or more execution environments supported by the cloud service provider.

- **Business intelligence** (18)**:** Platforms for the creation of business intelligence applications such as dashboards, reporting systems, and big data analysis.

- **Database** (18)**:** These services offer scalable database systems ranging from relational database solutions to massively scalable non-SQL datastores.

- **Development and testing** (18) **:** These platforms are only for the development and testing cycles of application development, which expand and contract as needed.

- **General purpose** (22)**:** Platforms suited for general-purpose application development. These services provide a database, a web application runtime environment, and typically support web services for integration.

- **Integration** (14)**:** Services for integrating applications ranging from cloud-to-cloud integration to custom application integration.

Infrastructure as a Service

Infrastructure
as a Service
(IaaS)

A group of capabilities offered via cloud computing in which the cloud service customer can provision and use processing, storage, or networking resources.

With **IaaS**, the customer has access to the resources of the underlying cloud infrastructure. IaaS provides virtual machines and other abstracted hardware and operating systems. IaaS offers the customer processing, storage, networks, and other fundamental computing resources so that the customer can deploy and run arbitrary software, which can include operating systems and applications. IaaS enables customers to combine basic computing services, such as number crunching and data storage, to build highly adaptable computer systems.

Typically, customers are able to self-provision this infrastructure, using a web-based graphical user interface that serves as an IT operations management console for the overall environment. API access to the infrastructure may also be offered as an option. Examples of IaaS are Amazon Elastic Compute Cloud (Amazon EC2), Microsoft Windows Azure, Google Compute Engine (GCE), and Rackspace.

The following list describes example IaaS services. The numbers in parentheses refer to the number of vendors currently offering each service:

- **Backup and recovery** (14)**:** Platforms providing services to backup and recover file systems and raw data stores on servers and desktop systems.

- **Cloud broker** (7)**:** Tools that manage services on more than one cloud infrastructure platform. Some tools support private-public cloud configurations.

- **Compute** (31)**:** Provides server resources for running cloud-based systems that can be dynamically provisioned and configured as needed.

- **Content delivery networks** (2)**:** CDNs store content and files to improve the performance and cost of delivering content for web based systems.

- **Services management** (7): Services that manage cloud infrastructure platforms. These tools often provide features that cloud providers do not provide or specialize in managing certain application technologies.

- **Storage** (12): Provides massively scalable storage capacity that can be used for applications, backups, archiving, file storage, and more.

Figure 13.3 compares the functions implemented by the cloud service provider for the three principal cloud service models.

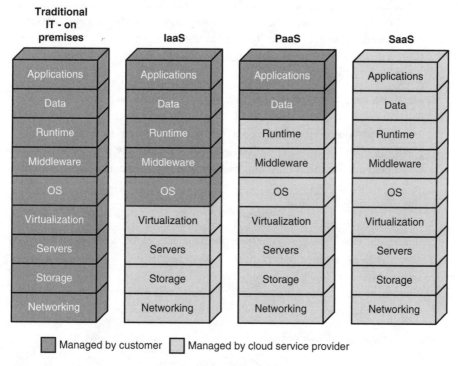

FIGURE 13.3   Separation of Responsibilities in Cloud Operation

Other Cloud Services

A number of other cloud services have been proposed, with some available as vendor offerings. A useful list of these additional services is provided by ITU-T Y.3500 (*Cloud Computing — Overview and Vocabulary*, August 2014).

In addition to SaaS, PaaS, and IaaS, Y.3500 lists the following as representative cloud service categories:

- **Communications as a Service (CaaS):** The integration of real-time interaction and collaboration services to optimize business processes. This service provides a unified interface and consistent user experience across multiple devices. Examples of services included are video teleconferencing, web conferencing, instant messaging, and voice over IP.

- **Compute as a Service (CompaaS):** The provision and use of processing resources needed to deploy and run software. CompaaS may be thought of as a simplified IaaS, with the focus on providing compute capacity.

- **Data Storage as a Service (DSaaS):** The provision and use of data storage and related capabilities. DSaaS describes a storage model where the client leases storage space from a third-party provider. Data is transferred from the client to the service provider via the Internet, and the client then accesses the stored data using software provided by the storage provider. The software is used to perform common tasks related to storage, such as data backups and data transfers.

- **Network as a Service (NaaS):** Transport connectivity services / intercloud network connectivity services. NaaS involves the optimization of resource allocations by considering network and computing resources as a unified whole. NaaS can include flexible and extended virtual private network (VPN), bandwidth on demand, custom routing, multicast protocols, security firewall, intrusion detection and prevention, wide-area network (WAN), content monitoring and filtering, and antivirus.

Y.3500 distinguishes between cloud capabilities and cloud services. The three capabilities types are application, platform, and infrastructure, corresponding to the basic service types of SaaS, PaaS, and IaaS. A cloud service category can include capabilities from one or more cloud capability types. Table 13.1 shows the relationship of the seven cloud service categories and the three cloud capabilities types.

TABLE 13.1   Cloud Service Categories and Cloud Capabilities Types

Cloud Service Categories	Cloud Capabilities Types		
	Infrastructure	Platform	Application
Compute as a Service	X		
Communications as a Service		X	X
Data Storage as a Service	X	X	X
Network as a Service	X	X	
Infrastructure as a Service	X		
Platform as a Service		X	
Software as a Service			X

Y.3500 also lists examples of emerging cloud service categories:

- **Database as a Service:** Database functionalities on demand where the installation and maintenance of the databases are performed by the cloud service provider.

- **Desktop as a Service:** The ability to build, configure, manage, store, execute, and deliver user desktop functions remotely. In essence, Desktop as a Service offloads common desktop apps plus data from the user's desktop or laptop computer into the cloud. Designed to provide a reliable, consistent experience for the remote use of programs, applications, processes, and files.

- **E-mail as a Service:** A complete e-mail service, including related support services such as storage, receipt, transmission, backup, and recovery of e-mail.

- **Identity as a Service:** Identity and access management (IAM) that can be extended and centralized into existing operating environments. This includes provisioning, directory management, and the operation of a single sign-on service.

- **Management as a Service:** Includes application management, asset and change management, capacity management, problem management (service desk), project portfolio management, service catalog, and service level management.

- **Security as a Service:** The integration of a suite of security services with the existing operating environment by the cloud service provider. This may include authentication, antivirus, antimalware/spyware, intrusion detection, and security event management, among others.

XaaS

XaaS is the latest development in the provisioning of cloud services. The acronym has three generally accepted interpretations, all of which mean pretty much the same thing:

- **Anything as a Service:** Where *anything* refers to any service other than the three traditional services.

- **Everything as a Service:** Although this version is sometimes spelled out, it is somewhat misleading, because no vendor offers every possible cloud service. This version is meant to suggest that the cloud service provider is providing a wide range of service offerings.

- **X as a Service:** Where *X* can represent any possible cloud service option.

XaaS providers go beyond the traditional "big three" services in three ways.

- Some providers package together SaaS, PaaS, and IaaS so that the customer can do one-stop shopping for the basic cloud services that enterprises are coming to rely on.

- XaaS providers can increasingly displace a wider range of services that IT departments typically offer internal customers. This strategy reduces the burden on the IT department to acquire, maintain, patch, and upgrade a variety of common applications and services.

- The XaaS model typically involves an ongoing relationship between customer and provider, in which there are regular status updates and a genuine two-way, real-time exchange of information. In effect, this is a managed service offering, enabling the customer to commit to only the amount of service needed at any time, and to expand both the amount and types of service as the customers needs evolve and as the offerings available expand.

XaaS is becoming increasingly attractive to customers because it offers these benefits:

- Total costs are controlled and lowered. By outsourcing the maximum range of IT services to a qualified expert partner, an enterprise sees both immediate and long-term cost reductions. Capital expenditures are drastically reduced because of the need to acquire far less hardware and software locally. Operating expenses are lower because the resources used are tailored to immediate needs and change only as needs change.

- Risks are lowered. XaaS providers offer agreed service levels. This eliminates the risks of cost overruns so common with internal projects. The use of a single provider for a wide range of services provides a single point of contact for resolving problems.

- Innovation is accelerated. IT departments constantly run the risk of installing new hardware and software only to find that later versions that are more capable, less expensive, or both are available by the time installation is complete. With XaaS, the latest offerings are more quickly available. Further, providers can react quickly to customer feedback.

13.3 Cloud Deployment Models

An increasingly prominent trend in many organizations is to move a substantial portion or even all information technology (IT) operations to enterprise cloud computing. The organization is faced with a range of choices as to cloud ownership and management. This section looks at the four most prominent deployment models for cloud computing.

Public Cloud

A public cloud infrastructure is made available to the general public or a large industry group and is owned by an organization selling cloud services. The cloud provider is responsible both for the cloud infrastructure and for the control of data and operations within the cloud. A public cloud may be owned, managed, and operated by a business, academic, or government organization, or some combination of them. It exists on the premises of the cloud service provider.

In a public cloud model, all major components are outside the enterprise firewall, located in a multitenant infrastructure. Applications and storage are made available over the Internet via secured IP, and can be free or offered at a pay-per-usage fee. This type of cloud supplies easy-to-use consumer-type services, such as: Amazon and Google on-demand web applications or capacity, Yahoo! Mail, and Facebook or LinkedIn social media providing free storage for photographs. Although public clouds are inexpensive and scale to meet needs, they typically provide no or lower service level agreements (SLAs) and may not offer the guarantees against data loss or corruption found with private or hybrid cloud offerings. The public cloud is appropriate for consumers and entities not requiring the same levels of service that are expected within the firewall. Also, the public IaaS clouds do not necessarily provide for restrictions and compliance with privacy laws, which remain the responsibility of the subscriber or corporate end user. In many public clouds, the focus is on the consumer and small and medium-size businesses where pay-per-use pricing is available, often equating to pennies per gigabyte. Examples of services here might be picture and music sharing, laptop backup, or file sharing.

The major advantage of the public cloud is cost. A subscribing organization pays only for the services and resources it needs and can adjust these as needed. Further, the subscriber has greatly reduced management overhead. The principal concern is security; however, a number of public cloud providers have demonstrated strong security controls and, in fact, such providers may have more resources and expertise to devote to security that would be available in a private cloud.

Private Cloud

A private cloud is implemented within the internal IT environment of the organization. The organization may choose to manage the cloud in house or contract the management function to a third party. In addition, the cloud servers and storage devices may exist on premises or off premises.

Private clouds can deliver IaaS internally to employees or business units through an intranet or the Internet via a virtual private network (VPN), as well as software (applications) or storage as services to its branch offices. In both cases, private clouds are a way to leverage existing infrastructure, and deliver and chargeback for bundled or complete services from the privacy of the organization's network. Examples of services delivered through the private cloud include database on demand, e-mail on demand, and storage on demand.

A key motivation for opting for a private cloud is security. A private cloud infrastructure offers tighter controls over the geographic location of data storage and other aspects of security. Other benefits include easy resource sharing and rapid deployment to organizational entities.

Community Cloud

A community cloud shares characteristics of private and public clouds. Like a private cloud, a community cloud has restricted access. Like a public cloud, the cloud resources are shared among a number of independent organizations. The organizations that share the community cloud have similar requirements and, typically, a need to exchange data with each other. One example of an industry that is using the community cloud concept is the healthcare industry. A community cloud can be implemented to comply with government privacy and other regulations. The community participants can exchange data in a controlled fashion.

The cloud infrastructure may be managed by the participating organizations or a third party and may exist on premises or off premises. In this deployment model, the costs are spread over fewer users than a public cloud (but more than a private cloud), so only some of the cost savings potential of cloud computing are realized.

Hybrid Cloud

The hybrid cloud infrastructure is a composition of two or more clouds (private, community, or public) that remain unique entities but are bound together by standardized or proprietary technology that enables data and application portability (for example, cloud bursting for load balancing between clouds). With a hybrid cloud solution, sensitive information can be placed in a private area of the cloud, and less sensitive data can take advantage of the benefits of the public cloud.

A hybrid public/private cloud solution can be particularly attractive for smaller businesses. Many applications for which security concerns are less can be offloaded at considerable cost savings without committing the organization to moving more sensitive data and applications to the public cloud.

Table 13.2 lists some of the relative strengths and weaknesses of the four cloud deployment models.

TABLE 13.2 Comparison of Cloud Deployment Models

	Private	Community	Public	Hybrid
Scalability	Limited	Limited	Very high	Very high
Security	Most secure option	Very secure	Moderately secure	Very secure
Performance	Very good	Very good	Low to medium	Good
Reliability	Very high	Very high	Medium	Medium to high
Cost	High	Medium	Low	Medium

13.4 Cloud Architecture

To gain a better understanding of the elements of a cloud system, this section examines two reference architectures.

NIST Cloud Computing Reference Architecture

NIST SP 500-292, *NIST Cloud Computing Reference Architecture*, September 2011, establishes a reference architecture, described as follows:

> The NIST cloud computing reference architecture focuses on the requirements of "what" cloud services provide, not a "how to" design solution and implementation. The reference architecture is intended to facilitate the understanding of the operational intricacies in cloud computing. It does not represent the system architecture of a specific cloud computing system; instead it is a tool for describing, discussing, and developing a system-specific architecture using a common framework of reference.

NIST developed the reference architecture with the following objectives in mind:

- To illustrate and understand the various cloud services in the context of an overall cloud computing conceptual model.

- To provide a technical reference for consumers to understand, discuss, categorize, and compare cloud services.

- To facilitate the analysis of candidate standards for security, interoperability, and portability and reference implementations.

Cloud Computing Actors

The reference architecture depicted in Figure 13.4 defines five major actors in terms of the roles and responsibilities, as defined in the list that follows.

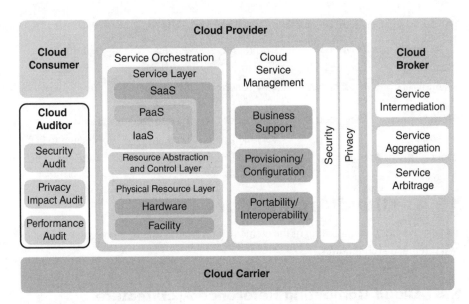

FIGURE 13.4   NIST Cloud Computing Reference Architecture

- **Cloud consumer**: A person or organization that maintains a business relationship with and uses services from cloud providers.

- **Cloud provider (CP)**: A person, organization, or entity responsible for making a service available to interested parties.

- **Cloud auditor**: A party that can conduct independent assessment of cloud services, information system operations, performance, and security of the cloud implementation.

- **Cloud broker**: An entity that manages the use, performance and delivery of cloud services and negotiates relationships between CPs and cloud consumers.

- **Cloud carrier**: An intermediary that provides connectivity and transport of cloud services from CPs to cloud consumers.

The roles of the cloud consumer and provider have already been discussed. To summarize, a **cloud provider** can provide one or more of the cloud services to meet IT and business requirements of **cloud consumers**. For each of the three service models (SaaS, PaaS, IaaS), the CP provides the storage and processing facilities needed to support that service model, together with a cloud interface for cloud service consumers. For SaaS, the CP deploys, configures, maintains, and updates the operation of the software applications on a cloud infrastructure so that the services are provisioned at the expected service levels to cloud consumers. The consumers of SaaS can be organizations that provide their members with access to software applications, end users who directly use software applications, or software application administrators who configure applications for end users.

For PaaS, the CP manages the computing infrastructure for the platform and runs the cloud software that provides the components of the platform, such as runtime software execution stack, databases, and other middleware components. Cloud consumers of PaaS can employ the tools and execution resources provided by CPs to develop, test, deploy, and manage the applications hosted in a cloud environment.

For IaaS, the CP acquires the physical computing resources underlying the service, including the servers, networks, storage, and hosting infrastructure. The IaaS cloud consumer in turn uses these computing resources, such as a virtual computer, for their fundamental computing needs.

The **cloud carrier** is a networking facility that provides connectivity and transport of cloud services between cloud consumers and CPs. Typically, a CP will set up SLAs with a cloud carrier to provide services consistent with the level of SLAs offered to cloud consumers, and may require the cloud carrier to provide dedicated and secure connections between cloud consumers and CPs.

A **cloud broker** is useful when cloud services are too complex for a cloud consumer to easily manage. Three areas of support can be offered by a cloud broker:

- **Service intermediation:** These are value-added services, such as identity management, performance reporting, and enhanced security.

- **Service aggregation:** The broker combines multiple cloud services to meet consumer needs not specifically addressed by a single CP, or to optimize performance or minimize cost.

- **Service arbitrage:** This is similar to service aggregation except that the services being aggregated are not fixed. Service arbitrage means a broker has the flexibility to choose services from multiple agencies. The cloud broker, for example, can use a credit-scoring service to measure and select an agency with the best score.

A **cloud auditor** can evaluate the services provided by a CP in terms of security controls, privacy impact, performance, and so on. The auditor is an independent entity that can assure that the CP conforms to a set of standards.

Figure 13.5 illustrates the interactions between the actors. A cloud consumer may request cloud services from a cloud provider directly or via a cloud broker. A cloud auditor conducts independent audits and may contact the others to collect necessary information. This figure shows that cloud networking issues in fact involve three separate types of networks. For a cloud producer, the network architecture is that of a typical large data center, which consists of racks of high-performance servers and storage devices, interconnected with high-speed top-of-rack Ethernet switches. The concerns in this context focus on virtual machine placement and movement, load balancing, and availability issues. The enterprise network is likely to have a quite different architecture, typically including a number of LANs, servers, workstations, PCs, and mobile devices, with a broad range of network performance, security, and management issues. The concern of both producer and consumer with respect to the cloud carrier, which is shared with many users, is the ability to create virtual networks, with appropriate SLA and security guarantees.

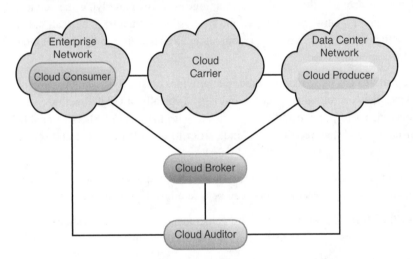

FIGURE 13.5   Interactions Between Actors in Cloud Computing

Cloud Provider Architectural Components

Figure 13.4 shows four main architectural components of the cloud provider. **Service orchestration** refers to the composition of system components to support the cloud provider activities in arrangement, coordination, and management of computing resources to provide cloud services to cloud consumers. Orchestration is shown as a three-layer architecture. We see here the familiar mapping of physical resources to consumer-visible services by a resource abstraction layer. Examples of resource abstraction components include software elements such as hypervisors, virtual machines, virtual data storage, and other computing resource abstractions.

Cloud service management includes all the service-related functions necessary for the management and operation of those services required by or proposed to cloud consumers. It covers three main areas:

- **Business support:** This consists of business-related services dealing with customers, such as accounting, billing, reporting, and auditing.

- **Provisioning/configuration:** This includes automated tools for rapid deployment of cloud systems for consumers, adjusting configuration and resource assignment, and monitoring and reporting on resource usage.

- **Portability/interoperability:** Consumers are interested in cloud offering that support data and system portability and service interoperability. This is particularly useful in a hybrid cloud environment, in which the consumer may want to change the allocation of data and applications between on-premises and off-premises sites.

Security and **privacy** are concerns that encompass all layers and elements of the cloud provider's architecture.

ITU-T Cloud Computing Reference Architecture

It is useful to look at an alternative reference architecture, published in ITU-T Y.3502, *Cloud Computing Architecture*, August 2014. This architecture is somewhat broader in scope than the NIST architecture and views the architecture as a layered functional architecture.

Cloud Computing Actors

Before looking at the four-layer reference architecture, we need to note the differences between NIST and ITU-T in defining cloud actors. The ITU-T document defines three actors:

- **Cloud service customer or user:** A party that is in a business relationship for the purpose of using cloud services. The business relationship is with a cloud service provider or a cloud service partner. Key activities for a cloud service customer include, but are not limited to, using cloud services, performing business administration, and administering use of cloud services.

- **Cloud service provider:** A party that makes cloud services available. The cloud service provider focuses on activities necessary to provide a cloud service and activities necessary to ensure its delivery to the cloud service customer as well as cloud service maintenance. The cloud service provider includes an extensive set of activities (for example, provide service, deploy and monitor service, manage business plan, provide audit data) as well as numerous subroles (for example, business manager, service manager, network provider, security and risk manager).

- **Cloud service partner:** A party which is engaged in support of, or auxiliary to, activities of either the cloud service provider or the cloud service customer, or both. A cloud service partner's activities vary depending on the type of partner and their relationship with the cloud service provider and the cloud service customer. Examples of cloud service partners include cloud auditor and cloud service broker.

Figure 13.6 depicts the actors with some of their possible roles in a cloud ecosystem.

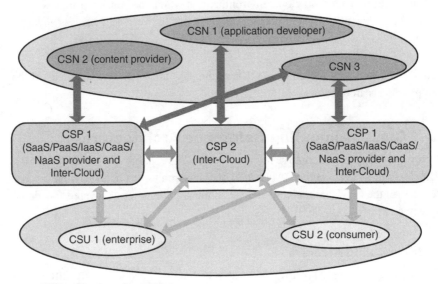

CSN = Cloud service partner
CSP = Cloud service provider
CSU = Cloud service user

FIGURE 13.6   Actors with Some of Their Possible Roles in a Cloud Ecosystem

Layered Architecture

Figure 13.7 shows the four-layer ITU-T cloud computing reference architecture. The user layer is the user interface through which a cloud service customer interacts with a cloud service provider and with cloud services, performs customer related administrative activities, and monitors cloud services. It can also offer the output of cloud services to another resource layer instance. When the cloud receives service requests, it orchestrates its own resources and/or other clouds' resources (if other clouds' resources are received via the intercloud function) and provides back cloud services through the user layer. The user layer is where the CSU resides.

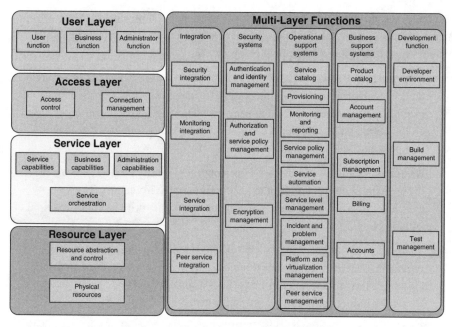

FIGURE 13.7 ITU-T Cloud Computing Reference Architecture

The access layer provides a common interface for both manual and automated access to the capabilities available in the services layer. These capabilities include both the capabilities of the services and also the administration and business capabilities. The access layer accepts user/partner/other provider cloud service consumption requests using cloud application programming interfaces (APIs) to access the provider's services and resources.

The access layer is responsible for presenting cloud service capabilities over one or more access mechanisms—for example, as a set of web pages accessed via a browser, or as a set of web services that can be accessed programmatically. The access layer also deals with security and QoS.

The service layer contains the implementation of the services provided by a cloud service provider (for example, SaaS, PaaS, IaaS). The service layer contains and controls the software components that implement the services (but not the underlying hypervisors, host operating systems, device drivers, and so on), and arranges to offer the cloud services to users via the access layer.

The resource layer consists of physical resources available to the provider and the appropriate abstraction and control mechanisms. For example, hypervisor software can provide virtual network, virtual storage, and virtual machine capabilities. It also houses the cloud core transport network functionality that is required to provide underlying network connectivity between the provider and users.

The multilayer functions include a series of functional components that interact with functional components of the four other layers to provide supporting capabilities. It includes five categories of functional components:

- **Integration:** Responsible for connecting functional components in the architecture to create a unified architecture. The integration functional components provide message routing and message exchange mechanisms within the cloud architecture and its functional components as well as with external functional components.

- **Security systems:** Responsible for applying security related controls to mitigate the security threats in cloud computing environments. The security systems functional components encompass all the security facilities required to support cloud services.

- **Operational support systems (OSS):** Encompass the set of operational related management capabilities that are required to manage and control the cloud services offered to customers. OSS is also involved in system monitoring, including the use of alarms and events.

- **Business support systems (BSS):** Encompass the set of business-related management capabilities dealing with customers and supporting processes, such as billing and accounts.

- **Development function:** Supports the cloud computing activities of the cloud service developer. This includes support of the development/composition of service implementations, build management and test management.

13.5 SDN and NFV

Cloud computing predates software-defined networking (SDN) and network functions virtualization (NFV). While cloud computing can be, and has been, deployed and managed without SDN and NFV, both of these technologies are compelling for both private cloud operators and public cloud service providers.

In simplified and generalized terms, what SDN offers is centralized command and control of network resources and traffic patterns. A single central controller, or a few distributed cooperating controllers, can configure and manage virtual networks and provide QoS and security services. This relieves network management of the need to individually configure and program each networking device.

What NFV offers is automated provisioning of devices. NFV virtualizes network devices, such as switches and firewalls, as well as compute and storage devices, and provides tools for scaling out and automatically deploying devices as needed. Therefore, each project or cloud customer does not require separate equipment or reprogramming of existing equipment. Relevant devices can be centrally deployed via a hypervisor management platform and configured with rules and policies.

Service Provider Perspective

A large cloud service provider will deal with thousands of customers, with dynamic needs for capacity, both in terms of traffic-carrying capacity and in terms of compute and storage resources. The provider needs to be able to rapidly manage the entire network to handle traffic bottlenecks, manage numerous traffic flows with differing QoS requirements, and deal with outages and other problems. All of this must be done in a secure manner. SDN can provide the needed overall view of the entire network and secure, centralized management of the network. The provider needs to be able to deploy and scale in/out and up/down virtual switches, servers, and storage rapidly and transparently for the customer. NFV provides the automated tools for managing this process.

Private Cloud Perspective

Large and medium-size enterprises see a number of advantages to moving much of their network-based operations to a private cloud or a hybrid cloud. Their customers are end users, IT managers, and developers. Individual departments may have substantial, dynamic IT resource needs. The enterprise typically will need to develop one or multiple server farms / data centers. As the overall resource demand grows, the ability to deploy and manage all of the equipment becomes more challenging. In addition, there are security requirements, such as firewalls, and antivirus deployments. Further complicating the scenario is the need for load balancing as projects grow and consume more resources, thus the need for rapid scalability and provisioning of devices becomes more pronounced. The need for automated provisioning of virtual networking equipment almost becomes a requirement, and with all the new virtual devices (especially in conjunction with the existing physical devices), centralized command and control becomes a must. SDN and NFV provide the enterprise with the tools to successfully develop and manage private cloud resources for internal use.

ITU-T Cloud Computing Functional Reference Architecture

Figure 13.7 showed the four-layer cloud computing reference architecture defined in Y.3502. For our discussion of the relationship between cloud networking and NFV, it is instructive to look at an earlier version of this architecture, defined in *ITU-T Focus Group on Cloud Computing Technical Report, Part 2: Functional Requirements and Reference Architecture*, February 2012 and shown in Figure 13.8. This architecture has the same four-layer structure as that of Y.3502, but provides more detail of the lowest layer, called the resources and network layer. This layer consists of three sublayers as defined in the list that follows.

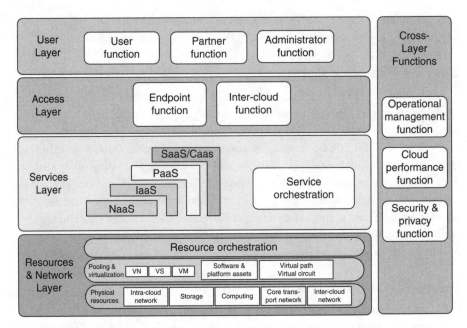

FIGURE 13.8   ITU-T Cloud Computing Functional Reference Architecture

- **Resource orchestration:** The management, monitoring, and scheduling of computing, storage, and network resources into consumable services by the upper layers and users. It controls the creation, modification, customization and release of virtualized resources.

- **Pooling and virtualization:** The virtualization function turns physical resources into virtual machines, virtual storage, and virtual networks. These virtual resources are in turn managed and controlled by the resource orchestration, based on user demand. Software and platform assets in the pooling and virtualization layer are the runtime environment, applications, and other software assets used to orchestrate and implement cloud services.

- **Physical resources:** The computing, storage, and network resources that are fundamental to providing cloud services. These resources may include those that reside inside cloud-data centers (for example, computing servers, storage servers, and intracloud networks), and those that reside outside of data centers, typically networking resources, such as intercloud networks and core transport networks.

A comparison of the resources and network layer of the ITU-T architecture to the NFV architectural framework (refer to Figure 7.7 in Chapter 7, "Network Functions Virtualization: Concepts and Architecture") suggests that the resources and network layer can be implemented using the network functions virtualization infrastructure (NFVI) for the lower two sublayers and virtualized infrastructure manager (VIM) for the resource orchestration sublayer. Thus, the general-purpose tools, often in the form of open software, plus commercial off-the-shelf physical resources, enable the cloud provider to effectively deploy and manage cloud services and resources. It should also be an effective strategy to map many of the upper layer functions in the cloud architecture to either virtual network functions or SDN control and application layer functions. Thus, both NFV and SDN contribute to the deployment of cloud services.

Similar reasoning applies to the NIST reference architecture shown previously in Figure 13.4. The service orchestration component consists of three layers: physical resource, resource abstraction and control, and service layers. The lower two layers correspond quite well to the NFVI portion of the NFV architecture.

13.6 Key Terms

After completing this chapter, you should be able to define the following terms.

Anything as a Service (XaaS)	Communications as a Service (CaaS)
cloud auditor	community cloud
cloud broker	Compute as a Service (CompaaS)
cloud carrier	Data Storage as a Service (DSaaS)
cloud computing	hybrid cloud
cloud consumer	Infrastructure as a Service (IaaS)
cloud networking	Network as a service (NaaS)
cloud provider	Platform as a Service (PaaS)
cloud service customer	private cloud
cloud service management	public cloud
cloud service partner	service orchestration
cloud service provider	Software as a Service (SaaS)
cloud storage	

Chapter | **14**

The Internet of Things: Components

Within our grasp is the leisure of the Greek citizen, made possible by our mechanical slaves, which far outnumber his twelve to fifteen per free man. These mechanical slaves jump to our aid. As we step into a room, at the touch of a button a dozen light our way. Another slave sits twenty-four hours a day at our thermostat, regulating the heat of our home. Another sits night and day at our automatic refrigerator. They start our car; run our motors; shine our shoes, and cut our hair. They practically eliminate time and space by their very fleetness.

— *Spectatoritis*, Jay B. Nash, 1932

Chapter Objectives

After studying this chapter, you should be able to

- Explain the scope of the Internet of Things.
- List and discuss the five principal components of IoT-enabled things.

Section 1.7 provided a brief overview of the concept of the Internet of Things (IoT). This chapter and the next provide a more detailed treatment. This chapter begins with a discussion of the basic concepts and scope of IoT. Then, Section 14.3 lists and discusses the main components of IoT-enabled things. Chapter 15, "The Internet of Things: Architecture and Implementation," discusses IoT architecture and implementation.

14.1   The IoT Era Begins

The future Internet will involve large numbers of objects that use standard communications architectures to provide services to end users. It is envisioned that tens of billions of such devices will be interconnected in a few years. This will provide new interactions between the physical world and computing, digital content, analysis, applications, and services. This resulting networking paradigm is being called the Internet of Things (IoT). This will provide unprecedented opportunities for users, manufacturers, and service providers in a wide variety of sectors. Areas that will benefit from IoT data collection, analysis, and automation capabilities include health and fitness, healthcare, home monitoring and automation, energy savings and smart grid, farming, transportation, environmental monitoring, inventory and product management, security, surveillance, education, and many others.

Technology development is occurring in many areas. Not surprisingly, wireless networking research is being conducted and actually has been conducted for quite a while now, but under previous titles such as mobile computing, pervasive computing, wireless sensor networks, and cyber-physical systems. Many proposals and products have been developed for low power protocols, security and privacy, addressing, low cost radios, energy efficient schemes for long battery life, and reliability for networks of unreliable and intermittently sleeping nodes. These wireless developments are crucial for the growth of IoT. In addition, areas of development have also involved giving IoT devices social networking capabilities, taking advantage of machine-to-machine communications, storing and processing large amounts of real-time data, and application programming to provide end users with intelligent and useful interfaces to these devices and data.

Many have provided a vision for the IoT. In a 2014 paper in the *Internet of Things Journal* [STAN14], the author suggests personal benefits such as digitizing daily life activities, patches of bionic skin to communicate with surrounding smart spaces for improved comfort, health, and safety, and smart watches and body nodes that optimize access to city services. Citywide benefits could include efficient, delay-free transportation with no traffic lights. Smart buildings could not only control energy and security, but also support health and wellness activities. In the same ways people have been provided new ways of accessing the world through smartphones, the IoT will create a new paradigm in the ways we have continuous access to needed information and services. Regardless of the level of positivity in one's view of the IoT or predictions about how soon this will be realized, it is certainly exciting to consider this future.

14.2   The Scope of the Internet of Things

ITU-T Y.2060, *Overview of the Internet of Things*, June 2012, provides the following definitions that suggest the scope of IoT:

- **Internet of Things (IoT):** A global infrastructure for the information society, enabling advanced services by interconnecting (physical and virtual) things based on existing and evolving interoperable information and communication technologies.

- **Thing:** With regard to the IoT, this is an object of the physical world (physical things) or the information world (virtual things), which is capable of being identified and integrated into communication networks.

- **Device:** With regard to the IoT, this is a piece of equipment with the mandatory capabilities of communication and the optional capabilities of sensing, actuation, data capture, data storage, and data processing.

Most of the literature views the IoT as involving intercommunicating smart objects. Y.2060 extends this to include virtual things, a topic examined in Section 14.4.

Y.2060 characterizes the IoT as adding the dimension "Any THING communication" to the information and communication technologies which already provide "any TIME" and "any PLACE" communication (see Figure 14.1).

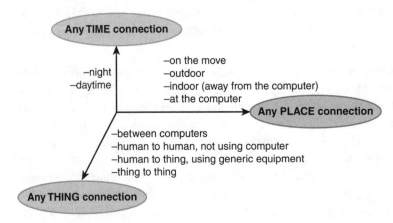

FIGURE 14.1   The New Dimension Introduced in the Internet of Things

In *Designing the Internet of Things* [MCEW13], the author condenses the elements of the IoT into a simple equation:

Physical objects + Controllers, Sensors, Actuators + Internet = IoT

This equation neatly captures the essence of the Internet of Things. An instance of the IoT consists of a collection of physical objects, each of which

- Contains a microcontroller that provides intelligence

- Contains a sensor that measures some physical parameter/actuator that acts on some physical parameter

- Provides a means of communicating via the Internet or some other network

One item not covered in the equation, and referred to in the Y.2060 definition, is a means of identification of an individual thing, usually referred to as a *tag*. We discuss tags in Section 14.3.

Note that although the phrase *the Internet of Things* is always used in the literature, a more accurate description would be *an Internet of Things*, or *a network of things*. A smart home installation, for example, consists of a number of things in the home that are interconnected via Wi-Fi or Bluetooth with some central controller. In a factory or farm setting, there may be a network of things enabling enterprise applications to interact with the environment and run applications to exploit the network of things. In these examples, it is usually but not invariably the case that remote access over the Internet is available. Whether such Internet connection is available, the collection of smart objects at a site, plus any other local compute and storage device, can be characterized as a network or an Internet of Things.

Table 14.1, based on a graphic from Beechem Research, gives an idea of the scope of IoT.

TABLE 14.1 The Internet of Things

Service Sectors	Application Groups	Locations	Device Examples
IT and networks	Public	Services, e-commerce, data centers, mobile carriers, fixed carriers	Servers, storage, PCs, routers, switches, PBXs
		ISPs	
	Enterprise	IT/data center, office, private nets	
Security/public safety	Surveillance equipment, tracking	Radar/satellite, military security, unmanned, weapons, vehicles, ships, aircraft, gear	Tanks, fighter jets, battlefield communications, jeeps
	Public infrastructure	Human, animal, postal, food/health, packaging, baggage, water treatment, building environmental, general environmental	Cars, breakdown lane worker, homeland security, fire, environmental monitor
	Emergency services	Equipment and personnel, police, fire, regulatory	Ambulances, public security vehicles

Service Sectors	Application Groups	Locations	Device Examples
Retail	Specialty	Fuel stations, gaming, bowling, cinema, discos, special events	POS terminals, tags, cash registers, vending machines, signs
	Hospitality	Hotels, restaurants, bars, cafes, clubs	
	Stores	Supermarkets, shopping centers, single site, distribution center	
Transportation	Nonvehicular	Air, rail, marine	Vehicles, lights, ships, planes, signage, tolls
	Vehicles	Consumer, commercial, construction, off-road	
	Transportation systems	Tolls, traffic management, navigation	
Industrial	Distribution	Pipelines, materials handling, conveyance	Pumps, valves, vats, conveyers, pipelines, motors, drives, converting, fabrication, assembly/packing, vessels, tanks
	Converting, discrete	Metals, paper, rubber, plastic, metalworking, electronics assembly, test	
	Fluid/processes	Petro-chemical, hydrocarbon, food, beverage	
	Resource automation	Mining, irrigation, agricultural, woodland	
Healthcare and life science	Care	Hospital, ER, mobile PoC, clinic, labs, doctor office	MRIs, PDAs, implants, surgical equipment, pumps, monitors, telemedicine
	In-vivo, home	Implants, home monitoring systems	
	Research	Drug discovery, diagnostics, labs	
Consumer and home	Infrastructure	Wiring, network access, energy mgt	Digital camera, power systems, dishwashers, eReaders, desktop computers, washer/dryer, meters, lights, TVs, MP3, games console, lighting, alarms
	Awareness and safety	Security/alert, fire safety, environmental safety, elderly, children, power protection	
	Convenience and entertainment	HVAC/climate, lighting, appliance, entertainment	

Service Sectors	Application Groups	Locations	Device Examples
Energy	Supply/ demand	Power generation, transport and distribution, low voltage, power quality, energy management	Turbines, wind-mills, uninterruptible power supply (UPS), batteries, generators, meters, drills, fuel cells
	Alternative	Solar, wind, co-generation, electro-chemical	
	Oil/gas	Rigs, derricks, well heads, pumps, pipelines	
Buildings	Commercial, institutional	Office, education, retail, hospitality, healthcare, airports, stadiums	HVAC, transport, fire and safety, lighting, security, access
	Industrial	Process, clean room, campus	

Source: Beecham Research

14.3 Components of IoT-Enabled Things

The key ingredients of an IoT-enabled thing are sensors, actuators, a microcontroller, a means of communication (transceiver), and a means of identification (radio-frequency identification [RFID]). A means of communication is an essential ingredient; otherwise, the device cannot participate in a network. Nearly all IoT-enabled things have some sort of computing capability, no matter how rudimentary. And a device may have one or more of the other ingredients. We examine each of these ingredients in this section.

Sensors

A **sensor** measures some parameter of a physical, chemical, or biological entity and delivers an electronic signal proportional to the observed characteristic, either in the form of an analog voltage level or a digital signal. In both cases, the sensor output is typically input to a microcontroller or other management element.

sensor
A device that converts a physical, biological, or chemical parameter into an electrical signal.

The left side of Figure 14.2, adapted from a figure in *Middleware Architecture with Patterns and Frameworks* [KRAK09], shows the interface between a sensor and the controller for that sensor. A sensor may take the initiative in sending sensor data to the controller, either periodically or when a defined threshold is crossed; this is the active mode. Alternatively, or in addition, the sensor may operate in the passive mode, providing data when requested by the controller.

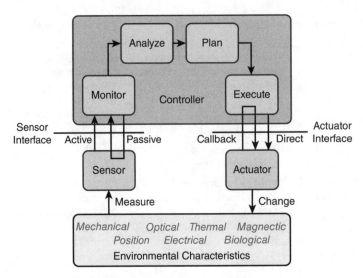

FIGURE 14.2   Interfaces for Sensors and Actuators

Types of Sensors

The variety of sensors used in IoT deployments is huge. Sensors may be extremely tiny, using nanotechnology, or quite substantial, such as a surveillance camera. Sensors may be deployed individually or in very small numbers on the one hand, or in large numbers on the other. Table 14.2, from *Practical Electronics for Inventors* [SCHE13], lists various types of sensors, with examples of each type.

TABLE 14.2   Types of Sensors

Category	What It Does	Device Examples
Position measuring devices	Designed to detect and respond to changes in angular position or in linear position of the device	Potentiometer, linear position sensor, hall effect position sensor, magnetoresistive angular, encoders (quadrature, incremental rotary, absolute rotary, optical)
Proximity, motion sensors	Designed to detect and respond to movement outside of the component but within the range of the sensor	Ultrasonic proximity, optical reflective, optical slotted, PIR (passive infrared), inductive proximity, capacitive proximity, reed switch, tactile switch
Inertial devices	Designed to detect and respond to changes in the physical movement of the sensor	Accelerometer, potentiometer, inclinometer, gyroscope, vibration sensor/switch, tilt sensor, Piezo shock sensor, LVDT/RVDT
Pressure/force	Designed to detect a force being exerted against it	IC barometer, strain gauge, pressure potentiometer, LVDT, silicon transducer, Piezoresistive sensor, capacitive transducer

Category	What It Does	Device Examples
Optical devices	Designed to detect the presence of light or a change in the amount of light on the sensor	LDR, photodiodes, phototransistors, photo interrupters, reflective sensors, IrDA transceiver, solar cells, LTV (light voltage) sensors
Image, camera devices	Designed to detect and change a viewable image into a digital signal	CMOS image sensor
Magnetic devices	Designed to detect and respond to the presence of a magnetic field	Hall effect sensor, magnetic switch, linear compass IC, Reed sensor
Media devices	Designed to detect and respond to the presence or the amount of a physical substance on the sensor	Gas, smoke, humidity, moisture, dust, float level, fluid flow
Current and voltage devices	Designed to detect and respond to changes in the flow of electricity in a wire or circuit	Hall effect current sensor, DC current sensor, AC current sensor, voltage transducer
Temperature	Designed to detect the amount of heat using different techniques and in different mediums	Thermistor NTC, thermistor PTC, resistance temp detectors (RTD)s, thermocouple, thermopile, digital IC, analog IC, infrared thermometer/pyrometer
Specialized	Designed to provide detection, measurement, or response in specialized situations, which also may include multiple functions	Audio Microphone, Geiger-Müller tube, chemical

Precision, Accuracy, and Resolution

Two key concepts need to be distinguished in discussing sensors: precision and accuracy. **Accuracy** refers to how close a measurement comes to the truth, represented as a bull's eye in Figure 14.3. **Precision** refers to how close multiple measurements of the same physical quantity are to each other. If a sensor has low accuracy, this produces a systematic error. If a sensor has low precision, it produces a reproducibility error.

accuracy

The closeness of agreement between the result of a measurement and the true value of the measurand. It can be expressed as a qualitative assessment of correctness, or freedom from error, or a quantitative measure of the expected magnitude of error.

precision

The degree of agreement of repeated measurements of the same property, expressed quantitatively as the standard deviation computed from the results of the series of measurements.

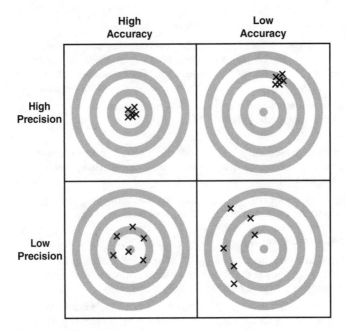

FIGURE 14.3   Precision and Accuracy

resolution

The smallest distinguishable increment into which a measured quantity is divided.

Related to precision is the concept of **resolution**. If a sensor has high precision, a very small change in the value of a physical quantity results in a very small change in the value of the sensor measurement. If the sensor output is digital, more bits are needed to represent the measurement to capture these small changes in the underlying physical parameter.

Actuators

actuator

A device that accepts an electrical signal and converts it into a physical, chemical, or biological action.

An **actuator** receives an electronic signal from a controller and responds by interacting with its environment to produce an effect on some parameter of a physical, chemical, or biological entity. The right side of Figure 14.2 shows the interface between an actuator and the controller for that actuator. In the direct mode of operation, the controller sends a signal that activates the actuator. In callback mode, the actuator responds to the controller to report completion or a problem, and requests further instructions.

Actuators are generally classified as follows:

- **Hydraulic:** Hydraulic actuators consist of a cylinder or fluid motor that utilizes hydraulic power to facilitate mechanical process. The mechanical motion gives an output in terms of linear, rotary, or oscillatory motion.

- **Pneumatic:** Pneumatic actuators work on the same concept as hydraulic actuators except compressed gas is used instead of liquid. Energy, in the form of compressed gas, is converted into linear or rotary motion, depending on the type of actuator.

- **Electric:** Electric actuators are devices powered by motors that convert electrical energy to mechanical torque.

- **Mechanical:** Function through converting rotary motion to linear motion. Devices such as gears, rails, pulley, chain, and others are used to help convert the motion.

Microcontrollers

The "smart" in a smart device is provided by a deeply embedded microcontroller. This section defines some key terms and explains the concept of a microcontroller.

Embedded System

The term **embedded system** refers to the use of electronics and software within a product that has a specific function or set of functions, as opposed to a general-purpose computer, such as a laptop or desktop system. Hundreds of millions of computers are sold every year, including laptops, personal computers, workstations, servers, mainframes, and supercomputers. In contrast, tens of billions of microcrontrollers are produced each year that are embedded within larger devices. Today, many, perhaps most, devices that use electric power have an embedded computing system. It is likely that in the near future nearly all such devices will have embedded computing systems.

embedded system

Any device that includes a computer chip, but that is not a general-purpose workstation, desktop, or laptop computer.

Types of devices with embedded systems are almost too numerous to list. Examples include cell phones, digital cameras, video cameras, calculators, microwave ovens, home security systems, washing machines, lighting systems, thermostats, printers, various automotive systems (for example, transmission control, cruise control, fuel injection, anti-lock brakes, and suspension systems), tennis rackets, toothbrushes, and numerous types of sensors and actuators in automated systems.

Often, embedded systems are tightly coupled to their environment. This can give rise to real-time constraints imposed by the need to interact with the environment. Constraints, such as required speeds of motion, required precision of measurement, and required time durations, dictate the timing of software operations. If multiple activities must be managed simultaneously, this imposes more complex real-time constraints.

Figure 14.4 shows in general terms an embedded system organization. In addition to the processor and memory, there are a number of elements that differ from the typical desktop or laptop computer:

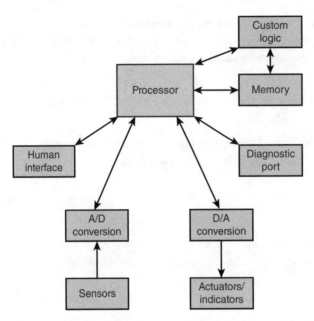

FIGURE 14.4   Possible Organization of an Embedded System

■ There may be a variety of interfaces that enable the system to measure, manipulate, and otherwise interact with the external environment. Embedded systems often interact (sense, manipulate, and communicate) with the external world through sensors and actuators and hence are typically reactive systems; a reactive system is in continual interaction with the environment and executes at a pace determined by that environment.

■ The human interface may be as simple as a flashing light or as complicated as real-time robotic vision. In many cases, there is no human interface.

■ The diagnostic port may be used for diagnosing the system that is being controlled—not just for diagnosing the computer.

■ Special-purpose field programmable (FPGA), application-specific (ASIC), or even nondigital hardware may be used to increase performance or reliability.

■ Software often has a fixed function and is specific to the application.

■ Efficiency is of paramount importance for embedded systems. They are optimized for energy, code size, execution time, weight and dimensions, and cost.

There are several noteworthy areas of similarity to general-purpose computer systems as well:

- Even with nominally fixed function software, the ability to field upgrades to fix bugs, improve security, and add functionality has become very important for embedded systems, and not just in consumer devices.

- One comparatively recent development has been of embedded system platforms that support a wide variety of apps. Good examples of this are smartphones and audio/visual devices, such as smart TVs.

Application Processors versus Dedicated Processors

Application processors are defined by the processor's ability to execute complex operating systems, such as Linux, Android, and Chrome. Thus, the application processor is general-purpose in nature. A good example of the use of an embedded application processor is the smartphone. The embedded system is designed to support numerous apps and perform a wide variety of functions.

Most embedded systems employ a **dedicated processor**, which, as the name implies, is dedicated to one or a small number of specific tasks required by the host device. Because such an embedded system is dedicated to a specific task or tasks, the processor and associated components can be engineered to reduce size and cost.

Microprocessors

Early **microprocessor** chips included registers, an arithmetic/logic unit (ALU), and some sort of control unit or instruction processing logic. As transistor density increased, it became possible to increase the complexity of the instruction set architecture, and ultimately to add memory and more than one processor. Contemporary microprocessor chips include multiple processors, called cores, and a substantial amount of cache memory. However, as shown in Figure 14.5, a microprocessor chip includes only some of the elements that make up a computer system.

microprocessor

A processor whose elements have been miniaturized into one or a few integrated circuits.

Most computers, including embedded computers in smartphones and tablets, plus personal computers, laptops, and workstations, are housed on a motherboard. Before describing this arrangement, we need to define some terms. A **printed circuit board** is a rigid, flat board that holds and interconnects chips and other electronic components. The board is made of layers, typically two to ten, that interconnect components via copper pathways that are etched into the board. The main printed circuit board (PCB) in a computer is called a system board or **motherboard**, and smaller ones that plug into the slots in the main board are called expansion boards.

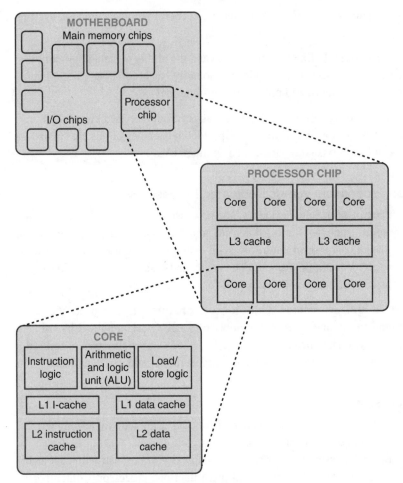

FIGURE 14.5   Simplified View of Major Elements of a Multicore Computer

The most prominent elements on the motherboard are the chips. A **chip** is a single piece of semiconducting material, typically silicon, upon which electronic circuits and logic gates are fabricated. The resulting product is referred to as an **integrated circuit**.

The motherboard contains a slot or socket for the processor chip, which typically contains multiple individual cores, in what is known as a *multicore processor*. There are also slots for memory chips, I/O controller chips, and other key computer components. For desktop computers, expansion slots enable the inclusion of more components on expansion boards. Thus, a modern motherboard connects only a few individual chip components, with each chip containing from a few thousand up to hundreds of millions of transistors.

Microcontrollers

A **microcontroller** chip makes a substantially different use of the logic space available. Figure 14.6 shows in general terms the elements typically found on a microcontroller chip. As shown, a microcontroller is a single chip that contains the core, nonvolatile memory for the program (ROM), volatile memory for input and output (RAM), a clock, and an I/O control unit. The processor portion of the microcontroller has a much lower silicon area than other microprocessors and much higher energy efficiency.

microcontroller

A single chip that contains the processor, nonvolatile memory for the program (ROM or flash), volatile memory for input and output (RAM), a clock and an I/O control unit. Also called a *computer on a chip*.

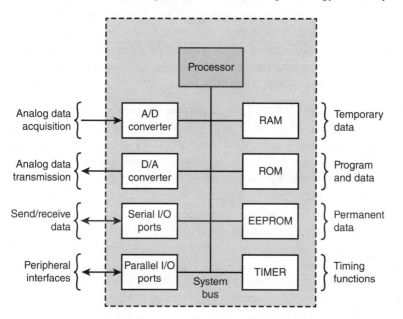

FIGURE 14.6   Typical Microcontroller Chip Elements

Also called a computer on a chip, billions of microcontroller units are embedded each year in myriad products from toys to appliances to automobiles. For example, a single vehicle can use 70 or more microcontrollers. Typically, especially for the smaller, less expensive microcontrollers, they are used as dedicated processors for specific tasks. For example, microcontrollers are heavily utilized in automation processes. By providing simple reactions to input, they can control machinery, turn fans on and off, open and close valves, and so forth. They are integral parts of modern industrial technology and are among the most inexpensive ways to produce machinery that can handle extremely complex functionalities.

Microcontrollers come in a range of physical sizes and processing power. Processors range from 4-bit to 32-bit architectures. Microcontrollers tend to be much slower than microprocessors, typically operating in the megahertz (MHz) range rather than the gigahertz (GHz) speeds of microprocessors. Another typical feature of a micro-controller is that it does not provide for human interaction. The microcontroller is programmed for a specific task, embedded in its device, and executes as and when required.

Deeply Embedded Systems

A subset of embedded systems, and a quite numerous subset, is referred to as **deeply embedded systems**. Although this term is widely used in the technical and commercial literature, you will search the Internet in vain (at least the writer did) for a straightforward definition. Generally, we can say that a deeply embedded system has a processor whose behavior is difficult to observe both by the programmer and the user. A deeply embedded system uses a microcontroller rather than a microprocessor, is not programmable once the program logic for the device has been burned into ROM (read-only memory), and has no interaction with a user.

Deeply embedded systems are dedicated, single-purpose devices that detect something in the environment, perform a basic level of processing, and then do something with the results. Deeply embedded systems often have wireless capability and appear in networked configurations, such as networks of sensors deployed over a large area (for example, factory, agricultural field). The Internet of Things depends heavily on deeply embedded systems. Typically, deeply embedded systems have extreme resource constraints in terms of memory, processor size, time, and power consumption.

Transceivers

transceiver

A device that is capable of both transmitting and receiving information.

A **transceiver** contains the electronics needed to transmit and receive data. Most IoT devices contain a wireless transceiver, capable of communication using Wi-Fi, ZigBee, or some other wireless scheme.

Figure 14.7 is a simplified block diagram showing the basic elements of a transceiver. The upper part of the figure is the transmitter, which takes some analog or digital input signal as input. This signal is modulated onto a carrier frequency. This is done by a modulator whose input is the source signal plus a carrier wave generated by an oscillator. The resulting signal goes through one or more amplifiers and then is transmitted by an antenna.

The lower part of Figure 14.7 is the receiver. The input to the receiver is the signal captured by the antenna. A low-noise amplifier (LNA) is an electronic amplifier used to amplify very weak signals (for example, captured by an antenna). The LNA is designed to boost the desired signal power while adding as little noise and distortion as possible. Following the LNA, a filter is used to eliminate or reduce unwanted noise and signal components. Then a demodulator converts the filter output to the desired baseband analog or digital signal.

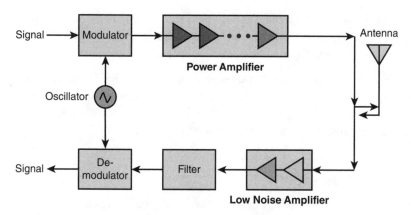

FIGURE 14.7 Simplified Transceiver Block Diagram

RFID

Radio-frequency identification (RFID) technology, which uses radio waves to identify items, is increasingly becoming an enabling technology for IoT. The main elements of an RFID system are tags and readers. RFID tags are small programmable devices used for object, animal and human tracking. They come in a variety of shapes, sizes, functionalities, and costs. RFID readers acquire and sometimes rewrite information stored on RFID tags that come within operating range (a few inches up to several feet). Readers are usually connected to a computer system that records and formats the acquired information for further uses.

Applications

The range of applications of RFID is wide and ever expanding. Four major categories of application are tracking and identification, payment and stored-value systems, access control, and anticounterfeiting.

The most widespread use of RFID is for tracking and identification. Early use of RFID was for large high-value items such as train cars and shipping containers. As the price has dropped and the technology improved, this application has expanded dramatically. For example, millions of pets have implanted RFID devices allowing lost animals to be identified and returned to their owner. Another example: tracking and managing the billions of consumer items and components that flow through supply changes is a formidable task and there has been widespread adoption of RFID tags to simplify the task. To make this process as inexpensive and interoperable as possible, standardized identification schemes have been developed, known as **electronic product codes (EPCs)**.

Another key area is payment and stored value systems. Electronic toll systems on highways are one example. Another is the use of electronic key "fobs" for payment at retail stores and entertainment venues.

radio-frequency identification (RFID)

A data collection technology that uses electronic tags attached to items to allow the items to be identified and tracked by a remote system. The tag consists of an RFID chip attached to an antenna.

electronic product code (EPC)

A standard code for RFID tags. The EPC ranges from 64 to 256 bits and contains, at minimum, the product number, serial number, company ID, and EPC version. Several bodies are involved in developing standards, including GS1 and EPCglobal.

Access control is another widespread application area. RFID proximity cards control building access at many companies and universities. Ski resorts and other leisure venues are also heavy users of this technology.

RFID also is effective as an anti-counterfeiting tool. Casinos use RFID tags on chips to prevent the use of counterfeit chips. The prescription drug industry uses RFID tags to cope with the counterfeit drug market. The tags are used to ensure the pedigree of drugs as they move through the supply chain and also to detect theft.

Here is a partial list of applications in these four areas:

- **Tracking and identification:**
    - Large assets, for example, railway cars and shipping containers
    - Livestock with rugged tags
    - Pets with implanted tags
    - Supply-chain management with EPC
    - Inventory control with EPC
    - Retail checkout with EPC
    - Recycling and waste disposal
    - Patient monitoring
    - Tagging children at school
    - Drivers' licenses and passports

- **Payment and stored-value systems:**
    - Electronic toll systems
    - Contact-less credit cards (for example, American Express Blue card)
    - Stored-valued systems (for example, ExxonMobil Speedpass)
    - Subway and bus passes
    - Casino tokens and concert tickets

- **Access control:**
    - Building access with proximity cards
    - Ski lift passes
    - Concert tickets
    - Automobile ignition systems

- **Anticounterfeiting:**
    - Casino tokens (for example, Wynn Casino Las Vegas)
    - High-denomination currency notes

- Luxury goods (for example, Prada)
- Prescription drugs

Tags

Figure 14.8 shows the key elements of an RFID system. Primary wireless communication is between a tag and a reader. The reader retrieves identification information and, depending on the application, other information about the tagged item. The reader then communicates this to a computer system which includes an RFID-related database and RFID-related applications.

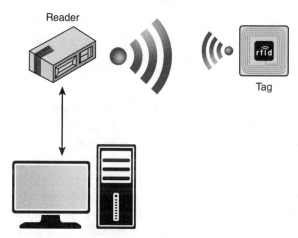

FIGURE 14.8 Elements of an RFID System

Figure 14.9 shows the two key components of a tag. The antenna is a metallic path in the tag whose layout depends on the size and shape of the tag and the operating frequency. Attached to the antenna is a simple microchip with very limited processing and nonvolatile storage.

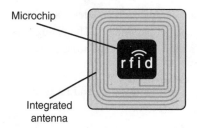

FIGURE 14.9 RFID Tag

RFID tags are classified as active, semi-passive, or passive (see Table 14.3). Active RFID tags produce their own signal from a battery, whereas passive RFID tags obtain their power from an RF signal impinging on the tag. Semi-passive tags do have a battery but behave like passive tags.

TABLE 14.3   Types of Tags

	Passive	Semi-Passive	Active
Power source	Harvesting RF energy	Battery	Battery
Required signal strength from reader to tag	High	Low	Low
Communication	Response only	Response only	Respond or initiate
Typical maximum passive read distance	10 m	> 100 m	> 100 m
Relative cost	Least expensive	More expensive	Most expensive
Example applications	EPC Proximity cards	Electronic tolls Pallet tracking	Large-asset tracking Livestock tracking

read range

The maximum distance between RFID tag and reader at which communication is reliable.

Active tags are considerably more expensive than passive tags and typically are physically larger. Active tags can generate a stronger signal and thus have a much further **read range** and can be read at high speed. Active RFIDs are the focus of the IEEE 802.15.4f standards effort.

For auto-ID and electronic key purposes, passive tags are the most common since they can be fabricated thin enough to be labels and are inexpensive. With a passive tag, the reader actually powers the tag, which then sends back its data to the reader.

Readers

RFID readers communicate with tags through an RF channel. The reader may obtain simple identification information or a more complex set of parameters. The dialogue is often a simple ping and response but may involve a more complex multiple exchange of information.

There is a wide variety of different readers in terms of functionality and basic operating style. In general, there are three categories of readers:

- **Fixed:** Fixed readers create portals for automated reading of tags as they pass by. Common applications are to read tags as the associated items enter a room, pass through warehouse dock doors, or travel on a conveyor line.

■ **Mobile:** Mobile readers are hand-held devices with an RFID antenna and reader and some computing capability. They are made for manually reading tags on the move. They are useful for inventory applications.

■ **Desktop:** This type of reader is typically attached to a PC or point-of-sale terminal and provides easy input.

Operating Frequency

True physical tag maximum read distance is determined by the individual RFID reader and antenna power, the chip used in the RFID tag, the material and thickness of material the tag is coated or covered with, the type of antenna the tag uses, the material the tag is attached to, and so on. The frequency range used by tag and reader is a limiting factor on read range. Table 14.4 lists standard frequencies and their respective passive read distances. Higher frequencies provide greater read range and the ability to transfer greater amounts of data. These frequencies can also be used for active tags. In addition, active tags can use the 433-MHz and 2.4-GHz bands with ranges in the hundreds of meters.

TABLE 14.4 Common RFID Operating Frequencies

Frequency Range	Frequencies	Passive Read Distance
Low frequency (LF)	120–140 KHz	10–20 cm
High frequency (HF)	13.56 MHz	10–20 cm
Ultra-high frequency (UHF)	868–928 MHz	3 meters
Microwave	2.45 and 5.8 GHz	3 meters
Ultra-wide band (UWB)	3.1–10.6 GHz	10 meters

Functionality

As the name suggests, the basic functionality of RFID is identification of tagged items. Tags may offer a number of other functionalities that are compatible with the RFID technology and systems. Table 14.5 lists six general classes defined by the standards group EPCglobal.

TABLE 14.5 Tag Functionality Classes

Class	Description
Class 0	UHF read-only, preprogrammed passive tag
Class 1	UHF or HF; write once, read many (WORM)
Class 2	Passive read-write tags that can be written to at any point in the supply chain
Class 3	Read-write with onboard sensors capable of recording parameters like temperature, pressure, and motion; can be semi-passive or active

Class	Description
Class 4	Read-write active tags with integrated transmitters; can communicate with other tags and readers
Class 5	Similar to Class 4 tags but with additional functionality; can provide power to other tags and communicate with devices other than readers

The Class 0 tags provide the most basic identification functionality, such as a product code or a unique identifier. The identifier is set when the tag is manufactured. These are fairly simple and inexpensive. Class 1 Tags are similar but provide the ability to set the identification information after manufacture time by the end user. Class 2 tags may be used as a logging device, in which the tagged item is logged into some system when first encountered and then provides identification information as needed. Class 3 tags provide two additional capabilities: read-write memory and onboard sensor capability. A sensor tag may log and store environmental data without the aid of a reader. Many sensor tags may form a "sensor net" that monitors a physical area's environmental properties. This may include temperature changes, rapid acceleration, changes in orientation, vibrations, the presence of biological or chemical agents, light, sound, and so on. Because they operate without a reader present, sensor tags must necessarily be semi-passive or active.

Class 4 tags, referred to as *motes*, or *smart dust*, are able to initiate communication with peers and form ad hoc networks. This leads to a wide variety of applications for small, inexpensive devices with limited communication range. Motes can be implanted or scattered over a region to collect data and pass it on from one to another to some central collection point. For example, a farmer, vineyard owner, or ecologist could equip motes with sensors that detect temperature, humidity, and so forth, making each mote a mini weather station. Scattered throughout a field, vineyard, or forest, these motes would allow the tracking of microclimates. This goes far beyond basic RFID functionality but is included by EPCglobal as a functional extension. Class 5 extends Class 4 to include the ability of one device to provide power to other tags and communicate with devices other than the reader. This opens up even more possibilities.

14.4 Key Terms

After completing this chapter, you should be able to define the following terms.

accuracy	microprocessor
actuators	operational technology (OT)
application processor	precision
dedicated processor	radio-frequency identification (RFID)
deeply embedded system	RFID reader
electronic product code (EPC)	read range
embedded systems	resolution
fog computing	sensors
information technology (IT)	RFID tag
Internet of Things (IoT)	transceiver
microcontrollers	

14.5 References

KRAK09: Krakowiak, S. *Middleware Architecture with Patterns and Frameworks.* 2009. http://sardes.inrialpes.fr/%7Ekrakowia/MW-Book/

MCEW13: McEwen, A., and Cassimally, H. *Designing the Internet of Things.* New York: Wiley, 2013.

SCHE13: Scherz, P., and Monk, S. *Practical Electronics for Inventors.* New York: McGraw-Hill, 2013.

STAN14: Stankovic, J. "Research Directions for the Internet of Things." *Internet of Things Journal*, Vol. 1, No. 1, 2014.

Chapter | **15**

The Internet of Things: Architecture and Implementation

Whenever logical processes of thought are employed—that is, whenever thought for a time runs along an accepted groove—there is an opportunity for the machine.

—"As We May Think," Vannevar Bush, *The Atlantic*, July 1945

Chapter Objectives

After studying this chapter, you should be able to

- Compare and contrast the ITU-T and IoT World Forum IoT reference models.
- Describe the open source IoTivity IoT implementation.
- Describe the commercial ioBridge IoT implementation.

This chapter concludes the discussion of the Internet of Things (IoT). It begins with a description of two important IoT reference models, which together provide insight into the architecture and functioning of an IoT. The chapter then examines three IoT implementations, one open source and two commercial.

15.1 IoT Architecture

Given the complexity of IoT, it is useful to have an architecture that specifies the main elements and their interrelationship. An IoT architecture can have the following benefits:

- It provides the IT or network manager with a useful checklist with which to evaluate the functionality and completeness of vendor offerings.

- It provides guidance to developers as to which functions are needed in an IoT and how these functions work together.

- It can serve as a framework for standardization, promoting interoperability and cost reduction.

We begin this section with an overview of the IoT architecture developed by ITU-T. We then look at one developed by IoT World Forum. The latter architecture, developed by an industry group, offers a useful alternative framework for understanding the scope and functionality of IoT.

ITU-T IoT Reference Model

The ITU-T IoT reference model is defined in Y.2060, *Overview of the Internet of Things*, June 2012. Unlike most of the other IoT reference models and architectural models in the literature, the ITU-T model goes into detail about the actual physical components of the IoT ecosystem. This is a useful treatment because it makes visible the elements in the IoT ecosystem that must be interconnected, integrated, managed, and made available to applications. This detailed specification of the ecosystem drives the requirements for the IoT capability.

An important insight provided by the model is that the IoT is in fact not a network of physical things. Rather, it is a network of devices that interact with physical things, together with application platforms, such as computers, tablets, and smartphones, that interact with these devices. So, we begin our overview of the ITU-T model with a discussion of devices.

Table 15.1 lists definitions of key terms used in Y.2060.

TABLE 15.1   Y.2060 IoT Terminology

Term	Definition
Communication network	An infrastructure network that connects devices and applications, such as an IP-based network or internet.
Thing	An object of the physical world (physical things) or the information world (virtual things) that can be identified and integrated into communication networks.
Device	A piece of equipment with the mandatory capability of communication and the optional capabilities of sensing, actuation, data capture, data storage and data processing.
Data-carrying device	A device attached to a physical thing to indirectly connect the physical thing with the communication networks. Class 3, 4, and 5 radio-frequency identification (RFID) tags are examples.
Data-capturing device	A reader/writer device with the capability to interact with physical things. The interaction can happen indirectly via data-carrying devices, or directly via data carriers attached to the physical things.
Data carrier	A battery-free data carrying object attached to a physical thing that can provide information to a suitable data capturing device. This category includes bar codes and QR codes attached to physical things.
Sensing device	Detects or measures information related to the surrounding environment and convert it into digital electronic signals.
Actuating device	Converts digital electronic signals from the information networks into operations.
General device	A general device has embedded processing and communication capabilities and may communicate with the communication networks via wired or wireless technologies. General devices include equipment and appliances for different IoT application domains, such as industrial machines, home electrical appliances, and smartphones.
Gateway	A unit in the IoT that interconnects the devices with the communication networks. It performs the necessary translation between the protocols used in the communication networks and those used by devices.

Devices

The unique aspect of IoT, compared to other network systems, of course, is the presence of a number of physical things and devices other than computing or data processing devices. Figure 15.1, adapted from one in Y.2060, shows the types of devices in the ITU-T model. The model views an IoT as functioning as a network of devices that are tightly coupled with things. Sensors and actuators interact with physical things in the environment. Data capturing devices read data from/write data to physical things via interaction with a data carrying device or a data carrier attached or associated in some way with a physical object.

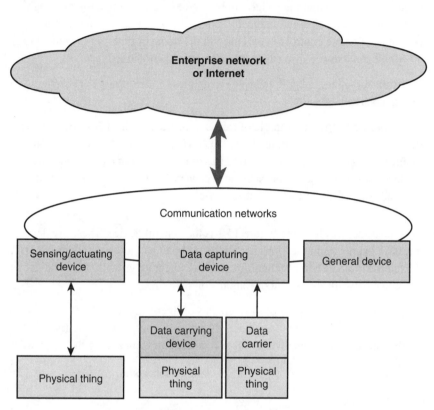

FIGURE 15.1   Types of Devices and Their Relationship with Physical Things

The model makes a distinction between data carrying devices and data carriers. A data-carrying device is a device in the Y.2060 sense. A device at minimum is capable of communication and may include other electronic capabilities. An example of a data-carrying device is an RFID tag. By contrast, a data carrier is an element attached to a physical thing for the purpose of identification of providing some other sort of information.

Y.2060 notes that technologies used for interaction between data-capturing devices and data-carrying devices or data carriers include radio frequency, infrared, optical, and galvanic driving. Examples of each include the following:

- **Radio frequency:** An RFID tag is an example.

- **Infrared:** Infrared badges are in use in military, hospital, and other settings where the location and movement of personnel needs to be tracked. Examples include infrared reflective patches used by the military and battery-operated badges that emit identifying information. The latter can include a button that must be pressed so that the badge can be used as a means of passing through a portal, and a badge that automatically repeats the signal as a means of tracking personnel. Remote control devices used in the home or other settings to control electronic devices can also easily be incorporated into an IoT.

- **Optical:** Bar codes and QR codes are examples of identifying data carriers that can be read optically.

- **Galvanic driving:** An example of this is implanted medical devices that use the conductive properties of the body [FERG11]. In implant-to-surface communication, galvanic coupling is used to send signals from an implanted device to electrodes on the skin. This scheme uses very little power and reduces the size and complexity of the implanted device.

The final type of device shown in Figure 15.1 is the general device. These are devices with processing and communications capability that can be incorporated into an IoT. A good example is smart home technology that can integrate virtually every device in the home into a network for central or remote control.

Figure 15.2 provides an overview of the elements of interest in IoT. The various ways that physical devices can be connected are shown on the left side of the figure. It is assumed that one or multiple networks support communication among the devices.

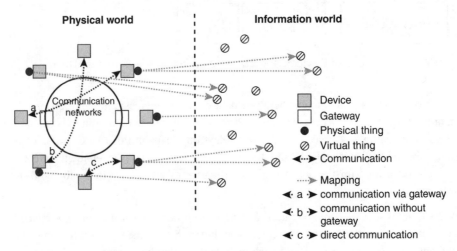

FIGURE 15.2   Technical Overview of the IoT (Y.2060)

Figure 15.2 introduces one additional IoT-related device: the gateway. At a minimum, a gateway functions as a protocol translator. Gateways address one of the greatest challenges in designing for IoT, which is connectivity, both among devices and between devices and the Internet or enterprise network. Smart devices support a wide variety of wireless and wired transmission technologies and networking protocols. Further, these devices typically have limited processing capability. Y.2067, *Common Requirements and Capabilities of a Gateway for Internet of Things Applications*, June 2014, lays out the requirements for IoT gateways, which generally fall into three categories:

- The gateway supports a variety of device access technologies, enabling devices to communicate with each other and across an Internet or enterprise network with IoT applications. The access schemes could include, for example, ZigBee, Bluetooth, and Wi-Fi.

- The gateway supports the necessary networking technologies for both local and wide-area networking. These could include Ethernet and Wi-Fi on the premises, and cellular, Ethernet, digital subscriber line (DSL), and cable access to the Internet and wide-area enterprise networks.

- The gateway supports interaction with application, network management, and security functions.

The first two requirements involve protocol translation between different network technologies and protocol suites. The third requirement is generally referred to as an **IoT agent** function. In essence, the IoT agent provides higher-level functionality on behalf of IoT devices, such as organizing/summarizing data from multiple devices to pass on to IoT applications, implementing security protocols and functions, and interacting with network management systems.

At this point, it should be noted that the term *communication network* is not directly defined in the Y.206x series of IoT standards. The communication network or networks supports communication among devices and may directly support application platforms. This may be the extent of a small IoT, such as a home network of smart devices. More generally, the device networks connect to enterprise networks or the Internet for communication with systems that host apps and servers that host databases related to the IoT.

We can now return to the left side of Figure 15.2, which illustrates the communication possibilities among devices. The first possibility is for communication between devices via the gateway. For example, a sensor or actuator with Bluetooth capability could communicate with a data-capturing device or general device that uses Wi-Fi by means of the gateway. The second possibility is communication across the communication network without a gateway. For example, all the devices in a smart home network may use Bluetooth and could be managed from a Bluetooth-enabled computer, tablet, or smartphone. The third possibility is devices that communicate directly with each other through a separate local network and then (not shown in the figure) communicate through the communication network via a local network gateway. An example of this third possibility is the following: A number of low-power sensor devices could be deployed in an extended area, such as farmland or a factory. These could communicate with one another to pass data on toward a device connected to a gateway to the communication network.

The right side of Figure 15.2 emphasizes that each physical thing in an IoT may be represented in the information world by one or more virtual things but a virtual thing can also exist without any associated physical thing. Physical things are mapped to virtual things stored in databases and other data structures. Applications process and deal with virtual things.

The Reference Model

Figure 15.3 depicts the ITU-T IoT reference model, which consists of four layers as well as management capabilities and security capabilities that apply across layers. We have so far been considering the device layer. In terms of communications functionality, the device layer includes, roughly, the OSI physical and data link layers. We now look at the other layers.

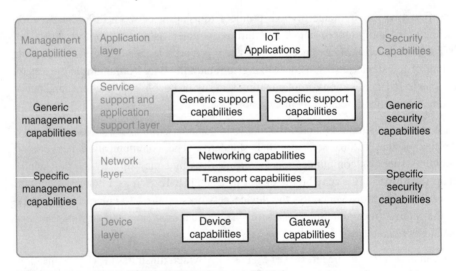

FIGURE 15.3 ITU-T Y.2060 IoT Reference Model

The **network layer** performs two basic functions. Networking capabilities refer to the interconnection of devices and gateways. Transport capabilities refer to the transport of IoT service and application specific information as well as IoT-related control and management information. Roughly, these correspond to OSI network and transport layers.

The **service support and application support layer** provides capabilities that are used by applications. Generic support capabilities can be used by many different applications. Examples include common data processing and database management capabilities. Specific support capabilities are those that cater for the requirements of a specific subset of IoT applications.

The **application layer** consists of all the applications that interact with IoT devices.

The **management capabilities layer** covers the traditional network-oriented management functions of fault, configuration, accounting, and performance management. Y.2060 lists the following as examples of generic support capabilities:

- **Device management:** Such as device discovery, authentication, remote device activation and de-activation, configuration, diagnostics, firmware/software updating, device working status management

- **Local network topology management:** Such as network configuration management

- **Traffic and congestion management:** Such as the detection of network overflow conditions and the implementation of resource reservation for time-critical/life-critical data flows

Specific management capabilities are tailored to specific classes of applications. An example is smart grid power transmission line monitoring.

The **security capabilities layer** includes generic security capabilities that are independent of applications. Y.2060 lists the following as examples of generic security capabilities:

- **Application layer:** Authorization, authentication, application data confidentiality and integrity protection, privacy protection, security audit, and antivirus

- **Network layer:** Authorization, authentication, user data and signaling data confidentiality, and signaling integrity protection

- **Device layer:** Authentication, authorization, device integrity validation, access control, data confidentiality, and integrity protection

Specific security capabilities relate to specific application requirements, such as mobile payment security requirements.

IoT World Forum Reference Model

The IoT World Forum (IWF) is an industry-sponsored annual event that brings together representatives of business, government, and academia to promote the market adoption of IoT. The IoT World Forum Architecture Committee, made up of industry leaders including IBM, Intel, and Cisco, released an IoT reference model in October 2014. This model serves as a common framework to help the industry accelerate IoT

IoT World Forum

deployments. The reference model is intended to foster collaboration and encourage the development of replicable deployment models.

This reference model is a useful complement to the ITU-T reference model. The ITU-T documents focus on the device and gateway level with only a broad depiction of the upper layers. Indeed, Y.2060 describes the application layer with a single sentence. The ITU-T Y.206x series seems most concerned with defining a framework to support development of standards for interaction with IoT devices. The IWF is concerned with the broader issue of developing the applications, middleware, and support functions for an enterprise-based IoT.

Figure 15.4 depicts the seven-level model. The white paper in the IWF model issued by Cisco [CISC14b] indicates that the model is designed to have the following characteristics:

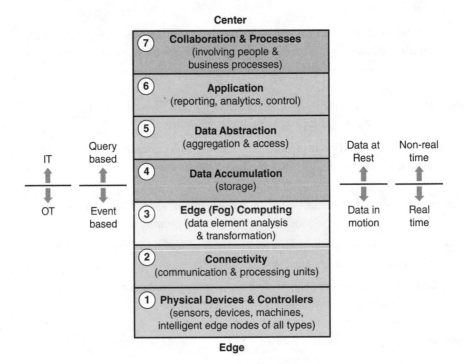

FIGURE 15.4   IoT World Forum Reference Model

- **Simplifies:** It helps break down complex systems so that each part is more understandable.

- **Clarifies:** It provides additional information to precisely identify levels of the IoT and to establish common terminology.

- **Identifies:** It identifies where specific types of processing is optimized across different parts of the system.

- **Standardizes:** It provides a first step in enabling vendors to create IoT products that work with each other.

- **Organizes:** It makes the IoT real and approachable, instead of simply conceptual.

Physical Devices and Controllers Level

Level 1 consists of physical devices and controllers that might control multiple devices. Level 1 of the IWF model corresponds approximately to the device level of the ITU-T model (Figure 15.3). As with the ITU-T model, the elements at this level are not physical things as such, but rather devices that interact with physical things, such as sensors and actuators. Among the capabilities that devices may have are analog-to-digital and digital-to-analog conversion, data generation, and the ability to be queried/controlled remotely.

Connectivity Level

From a logical point of view, this level enables communication between devices and communication between devices and the low-level processing that occurs at level 3. From a physical point of view, this level consists of networking devices, such as routers, switches, gateways, and firewalls that are used to construct local and wide-area networks and provide Internet connectivity. This level enables devices to communicate with one another and to communicate, via the upper logical levels, with application platforms such as computers, remote control devices, and smartphones.

Level 2 of the IWF model corresponds approximately to the network level of the ITU-T model. The main difference is that the IWF model includes gateways in level 2 whereas the ITU-T model puts the gateway at level 1. Because the gateway is a networking and connectivity device, its placement and level 2 seems to make more sense.

Edge Computing Level

In many IoT deployments, massive amounts of data may be generated by a distributed network of sensors. For example, offshore oil fields and refineries can generate a terabyte of data per day. An airplane can create multiple terabytes of data per hour. Rather than store all of that data permanently (or at least for a long period) in central storage accessible to IoT applications, it is often desirable to do as much data processing close to the sensors as possible. Thus, the purpose of the edge computing level is to convert network data flows into information that is suitable for storage and higher level processing. Processing elements at this level may deal with high volumes of data and perform data transformation operations, resulting in the storage of much lower volumes of data. The Cisco white paper on the IWF model [CISC14b] lists the following examples of edge computing operations:

- **Evaluation:** Evaluating data for criteria as to whether it should be processed at a higher level

- **Formatting:** Reformatting data for consistent higher-level processing

- **Expanding/decoding:** Handling cryptic data with additional context (such as the origin)

- **Distillation/reduction:** Reducing/summarizing data to minimize the impact of data and traffic on the network and higher-level processing systems

- **Assessment:** Determining whether data represents a threshold or alert; this could include redirecting data to additional destinations

Processing elements at this level correspond to general devices in the ITU-T model (Figure 15.1; Table 15.1). Generally, they are deployed physically near the edge of the IoT network; that is, near the sensors and other data-generating devices. So, some of the basic processing of large volumes of generated data is offloaded and outsourced from IoT application software located at the center.

fog computing

A scenario in which a massive number of heterogeneous, decentralized devices communicate with each other and with the network to perform storage and processing tasks without the intervention of third parties.

Processing at the edge computing level is sometimes referred to as **fog computing**. Fog computing and fog services are expected to be a distinguishing characteristic of the IoT. Figure 15.5 illustrates the concept. Fog computing represents an opposite trend in modern networking from cloud computing. With cloud computing, massive, centralized storage and processing resources are made available to distributed customers over cloud networking facilities to a relatively small number of users. With fog computing, massive numbers of individual smart objects are interconnected with fog networking facilities that provide processing and storage resources close to the edge devices in an IoT. Fog computing addresses the challenges raised by the activity of thousand or millions of smart devices, including security, privacy, network capacity constraints, and latency requirements. The term *fog computing* is inspired by the fact that fog tends to hover low to the ground, whereas clouds are high in the sky.

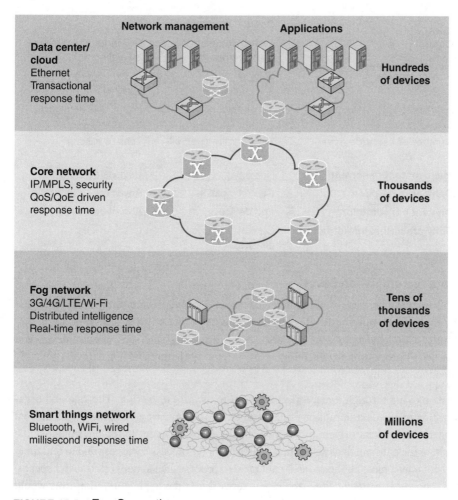

FIGURE 15.5   Fog Computing

Table 15.2, based on one in a paper by Vaquero and Rodero-Merino [VAQU14], compares cloud and fog computing.

TABLE 15.2   Comparison of Cloud and Fog Features

	Cloud	Fog
Location of processing/storage resources	Center	Edge
Latency	High	Low
Access	Fixed or wireless	Mainly wireless
Support for mobility	Not applicable	Yes

	Cloud	Fog
Control	Centralized/hierarchical (full control)	Distributed/hierarchical (partial control)
Service access	Through core	At the edge/on handheld device
Availability	99.99 percent	Highly volatile/highly redundant
Number of users/devices	Tens/hundreds of millions	Tens of billions
Main content generator	Human	Devices/sensors
Content generation	Central location	Anywhere
Content consumption	End device	Anywhere
Software virtual infrastructure	Central enterprise servers	User devices

Data Accumulation Level

This level is where data coming from the numerous devices, and filtered and processed by the edge computing level, is placed in storage that will be accessible by higher levels. This level marks a clear distinction in the design issues, requirements, and method of processing between lower-level (fog) computing and upper-level (typically cloud) computing.

Data moving through a network is referred to as *data in motion*. The rate and organization of the data in motion is determined by the devices generating the data. Data generation is event driven, either periodically or by an event in the environment. To capture the data and deal with it in some fashion, it is necessary to respond in real time. By contrasts, most applications do not need to process data at network transfer speeds. As a practical matter, neither the cloud network nor the application platforms would be able to keep up with data volume generated by a huge number of IoT devices. Instead, applications deal with *data at rest*, which is data in some readily accessible storage facility. Applications can access the data as needed, on a non-real-time basis. Thus, the upper levels operate on a query or transaction basis, whereas the lower three levels operate on an event basis.

The Cisco white paper on the IWF model [CISC14b] lists the following as operations performed at the data accumulation level:

1. Converts data-in-motion to data-at-rest

2. Converts format from network packets to database relational tables

3. Achieves transition from event based to query based computing

4. Dramatically reduces data through filtering and selective storing

Another way of viewing the data accumulation level is that it marks the boundary between **IT** and **OT**.

Data Abstraction Level

The data accumulation level absorbs large quantities of data and places them in storage, with little or no tailoring to specific applications or groups of applications. A number of different types of data in varying formats and from heterogeneous processors may be coming up from the edge computing level for storage. The data abstraction level can aggregate and format this data in ways that make access by applications more manageable and efficient. Tasks involved could include the following:

1. Combining data from multiple sources. This includes reconciling multiple data formats.

2. Perform necessary conversions to provide consistent semantics of data across sources.

3. Place formatted data in appropriate database. For example, high-volume repetitive data may go into a big data system such as Hadoop. Event data would be steered to a relational database management system, which provides faster query times and an appropriate interface for this type of data.

4. Alerting higher-level applications that data is complete or had accumulated to a defined threshold.

5. Consolidating data into one place (with ETL [extract, transform, load], ELT [extract, load, transform], or data replication) or providing access to multiple data stores through data virtualization.

6. Protecting data with appropriate authentication and authorization.

7. Normalizing or denormalizing and indexing data to provide fast application access.

Application Level

This level contains any type of application that uses IoT input or controls IoT devices. Generally, the applications interact with level 5 and the data at rest, and so do not have to operate at network speeds. Provision should be available for streamlined operation that allows applications to bypass intermediate layers and interact directly with Layer 3 or even Layer 2. The IWF model does not strictly define applications, considering this beyond the scope of IWT model discussion.

Collaboration and Processes Level

This level recognizes the fact that people must be able to communicate and collaborate to make an IoT useful. This may involve multiple applications and exchange of data and control information across the Internet or an enterprise network.

---

information technology (IT)

The common term for the entire spectrum of technologies for information processing, including software, hardware, communications technologies, and related services. In general, IT does not include embedded technologies that do not generate data for enterprise use.

operational technology (OT)

Hardware and software that detects or causes a change through the direct monitoring/control of physical devices, processes and events in the enterprise.

Summary of the IoT Reference Model

The IWF views the IoT reference model as an industry-accepted framework aimed at standardizing the concepts and terminology associated with IoT. More importantly, the IWF model sets out the functionalities required and concerns that must be addressed before the industry can realize the value of the IoT. This model is useful both for suppliers who develop functional elements within the model and customers for developing their requirements and evaluating vendor offerings.

Figure 15.6, adapted from one in a Cisco presentation on the IWF model [CISC14c], pulls together the key concepts in the IWF model.

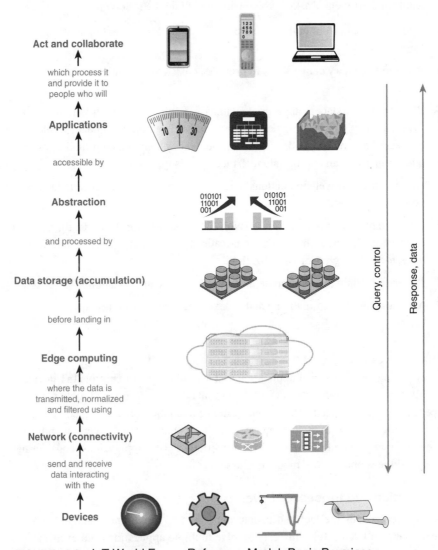

FIGURE 15.6 IoT World Forum Reference Model: Basic Premises

15.2 IoT Implementation

The preceding section looked at two reference models, which provide a good overview of the desired functionality in an IoT design. This section turns to the practical issue of deploying IoT devices and software, by looking at three implementation efforts. First, we examine an open source software initiative, and then look at two vendor offerings.

IoTivity

IoTivity is an open source software initiative. Their objective is to provide a standard and open source implementation so devices and services will be able to work together regardless of who makes them.

IoTivity

Two organizations are playing a key role in the IoTivity project. The project is sponsored by the Open Interconnect Consortium (OIC). OIC is an industry consortium whose purpose is to promote an open source implementation to improve interoperability between the billions of devices making up the IoT. To this end, OIC is working on developing standards and an overall framework that will establish a single solution covering interoperability across multiple vertical markets and use cases. The charter of the IoTivity project is to develop and maintain an open source implementation compliant with OIC final specifications and which passes OIC certification testing.

Open Interconnect Consortium

The IoTivity Project is hosted by the Linux Foundation, the nonprofit consortium dedicated to fostering the growth of Linux and collaborative development. As a Linux Foundation project, IoTivity is overseen by an independent steering group that will work with the OIC. Developers who want to get involved with the project can access RESTful-based application programming interfaces (APIs) and submit code for peer review through the project's server. It will be made available across a range of programming languages, operating systems, and hardware platforms.

Linux Foundation

Although OIC, at the time of this writing, has not released any specifications, IoTivity has moved forward with developing an initial "preview" release of its open source code. The initial release includes builds and Getting Started Guides for Linux, Arduino, and Tizen. The code is designed to be portable and future releases will include builds for additional operating systems.

Protocol Architecture

The IoTivity software provides a number of general-purpose query/response functions to be implemented in IoT devices and in application platforms.

IoTivity makes a distinction between a **constrained device** and an unconstrained device. Many devices in the IoT, particularly the smaller, more numerous devices, are resource constrained. As pointed out in a paper by Seghal, et al [SEGH12], technology improvements following Moore's law continue to make embedded devices

constrained device

In an IoT, a device with limited volatile and nonvolatile memory, limited processing power, and a low data rate transceiver.

cheaper, smaller, and more energy-efficient but not necessarily more powerful. Typical embedded IoT devices are equipped with 8- or 16-bit microcontrollers that possess very little RAM and storage capacities. Resource-constrained devices are often equipped with an IEEE 802.15.4 radio, which enables low-power low-data-rate wireless personal-area networks (WPANs) with data rates of 20 to 250 kbps and frame sizes of up to 127 octets.

The term *unconstrained device* simply refers to any device without severe resources constraints. Such devices might run a general-purpose operating system, such as iOS, Android, Linux, or Windows. Unconstrained devices would include IoT devices with a good amount of processing power and memory, and application platforms for IoT applications.

To accommodate constrained devices, the overall protocol architecture (see Figure 15.7) is implemented in both constrained and unconstrained devices. At the transport level, the software relies on User Datagram Protocol (UDP), which requires minimal processing power and memory, running on top of Internet Protocol (IP). Running on top of UDP is the Constrained Application Protocol (CoAP), which is a simplified query/response protocol designed for constrained devices, and which is described subsequently. The IoTivity implementation uses libcoap, which is a C implementation of CoAP that can be used both on constrained and unconstrained devices.

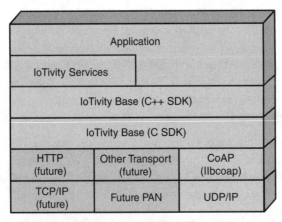

(a) **Resource API stack for unified block devices**

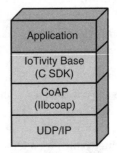

(b) **Resource API stack for constrained devices**

CoAP = Constrained Application Protocol
SDK = software developer's kit
PAN = personal area network

FIGURE 15.7   IoTivity Stack Blocks

The IoTivity base is a set of software development tools that support the creation of applications for communication between clients that host IoT applications and servers, which are IoT devices. The base is implemented in C, with additional tools in

C++ for unconstrained devices. This software is a base for the development of open source applications that will be part of the IoTivity package, in addition to proprietary, value-added applications developed by vendors.

Constrained Application Protocol

CoAP is defined in RFC 7252, *The Constrained Application Protocol*, June 2014. The RFC describes CoAP as a specialized web transfer protocol for use with constrained nodes and constrained networks in the IoT. The protocol is designed for machine-to-machine (M2M) applications such as smart energy and building automation. CoAP provides a request/response interaction model between application endpoints, supports built-in discovery of services and resources, and includes key concepts of the web such as URIs and Internet media types. CoAP is designed to easily interface with HTTP for integration with the web while meeting specialized requirements such as multicast support, very low overhead, and simplicity for constrained environments.

CoAP website

Although CoAP is designed for streamlined use in constrained devices, the protocol, with all its features, is surprisingly complex; RFC 7252 is 112 pages long. Here we provide a brief overview.

An instructive way to begin is to describe the protocol message format, shown in Figure 15.8. There are three categories of messages: Request, Response, and Empty, all of which use the same format. All messages begin with a 32-bit fixed header consisting of the following fields:

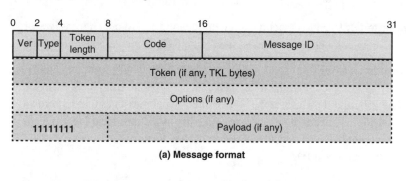

(a) Message format

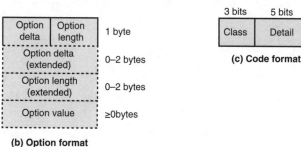

(b) Option format

(c) Code format

FIGURE 15.8   CoAP Formats

- **Version:** Current version is 1.

- **Type:** Message type. There are four message types:

  - **Confirmable:** This message requires an acknowledgment using an ACK or Reset message. CoAP normally runs on top of UDP (UDP port number 5683), which provides an unreliable service. Thus the confirmable message type provides reliable delivery when needed.

  - **Noncomfirmable:** No acknowledgment required. This is particularly true for messages that are repeated regularly for application requirements, such as repeated readings from a sensor.

  - **Acknowledgment:** Acknowledges receipt of a specific confirmable message.

  - **Reset:** Indicates that a specific message (confirmable or nonconfirmable) was received, but some context is missing to properly process it.

- **Token length:** Indicates the length of the variable-length token field, if any.

- **Code:** Consists of a 3-bit class and a 5-bit detail. The class indicates one of the following: request, success response, client error response, or server error response. In case of a request, the detail bits indicate the request method, which can be GET, POST, PUT, or DELETE. In case of a response, detail bits indicate the response code (see Table 15.3 and Table 15.4).

- **Message ID:** Used to detect message duplication and to match messages of type acknowledgment/reset to messages of type confirmable/nonconfirmable.

- **Token:** Used to match responses to requests independently from the underlying messages. Note that the token is a concept separate from the message ID. The message ID works at the level of individual messages that require an acknowledgment. The token is intended for use as a client-local identifier for differentiating between concurrent requests (see Section 5.3); it could have been called a request ID.

- **Options:** A sequence of zero or more CoAP options in Type-Length-Value (TLV) format.

TABLE 15.3   CoAP Messages: Classes, Types, and Codes

Message Class	Response Message Codes	
Request	Created	Precondition failed
Success response	Deleted	Request entity too large
Client error response	Valid	
Server error response	Changed	Unsupported content-format
Empty	Content	Internal server error
Message Types	Bad Request	Not implemented
Confirmable	Unauthorized	Bad gateway
Nonconfirmable	Bad option	
Acknowledgment	Forbidden	Service unavailable
Reset	Not Found	Gateway timeout
Request Message Method Codes	Method not allowed	Proxying not supported
GET	Not acceptable	
POST		
PUT		
DELETE		

TABLE 15.4   CoAP Messages: Message Type Use by Message Class

Message Class	Message Type			
	Confirmable	Noncomfirmable	Acknowledgment	Reset
Request	✓	✓	—	—
Success response	✓	✓	✓	—
Client error response	✓	✓	✓	—
Server error response	✓	✓	✓	—
Empty	*	—	✓	✓

— Not used

* Not used in normal operation but only to elicit a reset message ("CoAP ping")

To understand the operation of CoAP, we need to distinguish among message class, message type, and message method. The message method is designed to provide a RESTful API to the next higher layer of software, and includes the typical REST functions, defined in CoAP as follows:

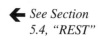

← *See Section 5.4, "REST"*

- **GET:** Retrieves a representation for the information that currently corresponds to the resource identified by the request URI. If the request includes an accept option, that indicates the preferred content-format of a response. If the request includes an ETag option, GET requests that ETag be validated and that the representation be transferred only if validation failed. Upon success, a content or valid response code should be present in the response message.

- **POST:** Requests that the representation enclosed in the request be processed. The actual function performed is determined by the origin server and dependent on the target resource. In essence, POST sends some data to a specified URL and, depending on context, some action is taken.

- **PUT:** Requests that the resource identified by the request URI be updated or created with the enclosed representation. In essence, PUT puts a page at a specific URL. If there's already a page there, it is replaced in its entirety. If there is no page there, a new one is created.

- **DELETE:** Requests that the resource identified by the request URI be deleted.

The simple but powerful API enables upper layer software to read and control IoT devices without worrying about the details of the protocol used to convey information. Each of the four message methods is conveyed in the Request message class and a response, if appropriate is conveyed in one of the three response message classes. Depending on the nature of the request, both the request and response may be confirmable or nonconfirmable (Table 13.8b). A response can also be carried in an acknowledgment message type (piggybacked response).

Figure 15.9, from RFC 7252, provides a simple example of CoAP message exchange. It shows a basic GET request causing a piggybacked response. The client sends a confirmable GET request for the resource coap://server/temperature to the server with a message ID of 0x7d34. The request includes one Uri-Path option (Delta 0 + 11 = 11, Length 11, Value "temperature"); the token is left empty. A 2.05 (content) response is returned in the acknowledgment message that acknowledges the confirmable request, echoing both the message ID 0x7d34 and the empty token value. The response includes a payload of "22.3 C".

There are other aspects of CoAP that are beyond the scope of this discussion, including security, caching, and proxy capabilities.

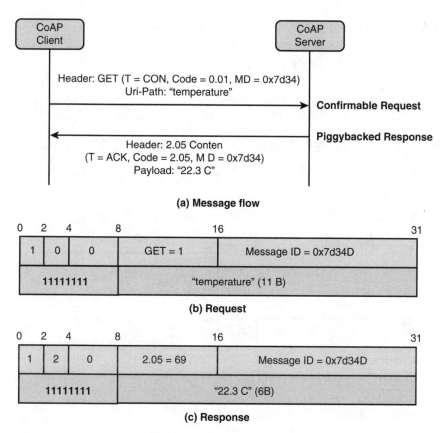

(a) Message flow

0	2	4	8	16	31
1	0	0	GET = 1	Message ID = 0x7d34D	
11111111			"temperature" (11 B)		

(b) Request

0	2	4	8	16	31
1	2	0	2.05 = 69	Message ID = 0x7d34D	
11111111			"22.3 C" (6B)		

(c) Response

FIGURE 15.9 CoAP Example

IoTivity Base Services

The IoTivity Base is software that runs on top of the CoAP API. It presents a resource model to higher layers, consisting of clients and servers. A server hosts resources, which are of two kinds: entity and entity handler. An entity corresponds to an IoT thing, either an actuator or a sensor. An entity handler is an associated device, such as one that caches data from one or more sensors, or a proxy for gateway type protocol conversion. The IoTivity Base provides the following services to higher layers:

- **Resource registration:** This is used to register a resource for future access.

- **Resource and device discovery:** This operation returns identification information for all resources of a given type on the network service. The operation is sent via multicast to all services.

- **Querying resource (GET):** Get information from resource.

- **Setting a resource state (PUT):** This operation sets the value of a simple resource.

■ **Observing resource state:** This operation fetches and registers as an ob-server for the value of a simple resource. Notifications are then provided to the client on an application-specific schedule.

The following example of querying a resource is from the IoTivity website. This example fetches the state from a light source in the following steps (see Figure 15.10):

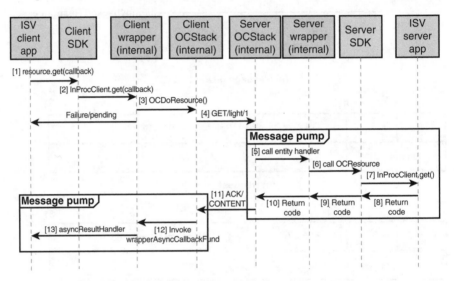

FIGURE 15.10   Sequence Diagram for Querying Resource State

1. The client application calls resource.get(...) to retrieve a representation from the resources.

2. The call is marshaled to the stack, which is either running in process or out of process (daemon).

3. The C API is called to dispatch the request. The call may look like the following: OCDoResource(OC_REST_GET, "//192.168.1.11/light/1, 0, 0, OC_CONFIRMABLE, callback);

4. Where CoAP is used as a transport, the lower stack will send a GET request to the target server.

5. On the server side, the OCProcess() function (message pump) receives and parses the request from the socket, then dispatches it to the correct entity handler based on the URI of the request.

6. Where the C++ API is used, the C++ entity handler parses the payload and marshals it to the client application depending on if the server stack is running in process or out of process (daemon).

7. The C++ SDK passes it up the C++ handler associated with the OCResource.

8. The handler returns the result code and representation to the SDK.

9. The SDK marshals the result code and representation to the C++ entity handler.

10. The entity handler returns the result code and representation to the CoAP protocol.

11. The CoAP protocol transports the results to the client device.

12. The results are returned the OCDoResource callback.

13. The results are returned to the C++ client application's syncResultCallback.

IoTivity Services

The IoTivity Base services provide a RESTful API for the basic functions outlined in the preceding subsection. On top of this, the current release includes four applications referred to as IoTivity Services. IoTivity Services provide a common set of functionalities to application development. These primitive services are designed to provide easy, scalable access to applications and resources and are fully managed by themselves. The four services are as follows:

- **Protocol Plugin Manager:** Makes IoTivity applications communicate with non-IoTivity devices by plug-in protocol converters. It provides several reference protocol plug-ins and plug-in manager APIs to start/stop plug-ins.

- **Soft Sensor Manager:** Provides physical and virtual sensor data on IoTivity in a robust manner useful for application developers. It also provides a deployment and execution environment on IoTivity for higher level virtual sensors. Its functions include the following: collect physical sensor data; manipulate collected data by aggregating based on its own composition algorithms; providing data to applications; detect specific events and changes.

- **Things Manager:** Creates groups, finds appropriate member things in the network, manages member presence, and makes group action easy. This service eases the task of applications by enabling them to deal with a group of things with single commands/responses.

- **Control Manager:** provides framework and services to implement a controller, a controllee, and REST framework for a controller. It also provides APIs for application developers.

To provide a better understanding of IoTivity, let's consider one of these services, the Control Manager (CM), shown in Figure 15.11. The CM runs on top of the IoTivity

Base on both client and server platforms. CM provides software developer kit (SDK) APIs for discovery of controlled devices and controlling them with RESTful resource operations. CM also provides subscription/notification functionality for monitoring the device operations or state changes.

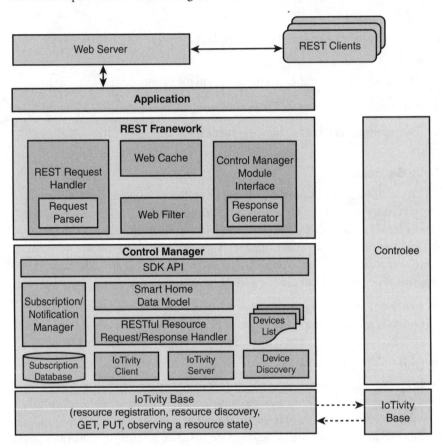

FIGURE 15.11   IoTivity Control Manager Architecture

In its current release, the CM is best suited to a smart home application. The CM makes use of the Samsung Smart Home Profile. Samsung introduced the Samsung Smart Home in early 2014. It is a service enabling Smart TVs, home appliances and smartphones to be connected and managed through a single integrated platform. Its functionality enables users to control and manage their home devices through a single application by connecting personal and home devices—from refrigerators and washing machines to smart TVs, digital cameras, smartphones and even the wearable device GALAXY Gear—through an integrated platform and server. Although the Samsung Smart Home was introduced by Samsung as a platform for controlling Samsung devices, the profile that defines the functionality can be used in other contexts and was adopted by IoTivity as an effective basis for its CM application.

The CM includes the following components:

- **SDK API:** A RESTful interface for the REST framework, discussed later in this chapter.

- **Smart home data model:** A data schema for all the available home devices and appliances, defining a hierarchical resource model and device attributes. A common set of resources provides information related to device capabilities, device configuration and supported resources. Function specific resources provide resources specific to a device function such as thermostat, light, door, and so on. With the help of a data model, application developers can easily compile device information, state and control the device.

- **RESTful resource request/response handler:** Provides the functionality of sending the requests from the controller to the controlled device by serializing it from the data model to a message format. It translates received response messages to the smart home data model for delivery to the controller. It uses the Client module for sending requests and receiving responses.

- **IoTivity client:** Implements the client using the IoTivity base framework for performing messaging with other IoTivity devices per IoTivity protocol. It supports sending requests to other IoTivity devices (for example, the controlled device) and receiving responses from them.

- **IoTivity server:** Implements the server using the IoTivity base framework for responding to requests from other IoTivity devices. CM acts like a server for responding to the discovery requests from other IoTivity devices and for receiving notifications sent from other IoTivity devices.

- **Device discovery:** Uses the IoTivity discovery mechanism of the base framework for discovering other IoTivity devices. Apart from initial device discovery, the CM discovery mechanism retrieves device specific information and capability and maintains the discovered device's information in the devices list.

- **Subscription/notification manager:** Provides functionality of subscribing to other devices and receiving notifications from other devices as defined in the Samsung Smart Home Profile. This is a RESTful subscription/notification mechanism that CM subscribes to resources of other IoTivity devices. The notifying device notifies the CM server with the REST URI specified by the CM during subscription request. CM also maintains the subscription information for the devices and resources it has already subscribed.

Referring back to Figure 15.11, we see that the CM provides a set of functions specific to smart home management and builds these on top of the more primitive functions provided by the IoTivity Base. To make the CM accessible to applications using a web-style interface, the IoTivity software release includes a REST framework software layer on top of the CM. The framework includes the following modules:

- **REST Request Handler**: Receives the REST request from the Application module, parses it, validates the request body (only schema validation) and forwards the request to the CM module via its interface. REST request handler return an error in case of invalid content (invalid URI/invalid request body, and so on).

- **Web Cache**: Caches the REST requests received from application. It responds with "304 Not Modified" when there is no change in the system after the same request was processed previously.

- **Web Filter**: Parses the filter parameters from the request URI.

- **CM Module Interface**: Acts as an interface between REST framework and the CM. It is mainly responsible for forwarding the processed REST requests to the CM. It creates and registers response listeners with the CM, which uses them to respond back asynchronously. Also, a timeout of 30 seconds is maintained here, after which if no response is received from CM, an error is sent back to the application.

Figure 15.11 shows three other elements. The execution model is that clients will interact with IoTivity through a web interface to a web server using HTTP. The web server provides a user-friendly interface for enabling the user to manage smart home devices. Each user request is passed on to the Application module, parses the HTTP request to extract information (method, URI, request body, and so on) and forwards them to the REST framework REST request handler. Responses are returned via the response generator in a similar fashion.

Cisco IoT System

In 2015, Cisco introduced a suite of integrated and coordinated products known as the Cisco IoT System. The philosophy guiding product development is based on the following observations. Cisco estimates that 50 billion devices and objects will be connected to the Internet by 2020. Yet today, more than 99 percent of things in the physical world remain unconnected. To capitalize on the unprecedented opportunities presented by this wave of digitization, companies and cities are increasingly deploying IoT solutions.

However, digitization is complex. Customers are often connecting devices and objects, or converging unrelated networks, at previously unprecedented scales. Furthermore, they can only realize the value of these connections through the application of advanced data analytics, and even then, customers often still need to create a new class of intelligent applications capable of accelerating new business models or increasing productivity. And all this has to happen without sacrificing security at any point in the system, from the device to the data center and via the cloud.

Cisco IoT System addresses the complexity of digitization with an infrastructure that is designed to manage large-scale systems of diverse endpoints and platforms, and the data deluge they create. The system consists of six critical technology pillars that, when combined together into an architecture, help reduce the complexities of digitization. Cisco also announced a number of IoT products within the six pillars and will continue to roll out new products as part of the Cisco IoT System.

Figure 15.12 illustrates the six IoT system pillars as described in the list that follows.

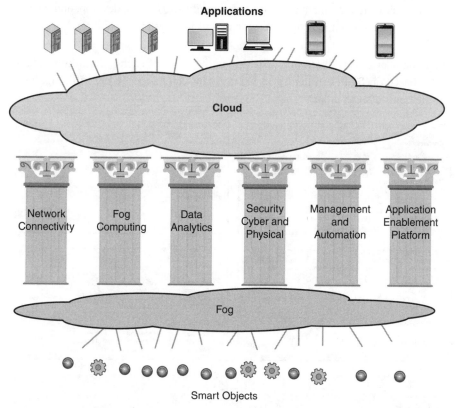

FIGURE 15.12   Cisco IoT System

- **Network connectivity:** Includes purpose-built routing, switching, and wireless products available in ruggedized and nonruggedized form factors.

- **Fog computing:** Provides Cisco's fog computing, or edge data processing platform, IOx.

- **Data analytics:** An optimized infrastructure to implement analytics and harness actionable data for both the Cisco Connected Analytics Portfolio and third-party analytics software.

- **Security:** Unifies cyber and physical security to deliver operational benefits and increase the protection of both physical and digital assets. Cisco's IP surveillance portfolio and network products with TrustSec security and cloud/cyber security products allow users to monitor, detect and respond to combined IT and operational technology (OT) attacks.

- **Management and automation:** Tools for managing endpoints and applications.

- **Application enablement platform:** A set of APIs for industries and cities, ecosystem partners and third-party vendors to design, develop, and deploy their own applications on the foundation of IoT System capabilities.

The remainder of this discussion provides an overview of each pillar in turn. Figure 15.13, based on figures in the Cisco IoT System white paper [CISC15b], highlights key elements of each pillar.

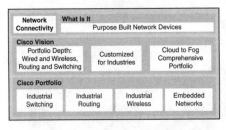

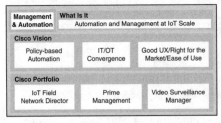

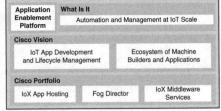

FIGURE 15.13   The Cisco IoT Pillars

Network Connectivity

The network connectivity component of Cisco IoT System is a collection of network products for the edge of the network, to support connectivity of smart objects, gateways, and other edge computing devices. Many smart objects are deployed in harsh or demanding environments, such as factories, farms, and other outdoor environments. Typically, these devices communicate wirelessly with limited transmit/receive range. Therefore, edge networking devices need to meet a number of unique requirements, including the following:

- Supporting large numbers of end systems

- Operating in demanding and possibly remote environments

- Close proximity to supported IoT objects

The network connectivity component brings together a number of preexisting and new products designed to support IoT. The product line include reliable, scalable, high-performance networking solutions with a broad portfolio of routing, switching, and wireless products, available in ruggedized and nonruggedized form factors, as well as software only solutions that integrate into third-party devices.

The product portfolio is organized into the following product categories:

- **Industrial switching:** A range of compact, ruggedized Ethernet switches that handle security, voice, and video traffic across industrial networks. A key feature of these products is that they implement Cisco's proprietary Resilient Ethernet Protocol (REP). REP provides an alternative to the Spanning Tree Protocol (STP). REP provides a way to control network loops, handle link failures, and improve convergence time. It controls a group of ports connected in a segment, ensures that the segment does not create any bridging loops, and responds to link failures within the segment. REP provides a basis for constructing complex networks and supports VLAN load balancing.

- **Industrial routing:** These products are certified to meet harsh environmental standards. They support a variety of communications interfaces, such as Ethernet, serial, cellular, WiMAX, and RF mesh.

- **Industrial wireless:** Designed for deployment in a variety of harsh or demanding environments. These products provide wireless access point functionality and implement Cisco VideoStream, which uses multicast encapsulated in unicast to improve multimedia applications.

- **Embedded networks:** Cisco Embedded Service switches are optimized for mobile and embedded networks that require switching capability in harsh environments. The primary product offering is the Cisco Embedded Service 2020 series switches product family of routers. These products are implemented on cards that can be incorporated in a variety of hardware devices. Also in this category, Cisco offers a software router application designed for small, low-powered Linux devices.

Fog Computing

The fog computing component of IoT System consists of software and hardware that extends IoT applications to the network edge, enabling data to be efficiently analyzed and managed where generated, thus reducing latency and bandwidth requirements.

The goal of the fog computing component is to provide a platform for IoT-related apps to be deployed in routers, gateways, and other IoT devices. To host new and existing applications on fog nodes, Cisco provides a new software platform, called IOx, and an API for deploying applications on IOx. The IOx platform combines the Cisco IOS operating system and Linux (see Figure 15.14). Currently, IOx is implemented on Cisco routers.

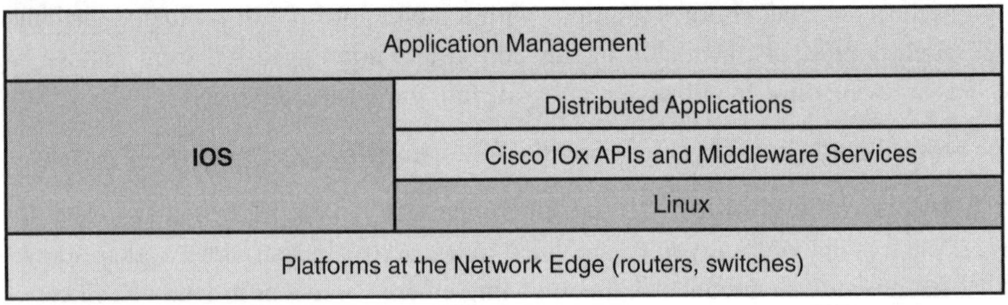

Application Management		
IOS	Distributed Applications	
	Cisco IOx APIs and Middleware Services	
	Linux	
Platforms at the Network Edge (routers, switches)		

FIGURE 15.14   Cisco IOx

Cisco IOS (originally Internetwork Operating System) is software used on most Cisco Systems routers and current Cisco network switches. IOS is a package of routing, switching, internetworking, and telecommunications functions integrated into a multitasking operating system. This is not to be confused with Apple's iOS operating system that runs on iPhones and iPads.

With IOS as a base, IOx combines the communication and computing resources that are required for IoT into a single platform for application enablement at the network edge. As Figure 15.14 shows, an IOx platform, such as a router, runs IOS and Linux in parallel, using the multitasking capability of the multicore processor. Linux is used as a base to support APIs and middleware services that enable partner companies to implement fog applications on the IOx platform.

Data Analytics

The data analytics component of IoT System consists of distributed network infrastructure elements and IoT-specific APIs that run business-specific software analytics packages throughout the network architecture—from the cloud to the fog—and that allow customers to feed IoT data intelligently into business analytics.

The Cisco IoT analytics infrastructure includes the following:

- **Infrastructure for real-time analytics:** The integration of network, storage, and compute capabilities on select Cisco routers, switches, Unified Communications System (UCS) servers, and IP cameras allows analytics to run directly on fog nodes for real-time collection, storage, and analysis at the network edge.

- **Cloud to fog:** Cisco Fog Data Services includes APIs to apply business rules and control which data remains in the fog for real-time analytics and which is sent to the cloud for long-term storage and historical analysis.

- **Enterprise analytics integration:** Using IOx APIs, enterprises can run analytics on fog nodes for real-time intelligence. Fog Data Services allows IoT data exporting to the cloud. Integration of IoT data can increase operational efficiency, improve product quality, and lower costs.

- **Analytics for security:** Cisco IP cameras with storage and compute capabilities support video, audio, and data analytics at the network edge so enterprises gain real-time security intelligence, including event processing and classification.

Security

The intent of the security component is to provide solutions from the cloud to the fog that address the full attack continuum—before, during, and after an attack. The component includes cloud-based threat protection, network and perimeter security, user- and group-based identity services, video analytics, and secure physical access.

The security portfolio includes the following elements:

- **Cloud-based threat protection:** Provided by Cisco's Advanced Malware Protection (AMP) package. This is a broad spectrum of products that can be deployed on a variety of Cisco and third-party platforms. AMP products use big data analytics, a telemetry model, and global threat intelligence to help enable continuous malware detection and blocking, continuous analysis, and retrospective alerting.

- **Network and perimeter security:** Products include firewall and intrusion prevention systems.

- **User- and group-based identity services:** Products include an Identity Service Engine, which is a security policy management platform that automates and enforces context-aware security access to network resources; and

Cisco TrustSec technology, which uses software-defined segmentation to simplify the provisioning of network access, accelerate security operations, and consistently enforce policy anywhere in the network.

- **Physical security:** Cisco's physical security approach consists of hardware devices and software for security management. Products include video surveillance, IP camera technology, electronic access control, and incident response. Cisco physical security solutions can be integrated with other Cisco and partner technologies to provide a unified interface that delivers situational awareness and rapid, informed decisions.

Management and Automation

The management and automation component is designed to provide simplified management of large IoT networks with support for multiple siloed functions, and to enable the convergence of OT data with the IT network. It includes the following elements:

- **IoT Field Network Director:** A software platform that provides a variety of tools for managing routers, switches, and endpoint devices. These tools include fault management, configuration management, accounting management, performance management, diagnostic and troubleshooting, and a northbound API for industry-specific applications.

- **Cisco Prime Management Portfolio:** A remote management and provisioning solution that provides visibility into the home network. The package discovers detailed information about all connected devices in the home and enables remote management.

- **Cisco Video Surveillance Manager:** Provides video, analytics and IoT sensor integration for providing physical security management.

Application Enablement Platform

This component provides a platform for cloud-based app development and deployment from cloud to fog, simply and at scale. Also offers open APIs and app development environments for use by customers, partners, and third parties. It features the following elements:

- **Cisco IOx App Hosting:** With IOx capability, customers from all segments and solution providers across industries will be able to develop, manage, and run software applications directly on Cisco industrial networked devices, including hardened routers, switches, and IP video cameras.

- **Cisco Fog Director:** Allows central management of multiple applications running at the edge. This management platform gives administrators control of application settings and lifecycle, for easier access and visibility into large-scale IoT deployments.

- **Cisco IOx Middleware Services:** Middleware is the software "glue" that helps programs and databases (which may be on different platforms) work together. Its most basic function is to enable communication between different pieces of software. This element provides tools necessary for IoT and cloud apps to communicate.

ioBridge

IoBridge provides software, firmware, and web services designed to make it simple and cost-effective to Internet-enable devices and products for manufacturers, professionals and casual users. By providing all the components necessary to web-enable things, ioBridge's customers avoid the complexity and cost associated with piecing together solutions from multiple vendors. The ioBridge offering is essentially a turnkey solution for a broad range of IoT users.

ioBridge

ioBridge Platform

IoBridge provides a complete end-to-end platform that is secure, private, and scalable for everything from do-it-yourself (DIY) home projects to commercial products and professional applications. ioBridge is both a hardware and cloud services provider. The IoT platform enables the user to create the control and monitoring applications using scalable Web technologies. ioBridge features end-to-end security, real-time I/O streaming to web and mobile apps, and easy-to-install and easy-to-use products.

Figure 15.15 illustrates some of the major features of ioBridge's technology. The tight integration between the embedded devices and the cloud services enable many of the features shown in the diagram that are not possible with traditional web server technology. Note that the off-the-shelf ioBridge embedded modules also include web-programmable control or "rules and actions." This enables the ioBridge embedded module to control devices even when it is not connected to the ioBridge cloud server.

The major offerings on the device side are firmware, Iota modules, and gateways. Firmware is added where possible to devices to add the functionality to communicate with ioBridge services. Iotas are tiny embedded firmware or hardware modules with either Ethernet or Wi-Fi network connectivity. Gateways are small devices that can act as protocol converters and bridges between IoT devices and ioBridge services.

In essence, the IoT platform provides a seamless mashup of embedded devices with web services. IoBridge markets hardware boards, firmware, and software that can be installed in embedded devices together with apps that can run on platforms such as smartphones and tablets, as well as web services.

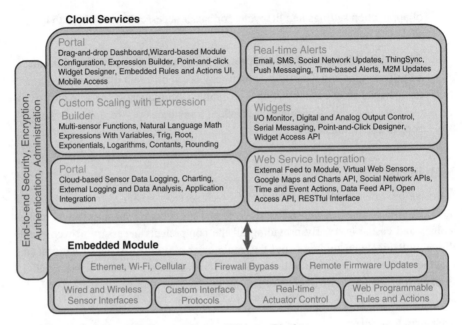

FIGURE 15.15   The ioBridge Internet of Things Platform

ThingSpeak

ThingSpeak

ThingSpeak is an open source IoT platform developed by ioBridge. ThingSpeak enables the creation of sensor logging applications, location-tracking applications, and a social network of things with status updates. It offers the capabilities of real-time data collection, visualizing the collected data in the form of charts, the ability to create plug-ins and apps for collaborating with web services, social networks, and other APIs.

The basic element of ThingSpeak is a ThingSpeak channel, which is hosted on the ThingSpeak website. A channel stores data sent to ThingSpeak and consists of the following elements:

- **Eight fields for storing data of any type:** These can be used to store the data from a sensor or from an embedded device.

- **Three location fields:** Can be used to store the latitude, longitude and the elevation. These are very useful for tracking a moving device.

- **One status field:** A short message to describe the data stored in the channel.

IoBridge-enabled devices and platforms with ioBridge apps can communicate via a channel. A ThingSpeak channel can also connect with Twitter so that sensor updates and other data can be communicated via tweet. Note that ThingSpeak is not limited to ioBridge devices; it can work with any device that includes the software necessary to communicate via a ThingSpeak channel.

A user begins by defining a channel on the ThingSpeak website. This is an easy interactive process that includes the following steps:

1. Create new channel with unique ID.

2. Specify whether the channel will be public (open to view by anyone) or private.

3. Create from one to eight fields, which can hold any type of data, giving each field a name.

4. Create API keys. A channel has one write API key. Any data communicated to the channel will only be written into one or more fields if the data is accompanied by the API key. A channel may have multiple read API keys. If the channel is private, data can only be read by presenting the API key. A user can define an app to an API key to perform some sort of data processing or directing.

ThingSpeak provides apps that allow for an easier integration with web services, social networks, and other APIs. Some of the apps provided by ThingSpeak are the following:

- **ThingTweet:** Allows the user to post messages to twitter via ThingSpeak. In essence, this is a TwitterProxy which redirects your posts to Twitter.

- **ThingHTTP:** Allows the user to connect to web services and supports GET, PUT, POST, and DELETE methods of HTTP.

- **TweetControl:** Enables user to monitor Twitter feeds for a specific keyword and then process the request. Once the specific keyword is found in the Twitter feed, the user can then use ThingHTTP to connect to a different web service or execute a specific action.

- **React:** Sends a tweet or trigger a ThingHTTP request when the channel meets a certain condition.

- **TalkBack:** Queues up commands and then allows a device to act upon these queued commands.

- **TimeControl:** Can perform a ThingTweet, ThingHTTP, or a TalkBack at a specified time in the future. Can also be used to allow these actions to happen at a specified time throughout the week.

In addition to the listed apps, ThingSpeak allows users to create ThingSpeak applications as plug-ins using HTML, CSS, and JavaScript, which can be embedded inside a website or inside a ThingSpeak channel.

RealTime.io

RealTime.io

Another offering of ioBridge is RealTime.io. This technology is similar to, but more powerful and sophisticated than, ThingSpeak. RealTime.io is a cloud platform that enables any device to connect to cloud services and mobile phones to provide control, alerts, data analytics, customer insights, remote maintenance, and feature selection. The intent is that product manufacturers that leverage ioBridge's technology will be able to quickly and securely bring new connected home products to market while slashing their cost-per-connected device.

The RealTime.io App Builder allows the user to build web apps directly on the RealTime.io cloud platform. The user can write web applications based on HTML5, CSS, and JavaScript and create interactions with devices, social networks, external APIs, and ioBridge web services. There is an in-browser code editor, JavaScript library, app update tracking, device manager, and single sign on with existing ioBridge user accounts. RealTime.io natively works with ioBridge Iota-based devices and firmware.

RealTime.io has built-in template apps or custom apps. Template apps are prebuilt apps that the user can start with and then customize. Custom apps allow the user to upload their own files and images without any starter templates.

Figure 15.16 shows the overall ioBridge environment.

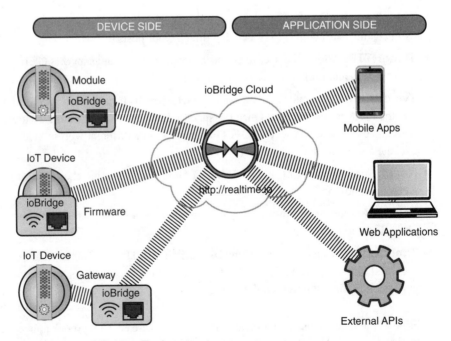

FIGURE 15.16   ioBridge Environment

15.3   Key Terms

After completing this chapter, you should be able to define the following terms.

accuracy	microcontrollers
actuators	microprocessor
application processor	operational technology (OT)
Constrained Application Protocol (CoAP)	precision
constrained device	radio-frequency identification (RFID)
dedicated processor	RFID reader
deeply embedded system	read range
electronic product code (EPC)	resolution
embedded systems	unconstrained device
fog computing	sensors
information technology (IT)	RFID tag
Internet of Things (IoT)	transceiver

15.4   References

CISC14b: Cisco Systems. *The Internet of Things Reference Model.* White paper, 2014. http://www.iotwf.com/.

CISC14c: Cisco Systems. *Building the Internet of Things.* Presentation, 2014. http://www.iotwf.com/.

CISC15b: Cisco Systems. *Cisco IoT System: Deploy, Accelerate, Innovate.* Cisco white paper, 2015.

FERG11: Ferguson, J., and Redish, A. "Wireless Communication with Implanted Medical Devices Using the Conductive Properties of the Body." *Expert Review of Medical Devices*, Vol. 6, No. 4, 2011. http://www.expert-reviews.com.

SEGH12: Seghal, A., et al. "Management of Resource Constrained Devices in the Internet of Things." *IEEE Communications Magazine*, December 2012.

VAQU14: Vaquero, L., and Rodero-Merino, L. "Finding Your Way in the Fog: Towards a Comprehensive Definition of Fog Computing." *ACM SIGCOMM Computer Communication Review*, October 2014.

PART VI

Related Topics

The reader who has persevered thus far in this account will realize the difficulties that were coped with, the hazards that were encountered, the mistakes that were made, and the work that was done.

—*The World Crisis*, Winston Churchill

Chapter 16 provides an overview of security issues that have emerged with the evolution of modern networking. Separate sections deal with software-defined networking (SDN), network functions virtualization (NFV), cloud, and IoT security, respectively. Chapter 17 concludes the book with some observations and advice about careers for the network professional.

Chapter | **16**

Security

To guard against the baneful influence exerted by strangers is therefore an elementary dictate of savage prudence. Hence before strangers are allowed to enter a district, or at least before they are permitted to mingle freely with the inhabitants, certain ceremonies are often performed by the natives of the country for the purpose of disarming the strangers of their magical powers, or of disinfecting, so to speak, the tainted atmosphere by which they are supposed to be surrounded.

—The Golden Bough, Sir James George Frazer

Chapter Objectives

After studying this chapter, you should be able to

- Describe the key security requirements of confidentiality, integrity, availability, authenticity, and accountability.
- Present an overview of SDN security.
- Present an overview of NFV security.
- Present an overview of cloud security.
- Present an overview of IoT security.

This chapter provides an introduction to security issues related to the main networking technologies discussed in this book. The chapter begins with a brief overview of the general security requirements that are relevant in any networking or computer environment. The remaining four sections of the chapter look at security for software-defined networking (SDN), network functions virtualization (NFV), cloud, and Internet of Things (IoT), respectively.

16.1   Security Requirements

It will be useful in the discussion in this chapter to start with an enumeration of the general security functions required to protect computer and network data and services. The five basic security functions that are widely accepted as required in most contexts consist of the following (see Figure 16.1):

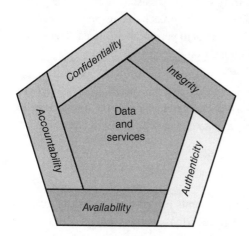

FIGURE 16.1   Essential Network and Computer Security Requirements

- **Confidentiality**: This term covers two related concepts:
  - **Data confidentiality:** Ensures that private or confidential information is not made available or disclosed to unauthorized individuals.
  - **Privacy:** Ensures that individuals control or influence what information related to them may be collected and stored and by whom and to whom that information may be disclosed.
- **Integrity**: This term covers two related concepts:
  - **Data integrity:** Ensures that information (both stored and in transmitted packets) and programs are changed only in a specified and authorized manner.
  - **System integrity:** Ensures that a system performs its intended function in an unimpaired manner, free from deliberate or inadvertent unauthorized manipulation of the system.
- **Availability**: Ensures that systems work promptly and service is not denied to authorized users.
- **Authenticity**: The property of being genuine and being able to be verified and trusted; confidence in the validity of a transmission, a message, or message

originator. This means verifying that users are who they say they are and that each input arriving at the system came from a trusted source.

- **Accountability**: The security goal that generates the requirement for actions of an entity to be traced uniquely to that entity. This supports nonrepudiation, deterrence, fault isolation, intrusion detection and prevention, and after-action recovery and legal action. Because truly secure systems are not yet an achievable goal, it must be possible to trace a security breach to a responsible party. Systems must keep records of their activities to permit later forensic analysis to trace security breaches or to aid in transaction disputes.

These concepts are worth keeping in mind as we discuss the specific security requirements for SDN, NFV, cloud, and IoT. For a more comprehensive discussion of network security, see the author's book, *Cryptography and Network Security* [STAL15b].

16.2   SDN Security

This section considers SDN security from two points of view: the security threats to SDN, and the use of SDN to enhance network security.

Threats to SDN

SDN represents a significant departure from traditional network architecture and may not mesh well with existing network security approaches. SDN involves a three-layer architecture (application, control, data) and new techniques for network control. All of this introduces the potential for new targets for attack.

Figure 16.2, from a 2014 *Network World* article [HOGG14], illustrates the potential locations of security threats in an SDN architecture. Threats can occur at any of the three layers or in the communication between layers. As shown, hardware/software platforms at any layer are potential targets for malware or intruder attacks. In addition, the protocols and application programming interfaces (APIs) related to SDN provide a new target for security attacks. This section discusses SDN-specific security threats.

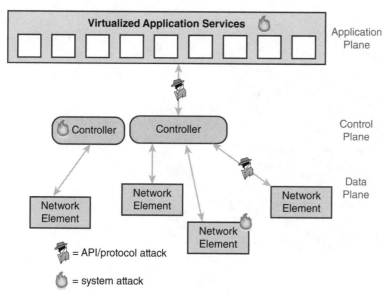

FIGURE 16.2 SDN Security Attack Surfaces

Data Plane

The key area of risk with respect to the data plane is the southbound API, such as OpenFlow and Open vSwitch Database Management Protocol (OVSDB). This API is a powerful tool for managing the data plane network elements, and increases the **attack surface** of the network infrastructure considerably because security is no longer limited to the network equipment supplier. The security of the network could be compromised by unsecure implementation of the southbound protocol. This could enable attackers to add their own flows into the flow table and spoof traffic that would otherwise be disallowed on the network. For example, the attacker might be able to define flows that bypass a firewall to introduce unwanted traffic or provide a means of eavesdropping. More generally, compromising southbound APIs would allow attackers to directly control the network elements as a whole.

attack surface
The reachable and exploitable vulnerabilities in a system.

One way to enhance security is the use of Transport Layer Security (TLS), which evolved from the earlier Secure Sockets Layer (SSL). Figure 14.3 illustrates the position of TLS in the TCP/IP architecture. Before discussing this architecture, we need to define the term *socket*. In essence, a socket is a method of directing data to the appropriate application in a IP-based network. The combination of the IP address of the host and a TCP or UDP port number make up a socket address. From the application point of view, a socket interface is an API. The socket interface is a generic communication programming interface implemented on UNIX and many other systems. Two applications communicate through TCP sockets. An application connects to TCP through a socket address and tells TCP what remote application is requested by means of the remote application's socket address.

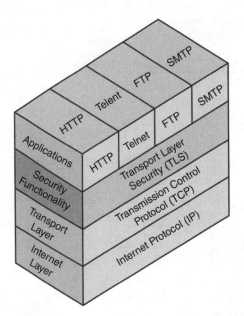

FIGURE 16.3   The Role of TLS in the TCP/IP Architecture

With TLS in place, an application has a TLS socket address and communicates to the TLS socket of the remote application. The security functions provided by TLS are transparent to the application and also to TCP. Thus, neither TCP nor the application needs to be modified to invoke the security features of TLS. As shown in Figure 14.3, TLS supports not only HTTP but also any other application that uses TCP.

TLS provides three categories of security:

- **Confidentiality**: All data that pass between the two applications (for example, the two HTTP modules) are encrypted so that they cannot be eaves-dropped.

- **Message integrity**: TLS ensures that the message is not altered or substituted for en route.

- **Authentication**: TLS can validate the identity of one or both partners to the exchange using public-key certificates. This helps prevent against a rogue controller or attacker trying to instantiate rogue flows into the network devices.

TLS consists of two phases: handshake and data transfer. During handshake, the two sides perform an authentication function and establish an encryption key to be used for data transfer. During data transfer, the two sides use the encryption key to encrypt all transmitted data.

The latest version of the OpenFlow Switch Specification, at the time of this writing (Version 1.5.1, March 26, 2015) states:

> "Between the datapath and the OpenFlow channel, the interface is implementation-specific, however all OpenFlow channel messages must be formatted according to the OpenFlow switch protocol. The OpenFlow channel is usually encrypted using TLS, but may be run directly over TCP."

However, because it is impossible to secure the data plane without securing the southbound communication channel (between control plane and data plane), TLS or an equivalent capability is necessary.

Control Plane

With SDN, the overall management, orchestration, routing, and other aspects of network traffic flow are concentrated in a single controller or a few distributed controllers. If an attacker can successfully penetrate a controller, the attacker can gain a considerable measure of control over the entire network. So, the SDN controller is a high-value target that needs a high level of protection.

Protection of the controller involves the usual repertoire of computer security techniques, including the following:

- Prevention/protection against distributed denial-of-service (DDoS) attacks. A high-availability controller architecture could go some way to mitigating a DDoS attack by using redundant controllers to make up for the loss of other controllers.

- Access control. A number of standard access control technologies can be employed, including role-based access control (RBAC) and attribute-based access control (ABAC).

- Antivirus/antiworm techniques.

- Firewalls, intrusion detection systems (IDS), and intrusion prevention systems (IPS).

Application Plane

Northbound APIs and protocols present a likely target for attackers. A successful attack here could allow the attacker to gain control of the networking infrastructure. Thus, SDN security in this area focuses on preventing unauthorized users and applications from exploiting the controller. In addition, the applications themselves are a vulnerable point. If an attacker can gain control of an application and if that application is then authenticated to the control plane, the amount of damage that can be done is considerable. An authenticated application with a broad range of privileges can exercise considerable control over the configuration and operation of the network.

There are two aspects of countering these threats: Mechanisms are needed to authenticate an application's access to the control plane and prevent this authenticated application from being hacked. To counter threats throughout the authentication process involving communication between applications and the controller, the communication needs to be secured by TLS or an equivalent functionality. To protect applications, they need to be coded securely and the application platform needs to be secured against hacking.

Software-Defined Security

Although SDN presents new security challenges for network designers and managers, it also provides a platform for implementing consistent, centrally managed security policies and mechanisms for the network. SDN allows the development of SDN security controllers and SDN security applications that can provision and orchestrate security services and mechanisms.

For security management, security controllers need to provide a secure API for relevant applications. For example, as an application creates virtual machines (VMs) and configures traffic paths, it needs to be able to associate the virtual components with the appropriate security capabilities, such as IDS, IPS, and security information and event management (SIEM).

In fact, security demands may turn out to be one of the key motivating factors for deploying SDN. On the one hand, key networking trends place an increasing burden on system and networking administrators, including the following:

- The increase in network traffic volume

- The use of VMs for servers, storage, and networking devices

- Cloud computing

- The growth in the size and complexity of data centers

- The growth of IoT applications

On the other hand, there is an increasing agility and sophistication of malware. Therefore, IT manpower becomes a major security bottleneck. Security managers cannot keep up with the increasing pace of incidents and alerts and the need to fine-tune security controls in response. SDN enables security managers to bridge this response resource gap through intelligent incident detection and automated response.

The use of SDN-enabled automated tools has a benefit in itself, but this is augmented by the ability to respond on a granular basis, such as per flow, per application, or per user.

A wide variety of security applications has been developed with more on the way. A good example is OpenDaylight's DDoS application, described in Chapter 6, "SDN Application Plane."

16.3 NFV Security

NFV dramatically changes how networks are designed, built, and managed. NFV moves network functions and network-associated functions from proprietary hardware and places them as VMs on servers that can be deployed where needed within the physical network environment. The security challenge with NFV is that it increases the attack surface and increases security complexity.

Attack Surfaces

To see this challenge, consider Figure 16.4. This repeats Figure 7.8 and indicates potential attack surfaces, as suggested in a white paper from Nakina Systems [NAKI15]. In contrast to traditional hardware-based networks, NFV blurs the hard boundaries that existed between physical network functions, making defining and administering security roles, responsibilities, and privilege levels more complex.

Security needs to address multiple levels and domains and their interactions, including the following:

- **The NFV infrastructure (NFVI):** This is the domain of the underlying network, compute, and storage systems, supporting virtual computing and storage, and virtual networks.

- **Virtual network functions (VNF):** These are the network functions running on NFVI VMs.

- **MANO and OSS/BSS:** Users employ the NFV management and orchestration (MANO) facility as well as OSS/BSS facilities to manage the network and orchestrate resources.

- **Management interfaces:** These are the critical interfaces between major domains of an NFV deployment.

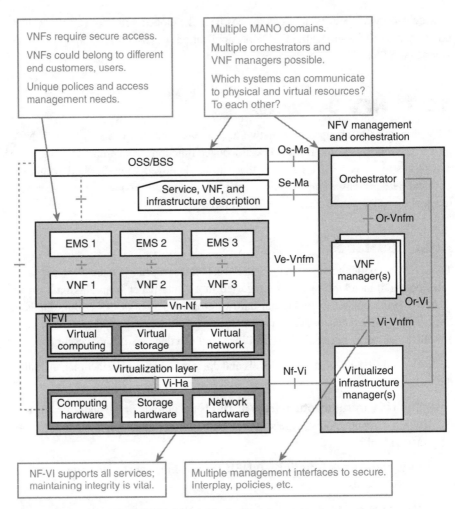

FIGURE 16.4   Potential NFV Attack Surfaces

A key security concern is for the system administration to control which users and/ or systems can view, set, or change configuration parameters and effect network policies. This is especially important given the interdependencies between NFVIs and VNFs, and overall service performance and availability. Moreover, as multiple automated software systems access the same shared pool of network resources, ensuring that security permissions and policies do not conflict will be crucial. Software-enabled provisioning processes can lead to orchestration vulnerabilities including network configuration exploits and malicious configurations.

Figure 16.4 depicts potential NFV attack surfaces from a logical point of view. Another useful perspective is from the physical and software point of view. In particular, we are concerned with the different levels of hardware and software and what entity is in control and responsible for each element at each level. Table 16.1, which repeats Table 7.4 from Chapter 7, "Network Functions Virtualization: Concepts and Architecture," summarizes different deployment scenarios that include the physical location (building), the server hardware, the hypervisor virtualizing software, and the VNFs. Figure 16.5, which follows, illustrates these key elements.

TABLE 16.1 NFV Deployment Scenarios

Deployment Scenario	Building	Host Hardware	Hypervisor	Guest VNF
Monolithic operator	N	N	N	N
Network operator hosting virtual network operators	N	N	N	N, N1, N2
Hosted network operator	H	H	H	N
Hosted communications providers	H	H	H	N1, N2, N3
Hosted communications and application providers	H	H	H	N1, N2, N3, P
Managed network service on customer premises	C	N	N	N
Managed network service on customer equipment	C	C	N	N

Note: The different letters represent different companies or organizations, and are chosen to represent different roles (for example, H = hosting provider, N = network operator, P = public, C = customer). The numbered network operators (N1, N2, and so on) represent multiple individual hosted network operators.

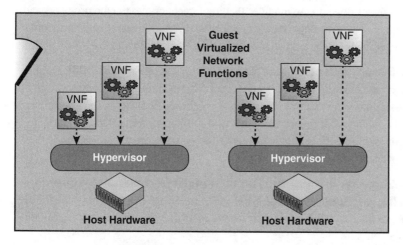

FIGURE 16.5 NFV Deployment Scenario Elements

Each of the levels indicated in Figure 16.5 (building, host hardware, hypervisor, VNFs) is a potential attack surface. But the design of an adequate set of security mechanisms and policies is complicated by the fact that different parties may operate at each of the levels. Therefore, the security requirements need to take this into account. Further, if there is a shared use of lower-level resources by multiple parties, then appropriate protection measures are needed. For example, if multiple VNFs from different users are running on the same physical server using the same hypervisor, then isolation of resources (for example, main memory, secondary memory, I/O ports) assigned to each user becomes a design issue.

ETSI Security Perspective

The European Telecommunications Standards Institute (ETSI), which is the lead organization in developing NFV standards, has issued four documents relating to security as part of their standards suite. The scope and field of application of each document, as defined by ETSI, is as follows:

- **NFV Security; Problem Statement (NFV-SEC 001):** Define NFV sufficiently to understand its security impact. Provide a reference list of deployment scenarios. Identify new security vulnerabilities resulting from NFV.

- **NFV Security; Cataloguing Security Features in Management Software Relevant to NFV (NFV-SEC 002):** Aims to catalogue security features in management software relevant to NFV. It covers OpenStack as the first case study. The initial deliverable is a catalogue of OpenStack modules that provide security services (such as authentication, authorization, confidentiality, integrity protection, logging, and auditing) with the full graphs of their respective dependencies down to the modules that implement cryptographic protocols and algorithms. Once the dependency graph is established, recommendations could be made on which options are appropriate for NFV deployment.

- **NFV Security; Security and Trust Guidance (NFV-SEC 003):** Define areas of consideration where security and trust technologies, practices, and processes have different requirements than non-NFV systems and operations. Supply guidance for the environment that supports and interfaces with NFV systems and operations, but avoid redefining any security considerations that are not specific to NFV.

- **NFV Security; Privacy and Regulation; Report on Lawful Interception (LI) Implications (NFV-SEC 004):** Identifies the necessary capabilities to be provided by NFV to support LI and identifies the challenges of providing LI in an NFV.

The ETSI documents classify the set of all security threats to a network comprising VNFs as illustrated in Figure 16.6 and described in the list that follows.

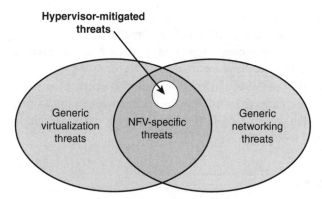

FIGURE 16.6   Classification of Threats in an NFV Networking Environment

- **Generic virtualization threats:** Threats faced by any virtualization implementation, such as failure to isolate guest users.

- **Generic networking threats:** Threats specific to the system of physical network functions prior to virtualization (for example, DDoS, firewall breach or bypass).

- **NFV-specific threats:** Threats that arise with the combining of virtualization technology and networking.

Examples of NFV-specific threats include the following:

- The use of hypervisors may introduce additional security vulnerabilities. Third-party certification of hypervisors should help shed light on their security properties. In general, to reduce the vulnerabilities of the hypervisors in use, it is essential to follow the best practices on hardening and patch management. To ensure that the right hypervisor is being executed calls for authenticating the hypervisor at the boot time through secure boot mechanisms.

- The usage of shared storage and shared networking may also add additional dimensions of vulnerability.

- The interconnectivity among NFV end-to-end architectural components (for example, hardware resources, VNFs, and management systems) exposes new interfaces that, unless protected, can create new security threats.

- The execution of diverse VNFs over the NFV infrastructure can also create additional security issues, in particular if VNFs are not properly isolated from others.

hypervisor introspection

The hypervisor capability to monitor each guest OS or VM as it is running, for security purposes.

ETSI also makes the observation that virtualization can eliminate some and mitigate other threats inherent to nonvirtualized network functions through the use of **hypervisor introspection** and other techniques. Hypervisor introspection has become a common security technique in virtualized environments. Hypervisor-based introspection can help detect attacks on VMs and guest operating systems, even when the guest operating systems are tampered with. Introspection is through monitoring of memory, program execution, access to data files, and network traffic. It can, in particular, thwart kernel-level rootkits (KLRs).

Security Techniques

It will be useful to examine a somewhat different perspective, provided in a paper by Hawilo, et al. [HAWI14]. This paper classifies the NFV environment into three functional domains, and specifies the risks and potential solutions for each as summarized in Table 16.2.

TABLE 16.2   NFV Security Risks

Functional Domain	Security Risks	Solutions and Requirements
Virtualized environment domain (hypervisor)	Unauthorized access or data leakage	Isolation of the served VM space, with access provided only with authentication controls.
Computing domain	Shared computing resources (CPU, memory, and so on)	Secured threads.
		Private and shared memory allocations should be erased before re-allocation.
		Data should be used and stored in an encrypted manner by which exclusive access is provided only to the VNF.
Infrastructure domain	Shared logical networking layer (vSwitches)	Usage of secure networking techniques (TLS, IPsec, SSH).
	Shared physical network interface cards (NICs)	

16.4 Cloud Security

There are numerous aspects to cloud security and numerous approaches to providing cloud security measures. A good example of the scope of cloud security concerns and issues is seen in the NIST guidelines for cloud security, specified in SP-800-144, *Guidelines on Security and Privacy in Public Cloud Computing*, December 2011, and listed in Table 16.3. Thus, a full discussion of cloud security is well beyond the scope of this chapter. In this section, we discuss some important cloud security topics related to the focus of this book.

The section begins with an overview of key cloud security issues and concerns. This is followed by a discussion of specific cloud security risks and their corresponding countermeasures. The next topic deals with one of the most important cloud security issues: the protection of data stored in the cloud. The discussion then introduces the concept of cloud security as a service. A final subsection looks at technical, operational, and management control functions related to cloud security.

TABLE 16.3 NIST Guidelines on Cloud Security and Privacy Issues and Recommendations

Cloud Security Feature	Guidelines
Governance	Extend organizational practices pertaining to the policies, procedures, and standards used for application development and service provisioning in the cloud, as well as the design, implementation, testing, use, and monitoring of deployed or engaged services.
	Put in place audit mechanisms and tools to ensure organizational practices are followed throughout the system lifecycle.
Compliance	Understand the various types of laws and regulations that impose security and privacy obligations on the organization and potentially impact cloud computing initiatives, particularly those involving data location, privacy and security controls, records management, and electronic discovery requirements.
	Review and assess the cloud provider's offerings with respect to the organizational requirements to be met and ensure that the contract terms adequately meet the requirements.
	Ensure that the cloud provider's electronic discovery capabilities and processes do not compromise the privacy or security of data and applications.
Trust	Ensure that service arrangements have sufficient means to allow visibility into the security and privacy controls and processes employed by the cloud provider, and their performance over time.
	Establish clear, exclusive ownership rights over data.
	Institute a risk management program that is flexible enough to adapt to the constantly evolving and shifting risk landscape for the lifecycle of the system.
	Continuously monitor the security state of the information system to support ongoing risk management decisions.

Cloud Security Feature	Guidelines
Architecture	Understand the underlying technologies that the cloud provider uses to provision services, including the implications that the technical controls involved have on the security and privacy of the system, over the full system lifecycle and across all system components.
Identity and access management	Ensure that adequate safeguards are in place to secure authentication, authorization, and other identity and access management functions, and are suitable for the organization.
Software isolation	Understand virtualization and other logical isolation techniques that the cloud provider employs in its multitenant software architecture, and assess the risks involved for the organization.
Data protection	Evaluate the suitability of the cloud provider's data management solutions for the organizational data concerned and the ability to control access to data, to secure data while at rest, in transit, and in use, and to sanitize data.
	Take into consideration the risk of collating organizational data with those of other organizations whose threat profiles are high or whose data collectively represent significant concentrated value.
	Fully understand and weigh the risks involved in cryptographic key management with the facilities available in the cloud environment and the processes established by the cloud provider.
Availability	Understand the contract provisions and procedures for availability, data backup and recovery, and disaster recovery, and ensure that they meet the organization's continuity and contingency planning requirements.
	Ensure that during an intermediate or prolonged disruption or a serious disaster, critical operations can be immediately resumed, and that all operations can be eventually reinstituted in a timely and organized manner.
Incident response	Understand the contract provisions and procedures for incident response and ensure that they meet the requirements of the organization.
	Ensure that the cloud provider has a transparent response process in place and sufficient mechanisms to share information during and after an incident.
	Ensure that the organization can respond to incidents in a coordinated fashion with the cloud provider in accordance with their respective roles and responsibilities for the computing environment.

Security Issues and Concerns

Security is important to any computing infrastructure. Companies go to great lengths to secure on-premises computing systems, so it is not surprising that security looms as a major consideration when augmenting or replacing on-premises systems with cloud services. Allaying security concerns is frequently a prerequisite for further discussions about migrating part or all of an organization's computing architecture to the cloud. Availability is another major concern: "How will we operate if we can't access the Internet? What if our customers can't access the cloud to place orders?" are common questions.

Generally speaking, such questions only arise when businesses contemplating moving core transaction processing, such as enterprise resource planning (ERP) systems, and other mission critical applications to the cloud. Companies have traditionally demonstrated less concern about migrating high maintenance applications such as e-mail and payroll to cloud service providers even though such applications hold sensitive information.

Auditability is another concern for many organizations, especially those who must comply with Sarbanes-Oxley and/or Health and Human Services Health Insurance Portability and Accountability Act (HIPAA) regulations. The auditability of their data must be ensured whether it is stored on-premises or moved to the cloud.

Before moving critical infrastructure to the cloud, businesses should perform due diligence on security threats both from outside and inside the cloud. Many of the security issues associated with protecting clouds from outside threats are similar to those that have traditionally faced centralized data centers. In the cloud, however, responsibility for assuring adequate security is frequently shared among users, vendors, and any third-party firms that users rely on for security-sensitive software or configurations. Cloud users are responsible for application-level security. Cloud vendors are responsible for physical security and some software security such as enforcing external firewall policies. Security for intermediate layers of the software stack is shared between users and vendors.

A security risk that can be overlooked by companies considering a migration to the cloud is that posed by sharing vendor resources with other cloud users. Cloud providers must guard against theft or denial-of-service attacks by their users and users need to be protected from one another. Virtualization can be a powerful mechanism for addressing these potential risks because it protects against most attempts by users to attack one another or the provider's infrastructure. However, not all resources are virtualized and not all virtualization environments are bug-free. Incorrect virtualization may allow user code access to sensitive portions of the provider's infrastructure or the resources of other users. Once again, these security issues are not unique to the cloud and are similar to those involved in managing noncloud data centers, where different applications need to be protected from one another.

Another security concern that businesses should consider is the extent to which subscribers are protected against the provider, especially in the area of inadvertent data loss. For example, in the event of provider infrastructure improvements, what happens to hardware that is retired or replaced? It is easy to imagine a hard disk being disposed of without being properly wiped clean of subscriber data. It is also easy to imagine permissions bugs or errors that make subscriber data visible to unauthorized users. User-level encryption may be an important self-help mechanism for subscribers, but businesses should ensure that other protections are in place to avoid inadvertent data loss.

Cloud Security Risks and Countermeasures

In general terms, security controls in cloud computing are similar to the security controls in any IT environment. However, because of the operational models and technologies used to enable cloud service, cloud computing may present risks that are specific to the cloud environment. The essential concept in this regard is that the enterprise loses a substantial amount of control over resources, services, and applications but must maintain accountability for security and privacy policies.

In a 2013 report (*The Notorious Nine Cloud Computing Top Threats*), The Cloud Security Alliance [CSA13] lists the following as the top cloud-specific security threats:

- **Abuse and nefarious use of cloud computing**: For many cloud providers (CPs), it is relatively easy to register and begin using cloud services, some even offering free limited trial periods. This enables attackers to get inside the cloud to conduct various attacks, such as spamming, malicious code attacks, and denial of service. Platform as a Service (PaaS) providers have traditionally suffered most from this kind of attacks; however, recent evidence shows that hackers have begun to target Infrastructure as a Service (IaaS) vendors as well. The burden is on the CP to protect against such attacks, but cloud service clients must monitor activity with respect to their data and resources to detect any malicious behavior.

  Countermeasures include (1) stricter initial registration and validation processes, (2) enhanced credit card fraud monitoring and coordination, (3) comprehensive inspection of customer network traffic, and (4) monitoring public blacklists for one's own network blocks.

- **Unsecure interfaces and APIs**: CPs expose a set of software interfaces or APIs that customers use to manage and interact with cloud services. The security and availability of general cloud services is dependent upon the security of these basic APIs. From authentication and access control to encryption and activity monitoring, these interfaces must be designed to protect against both accidental and malicious attempts to circumvent policy.

Countermeasures include (1) analyzing the security model of CP interfaces, (2) ensuring that strong authentication and access controls are implemented in concert with encrypted transmission, and (3) understanding the dependency chain associated with the API.

- **Malicious insiders**: Under the cloud computing paradigm, an organization relinquishes direct control over many aspects of security and, in doing so, confers an unprecedented level of trust onto the CP. One grave concern is the risk of malicious insider activity. Cloud architectures necessitate certain roles that are extremely high-risk. Examples include CP system administrators and managed security service providers.

  Countermeasures include (1) enforcing strict supply chain management and conduct a comprehensive supplier assessment, (2) specifying human resource requirements as part of legal contract, (3) requiring transparency into overall information security and management practices (as well as compliance reporting), and (4) determining security breach notification processes.

- **Shared technology issues**: IaaS vendors deliver their services in a scalable way by sharing infrastructure. Often, the underlying components that make up this infrastructure (CPU caches, GPUs, and so on) were not designed to offer strong isolation properties for a multitenant architecture. CPs typically approach this risk by the use of isolated VMs for individual clients. This approach is still vulnerable to attack, by both insiders and outsiders, and so can only be a part of an overall security strategy.

  Countermeasures include (1) implementing security best practices for installation/configuration, (2) monitoring environment for unauthorized changes/activity, (3) promoting strong authentication and access control for administrative access and operations, (4) enforcing service level agreements (SLAs) for patching and vulnerability remediation, and (5) conducting vulnerability scanning and configuration audits.

- **Data loss or leakage**: For many clients, the most devastating impact from a security breach is the loss or leakage of data. We address this issue in the next section.

  Countermeasures include (1) implementing strong API access control, (2) encrypting and protecting integrity of data in transit and at rest, (3) analyzing data protection at both design and run time, and (4) implementing strong key generation, storage and management, and destruction practices.

- **Account or service hijacking**: Account and service hijacking, usually with stolen credentials, remains a top threat. With stolen credentials, attackers can often access critical areas of deployed cloud computing services, allowing them to compromise the confidentiality, integrity, and availability of those services.

Countermeasures include (1) prohibiting the sharing of account credentials between users and services, (2) leveraging strong two-factor authentication techniques where possible, (3) employing proactive monitoring to detect unauthorized activity, and (4) understanding CP security policies and SLAs.

- **Unknown risk profile**: In using cloud infrastructures, the client necessarily cedes control to the cloud provider on a number of issues that may affect security. Thus the client must pay attention to and clearly define the roles and responsibilities involved for managing risks. For example, employees may deploy applications and data resources at the CP without observing the normal policies and procedures for privacy, security, and oversight.

    Countermeasures include (1) disclosure of applicable logs and data, (2) partial/full disclosure of infrastructure details (for example, patch levels and firewalls), and (3) monitoring and alerting on necessary information.

Similar lists have been developed by the European Network and Information Security Agency and NIST.

Data Protection in the Cloud

There are many ways to compromise data. Deletion or alteration of records without a backup of the original content is an obvious example. Unlinking a record from a larger context may render it unrecoverable, as can storage on unreliable media. Loss of an encoding key may result in effective destruction. Finally, unauthorized parties must be prevented from gaining access to sensitive data.

The threat of data compromise increases in the cloud, due to the number of, and interactions between, risks and challenges that are either unique to the cloud or more dangerous because of the architectural or operational characteristics of the cloud environment.

Database environments used in cloud computing can vary significantly. Some providers support a **multi-instance model**, which provide a unique DBMS running on a VM instance for each cloud subscriber. This gives the subscriber complete control over role definition, user authorization, and other administrative tasks related to security. Other providers support a **multitenant model**, which provides a predefined environment for the cloud subscriber that is shared with other tenants, typically through tagging data with a subscriber identifier. Tagging gives the appearance of exclusive use of the instance, but relies on the cloud provider to establish and maintain a sound secure database environment.

Data must be secured while at rest, in transit, and in use, and access to the data must be controlled. The client can employ encryption to protect data in transit, though this involves key management responsibilities for the CP. The client can enforce access control techniques but, again, the CP is involved to some extent depending on the service model used.

For data at rest, the ideal security measure is for the client to encrypt the database and only store encrypted data in the cloud, with the CP having no access to the encryption key. So long as the key remains secure, the CP has no ability to decipher the data, although corruption and other denial-of-service attacks remain a risk.

There are a number of ways in which an encryption scheme could be implemented. A very simple arrangement is as follows. Suppose that each individual item in the database is encrypted separately, all using the same encryption key. The encrypted database is stored at the server, but the server does not have the key, so that the data are secure at the server. Even if someone were able to hack into the server's system, all he or she would have access to is encrypted data. The client system does have a copy of the encryption key. A user at the client can retrieve a record from the database with the following sequence:

1. The user issues an SQL query for fields from one or more records with a specific value of the primary key.

2. The query processor at the client encrypts the primary key, modifies the SQL query accordingly, and transmits the query to the server.

3. The server processes the query using the encrypted value of the primary key and returns the appropriate record or records.

4. The query processor decrypts the data and returns the results.

More efficient and flexible systems have been implemented. See the author's book, *Computer Security: Principles and Practice* for details [STAL15a].

Cloud Security as a Service

The term *Security as a Service* has generally meant a package of security services offered by a service provider that offloads much of the security responsibility from an enterprise to the security service provider. Among the services typically provided are authentication, anti-virus, antimalware/spyware, intrusion detection, and security event management. In the context of cloud computing, Cloud Security as a Service, designated SecaaS, is a segment of the SaaS offering of a CP.

The Cloud Security Alliance defines SecaaS as the provision of security applications and services via the cloud either to cloud-based infrastructure and software or from the cloud to the customers' on-premise systems [CSA11]. The Cloud Security Alliance has identified the following SecaaS categories of service:

- Identity and access management
- Data loss prevention
- Web security
- E-mail security
- Security assessments
- Intrusion management
- Security information and event management
- Encryption
- Business continuity and disaster recovery
- Network security

This section covers these categories with a focus on security of the cloud-based infrastructure and services (see Figure 16.7).

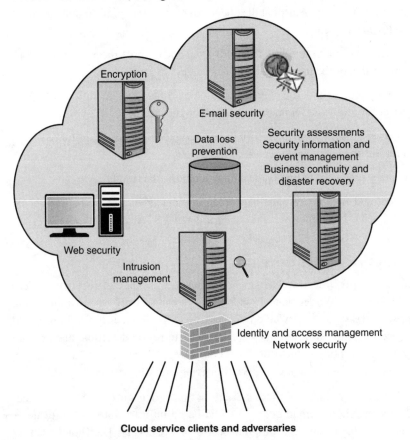

Cloud service clients and adversaries

FIGURE 16.7   Elements of Cloud Security as a Service

- **Identity and access management (IAM)** includes people, processes, and systems that are used to manage access to enterprise resources by assuring that the identity of an entity is verified, and then granting the correct level of access based on this ensured identity. One aspect of identity management is identity provisioning, which has to do with providing access to identified users and subsequently deprovisioning, or denying access, to users when the client enterprise designates such users as no longer having access to enterprise resources in the cloud. Another aspect of identity management is for the cloud to participate in the federated identity management scheme used by the client enterprise. Among other requirements, the cloud service provider (CSP) must be able to exchange identity attributes with the enterprise's chosen identity provider.

  The access management portion of IAM involves authentication and access control services. For example, the CSP must be able to authenticate users in a trustworthy manner. The access control requirements in SPI environments include establishing trusted user profile and policy information, using it to control access within the cloud service, and doing this in an auditable way.

- **Data loss prevention (DLP)** is the monitoring, protecting, and verifying the security of data at rest, in motion, and in use. Much of DLP can be implemented by the cloud client, such as discussed in the preceding subsection, "Data Protection in the Cloud." The CSP can also provide DLP services, such as implementing rules about what functions can be performed on data in various contexts.

- **Web security** is real-time protection offered either on premise through software/appliance installation or via the cloud by proxying or redirecting web traffic to the CP. This provides an added layer of protection on top of things such as antivirus to prevent malware from entering the enterprise via activities such as web browsing. In addition to protecting against malware, a cloud-based web security service might include usage policy enforcement, data backup, traffic control, and web access control.

- A CSP may provide a web-based e-mail service, for which security measures are needed. **E-mail security** provides control over inbound and outbound email, protecting the organization from phishing, malicious attachments, enforcing corporate polices such as acceptable use and spam prevention. The CSP may also incorporate digital signatures on all e-mail clients and provide optional e-mail encryption.

- **Security assessments** are third-part audits of cloud services. While this service is outside the province of the CSP, the CSP can provide tools and access points to facilitate various assessment activities.

■ **Intrusion management** encompasses intrusion detection, prevention, and response. The core of this service is the implementation of intrusion detection systems (IDS) and intrusion prevention systems (IPS) at entry points to the cloud and on servers in the cloud. An IDS is a set of automated tools designed to detect unauthorized access to a host system. An IPS incorporates IDS functionality but also includes mechanisms designed to block traffic from intruders.

■ **Security information and event management (SIEM)** aggregates (via push or pull mechanisms) log and event data from virtual and real networks, applications, and systems. This information is then correlated and analyzed to provide real-time reporting and alerting on information/events that may require intervention or other type of response. The CSP typically provides an integrated service that can put together information from a variety of sources both within the cloud and within the client enterprise network.

■ **Encryption** is a pervasive service that can be provided for data at rest in the cloud, e-mail traffic, client-specific network management information, and identity information. Encryption services provided by the CSP involve a range of complex issues, including key management, how to implement virtual private network (VPN) services in the cloud, application encryption, and data content access.

■ **Business continuity and disaster recovery** comprise measures and mechanisms to ensure operational resiliency in the event of any service interruptions. This is an area where the CSP, because of economies of scale, can offer obvious benefits to a cloud service client. The CSP can provide backup at multiple locations, with reliable failover and disaster recovery facilities. This service must include a flexible infrastructure, redundancy of functions and hardware, monitored operations, geographically distributed data centers, and network survivability.

■ **Network security** consists of security services that allocate access, distribute, monitor, and protect the underlying resource services. Services include perimeter and server firewalls and denial-of-service protection. Many of the other services listed in this section, including intrusion management, identity and access management, data loss protection, and web security, also contribute to the network security service.

Addressing Cloud Computer Security Concerns

Numerous documents have been developed to guide business thinking about the security issues associated with cloud computing. In addition to SP-800-144, which provides overall guidance, NIST has issued SP-800-146, *Cloud Computing Synopsis and Recommendations*, May 2012. NIST's recommendations systematically consider each of the major types of cloud services consumed by businesses including Software as a Service (SaaS), Infrastructure as a Service (IaaS), and Platform as a Service (PaaS). Security issues vary somewhat depending on the type of cloud service, but multiple NIST recommendations are independent of service type. Not surprisingly, NIST recommends selecting cloud providers that support strong encryption, have appropriate redundancy mechanisms in place, use authentication mechanisms, and offer subscribers sufficient visibility about mechanisms used to protect subscribers from other subscribers and the provider. SP-800-146 also lists the overall security controls that are relevant in a cloud computing environment and that must be assigned to the different cloud actors as listed in Table 16.4.

TABLE 16.4   Control Functions and Classes

Technical	Operational	Management
Access control	Awareness and training	Certification, accreditation, and security Assessment
Audit and accountability	Configuration and management	
Identification and authentication		Planning risk assessment
	Contingency planning	System and services acquisition
System and communication protection	Incident response	
	Maintenance	
	Media protection	
	Physical and environmental protection	
	Personnel security	
	System and information integrity	

As more businesses incorporate cloud services into their enterprise network infrastructures, cloud computing security will persist as an important issue. Examples of cloud computing security failures have the potential to have a chilling effect on business interest in cloud services, and this is inspiring service providers to be serious about incorporating security mechanisms that will allay concerns of potential subscribers. Some service providers have moved their operations to Tier 4 data centers to address user concerns about availability and redundancy. Because so many businesses remain reluctant to embrace cloud computing in a big way, cloud service providers will have to continue to work hard to convince potential customers that computing support for core business processes and mission critical applications can be moved safely and securely to the cloud.

16.5 IoT Security

IoT is perhaps the most complex and undeveloped area of network security. To see this, consider Figure 16.8, which shows the main elements of interest for IoT security. At the center of the network are the application platforms, data storage servers, and network and security management systems. These central systems gather data from sensors, send control signals to actuators, and are responsible for managing the IoT devices and their communication networks. At the edge of the network are IoT-enabled devices, some of which are quite simple constrained devices and some of which are more intelligent unconstrained devices. As well, gateways may perform protocol conversion and other networking service on behalf of IoT devices.

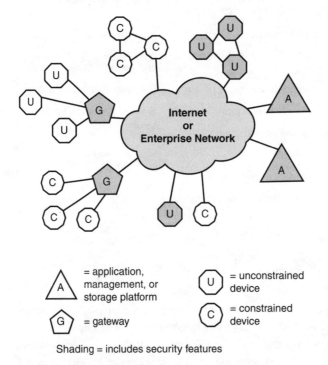

FIGURE 16.8 IoT Security: Elements of Interest

Figure 16.8 illustrates a number of typical scenarios for interconnection and the inclusion of security features.

The shading in Figure 16.8 indicates the systems that support at least some of these functions. Typically, gateways will implement secure functions, such as TLS and IPsec. Unconstrained devices may or may not implement some security capability. Constrained devices generally have limited or no security features. As suggested in the figure, gateway devices can provide secure communication between the gateway and the devices at the center, such as application platforms and management platforms. However, any constrained or unconstrained devices attached to the gateway are outside the zone of security established between the gateway and the central systems. As shown, unconstrained devices can communicate directly with the center and support security functions. However, constrained devices that are not connected to gateways have no secure communications with central devices.

The Patching Vulnerability

In an often-quoted 2014 article, security expert Bruce Schneier stated that we are at a crisis point with regard to the security of embedded systems, including IoT devices [SCHN14]. The embedded devices are riddled with vulnerabilities, and there is no good way to patch them. The chip manufacturers have strong incentives to produce their product with its firmware and software as quickly and cheaply as possible. The device manufacturers choose a chip based on price and features and do very little if anything to the chip software and firmware. Their focus is the functionality of the device itself. The end user may have no means of patching the system or, if so, little information about when and how to patch. The result is that the hundreds of millions of Internet-connected devices in the IoT are vulnerable to attack. This is certainly a problem with sensors, allowing attackers to insert false data into the network. It is potentially a graver threat with actuators, where the attacker can affect the operation of machinery and other devices.

IoT Security and Privacy Requirements Defined by ITU-T

ITU-T Recommendation Y.2066, *Common Requirements of the Internet of Things*, June 2014, includes a list of security requirements for the IoT. This list is a useful baseline for understanding the scope of security implementation needed for an IoT deployment. The requirements are defined as being the functional requirements during capturing, storing, transferring, aggregating and processing the data of things, as well as to the provision of services which involve things. These requirements are related to all the IoT actors. The requirements are as follows:

- **Communication security**: Secure, trusted, and privacy-protected communication capability is required, so that unauthorized access to the content of data can be prohibited, integrity of data can be guaranteed and privacy-related content of data can be protected during data transmission or transfer in IoT.

- **Data management security**: Secure, trusted, and privacy-protected data management capability is required, so that unauthorized access to the content of data can be prohibited, integrity of data can be guaranteed and privacy-related content of data can be protected when storing or processing data in IoT.

- **Service provision security**: Secure, trusted, and privacy-protected service provision capability is required, so that unauthorized access to service and fraudulent service provision can be prohibited and privacy information related to IoT users can be protected.

- **Integration of security policies and techniques**: The ability to integrate different security policies and techniques is required, so as to ensure a consistent security control over the variety of devices and user networks in IoT.

- **Mutual authentication and authorization**: Before a device (or an IoT user) can access the IoT, mutual authentication and authorization between the device (or the IoT user) and IoT is required to be performed according to predefined security policies.

- **Security audit**: Security audit is required to be supported in IoT. Any data access or attempt to access IoT applications are required to be fully transparent, traceable and reproducible according to appropriate regulation and laws. In particular, IoT is required to support security audit for data transmission, storage, processing, and application access.

A key element in providing security in an IoT deployment is the gateway. Y.2067, *Common Requirements and Capabilities of a Gateway for Internet of Things Applications*, June 2014, details specific security functions that the gateway should implement, some of which are illustrated in Figure 16.9. These consist of the following:

- Support identification of each access to the connected devices.

- Support authentication with devices. Based on application requirements and device capabilities, it is required to support mutual or one-way authentication with devices. With one-way authentication, either the device authenticates itself to the gateway or the gateway authenticates itself to the device, but not both.

- Support mutual authentication with applications.

- Support the security of the data that are stored in devices and the gateway, or transferred between the gateway and devices, or transferred between the gateway and applications. Support the security of these data based on security levels.

- Support mechanisms to protect privacy for devices and the gateway.

- Support self-diagnosis and self-repair as well as remote maintenance.

- Support firmware and software update.

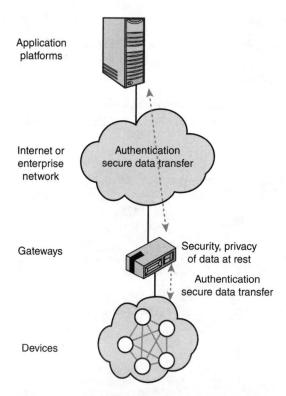

Application
platforms

Internet or
enterprise
network

Authentication
secure data transfer

Gateways

Security, privacy
of data at rest

Authentication
secure data transfer

Devices

FIGURE 16.9   IoT Gateway Security Functions

- Support auto configuration or configuration by applications. The gateway is required to support multiple configuration modes, for example, remote and local
  configuration, automatic and manual configuration, and dynamic configuration
  based on policies.

Some of these requirements may be difficult to achieve when they involve providing
security services for constrained devices. For example, the gateway should support
security of data stored in devices. Without encryption capability at the constrained
device, this may be impractical to achieve.

Note that the Y.2067 requirements make a number of references to privacy requirements. Privacy is an area of growing concern with the widespread deployment of IoT-
enabled things in homes, retail outlets, and vehicles and humans. As more things are
interconnected, governments and private enterprises will collect massive amounts of
data about individuals, including medical information, location and movement information, and application usage.

An IoT Security Framework

Cisco, which has played a lead role in the development of the IoT World Forum Reference Model (see Figure 15.4), has developed a framework for IoT security [FRAH15] that serves as a useful complement to the World Forum IoT Reference Model.

Figure 16.10 illustrates the security environment related to the logical structure of an IoT. The IoT model is a simplified version of the World Forum IoT Reference Model. It consists of the following levels:

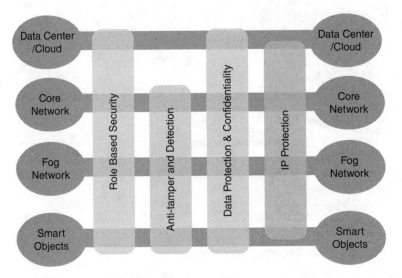

FIGURE 16.10 IoT Security Environment

- **Smart objects/embedded systems:** Consists of sensors, actuators, and other embedded systems at the edge of the network. This is the most vulnerable part of an IoT. The devices may not be in a physically secure environment and may need to function for years. Availability is certainly an issue. Also, network managers need to be concerned about the authenticity and integrity of the data generated by sensors and about protecting actuators and other smart devices from unauthorized use. Privacy and protection from eavesdropping may also be requirements.

- **Fog/edge network:** This level is concerned with the wired and wireless interconnection of IoT devices. In addition, a certain amount of data processing and consolidation may be done at this level. A key issue of concern is the wide variety of network technologies and protocols used by the various IoT devices and the need to develop and enforce a uniform security policy.

- **Core network:** The core network level provides data paths between network center platforms and the IoT devices. The security issues here are those confronted in traditional core networks. However, the vast number of endpoints to interact with and manage creates a substantial security burden.

- **Data center/cloud:** This level contains the application, data storage, and network management platforms. IoT does not introduce any new security issues at this level, other than the necessity of dealing with huge numbers of individual endpoints.

Within this four-level architecture, the Cisco model defines four general security capabilities that span multiple levels:

- **Role-based security: RBAC** systems assign access rights to roles instead of individual users. In turn, users are assigned to different roles, either statically or dynamically, according to their responsibilities. RBAC enjoys widespread commercial use in cloud and enterprise security and is a well-understood tool that can be used to manage access to IoT devices and the data they generate.

  > **role-based access control (RBAC)**
  > Controls access based on the roles that users have within the system and on rules stating what accesses are allowed to users in given roles.

- **Antitamper and detection:** This function is particularly important at the device and fog network levels but also extends to the core network level. All of these levels may involve components that are physically outside the area of the enterprise that is protected by physical security measures.

- **Data protection and confidentiality:** These functions extend to all level of the architecture.

- **Internet protocol protection:** Protection of data in motion from eavesdropping and snooping is essential between all levels.

Figure 16.10 maps specific security functional areas across the four layers of the IoT model. A 2015 Cisco White Paper on IoT security [FRAH15] also proposes a secure IoT framework that defines the components of a security facility for an IoT that encompasses all the levels, as shown in Figure 16.11, and described in the list that follows.

- **Authentication:** Encompasses the elements that initiate the determination of access by first identifying the IoT devices. In contrast to typical enterprise network devices, which may be identified by a human credential (for example, username and password or token), the IoT endpoints must be fingerprinted by means that do not require human interaction. Such identifiers include RFID, x.509 certificates, or the MAC address of the endpoint.

- **Authorization:** Controls a device's access throughout the network fabric. This element encompasses access control. Together with the authentication layer, it establishes the necessary parameters to enable the exchange of information between devices and between devices and application platforms and enables IoT-related services to be performed.

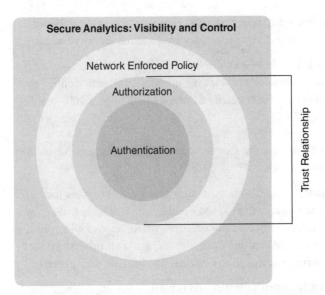

FIGURE 16.11   Secure IoT Framework

- **Network enforced policy:** Encompasses all elements that route and transport endpoint traffic securely over the infrastructure, whether control, management or actual data traffic.

- **Secure analytics, including visibility and control:** This component includes all the functions required for central management of IoT devices. This involves, first, visibility of IoT devices, which simply means that central management services are securely aware of the distributed IoT device collection, including identity and attributes of each device. Building on this visibility is the ability to exert control, including configuration, patch updates, and threat countermeasures.

An important concept related to this framework is that of trust relationship. In this context, trust relationship refers to the ability of the two partners to an exchange to have confidence in the identity and access rights of the other. The authentication component of the trust framework provides a basic level of trust, which is expanded with the authorization component. The Cisco IoT security white paper [FRAH15] gives the example that a car may establish a trust relationship with another car from the same vendor. That trust relationship, however, may only allow cars to exchange their safety capabilities. When a trusted relationship is established between the same car and its dealer's network, the car may be allowed to share additional information such as its odometer reading and last maintenance record.

Conclusion

Computer and network security protocols, technologies, and policies have developed and matured over the past decades, tailored to the needs of enterprises, governments, and other users. Although there is an ongoing arms race between attackers and defenders, it is possible to build a powerful security facility for traditional networks and for SDN/NFV networks. The sudden explosion of IoT networks with millions to billions of devices poses an unprecedented security challenge. A model and framework such as that of Figures 16.10 and 16.11 can serve as a foundation for the design and implementation of an IoT security facility.

16.6   Key Terms

After completing this chapter, you should be able to define the following terms.

accountability	data confidentiality	role-based access control (RBAC)
attack surface	data integrity	Security as a Service (SecaaS)
authenticity	hypervisor introspection	system integrity
availability	integrity	Transport Layer Security (TLS)
confidentiality	privacy	

16.7   References

CSA11: Cloud Security Alliance. *Security as a Service (SecaaS)*. CSA Report, 2011.

CSA13: Cloud Security Alliance. *The Notorious Nine Cloud Computing Top Threats in 2013*. CSA Report, February 2013.

HAWI14: Hawilo, H., et al. "NFV: State of the Art, Challenges, and Implementation in Next Generation Mobile Networks." *IEEE Network*, November/December 2014.

HOGG14: Hogg, S. "SDN Security Attack Vectors and SDN Hardening." *Network World*, Oct 28, 2014.

NAKI15: Nakina Systems. *Achieving Security Integrity in Service Provider NFV Environments*. Nakina Systems white paper, 2015.

STAL15: Stallings, W., and Brown, L. *Computer Security: Principles and Practice*. Englewood Cliffs, NJ: Pearson, 2015.

Chapter | **17**

The Impact of the New Networking on IT Careers

You don't understand! I coulda had class. I coulda been a contender. I could've been somebody, instead of a bum, which is what I am.

—Marlon Brando, *On the Waterfront*, 1954

Chapter Objectives

After studying this chapter, you should be able to

- Discuss the changing responsibilities of network professionals and the impact on job positions.
- Present an overview of DevOps.
- Understand the role of DevOps for implementing networking systems.
- Understand the relevance of training and certification programs.

The network landscape is changing rapidly in a variety of ways and in a number of directions. To further their careers, network professionals need to not only master new technical skills but also broaden the scope of their involvement in the many facets of network technology, management, and deployment. This chapter aims to provide some guidance and information that will be useful in protecting and enhancing your career prospects in the new networking landscape.

The chapter begins with some overall thoughts about the changing roles of network professionals. Next, the chapter focuses on one specific area that might be overlooked in developing your career-building skills: DevOps. This is followed by a discussion of training and certification. The chapter closes with a description of online resources that can be an ongoing source of information and support.

17.1 The Changing Role of Network Professionals

The emerging networking era has many ramifications that the alert network professional should consider. We mention some here:

- The network infrastructure is unlikely to be sourced from a single vendor. The infrastructure has multiple layers, defined interfaces (both horizontal and vertical), reliance on abstraction, and a mix of local and cloud/fog-based elements.

- Application workloads are changing, both in the variety and pace. Software modules that manage, utilize, and even define the network infrastructure need to be incorporated into the network software environment.

- The available toolset of the network professional is proliferating rapidly, including languages, scripting tools, and a growing variety of packaged products to help do network design, deployment, operations, management, and security. IT executives are aware of these tools and expect their networking team to use them.

- Network functions are increasingly being defined, implemented, and managed using software techniques, such as software-defined networking (SDN) and network functions virtualization (NFV). This "soft" nature of networks compels an increasingly collaborative approach to IT management and to network development and operations.

Network professionals cannot expect to move forward with skills learned in college or training so far obtained. SDN and NFV open up the network ecosystem to many more players so that the complex world of networking is accessible to people coming from a variety of backgrounds. Networking roles and responsibilities will be in flux, with job slots disappearing and opening up. Networking professionals need to seize opportunities for both in-house and third party training to maintain their competitive edge.

Changing Responsibilities

A Webtorials paper by Metzler [METZ14b] lists the following as key characteristics of the emerging role of network and IT infrastructure professionals:

- **More emphasis on programming:** At minimum, the proliferation of application programming interfaces (APIs) as part of the SDN and NFV network structure requires senior level IT professionals to have some level of understanding of programming to better interact with enterprise software development units. And organizations may want to leverage the API functionality newly available by having networking professionals write programs that utilize those APIs. This is discussed further in Section 17.2.

- **An increased knowledge of other IT disciplines:** IT will become less separated by specific areas of expertise (storage, networking, virtualization, and security) and more cross-functional as teams interoperate with each other. The increased emphasis on collaboration and DevOps (discussed in the next section) requires an amalgamation of skills spanning everything from IT security to database design and application architecture, plus everything in between. While each individual on the team has a particular strength, each one also needs to have working knowledge in other areas.

- **Heightened emphasis on security:** Security expertise becomes more critical as data is secured on premises, in the cloud, and on user devices. Data is the lifeblood of any company, and so determining and enforcing policies that keep things secure without impacting users' ability to get their work accomplished will be critical.

- **More focus on setting policy:** SDN and NFV enable IT organizations to implement a policy-driven infrastructure in a more dynamic and granular fashion than was previously possible.

- **More knowledge of the business:** SDN, NFV, and QoE provide management with the technology base for providing an agile response to business needs and customer requirements. New application software is generated to run on the network and the virtualized network elements are modified and repositioned rapidly to adjust to enterprise and user needs. This places the burden on the network professional to understand how the network is to be managed and configured to support this dynamic environment. Another consideration is that the ability of the IT organization to justify an investment in IT is increasingly tied to the ability of the organization to concretely demonstrate the business value of that investment.

- **More understanding of applications:** Cloud computing and IoT open up the range of applications that need to be supported on networks. The architecture of these applications is broadening as well, with simple client/server models supplanted or enhanced by applications structures that spread out vertically (mutitier) and horizontally (peer cooperation). Complex applications, such as customer relationship management (CRM), actually consist of several modules, with a range of network requirements. IT infrastructure and network professionals in particular need to better understand these new architectures and complex applications to ensure that the emerging set of technologies are designed and architected appropriately.

Another interesting take on what is needed to succeed in the new networking environment is provided in a paper by Pretz [PRET14], which lists the following five skills needed by network professionals:

- The ability to incorporate know-how from the IT and network domains, which have grown independently of each other over the years but are now converging.

- An understanding of industrial mathematics, a branch of applied mathematics. Those with this knowledge will be better able to understand technical issues, formulate precise and accurate mathematical models, and implement solutions using the latest computer techniques. An understanding of this field will help in developing systems by applying machine learning and cognitive algorithms, which are expected to lessen the complexity and dynamic nature of SDNs.

- A mastery of software architecture and open source software, which is needed to develop SDN tools and applications. It will also be helpful to understand software verification and validation processes, which ensure that software meets specifications and fulfills its intended purpose. Some engineers assume they'll need programming skills, but that's not necessarily so, because software applications for SDNs from third parties are already available.

- A background in big data analytics to understand how to handle the huge amounts of data expected from SDNs. Someone skilled in big data analytics will not only be able to manage more data but also know the right questions to ask should problems arise. Such analytics will also help engineers make smart, data-driven decisions.

- Expertise in cybersecurity, because security must be everywhere within SDNs. It needs to be built into the architecture and also must be delivered as a service to protect the availability, integrity, and privacy of connected resources and information.

Impact on Job Positions

In a Global Knowledge white paper, Hales [HALE14] lists the following as likely impacts of SDN and NFV on individual job positions:

- **Network administrator:** Those with the skills to design and manage software-dominated networks and to plan migration strategy from the existing environment will be in high demand.

- **Virtualization administrator:** Administrators with more advanced skills will be needed for figuring out how to implement cloud systems and make them work within an existing infrastructure. Virtualization administrators will need to work more closely with the storage, network, security, and application teams to make them seamlessly work together.

- **Applications administrator:** Applications administrators need to be aware of the many implications of SDN and NFV APIs on applications. This includes the fact that applications can request the network to provide them with the bandwidth and latency needed for the application to work correctly. Administrators will need to know what these requirements are and work with other application administrators to ensure that the needs of all applications are being met. Security needs will also change in unanticipated ways so that the applications administrator needs a good understanding of security services and mechanisms.

- **Security administrator:** The security administrator will likely need to work more closely with other types of administrators to ensure that appropriate policies and rules are designed, enforced, and audited to ensure compliance. As companies move more to the cloud and encourage users to bring your own device (BYOD), the need for this type of administrator will only increase.

- **Developer:** Developers might be used to integrate functionality into the APIs provided by the SDN and NFV controllers, or they may write applications that can make requests of the network. This may require additional general networking knowledge as well as knowledge of the specific APIs that need to be used for a given problem. Developers will need to think about security in greater detail and pass on security requirements to security, application, virtualization, and/or network teams to ensure that the requirements of the application are met and to modify the application as needed.

- **IT manager:** IT managers must become generalists with an ability to understand the new networking capabilities, the security demands of the new environment, and the need to integrate application development with network development. A collaborative mindset, such as is required by DevOps (discussed in Section 17.2), must be cultivated by all within the organization.

Bottom Line

The need for a strong staff of networking professionals is not going to go away, no matter how many automated tools are added to the new networking infrastructures. But the roles, responsibilities, and skills needed to thrive in the new networking environment are changing.

17.2   DevOps

A review of technical and management literature on SDN, NFV, cloud, and Internet of Things (IoT) shows a frequent reference to the need for personnel who understand and can use a DevOps approach to designing, installing, and managing these new network technologies. This section first provides an overview of the concept of DevOps and then looks at how it applies to modern networking technologies.

DevOps Fundamentals

In just a few short years, **DevOps** has gone from a buzzword to an accepted method of software development and deployment. Enterprises large and small are trying to get a grasp on what DevOps is and what impact it can have on their organizations. The attention is coming not just from IT executives and CIOs but also from business managers who are beginning to recognize the potential of DevOps to enable business units to become more efficient, deliver higher-quality product, and be more agile and innovative. Major software organizations, including IBM and Microsoft, are rapidly expanding their DevOps offerings.

DevOps (development operations)

The tighter integration between the developers of applications and the IT department that tests and deploys them. DevOps is said to be the intersection of software engineering, quality assurance, and operations.

The focus of DevOps has been the development of application software and support software. The essence of the DevOps philosophy is that all participants in creating a product or system should collaborate from the beginning, including business unit managers, developers, operations staff, security staff, and end-user groups.

To understand the DevOps approach, we need to briefly outline the typical stages in the development and deployment of applications. As described in *Application Release and Deployment for Dummies*, most application vendors and in-house application developers follow a lifecycle similar to the following [MINI14]:

- **Development (DEV):** Developers build and deploy code in a test environment, and the development team tests the application at the most basic level. When the application meets certain criteria for advancement, it moves to SIT.

- **System integration testing (SIT):** The application is tested to ensure that it works with existing applications and systems. When the application meets the criteria of this environment, it is deployed to UAT.

- **User acceptance testing (UAT):** The application is tested to ensure that it provides the required features for end users. This environment usually is production-like. When the application passes these requirements, it moves to production.

- **Production (PROD):** The application is made available to users. Feedback is captured by monitoring the application's availability and functionality. Any updates or patches are introduced in the DEV environment and follow the same cycle.

Traditionally, an information system development project proceeds sequentially through these stages, without delivering working pieces in between and without obtaining customer feedback on the way. The entire process is called **waterfall development**. With such large projects, once each stage is completed, it cannot be easily reversed, much like trying to move up a waterfall. Beginning in the early 2000s, **agile software development** began to gain favor. The agile methods emphasize teamwork, customer involvement and, most significantly, the creation of small or partial pieces of the total system that are tested in a user environment. For example, an application with 25 features might be prototyped with only 5 or 6 thoroughly completed before adding more, and so on. Agile development has proven to be more effective in dealing with changing requirements during the development phase, which always seem to occur.

Agile development is characterized by frequent releases, in an iterated loop fashion, with a certain amount of automation in the form of tools that can be used to support collaboration. DevOps takes this philosophy much further. It is characterized by rapid releases, feedback loops embedded throughout the process, and a comprehensive set of tools and documented best practices to automate the DevOps process.

Figure 17.1, from *DevOps for Dummies*, provides an overview of the DevOps process [SHAR15].

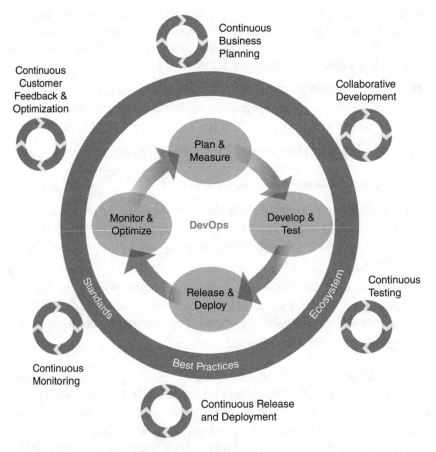

FIGURE 17.1   DevOps Reference Architecture

DevOps can be viewed as a repetitive cycle of four major activities:

- **Plan and measure:** Focuses on business units and their planning process. The planning process relates business needs to the outcomes of the development process. This activity can start with small, limited portions of the overall plan, identifying outcomes and resources needed to develop the required software. The plan must include developing measures that are used to evaluate software, adapt and adjust continually, relate to customer needs, and continually update the development plan and the measurement plan. The measurement function can also be applied to the DevOps process itself to ensure that the right automated tools are being used and that collaboration is ongoing.

- **Develop and test:** Focuses on collaborative development, continuous integration of new code, and continuous testing. It focuses on streamlining development and testing teams' capabilities. Useful tools are automated tracking of testing against measured outcomes and virtualized test beds that enable testing in an isolated but real-world environment.

- **Release and deploy:** Provide a continuous delivery pipeline that automates deployment to test and production environments. Releases are managed centrally in a collaborative environment that leverages automation. Deployments and middleware configurations are automated and then mature to a self-service model that provides individual developers, teams, testers, and deployment managers with a capability to continuously build, provision, deploy, test, and promote. Infrastructure and middleware provisioning evolves to an automated then self-service capability similar to application deployment. Operations engineers cease manually changing environments; instead, they focus on optimizing the automation.

- **Monitor and optimize:** Includes the practices of continuous monitoring, customer feedback, and optimization to monitor how applications are performing post-release, allowing businesses to adapt their requirements as needed. Customer experience is monitored to optimize experiences within business applications. Optimization to customer key performance indicators that reflect business value attainment is part of the continuous improvement program.

application lifecycle management
The administration and control of an application from inception to its demise. It embraces requirements management, system design, software development, and configuration management and implies an integrated set of tools for developing and controlling the project.

Figure 17.2, from the Microsoft white paper *Enterprise DevOps* [MICR15], provides another useful perspective on DevOps. DevOps is intended to improve the efficiency and effectiveness of the process of managing applications throughout their lifecycle. With the introduction of agile software development, organizations have developed **application lifecycle management (ALM)** practices to integrate the business, development, QA, and operations functions in a virtuous cycle for greater agility in delivering continuous value.

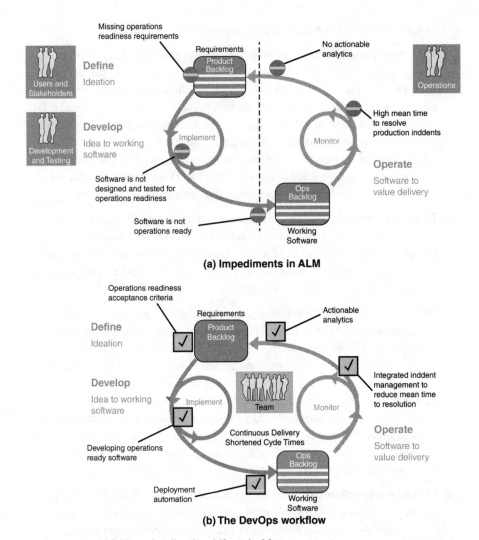

FIGURE 17.2   Modern Application Lifestyle Management

As part a of Figure 17.2 shows, ALM practices, as they have developed, have encountered a number of impediments to agile and effective delivery of the final product.
These arise from the conventional divide that exists between development and operations functions. A key theme illustrated here is the danger that operations requirements are being de-prioritized to accommodate functional needs. DevOps intends to
address these impediments, as shown in part b of Figure 17.2.

Fundamentally, DevOps rests on two key foundations: collaboration and automation.
Collaboration begins with management policy to encourage and require the various
actors in the software development and deployment process to work together.

Automation consists of tools that support that collaboration and are designed to automate as much as possible the cyclic process illustrated in Figures 17.1 and 17.2.

A number of companies now offer DevOps automation tools. For example, in 2014 Microsoft introduced a number of tools that work as part of their Visual Studio offerings. Visual Studio is a set of developer tools and services to assist users in creating apps on Microsoft platforms and in the cloud. One of the additions is releasing management software that automates many of the chores that are needed to be done to move a software program from development to production, such as alerting the appropriate managers, and preparing the production server to run the software. Another DevOps-minded feature Microsoft has introduced for Visual Studio is called Cloud Deployment Projects, which allows organizations to capture and reuse the configuration settings of new applications, in order to speed the deployment times. The configuration settings, or blueprints, are captured within a virtual machine (VM), which then can be deployed, holding the application, in the Microsoft Azure cloud. Microsoft also introduced its Application Insights software. Application Insights provides a way to instrument an application so the developers can determine if it is working correctly, and how people are using the software program. This could help developers pinpoint bugs, as well as get early insight into behavioral issues, such as a sudden fall-off of use due to a bad redesign.

The Demand for DevOps

IT departments are increasingly relying on DevOps. For example, a recent report [DICE15] on the job-listing site Dice stated that "senior system administrators with DevOps and an engineering background are in the right area of their careers. In markets like Silicon Valley, recruiting DevOps talent can be a headache. It's not unusual for multiple offers, counteroffers, and rising salaries for DevOps experience." Table 15.1 shows the number of active job listings for DevOps engineers, managers, architects, and so on within a 100-mile radius of six U.S. cities. DevOps clearly has "arrived" as a skill set that tech employers are seeking.

TABLE 17.1 Recent DevOps Job Listings on Dice by Location (May 2015)

City	Number of Listings
Boston	106
New York	183
Washington, D.C.	109
Chicago	53
San Francisco	319
Dallas	85

DevOps for Networking

Although DevOps was created and has evolved to support the application development and deployment process, it can also be applied in the networking context. This is because the networking infrastructure is increasingly software defined and software driven:

- **Software-defined networking (SDN):** SDN defines network behavior in software. Utilities and apps at the control and application level build on the basic capability provided by the split between the control and data planes. Network designers and network managers need to be able to rapidly respond to changing network conditions and requirements and the need for new customer-driven applications.

- **Network functions virtualization (NFV):** NFV defines the structure and functioning of the network in software, with the deployment of virtual compute, storage, and network functions. The NFV software environment is complex, involving the interaction of a host virtual network functions (VNFs) and management and operations software. This is an environment that requires rapid response to changing conditions and demands.

- **QoS/QoE:** The demands of quality of service (QoS) and especially quality of experience (QoE) dictate a process that is driven by end-user analytics and the is best served by a rapid development and deployment cycle to ensure that the network is responsive to the end user's needs.

- **Cloud:** Whether it be IaaS, PaaS, or SaaS, and whether it be public or private cloud, cloud managers and providers have a constant, ongoing need to modify and enhance cloud offerings. To meet user expectations, this must be done in a highly agile manner.

- **Internet of Things (IoT):** Although IoT involves lots of physical "stuff," the overall architecture from the fog computing edge to the central application platforms, requires rapid response to changing conditions to provide expected performance, as well as the need to constantly upgrade and modify the networks to deal with a rapidly changing mix of IoT devices.

In a nutshell, a DevOps approach is not just for applications, web server software, and the like; it is also for network infrastructure. For network managers and network engineers who are designing and deploying network infrastructure software and who are modifying the network infrastructure on demand, the DevOps approach can involve a number of aspects, including the following:

- Increased collaboration with network operations staff so as to anticipate how network changes will impact day-to-day operations, developing metrics for measuring the impact of changes, and developing procedures for creating a back-and-forth between development and operations.

- Examining the software and network infrastructure deployment pipeline with a focus on the processes that govern pipeline flow to determine how to enhance efficiency and remove impediments.

- Adopting automation tools to eliminate repetitious tasks.

All the networking technologies discussed in this book lend themselves to the DevOps approach. But perhaps the most prominent area is cloud computing/networking, where providers seem to be ahead of the curve in employing DevOps techniques. As pointed out in the Dice report, *Why DevOps Is CPR for Cloud Applications*, [DICE13], "The cloud lends itself naturally to DevOps in that it's heavily driven by APIs and frameworks that can easily be incorporated into automated, DevOps processes. It is the API-driven, self-service provisioning that makes the cloud the cloud, so DevOps is a natural fit where clouds are involved. That means a good way to succeed or move into a position in the cloud is to polish your scripting and API-targeting skills. Being able to demonstrate experience with public cloud provider APIs or private cloud management frameworks will go a long way toward building a portfolio of cloud skills that will make you more attractive to prospective (and current) employers."

An *Information Week* article [MACV15] points out a common concern among network engineers as the beating of the DevOps drum gets louder is the associated focus on programmability. In particular, engineers are concerned they may be required to, well, code (rightly so, given phrases like *infrastructure as code*). They are concerned about the skills and skill sets they need that they may not have. Two things need to be said about that. First, the type of coding likely to be involved is scripting, rather than large software development with C, C++, Java, and so on. Network engineers use tools such as Python, Perl, Bash, and Curl to script common tasks across a variety of devices. To move this scripting approach into the DevOps realm, the network engineer needs to learn some tools that are integral to a networking DevOps environment.

One such tool is a version control system, such as Git. In addition to being a repository for software source code, version control systems can hold configuration data for infrastructure such as routers, firewalls, switches, and Apache web servers. Maintaining configuration data in a version control system provides an element of change control. It allows you to track things such as when a firewall rule was introduced or when an Apache vhost was added. The scripts written for device tasks (for example, in Python) can be stored in Git, where they are versioned and controlled. Further, with Git, scripting can be used to automate much of the task of populating the version control data. In addition, configuration management tools, such as Puppet or Chef, can be used to generate templates that are stored in Git.

A second point to make is that DevOps for networking is broader than just scripting, such as working with relevant staff to optimize processes and manage the infrastructure in a collaborative fashion that takes into account development, operations, and user needs. Another ongoing task is determining what (and how) you need to measure to meet the business priorities that are driving DevOps in the first place: faster time to market, reduced risk, and lower costs.

Even so, the mastery of skills with particular software tools and packages is a good way to build DevOps credibility. The Dice report *Critical Skills for DevOps Engineers*, [DICE14] lists the following as the four main clusters of skills and tools to succeed in a DevOps role:

- **Puppet, Chef, Vagrant, CFEngine, and Bcfg2:** Maintaining consistent system performance is critical. This means being up and available, as well as fast and reliable. Experience with these configuration management tools will help you manage software and system changes repeatedly and predictably.

- **Jenkins, Maven, Ant, CruiseControl, and Hudson:** A key part of your job is making it faster and easier to create and deploy software. Experience with tools like these will help ensure you have what you need to keep things moving.

- **Git, SVN, CVS, Visual Studio Online, and Perforce:** Version control is important to DevOps so developers don't get in each other's way. Use of these source control systems allows for collaboration on software projects and makes it easy to manage changes and updates.

- **Nagios, Munin, Zabbix, Sensu, LogStash, CloudWatch, Splunk, and NewRelic:** As a DevOps professional, you must always keep tabs on performance. While the specifics of each tool are different, you should know the philosophy and principles behind each of them so that you can implement them effectively.

Strong experience with one technology in a cluster usually translates well to the others with only a few weeks of training, and because many of these tools are relatively new, you should be willing and able to apply your existing knowledge to new tools as needed for the role.

DevOps Network Offerings

A good indication of the growing awareness of the need for DevOps for modern network providers is found in the most recent annual NVF report from SDxCentral (SDxCentral Network Functions Virtualization Report, 2015 Edition). The following companies are listed as providing DevOps-related products:

- **Brocade Mobile Analytics:** Provides a full mobile network visibility capability stack. Modular product architecture lends itself to DevOps model for rapidly deploying custom solutions that fulfill mobile operators' unique needs.

- **Red Hat Enterprise Linux Atomic Host:** An NFV software platform. It includes tools to enable IT organizations to quickly realize the benefits of DevOps practices, including faster delivery of features and continual improvement.

- **SuperCloud:** A vendor-neutral NFV services orchestration platform. Enables data center and cloud service providers to deploy and manage VNF and SDN applications. Designed from DevOps and service automation mindset to fulfill the needs of network administrators that support IT application developers.

- **CloudShell:** A DevOps-oriented cloud management platform that provides self-service access to complex network environments comprised of bare metal as well as virtualized components. CloudShell is used to automate DevOps labs and data centers for development, testing, training, support, proof of concept, and open communities. CloudShell markets itself as the leading automation platform for network DevOps.

The list of NFV- and SDN-related vendors whose offerings reflect or support DevOps is likely to grow dramatically in the next few years.

Cisco DevNet

In 2015, Cisco announced a new approach, known as DevNet for Cisco customers and partners for employing DevOps. DevNet is meant to be a community of the enterprise network developers among its customers, its independent software vendors, independent systems integrators, and Cisco partners, producing software applications to run the programmable network of the future.

Cisco DevNet provides software developer kits (SDKs), visual modeling tools, ready-to-use code samples, and more accessible REST-based APIs through partner Mulesoft. Also, DevNet is a community where members may come to rely on each other for shared experience and support. In addition, DevNet will serve as an education and delivery vehicle for the Cisco approach to SDN, its Application Centric Infrastructure.

Conclusion on the Current State of DevOps

This chapter devotes considerable space to DevOps for two reasons. First, DevOps will become increasingly critical for managing the stupendously complex networks that can be deployed with technologies such as NFV and SDN. Second, it is perhaps less obvious to the career-minded individual that DevOps know-how is a key skill than is the need for an understanding of SDN, NFV, QoE, and so on. The employee or job seeker with DevOps skills will have a competitive advantage going forward.

17.3   Training and Certification

The technologies discussed in this book are rapidly coming to dominate the networking industry and both private sector and government users. Networking professionals who have got this far in the book should by now be convinced of the need to learn these technologies and demonstrate competence in them. With all the changes taking place, experts warn networking pros that they will be left behind if they do not add new skills. Training and certification are the ideal vehicles for this. In a 2013 survey [BORT13] of 700 network professionals, Some 60 percent said a certification led to a new job; 50 percent said they earned more pay, with 40 percent saying their pay increased by more than 10 percent directly because of a certification; and 29 percent said a certification led to a promotion.

Fortunately, there is a large and growing number of opportunities to learn how to use the new networking technologies through certification programs.

Certification Programs

Tables 17.2 through 17.4 show some of the certification programs available related to SDN, network virtualization, and the cloud, respectively. Many of these emphasize the products of the companies that offer the training and certification, and so networking professionals can choose programs that either enhance their skills for their current position or for positions they want to seek. As for IoT, there are few offerings from the traditional sources. One recently introduced offering is the Cisco Industrial Networking Specialist Certificate. This training and certification program is for information technology (IT) and operational technology (OT) professionals in the manufacturing, process control, and oil and gas industries, who will be involved with the implementation, operation, and support of networked industrial products and solutions. We can expect to see many more such offerings.

Table 17.5 lists a number of other certification offerings in networking-related fields.

TABLE 17.2 SDN Certification Programs

Certification Program	Description
Open Networking Foundation (ONF) Certified SDN Associate	The aim of this certification is to validate knowledge of foundational concepts in SDN.
ONF Certified SDN Engineer	Targeted at those SDN professionals who are actively engaged in the more technical components of the SDN ecosystem. In this case, the ONF-Certified SDN Engineer certification (OCSE) will validate the skills, knowledge, and abilities for technical professionals working in the SDN ecosystem.
HP ASE - SDN Application Developer	Certifies understanding of SDN environment and SDN application use cases and ability to write, test, and debug an SDN application.
VMware Certified Professional - Network Virtualization (VCP-NV)	Validates your ability to install, configure, and administer NSX virtual networking implementations, regardless of the underlying physical architecture.
Brocade NFV Certification	Designed for IT professionals to expand their skills and contributions to their company by gaining in-depth relevant NFV expertise.

TABLE 17.3 Network Virtualization Certification Programs

Certification Program	Description
Cisco Business Application Engineer Specialist	For application engineers who design, develop, and build business applications and who are looking to leverage the programmability capability of the new open network environment.
Cisco Network Programmability Developer Specialist	For software programmers who focus on the development of the network applications layer and will enable service provider, campus, and data center use cases. This certification and course develop the foundational skills needed to develop network applications in programmable environments.
Cisco Network Programmability Design Specialist	For engineers who have both architectural and application development expertise. You will learn how to better collect customer requirements and use this information combined with knowledge about the applications to leverage the infrastructure and translate requirements into a recommended open infrastructure.
Cisco Network Programmability Engineer Specialist	For engineers who deploy network applications into a programmable environment and make them operational. Key skills covered with this certification include implementing and troubleshooting an open network infrastructure designed by the network designers and architects.

TABLE 17.4 Cloud Certification Programs

Certification Program	Description
Amazon Web Services (AWS) Certified Solutions Architect - Associate	Designed for IT professionals with experience in designing distributed applications and systems on the AWS platform.
AWS Certified Solutions Architect - Professional	Ideal candidates for this certification are professionals with advanced technical skills and experience in designing distributed applications and systems on the AWS platform.
AWS Certified Developer - Associate	Intended for those with technical skills and knowledge in developing and maintaining applications on AWS.
AWS Certified SysOps Administrator - Associate	Recognizes professionals with technical expertise in deployment, management, and operations on the AWS platform.
AWS Certified DevOps Engineer - Professional	Designed for those with expertise in provisioning, operating, and managing distributed application systems on AWS.
IBM Certified Solution Advisor - Cloud Computing Architecture V4	For IT pros who want to be recognized for their skills and experience in cloud computing. It aims to impart knowledge about cloud computing concepts and benefits, cloud computing design principles, IBM cloud computing architecture, and IBM cloud computing solutions.
IBM Certified Solution Architect - Cloud Computing Infrastructure V1	Recognizes those with proven knowledge in the design, planning, architecture, and management principles of an IBM cloud computing infrastructure.
Microsoft Certified Solution Expert: Private Cloud	For those who have interest towards Microsoft-led technologies and want to improve and prove their knowledge and skills. The certification provides the skills to build a private cloud solution with the help of Windows Server and System Center.
Microsoft Specialist Certification in Microsoft Azure	For IT pros such as developers who have prior experience working with Azure, Microsoft offers three specialist certifications to expand their skills with an eye toward future business requirements.
Salesforce Administrators	For those with experience being a Salesforce administrator.
Salesforce Implementation Experts	For those who have experience applying Sales Cloud solutions in a customer-facing role.
Salesforce Pardot Consultant	Designed for IT pros who have experience in applying Pardot marketing automation technology with in-depth knowledge of users and prospects, automation and segmentation tools, and building e-mails, forms, and landing pages in a customer-facing role.

Certification Program	Description
Salesforce Developers	Intended for those who have cloud development experience and want to showcase their knowledge, skills, and abilities in creating bespoke application and analytic solutions using the Force.com platform.
Salesforce Technical Architect	For candidates who have experience measuring customer architecture and designing secure, high-performance technical solutions on the Force.com platform.
Google Qualified Developer	To be certified as a Google Qualified Developer, a candidate must pass at least one of the following exams: App Engine, Cloud Storage, Cloud SQL, BigQuery: Compute Engine.
Google Qualified Cloud Platform Developer	To be a certified Google Qualified Cloud Platform Developer, candidates must pass all five of the exams listed under Google Qualified Developer.

TABLE 17.5 Other Networking-Related Certification Programs

Type of Certification	Certification	Description
Virtualization Certification	VMware Certified Associate - Data Center Virtualization (VCA-DCV)	Enables IT pros to have greater credibility when discussing data center virtualization, and how to virtualize the data center with vSphere.
	VMware Certified Professional 5 - Data Center Virtualization (VCP5-DCV)	Designed to enable IT pros to effectively install, deploy, scale, and manage VMware vSphere environments, and also provides skills obtained from a minimum of 6 months experience with VMware infrastructure technologies. Candidates must complete a VMware-authorized training course and hands-on experience with VMware technologies.
	VMware Certified Advanced Professional 5 - Data Center Administration (VCAP5-DCA)	To earn this certification, IT pros must complete a VMware-authorized training course and conduct hands-on experience with VMware technologies. Candidates receive the knowledge required to effectively install, deploy, scale, and manage VMware vSphere environments, as well as the skills gained by a minimum of 6 months experience with VMware infrastructure technologies.

	VMware Certified Advanced Professional 5 - Data Center Design (VCAP5-DCD)	Requires candidates go through a lab-based exam, performing tasks using actual equipment to verify skills at installing, configuring, and administering large and complex virtualized environments. Receiving this credential gives an IT pro an advanced certificate that demonstrates expertise with VMware vSphere 5, as well as the ability to use automation tools and implement virtualized environments.
	VMware Certified Design Expert 5 - Data Center Virtualization (VCDX5-DCV)	Reserved for top design architects highly skilled in VMware enterprise deployments. This certification program is designed for veteran professionals who want to validate and demonstrate their expertise in VMware technology. The certification is completed through a design-defense process, where all candidates must submit and effectively secure a production-ready VMware solution before a board of veteran VCDX-DCV holders.
	Citrix Certified Associate - Virtualization (CCA-V)	Validates the skills and knowledge of IT operators and administrators to manage, maintain, monitor and troubleshoot XenDesktop 7 solutions.
	Citrix Certified Professional - Virtualization (CCP-V)	Validates the skills and knowledge of experienced IT solution builders, such as engineers and consultants, to install, configure, and roll out common XenDesktop 7 solutions.
	Citrix Certified Expert - Virtualization (CCE-V)	Recognizes the skills and knowledge of experienced IT solution designers, such as architects, engineers, and consultants, to assess and design comprehensive XenDesktop 7 solutions.
Networking Certification	Cisco Entry Level Certification	Designed for those who have a keen interest in networking and want to start a career in the same. This certification serves as a stepping stone.
	Cisco Associate Level Certification	Designed for candidates who already have an entry-level certification or some experience in networking, such as troubleshooting or network design. These certifications would serve as the foundation to a career in networking.

	Cisco Professional Level Certification	For networking pros who have significant experience and skills in networking domains and are ready to go to the next level. These certifications are ideal for candidates wanting to explore new avenues within networking, with varying roles and responsibilities.
	Cisco Expert Level Certification	For networking pros who are recognized for their expert network engineering skills and mastery of Cisco products and solutions. These certifications are designed for those who want deep technical networking knowledge and challenging assignments.
	Cisco Architect Certification	Recognizing deep technical expertise, these certifications are the highest level Cisco has to offer.
	Juniper Service Provider Routing and Switching	This track is designed for those who have been working with infrastructure or access products in a Juniper routing/switching end-to-end environment, predominantly within the telecommunications arena or a Fortune 100 enterprise environment.
	Juniper Enterprise Routing and Switching	Designed for candidates working in small to large enterprise settings that install and support Juniper-based networks in which LAN and WAN routers and switches reside.
	Juniper Junos Security	This track is directed toward those who design and implement Juniper secure networks.
Project Management Certification	Certified Associate in Project Management (CAPM)	Project Management Institute (PMI) certification designed for candidates who are less experienced project practitioners looking to demonstrate their commitment to project management and want to improve their ability to manage larger projects and earn additional responsibilities.
	PMI Agile Certified Practitioner (PMI-ACP)	Designed for candidates who are active users of agile practices in their organization or who are in the process of adopting agile methods, this certification is ideal for demonstrating commitment to this rapidly growing approach to project management.

	Project Management Professional (PMP)	Designed for those who want to demonstrate competence in leading and directing project teams. The ideal candidate is an experienced project manager looking to solidify skills, stand out to employers, and maximize their earning potential.
	Portfolio Management Professional (PfMP)	Those who hold this credential are portfolio managers looking to prove their ability to manage and line up a portfolio of projects and programs to achieve organizational strategy and objectives.
	PMI Professional in Business Analysis (PMI-PBA)	Designed for business analysts working on projects and programs, as well as project and program managers who perform business analysis as part of their role.
	Program Management Professional (PgMP)	Candidates for this certification are usually already program managers, looking to validate their ability to manage complex, multiple projects and line up results to organizational goals. Professionals can use this certification to increase visibility and communicate valuable skills.
Systems Engineer Certification	Microsoft MCSE: Enterprise Devices and Apps	Designed for candidates with the skills needed to manage devices in today's bring-your-own-device (BYOD) enterprise. The candidate with this certification can be placed as a traditional desktop support technician to enterprise management of BYOD devices and apps.
	Microsoft MCSE: Messaging	For IT pros with an interest in cloud-based services such as Microsoft Office 365. This certification qualifies the candidate for a position in network and computer systems administration.
	Microsoft MCSE: Communication	Designed for those who have an interest in creating a consistent communications experience at the workplace. This credential qualifies candidates for a place in network and computer systems administration.

	Red Hat Certified Systems Administrator (RHCSA)	Designed for experienced system administrators looking to validate their skills and knowledge. It also can be helpful to students who have attended Red Hat System Administration I and II and want to be RHCSA certified.
	Red Hat Certified Engineer (RHCE)	For IT pros who are already RHCSAs and want to obtain higher-level credentials. Candidates such as experienced senior system administrators who have not yet been certified may be interested in this certification.
IT Security Certification	Global Information Assurance Certification (GIAC) Security Essentials (GSEC)	Designed for IT pros who want to demonstrate skills in IT systems hands-on roles with respect to security tasks. Ideal candidates for this certification possess an understanding of information security beyond simple terminology and concepts.
	International Information System Security Certification Consortium (ISC)^2 Certified Information Systems Security Professional (CISSP)	Ideal candidates for this certification are information assurance pros who know how to define the information system architecture, design, management, and controls to ensure the security of business environments.
	(ISC)^2 Systems Security Certified Practitioner (SSCP)	Designed for those with proven technical skills and practical security knowledge in hands-on operational IT roles. The SSCP provides confirmation of a practitioner's ability to implement, monitor, and administer IT infrastructure in accordance with information security policies and procedures that ensure data confidentiality, integrity, and availability.
	ISACA Certified Information Security Manager (CISM)	For candidates who have an inclination toward organizational security and want to demonstrate the ability to create a relationship between an information security program and broader business goals and objectives. This certification ensures knowledge of information security, development, and management of an information security program.

IT Skills

A global survey of 1156 respondents by TechPro Research [TECH14] revealed that many people fear that their current IT skill set will become obsolete. To stave off obsolescence, many respondents are planning to obtain additional IT certifications or degrees, with 57 percent planning for IT certifications either within their current job role or outside of their current job role. There are vast opportunities for the networking professional both to obtain these credentials and to leverage their education to maintain a high level of job security.

A useful tool in considering what specific skills you might need are the Dice rankings of skills in demand. Some of these are not directly related to networking tasks, but given the collaborative nature of the new networking environment, these skills can strengthen the network professional's resume. Table 17.6 shows the skills that commanded the highest salaries in the latest Dice salary survey, while Table 17.7 shows those skills for which demand is growing the fastest.

TABLE 17.6 Top-Paying Skills

Skill	Description	Average Salary (US$)
PaaS	Platform as a Service	$130,081
Cassandra	A database management system developed by Facebook.	$128,646
MapReduce	A programming model from Google for processing huge data sets on large clusters of servers. It includes distribution, parallelizing, and fault-tolerant functions.	$127,315
Cloudera Impala	An open source MPP SQL query engine for mining data stored in Apache Hadoop clusters.	$126,816
Hbase	An open source, nonrelational, distributed database modeled after Google's BigTable and written in Java.	$126,369
Pig	A MapReduce programming tool used on Hadoop.	$124,563
ABAP	Advanced Business Application Programming. A high-level, COBOL-like programming language used to develop SAP applications.	$124,262
Chef	An open source configuration management tool.	$123,458
Flume	A service for collecting, aggregating, and moving large amounts of log data.	$123,816
Hadoop	An open source project from the Apache Software Foundation that provides a software framework for distributing applications on clusters of servers. Designed to handle huge amounts of data and inspired by Google's MapReduce programming model and file system.	$121,313

Source: 2015 Dice Tech Salary Survey

TABLE 17.7 Fastest Trending Skills

Skill	Description	Average Salary (US$)
Cloudera Impala	An open source MPP SQL query engine for mining data stored in Apache Hadoop clusters.	$139,784
Adobe Experience Manager	Designed for organizing and managing creative assets, is popular among marketers, advertising-agency creative professionals and others who craft content.	$123,599
Ansible	System administrators rely on this open source tool to help them configure and manage PCs.	$124,860
Xamarin	Developers who want to rapidly build iOS and Android apps can use this tool to develop cross-platform in C#.	$101,707
OnCue	A web-based video streaming service.	$125,067
Laravel	An open source PHP Web application framework.	$96,219
RStudio	This integrated development environment for R (a statistical programming language that's proven a lucrative specialty for skilled developers) allows teams to share workspaces.	$117, 257
Unified Functional Testing	Gives tech pros the ability to comprehensively test software platforms and ecosystems.	$102,419
Pascal	Although Pascal has been around for 45 years, it is still very much in use.	$77,907
Apache Kafka	An open source tool developed by the Apache Software Foundation for maintaining real-time data feeds, capable of handling hundreds of megabytes of writes and reads per second from thousands of clients.	$134,950

Note: Descending order of popularity. These are not the skills most in demand, but the skills for which demand is growing most rapidly.

Source: Dice, April 2015

17.4 Online Resources

Numerous online resources can help you maintain and further your career, including the following:

- **ACM Career Resources:** ACM is an excellent source of CS career information. Resources include the following:
  - **Online Resources for Graduating Students**, which has a useful list of links to career websites (http://www.acm.org/membership/membership/student/resources-for-grads).
  - **ACM Career and Job Center (http://jobs.acm.org/)** is a place for job seekers and employers in the computing industry to connect with each other.

- **Computer Careers website (http://computingcareers.acm. org/)** provides guidance and resources for preparing for a career in computer science.

- **IEEE Resume Lab:** Online service that allows IEEE members to develop a resume or CV using specialized tools tailored for each step of the job seeking process. Excellent resource (https://ieee.optimalresume.com/index.php).

- **IEEE Computer Society Build Your Career (http://www.computer. org/web/careers):** Another excellent source of career information.

- **IEEE Job Site:** Yet another excellent source of career information, plus specific job leads (http://careers.ieee.org/).

- **ComputerWorld IT Topic Center (http://careers.ieee.org/):** Wide range of material, including news, white papers, career center, in-depth reports, and so on.

- **Computer Jobs (http://computerjobs.com/us/en/IT-Jobs/):** Lists thousands of searchable job opportunities categorized by major metropolitan markets and skill sets.

- **Career Overview (http://www.careeroverview.com/):** Contains jobs, job search websites and employment resources for professionals seeking career opportunities in computers, information technology, or another high-tech field. Good source of links.

- **DICE (http://www.dice.com/):** Frequently rated the best job site for positions worldwide in the information technology industry. Site also includes monthly article on timely topics, salary surveys, and discussions of skills in demand.

Another resource that you might find useful is the Computer Science Student Resources site that I maintain at http://www.computersciencestudent.com. This site is for professionals as well as students. The purpose of this site is to provide documents, information, and links for computer science students and professionals. Links and documents are organized into these categories:

- **Math**: Includes a basic math refresher, a queuing analysis primer, a number system primer, and links to numerous math sites.

- **How-to**: Advice and guidance for literature searching, solving homework problems, writing technical reports, and preparing technical presentations.

- **Research resources**: Links to important collections of papers, technical reports, and bibliographies.

Computer Science
Student Resources

- **Writing**: A number of useful sites and documents for improving your writing skills.

- **Other useful**: A variety of other useful documents and links.

- **Careers**: Useful links and documents related to career building. This page includes links to all of the sites listed earlier in this chapter, plus more.

17.5 References

BORT13: Bort, J. "Will IT certs get you jobs and raises? Survey says yes." *Network World*, November 14, 2011.

DICE13: Dice. "Why DevOps Is CPR for Cloud Applications." *Dice Special Report*, November 2013.

DICE14: Dice. "Critical Skills for DevOps Engineers." *Dice Special Report*, August 2014.

DICE15: Dice. "Spotlight on DevOps." *Dice Special Report*, 2015.

HALE14: Hales, J. *SDN: How It Will Affect You and Why You Should Care.* Global Knowledge white paper, 2014.

MACV15: MacVitie, L. "Network Engineers: Don't Fear the Code." *Information Week*, March 2, 2015.

METZ14b: Metzler, J. *The Changing Role of the IT & Network Professional.* Webtorials, July 2014.

MICR15: Microsoft. *Enterprise DevOps.* Microsoft white paper, 2015.

MINI14: Minick, E., Rezabek, J., and Ring, C. *Application Release and Deployment for Dummies.* New York: Wiley, 2014.

PRET14: Pretz, K. "Five Skills for Managing Software-Defined Networks." *IEEE The Institute*, December 2014.

SHAR15: Sharma, S., and Coyne. B. *DevOps for Dummies.* Hoboken, NJ: Wiley, 2015.

TECH14: TechPro Research. *The Future of IT Jobs: Critical Skills and Obsolescent Roles.* TechPro Research Report, August 2014.

Appendix | A

References

In matters of this kind, everyone feels he is justified in writing and publishing the first thing that comes into his head when he picks up a pen, and thinks his own idea as axiomatic as the fact that two and two make four. If critics would go to the trouble of thinking about the subject for years on end and testing each conclusion against the actual history of war, as I have done, they would undoubtedly be more careful of what they wrote.

—On War, Carl von Clausewitz

Abbreviations

- **ACM**: Association for Computing Machinery
- **IEEE**: Institute of Electrical and Electronics Engineers
- **ITU-T**: International Telecommunication Union—Telecommunication Standardization Sector
- **NIST**: National Institute of Standards and Technology
- **RFC**: Request For Comments

References

AKAM15: Akamai Technologies. *Akamai's State of the Internet.* Akamai Report, Q4|2014. 2015.

BARI13: Bari, M. "PolicyCop: An Autonomic QoS Policy Enforcement Framework for Software Defined Networks," Proc. of IEEE SDN4FNS'13, Trento, Italy, Nov. 2013.

BENS11: Benson, T., et al. "CloudNaaS: A Cloud Networking Platform for Enterprise Applications." *Proceedings, SOCC'11*, October 2011.

BORT13: Bort, J. "Will IT certs get you jobs and raises? Survey says yes." *Network World*, November 14, 2011.

CISC14a: Cisco Systems. *Cisco Visual Networking Index: Forecast and Methodology, 2013–2018.* White Paper, 2014.

CISC14b: Cisco Systems. *The Internet of Things Reference Model.* White paper, 2014. http://www.iotwf.com/.

CISC14c: Cisco Systems. *Building the Internet of Things.* Presentation, 2014. http://www.iotwf.com/.

CISC15: Cisco Systems. *Internetworking Technology Handbook.* July 2015. http://docwiki.cisco.com/wiki/Internetworking_Technology_Handbook.

CISC15a: Cisco Systems. *Internetworking Technology Handbook.* July 2015. http://docwiki.cisco.com/wiki/Internetworking_Technology_Handbook.

CISC15b: Cisco Systems. *Cisco IoT System: Deploy, Accelerate, Innovate.* Cisco white paper, 2015.

CLAR98: Clark, D., and Fang, W. "Explicit Allocation of Best-Effort Packet Delivery Service." *IEEE/ACM Transactions on Networking*, August 1998.

COGE13: Cogent Communications. *Network Services SLA Global.* October 2013. http://www.cogentco.com.

CSA11: Cloud Security Alliance. *Security as a Service (SecaaS).* CSA Report, 2011.

CSA13: Cloud Security Alliance. *The Notorious Nine Cloud Computing Top Threats in 2013.* CSA Report, February 2013.

DICE13: Dice. "Why DevOps Is CPR for Cloud Applications." *Dice Special Report*, November 2013.

DICE14: Dice. "Critical Skills for DevOps Engineers." *Dice Special Report*, August 2014.

DICE15: Dice. "Spotlight on DevOps." *Dice Special Report*, 2015.

ETSI14: ETSI TS 103 294 V1.1.1 Speech and Multimedia Transmission Quality (STQ); Quality of Experience; A Monitoring Architecture (2014-12).

FERG11: Ferguson, J., and Redish, A. "Wireless Communication with Implanted Medical Devices Using the Conductive Properties of the Body." *Expert Review of Medical Devices*, Vol. 6, No. 4, 2011. http://www.expert-reviews.com.

FOST13: Foster, N. "Languages for Software-Defined Networks." *IEEE Communications Magazine*, February 2013.

FRAH15: Frahim, J., et al. *Securing the Internet of Things: A Proposed Framework.* Cisco white paper, March 2015.

GUPT14: Gupta, D., and Jahan, R. *Securing the Internet of Things: A Proposed Framework.* Tata Consultancy Services White Paper, 2014. http://www.tcs.com.

HALE14: Hales, J. *SDN: How It Will Affect You and Why You Should Care.* Global Knowledge white paper, 2014.

HAWI14: Hawilo, H., et al. "NFV: State of the Art, Challenges, and Implementation in Next Generation Mobile Networks." *IEEE Network*, November/December 2014.

HOGG14: Hogg, S. "SDN Security Attack Vectors and SDN Hardening." *Network World*, Oct 28, 2014.

HOSS13: Hossfeld, T., et al. " Internet Video Delivery in YouTube: From Traffic Measurements to Quality of Experience." Book chapter in *Data Traffic Monitoring and Analysis: From Measurement, Classification, and Anomaly Detection to Quality of Experience*, Lecture Notes in Computer Science, Volume 7754, 2013.

IBM11: IBM Study, "Every Day We Create 2.5 Quintillion Bytes of Data." Storage Newsletter, October 21, 2011. http://www.storagenewsletter.com/rubriques/market-reportsresearch/ibm-cmo-study/.

ISGN12: ISG NFV. *Network Functions Virtualization: An Introduction, Benefits, Enablers, Challenges & Call for Action*. ISG NFV white paper, October 2012.

ITUT12: ITU-T. Focus Group on Cloud Computing Technical Report Part 3: Requirements and Framework Architecture of Cloud Infrastructure. FG Cloud TR, February 2012.

KAND12: Kandula, A., Sengupta, S., and Patel, P. "The Nature of Data Center Traffic: Measurements and Analysis." ACM SIGCOMM Internet Measurement Conference, November 2009.

KETY10: Ketyko, I., De Moor, K., Joseph, W., and Martens, L. "Performing QoE-Measurements in an Actual 3G Network," IEEE International Symposium on Broadband Multimedia Systems and Broadcasting, March 2010.

KHAN09: Khan, A., Sun, L., and Ifeachor, E. "Content Clustering Based Video Quality Prediction Model for MPEG4 Video Streaming over Wireless Networks," *IEEE International Conference on Communications*, 2009.

KHAN15: Khan, F. *A Beginner's Guide to NFV Management & Orchestration (MANO)*. Telecom Lighthouse. April 9, 2015. http://www.telecomlighthouse.com.

KIM14: Kim, H., and Choi, S. "QoE Assessment Model for Multimedia Streaming Services Using QoS Parameters," *Multimedia Tools and Applications*, October 2014.

KRAK09: Krakowiak, S. *Middleware Architecture with Patterns and Frameworks*. 2009. http://sardes.inrialpes.fr/%7Ekrakowia/MW-Book/.

KREU15: Kreutz, D., et al. "Software-Defined Networking: A Comprehensive Survey." *Proceedings of the IEEE*, January 2015.

KUIP10: Kuipers, F. et al. "Techniques for Measuring Quality of Experience," 8th International Conference on Wired/Wireless Internet Communications, 2010.

KUMA13: Kumar, R. Software Defined Networking—a Definitive Guide. Smashwords.com, 2013.

MA14: Ma, H., Seo, B., and Zimmermann, R. "Dynamic Scheduling on Video Transcoding for MPEG DASH in the Cloud Environment," Proceedings of the 5th ACM Multimedia Systems Conference, March 2014.

MACV15: MacVitie, L. "Network Engineers: Don't Fear the Code." *Information Week*, March 2, 2015.

MARS06: Marsh, I., Grönvall, B., and Hammer, F. "The Design and Implementation of a Quality-Based Handover Trigger," 5th International IFIP-TC6 Networking Conference, Coimbra, Portugal.

MCEW13: McEwen, A., and Cassimally, H. *Designing the Internet of Things.* New York: Wiley, 2013.

MCMU14: McMullin, M. "SDN is from Mars, NFV is from Venus." *Kemp Technologies Blog*, November 20, 2014. http://kemptechnologies.com/blog/sdn-mars-nfv-venus.

METZ14a: Metzler, J. *The 2015 Guide to SDN and NFV.* Webtorials, December 2014.

METZ14b: Metzler, J. *The Changing Role of the IT & Network Professional.* Webtorials, July 2014.

MICR15: Microsoft. *Enterprise DevOps.* Microsoft white paper, 2015.

MINI14: Minick, E., Rezabek, J., and Ring, C. *Application Release and Deployment for Dummies.* New York: Wiley, 2014.

MOLL12: Moller, S., Callet, P., and Perkis, A. "Qualinet White Paper on Definitions on Quality of Experienced," European Network on Quality of Experience in Multimedia Systems and Services (COST Action IC 1003) (2012).

MURP07: Murphy, L. et al. "An Application-Quality-Based Mobility Management Scheme," Proceedings of 9th IFIP/IEEE International Conference on Mobile and Wireless Communications Networks, 2007.

NAKI15: Nakina Systems. *Achieving Security Integrity in Service Provider NFV Environments.* Nakina Systems white paper, 2015.

NETW14: Network World. Survival Tips for Big Data's Impact on Network Performance. White paper. April 2014.

NGUY13: Nguyen, X., et al. "Efficient Caching in Content-Centric Networks using OpenFlow," 2013 IEEE Conference on Computer Communications Workshops (INFOCOM WKSHPS), 2013.

NGUY14: Nguyen, X., Saucez, D,, and Thierry, T. "Providing CCN Functionalities over OpenFlow Switches," hal-00920554, 2013. https://hal.inria.fr/hal-00920554/.

ODCA14: Open Data Center Alliance. Open Data Center Alliance Master Usage Model: Software-Defined Networking Rev. 2.0. White Paper. 2014.

ONF12: Open Networking Foundation. *Software-Defined Networking: The New Norm for Networks.* ONF White Paper, April 13, 2012.

ONF14: Open Networking Foundation. *OpenFlow-Enabled SDN and Network Functions Virtualization.* ONF white paper, February 17, 2014.

POTT14: Pott, T. "SDI Wars: WTF Is Software Defined Center Infrastructure?" *The Register*, October 17, 2014. http://www.theregister.co.uk/2014/10/17/sdi_wars_what_is_software_defined_infrastructure/.

PRET14: Pretz, K. "Five Skills for Managing Software-Defined Networks." *IEEE The Institute*, December 2014.

QUIN12: M.R.Quintero, M., and Raake, A. "Is Taking into Account the Subjects' Degree of Knowledge and Expertise Enough When Rating Quality?" Fourth International Workshop on Quality of Multimedia Experience (QoMEX), pp.194,199, 5–7 July 2012.

SCHE13: Scherz, P., and Monk, S. *Practical Electronics for Inventors.* New York: McGraw-Hill, 2013.

SCHN14: Schneier, B. "The Internet of Things is Wildly Insecure—and Often Unpatchable." *Wired*, January 6, 2014.

SDNC14: SDNCentral. SDNCentral Network Virtualization Report, 2014 Edition, 2014.

SEGH12: Seghal, A., et al. "Management of Resource Constrained Devices in the Internet of Things." *IEEE Communications Magazine*, December 2012.

SHAR15: Sharma, S., and Coyne. B. *DevOps for Dummies.* Hoboken, NJ: Wiley, 2015.

SHEN11: Schenker, S. "The Future of Networking, and the Past of Protocols," October 2011.Video: http://www.youtube.com/watch?v=YHeyuD89n1Y; Slides: http://www.slideshare.net/martin_casado/sdn-abstractions.

STAL15a: Stallings, W., and Brown, L. *Computer Security: Principles and Practice.* Englewood Cliffs, NJ: Pearson, 2015.

STAL15b: Stallings, W. *Cryptography and Network Security.* Englewood Cliffs, NJ: Pearson, 2015.

STAN14: Stankovic, J. "Research Directions for the Internet of Things." *Internet of Things Journal*, Vol. 1, No. 1, 2014.

SZIG14: Szigeti, T., Hattingh, C., Barton, R., and Briley, K. *End-to-End QoS Network Design: Quality of Service for Rich-Media & Cloud Networks.* Englewood Cliffs, NJ: Pearson. 2014.

TECH14: TechPro Research. *The Future of IT Jobs: Critical Skills and Obsolescent Roles.* TechPro Research Report, August 2014.

VAQU14: Vaquero, L., and Rodero-Merino, L. "Finding Your Way in the Fog: Towards a Comprehensive Definition of Fog Computing." *ACM SIGCOMM Computer Communication Review*, October 2014.

WANG12: Wang, G.; Ng, E.; and Shikh, A. "Programming Your Network at Run-Time for Big Data Applications." *Proceedings, HotSDN'12*. August 13, 2012.

XI11: Xi, H. "Bandwidth Needs in Core and Aggregation Nodes in the Optical Transport Network." IEEE 802.3 Industry Connections Ethernet Bandwidth Assessment Meeting, November 8, 2011. http://www.ieee802.org/3/ad_hoc/bwa/public/nov11/index_1108.html.

Glossary

In studying the Imperium, Arrakis, and the whole culture which produced Maud'Dib, many unfamiliar terms occur. To increase understanding is a laudable goal, hence the definitions and explanations given below.

—*Dune*, Frank Herbert

3G: Third-generation wireless cellular communications technology. Designed to provide fairly high-speed wireless communications to support multimedia, data, and video in addition to voice. Target data rates are 144 and 384 kbps. Some 3G systems also provide support up to 2 Mbps for office use.

4G: Fourth generation wireless cellular communications technology. Based on all-IP packet switched network. Support peak data rates of up to approximately 100 Mbps for high-mobility mobile access and up to approximately 1 Gbps for low-mobility access such as local wireless access.

5G: Projected fifth-generation wireless cellular communications technology. The focus for 5G will be on building more intelligence into the network, to meet service quality demands by dynamic use of priorities, adaptive network reconfiguration, and other network management techniques.

access network: A network that connects directly to the end user or customer.

accuracy: The closeness of agreement between the result of a measurement and the true value of the measure. It can be expressed as a qualitative assessment of correctness, or freedom from error, or a quantitative measure of the expected magnitude of error.

actuator: A device that accepts an electrical signal and converts it into a physical, chemical, or biological action.

analytics: Analysis of massive amounts of data, particularly with a focus on decision making.

application lifecycle management: The administration and control of an application from inception to its demise. It embraces requirements management, system design, software development, and configuration management, and it implies an integrated set of tools for developing and controlling the project.

application programming interface (API): A language and message format used by an application program to communicate with the operating system or some other control program such as a database management system (DBMS) or communications protocol. APIs are implemented by writing function calls in the program, which provide the linkage to the required subroutine for execution. An open or standardized API can ensure the portability of the application code and the vendor independence of the called service.

application provider: An entity generating/selling user applications to be executed on the user's platform.

application service provider: An organization that hosts software applications within its own facilities. It provides network-accessible applications such as e-mail, web hosting, banking, and cloud-based services.

attack surface: The reachable and exploitable vulnerabilities in a system.

attack vector: The method or type of attack on a computer system or network.

autonomous system (AS): A network that is administered by a single set of management rules that are controlled by one person, group or organization. Autonomous systems often use only one routing protocol, although multiple protocols can be used. The core of the Internet is made up of many autonomous systems.

backbone network: Same as core network.

best effort: A network or Internet delivery technique that does not guarantee delivery of data and treats all packets equally. All packets are forwarded on a first-come, first-served basis. Preferential treatment based on priority or other concerns is not provided.

big data: A collection of data on such a large scale that standard data analysis and management tools are not adequate. More broadly, big data refers to the volume, variety and velocity of structured and unstructured data pouring through networks into processors and storage devices, along with the conversion of such data into business advice for enterprises.

blade server: A server architecture that houses multiple server modules (blades) in a single chassis. It is widely used in data centers to save space and improve system management. Either self-standing or rack mounted, the chassis provides the power supply, and each blade has its own CPU, memory, and hard disk.

broadcast: An address recognized by all hosts on a network or within a network domain. With broadcast addressing, one transmission stream is used to each switch, at which point data are distributed out to the end users on separate lines.

business support system (BSS): Software applications that support customer-facing activities. Billing, order management, customer relationship management and call center automation are all BSS applications. BSS may also encompass the customer-facing veneer of OSS application such as trouble-ticketing and service assurance; these are back-office activities but initiated directly by contact with the customer.

capital expenditure (CapEx): A business expense incurred to create future benefits. A CapEx is incurred when a business spends money either to buy fixed assets or to add to the value of an existing asset with a useful life that extends beyond the tax year.

client/server: A common form of distributed system in which software is split between server tasks and client tasks. A client sends requests to a server, according to some protocol, asking for information or action, and the server responds.

cloud computing: A loosely defined term for any system providing access via the Internet to processing power, storage, software or other computing services, often via a web browser. Often, these services are rented from an external company that hosts and manages them.

commercial off-the-shelf (COTS): Item that is commercially available, leased, licensed, or sold to the general public and that requires no special modification or maintenance over the lifecycle of the product to meet the needs of the procuring agency.

Communication as a Service (CaaS): A service offered via cloud computing in which the capability provided to the cloud service customer is real time interaction and collaboration.

congestion: The condition of a network when there is not enough capacity to support the current traffic load.

congestion control: Protocol mechanisms for relieving or avoiding congestion.

consortium: A group of independent organizations joined by common interests. In the area of standards development, a consortium typically consists of individual corporations and trade groups concerned with a specific area of technology.

constrained device: In an IoT, a device with limited volatile and nonvolatile memory, limited processing power, and a low-data-rate transceiver.

container: Hardware or software that provides an execution environment for software.

container virtualization: A technique where the underlying operating environment of an application is virtualized. This will commonly be the operating system kernel, and the result is an isolated container in which the application can run.

content provider: An organization or individual that creates information, including educational or entertainment content distributed via the Internet or enterprise networks. A content provider may or may not provide the software used to access the material.

core network: A central network that provides networking services to attached distribution and access networks. Also referred to as a backbone network.

core router: A router that resides within the middle of the network rather than at its periphery. The routers that make up the backbone of the Internet are core routers.

cross-section bandwidth: For a network, this is the maximum bidirectional data rate that can pass between two parts of the network if it is divided into two equal halves. Also referred to as *bisection bandwidth*.

data deduplication: The elimination of redundant data. It includes (1) compressing data by only storing changes to data, and (2) replacing duplicate copies of chunks of data or files with pointers to a single copy.

datagram: A packet that is treated independently of other packets for packet switching. A datagram carries information sufficient for routing from the source to the destination without the necessity of establishing a logical connection between the endpoints.

deep packet inspection: Analyzing network traffic to discover the type of application that sent the data. In order to prioritize traffic or filter out unwanted data, deep packet inspection can differentiate data, such as video, audio, chat, Voice over IP (VoIP), e-mail, and web. Inspecting the packets all the way up to the application layer, it can be used to analyze anything within the packet that is not encrypted. For example, it can determine not only that the packets contain the contents of a web page but also which website the page is from.

delay jitter: The variation in delay associated with the transfer of packets between two points. Typically measured as the maximum variation in delay experienced by packets in a single session.

denial of service (DoS): The prevention of authorized access to resources or the delaying of time-critical operations.

DevOps (development operations): The tighter integration between the developers of applications and the IT department that tests and deploys them. DevOps is said to be the intersection of software engineering, quality assurance, and operations.

differentiated services: Functionality in the Internet and private internets to support specific QoS requirements for a group of users, all of whom use the same service label in IP packets.

differentiated services codepoint (DSCP): A 6-bit field in the IP header that is used to classify packets for differentiated services (a form of QoS traffic management).

distributed denial of service (DDoS): An attack when multiple systems are used to flood servers or network devices or links with traffic in an attempt to overwhelm its available resources (bandwidth, memory, processing power, and so on), making it unavailable to respond to legitimate users.

distribution network: Connects access networks to a core network.

edge router: A router that sits at the periphery of a network. Also called an *access router* or *aggregation router*.

elastic traffic: Network traffic that is tolerant to variations in delay, jitter, and throughput. Typically carried over TCP or UDP.

embedded system: Any device that includes a computer chip, but that is not a general-purpose workstation, desktop or laptop computer.

electronic product code (EPC): A standard code for RFID tags. The EPC ranges from 64 to 256 bits and contains, at minimum, the product number, serial number, company ID and EPC version. Several bodies are involved in developing standards, including GS1 and EPCglobal.

end user: The ultimate consumer of applications, data and services on a computing platform.

Ethernet: The commercial name for a wired local-area network technology. It involves the use of a shared physical medium, a medium access control protocol, and transmission of data in packets. Standards for Ethernet products are defined by the IEEE 802.3 committee.

exterior router protocol (ERP): A protocol that distributes routing information to collaborating routers that connect autonomous systems. BGP is an example of an ERP. Historically, referred to as an exterior gateway protocol.

flow: A sequence of packets between a source and destination that are recognized by the network as related and are treated in a uniform fashion.

fog computing: A scenario in which a massive number of heterogeneous, decentralized devices communicate with each other and with the network to perform storage and processing tasks without the intervention of third parties.

hardware virtualization: The use of software to partition a computer's resources into separate and isolated entities called virtual machines. It enables multiple copies of the same or different operating systems to execute on the computer and prevents applications from different virtual machines from interfering with each other.

high-availability (HA) cluster: A multiple-computer architecture consisting of redundant network nodes that deliver a secondary or backup service when the primary service fails. Such clusters build redundancy into their computing environments to eliminate single points of failure, and they can incorporate multiple network connections, redundant data storage volumes, doubled-up power supplies, and other backup components and capabilities.

hypervisor introspection: The hypervisor capability to monitor each guest OS or virtual machine as it is running, for security purposes.

IEEE 802: A committee of the Institute of Electrical and Electronics Engineers (IEEE) responsible for developing standards for local- and metropolitan-area networks (LANs and MANs).

IEEE 802.1: An IEEE 802 working group responsible for developing standards in the following areas: 802 LAN/MAN architecture, internetworking among 802 LANs, MANs and other wide-area networks, 802 Security, 802 overall network management.

IEEE 802.3: An IEEE 802 working group responsible for developing standards for Ethernet local-area networks (LANs).

inelastic traffic: Network traffic that is relatively intolerant to variations in delay, jitter, and throughput. Real-time traffic is an example of inelastic traffic.

information technology (IT): The common term for the entire spectrum of technologies for information processing, including software, hardware, communications technologies, and related services. In general, IT does not include embedded technologies that do not generate data for enterprise use.

Infrastructure as a Service (IaaS): A group of capabilities offered via cloud computing in which the cloud service customer can provision and use processing, storage, or networking resources.

interior router protocol (IRP): A protocol that distributes routing information to collaborating routers within an autonomous system. RIP and OSPF are examples of IRPs. Historically, referred to as an interior gateway protocol.

Internet: A worldwide internetwork based on TCP/IP that interconnects thousands of public and private networks and millions of users.

internet (with lower case "i"): A large network made up of a number of smaller networks. Also referred to as an *internetwork*.

Internet of Things (IoT): The expanding connectivity, particularly via the Internet of a wide range of sensors, actuators, and other embedded systems. In almost all cases, there is no human user, with interaction fully automated.

Internet Protocol (IP): A standardized protocol that executes in hosts and routers to interconnect a number of independent networks.

IP security (IPsec): Suite of protocols for securing IP communications at the network layer by authenticating and/or encrypting each IP packet in a data stream. IPsec also includes protocols for cryptographic key management.

LAN switch: A packet-forwarding network device for (1) interconnecting end systems in a local area to form a local-area network (LAN) segment, (2) connecting with other LAN switches to for a larger LAN, and (3) providing connection to routers and other network devices for wide-area network connectivity.

Layer 3 (L3) switch: A high-performance device for network routing. Layer 3 switches are very similar to routers. The key difference between L3 switches and routers is that a L3 switch replaces some of a router's software logic with hardware to offer better performance. L3 switches often cost less than traditional routers. Designed for use within local networks, a Layer 3 switch will typically not possess the WAN ports and wide-area network features a traditional router has.

media access control (MAC) frame: : A group of bits that includes source and destination addresses and other protocol control information plus, optionally, data. It is the basic unit of transmission on Ethernet and Wi-Fi LANs.

microcontroller: A single chip that contains the processor, non-volatile memory for the program (ROM or flash), volatile memory for input and output (RAM), a clock and an I/O control unit. Also called a *computer on a chip*.

microprocessor: A processor whose elements have been miniaturized into one or a few integrated circuits.

Multiprotocol Label Switching (MPLS): A protocol developed the IETF for directing packets in a wide-area IP network, or other WAN. MPLS adds a 32-bit label to each packet to improve network efficiency and to enable routers to direct packets along predefined routes in accordance with the required quality of service.

Network as a Service (NaaS): A service offered via cloud computing in which the capability provided to the cloud service customer is transport connectivity and related network capabilities.

network convergence: The provision of telephone, video, and data communication services within a single network.

network interface card: An adapter circuit board installed in a computer to provide a physical connection to a network.

network functions virtualization: The virtualization of network functions by implementing these functions in software and running them on virtual machines.

network operating system (NOS): A server-based operating system oriented to computer networking. It may include directory services, network management, network monitoring, network policies, user group management, network security and other network-related functions.

network provider: An organization that delivers communications services over a typically large geographic area. It provides, maintains, and manages network equipment and networks, either public or private.

northbound API: In an SDN environment, the interface between the control and application planes.

Open Service Gateway Initiative (OSGi): A set of specifications that defines a dynamic component system for Java. These specifications reduce software complexity by providing a modular architecture for large-scale distributed systems as well as small, embedded applications.

open standard: A standard that is developed on the basis of an open decision-making procedure available for implementation to all interested parties, that is available to all on a royalty-free basis, and that is intended to promote interoperability among products from multiple vendors.

operational expenditure (OpEx): Refers to business expenses incurred in the course of ordinary business, such as maintenance and operation of equipment.

operational technology (OT): Hardware and software that detects or causes a change through the direct monitoring and/or control of physical devices, processes and events in the enterprise.

operations support system (OSS): Software (occasionally hardware) applications that support back-office activities which operate a network, and provision and maintain customer services. OSS is typically used by network planners, service designers, operations, architects, support, and engineering teams in the service provider.

packet: A unit of data sent across a network. A packet is a group of bits that includes data plus protocol control information. The term generally applies to protocol data units at the network layer.

packet forwarding: The function performed by a router of accepting a packing on an input link and transmitting it on an output link.

packet switching: A method of transmitting messages through a communications network, in which long messages are subdivided into short packets. Each packet is passed from source to destination through intermediate nodes. At each node, the entire message is received, stored briefly, and then forwarded to the next node.

peer: On the same level or providing the same function. In networking, a peer is a node that provides the same functionality as another. For example, two desktop PCs in a network are peers. A desktop PC and a server are not peers as they perform different operations. The desktop PC may query the server for business data, but the server does not query the PC for the same data.

peering: An agreement between two routers to accept each other's data packets and forward them. A peer relationship generally involves the exchange of routing information.

Platform as a Service (PaaS): A group of capabilities offered via cloud computing in which the cloud service customer can deploy, manage and run customer-created or customer-acquired applications using one or more programming languages and one or more execution environments supported by the cloud service provider.

Power over Ethernet (PoE): Distributing power over an Ethernet cable to a target device that is not plugged into an AC wall outlet. PoE enables remote network devices in locations far away from AC sources.

powerline carrier (PLC): A data network that uses a building's electrical system as the transmission medium and regular wall outlets as connecting points. It is commonly used to extend a wired Ethernet network into another room.

precision: The degree of agreement of repeated measurements of the same property, expressed quantitatively as the standard deviation computed from the results of the series of measurements.

protocol: A set of semantic and syntactic rules that describe how to transmit data, especially across a network. Low-level protocols define the electrical and physical standards to be observed, bit- and byte-ordering, and the transmission and error detection and correction of the bit stream. High-level protocols deal with the data formatting, including the syntax of messages, semantics of messages, character sets, and sequencing of messages.

protocol architecture: The software structure that implements the communications function. Typically, the protocol architecture consists of a layered set of protocols, with one or more protocols at each layer.

protocol control information: Information exchanged between entities of a given layer, via the service provided by the next lower layer, to coordinate their joint operation.

protocol data unit (PDU): Information that is delivered as a unit between peer entities of a network. A PDU typically contains control information and address information in a header. The PDU may also contain data.

quality of experience (QoE): A subjective measure of performance in a system. QoE relies on human opinion and differs from quality of service (QoS), which can be precisely measured.

quality of service (QoS): The measurable end-to-end performance properties of a network service, which can be guaranteed in advance by a service level agreement between a user and a service provider, so as to satisfy specific customer application requirements. Note: These properties may include throughput (bandwidth), transit delay (latency), error rates, priority, security, packet loss, packet jitter, and so on.

radio-frequency identification (RFID): A data collection technology that uses electronic tags attached to items to allow the items to be identified and tracked by a remote system. The tag consists of an RFID chip attached to an antenna.

real time: As fast as required. A real-time system must respond to a signal, event or request fast enough to satisfy some requirement.

real-time traffic: A data flow that must meet real-time requirements, such as low jitter and low delay.

Request For Comments (RFC): A document in the archival series that is the official channel for publications of the Internet Society, including IETF and IRTF publications. An RFC may be informational, best practice, draft standard, or an official Internet Standard.

resolution: The smallest distinguishable increment into which a measured quantity is divided.

role-based access control (RBAC): Controls access based on the roles that users have within the system and on rules stating what accesses are allowed to users in given roles.

router: A network device that forwards data packets from one network to another. The forwarding decision is based on network layer information and routing tables, often constructed by routing protocols. Routers require packets formatted in a routable protocol, the global standard being the Internet Protocol (IP).

routing: The determination of a path that a data unit (frame, packet, message) will traverse from source to destination.

routing protocol: A protocol used by routers to determine the appropriate path onto which data should be forwarded. The routing protocol also specifies how routers report changes and share information with the other routers in the network that they can reach.

scale out: Expand the capability of a single physical machine or virtual machine.

scale up: Expand capability by adding additional physical or virtual machines.

sensor: A device that converts a physical, biological, or chemical parameter into an electrical signal.

service provider: A network-accessible entity that can provide services to an end user.

Software as a Service (SaaS): A group of capabilities offered via cloud computing in which the cloud service customer can use the cloud service provider's applications.

software-defined networking (SDN): An approach to designing, building and operating large-scale networks based on programming the forwarding decisions in routers and switches via software from a central server. SDN differs from traditional networking, which requires configuring each device separately and which relies on protocols that cannot be altered.

software-defined storage (SDS): An approach to data storage management and use in which the software that controls storage-related tasks is decoupled from the physical storage hardware.

southbound API: In an SDN environment, the interface between the control and data planes.

standard: A document that provides requirements, specifications, guidelines, or characteristics that can be used consistently to ensure that materials, products, processes, and services are fit for their purpose. Standards are established by consensus among those participating in a standards-making organization and are approved by a generally recognized body.

standards-developing organization (SDO): An official national, regional, or international standards body that develop standards and/or that coordinate the standards activities of a specific country, region or the world. Some SDOs facilitate the development of standards through support of technical committee activities, and some may be directly involved in standards development.

TCP/IP protocol architecture: The protocol architecture built around the TCP and IP protocols, consisting of five layers: physical, data link, network/internet (usually IP), transport (usually TCP or UDP), and application.

token bucket: A data-flow control mechanism that adds tokens in periodical time intervals into a buffer (bucket) and allows a data packet to leave the sender only if there are at least as many tokens in the bucket as the packet length of the data packet. This strategy allows precise control of the time interval between two data packets in the network.

top-of-rack (ToR) switch: A blade server arrangement in which servers connect to one or two Ethernet switches installed inside the rack. The actual physical location of the switch does not necessarily need to be at the top of the rack. Other switch locations could be bottom of the rack or middle of rack. However, top of the rack is most common due to easier accessibility and cleaner cable management.

traffic engineering: That aspect of network engineering dealing with the issues of performance evaluation and performance optimization of operational networks. Traffic engineering encompasses the application of technology and scientific principles to the measurement, characterization, modeling, and control of network traffic.

transceiver: A device that can both transmit and receive information.

unicast: An address which only one host will recognize. With unicast addressing, even though multiple users might request the same data from the same server at the same time, duplicate data streams are transmitted, one to each user.

unified communications: The integration of real-time, enterprise, communication services such as instant messaging, presence information, voice (including IP telephony), web and video conferencing, and speech recognition with non-real-time communication services such as unified messaging (integrated voicemail, e-mail, SMS, and fax).

Uniform Resource Identifier (URI): A compact sequence of characters that identifies an abstract or physical resource. The URI specification (RFC 3986) defines a syntax for encoding arbitrary naming or addressing schemes, and provides a list of such schemes. The URL (Uniform Resource Locator) is a type of URI, in which an access protocol is designated and a specific Internet address is provided.

virtual local-area network (VLAN): A virtual network abstraction on top of a physical packet-switched network. A VLAN is essentially a broadcast domain for a specified set of switches. These switches are required to be aware of the existence of VLANs and configured accordingly, to perform switching of packets between devices belonging to the same VLAN.

virtual machine: One instance of an operating system along with one or more applications running in an isolated partition within the computer. It enables different operating systems to run in the same computer at the same time as well as prevents applications from interfering with each other.

virtual machine monitor (VMM): A system program that provides a virtual machine environment. Also called a *hypervisor*.

virtual network: An abstraction of physical network resources as seen by some upper software layer. Virtual network technology enables a network provider to support multiple virtual networks that are isolated from one another. Users of a single virtual network are not aware of the details of the underlying physical network or of the other virtual network traffic sharing the physical network resources.

virtual private network (VPN): The use of encryption and authentication in the lower protocol layers to provide a secure connection through an otherwise unsecure network, typically the Internet. VPNs are generally cheaper than real private networks using private lines but rely on having the same encryption and authentication system at both ends. The encryption may be performed by firewall software or possibly by routers.

virtualization: A variety of technologies for managing computer resources by providing an abstraction layer between the software and the physical hardware. These technologies effectively emulate or simulate a hardware platform, such as a server, storage device, or network resource, in software.

Wi-Fi: Refers to the wireless LAN technology standardized by the IEEE 802.11 committee. The term Wi-Fi designates products that have been certified by the Wi-Fi Alliance to conform to the 802.11 standards and have passed interoperability tests.

Index

Symbols

A

P